SUNY series in Queer Politics and Cultures
————————
Cynthia Burack and Jyl J. Josephson, editors

RESIST ORGANIZE BUILD

FEMINIST AND QUEER ACTIVISM IN BRITAIN AND THE UNITED STATES DURING THE LONG 1980S

EDITED BY

SARAH CROOK AND **CHARLIE JEFFRIES**

Published by State University of New York Press, Albany

© 2022 State University of New York

All rights reserved

Printed in the United States of America

No part of this book may be used or reproduced in any manner without written permission. No part of this book may be stored in a retrieval system or transmitted in any form or by any means including electronic, electrostatic, magnetic tape, mechanical, photocopying, recording, or otherwise without the prior permission in writing of the publisher.

For information, contact State University of New York Press, Albany, NY
www.sunypress.edu

Library of Congress Cataloging-in-Publication Data

Names: Crook, Sarah, 1988– editor. | Jeffries, Charlie, editor.
Title: Resist, organize, build : feminist and queer activism in Britain and the United States during the long 1980s / edited by Sarah Crook and Charlie Jeffries.
Description: Albany, NY : State University of New York Press, [2022] | Series: SUNY series in queer politics and cultures | Includes bibliographical references and index.
Identifiers: LCCN 2022005688 | ISBN 9781438489599 (hardcover : alk. paper) | ISBN 9781438489605 (ebook) | ISBN 9781438489582 (pbk. : alk. paper)
Subjects: LCSH: Feminism—Great Britain—History. | Gay liberation movement—Great Britain—History. | Conservatism—Great Britain—History. | Feminism—United States—History. | Gay liberation movement—United States—History. | Conservatism—United States—History.
Classification: LCC HQ1191.G7 R37 2022 | DDC 305.420941—dc23/eng/20220404
LC record available at https://lccn.loc.gov/2022005688

10 9 8 7 6 5 4 3 2 1

Contents

Acknowledgments ix

Introduction: Thinking through and beyond the 1980s 1
   Sarah Crook and Charlie Jeffries

Part I
Student Politics and the Body Politic

"Aggies are Not Queers" A History of *Gay Student Services v. Texas A&M University*, 1975–1985 31
   Michael S. Hevel and Charles J. Thompson

"Specialty" Listening: Creating Space for Queer Programming on American College Radio in the Long 1980s 53
   Katherine Rye Jewell

Part II
Anti-Racist, Anti-Imperialist, Anti-Borders Action

"We were fire-fighting against Thatcher and the system she was putting forward": The Black Women's Movement and the Boundaries of Nationhood in Thatcher's Britain 75
   Jade Bentil

"Spiritualists, ideologues, pragmatists, feminists, and women of all descriptions": The British Women's Liberation Movement, the UN Decade for Women, and Feminist Transnationalism in *Spare Rib* 117
    Charlotte Lydia Riley

Part III
Families, Reproduction, and Health

Making Queer Families: Foster Family Activism in Los Angeles, 1977–1985 147
    Nora Kassner

Thatcherism, the Black Women's Movement, and the Politics of Motherhood in Britain 171
    Kate Turner

A Framework for Choice: The Lasting Influence of 1980s Advocacy on Reproductive Rights in the United States 199
    Tamar Holoshitz

Opening DOORWAYS and Closing Others: Tactical Deployments of Respectability, Religion, and Race in the St. Louis Early-AIDS Response 229
    Katie Batza

Part IV
Grassroots Images, Speech, and Power

Polareyes: A Magazine by and for Black British Women Photographers as a Site of Resistance in London, 1987 255
    Taous R. Dahmani

The Business of Feminism Endures: Four Decades of Spinsters Ink and Aunt Lute Books Publishing Lesbian-Feminist Books in the United States 285
    Julie R. Enszer

Lesbians Talk: British Lesbian Politics and the Sex Wars 307
 Flora Dunster

Epilogues

Looking Back, Thinking Forward: Grassroots Activism and
Modern Histories 331
 Sarah Crook

Critically Reflecting (on) the 1980s 335
 Charlie Jeffries

Contributors 339

Index 343

Acknowledgments

This book is the result of several years of collaboration and enthusiasm across continents and time zones. We would like to thank our contributors for their expertise, patience, and work. It has been a pleasure to develop this book with them. We are enormously grateful to our editor at SUNY, Rebecca Colesworthy, who has been efficient, helpful, and wise throughout. Thank you also to Sneha Krishnan, Martin Johnes, and Christoph Laucht for invaluable insights and advice.

This book has been shaped by our students' questions and interests: thank you to students at Swansea, Oxford, Queen Mary, University of London, Birkbeck, UEA, and Cambridge for your curiosity and positivity.

Sarah would like to thank Calum, for everything.

Charlie would like to thank Christabel for all the support, ideas, and care.

Introduction

Thinking through and beyond the 1980s

Sarah Crook and Charlie Jeffries

Writing in *Lesbians Talk Making Black Waves*, a book that sought to document the history and experiences of Black lesbians living in Britain, Araba Mercer, a publisher for Sheba Feminist Press who had been involved with Manchester's Black Women's Group in the mid-1980s, reflected that "There seemed to be so much more going on in the 1980s, everything was new, things were possible. There was so much dialogue and political theorising."[1] Here we reaffirm the 1980s as a period of activist dialogue, creativity, and energy in the face of the rise of the New Right. As Mercer said, things were *going on*. In spring 1979, the inaugural National Black Women's Conference was held in London; in autumn that year tens of thousands of women and men took to the streets of London to defend women's access to abortion; in 1980, Sheba Feminist Press was founded to prioritize the work of marginalized women. On the precipice of the new decade, then, new organizations and lines of defense were being established. That is not to say that the new decade was welcomed with optimism by activists in Britain. This is perhaps unsurprising. The general election of May 1979 had ushered in a Conservative government led by Margaret Thatcher, which would go on to cut back the welfare state, disempower unions, and curb immigration. This conservative climate would provide the background against which British activists—both those concerned with the topics of this collection, and other groups, like the Campaign for Nuclear Disarmament and the trade unions—would agitate over the coming years. In the 1980s, activists established new frontiers of resistance, organized around new demands, and built new collaborations. New ways of thinking—and, indeed, arguing—about liberationist projects would develop. New communities, campaigns and solidarities would crystallize. Some of these communities and campaigns of resistance are the subjects of this edited collection.

Despite their decades of mobilization, feminist and queer activists in the United States also approached the 1980s with trepidation. President Jimmy Carter was shortly to be ousted by Republican Ronald Reagan, who rode into the White House on a wave of electoral support fostered by the New Right, a multifaceted conservative movement that included reactionaries of many stripes. Social conservatives fueling the New Right's electoral success via wide-reaching televangelism railed against the gains of the civil rights, feminist, and gay liberation movements of the 1970s, citing such activist successes as *Roe v. Wade* and more visible queer communities in American cities as signs of moral decline.[2] Fiscal conservatives gained speed in the same era, as a global neoliberal intellectual movement began to influence the policies of Thatcher in the United Kingdom, and those of the incoming US president. This movement, which sought to replace government spending on society with apparent increased individual responsibility, centralized welfare as a moral-political issue, and young Black women on welfare were frequently chastised by the Reagan campaign in a way that united the socially and economically conservative factions of the New Right and electorate.[3] Simultaneously, the HIV/AIDS pandemic took hold across the United States, initially arising in communities of gay men. Religious conservatives framed this as an act of "retribution from God," and the Reagan administration was extremely slow to publicly acknowledge the disease that was devastating the country and the world.[4] At the heart of both neoliberal and social conservatism in the United States in this era was an inextricable racism, misogyny, and homophobia—one which activists were sharply attuned to, and which drove continued social justice work in the United States as the decade progressed. These two forces—of progress away from the inequalities that defined the nation's history, and of the desire to conserve the traditional morals and myths of the United States—became so powerfully opposed in the lead-up to Reagan's election that the period would later be framed as the start of the country's most recent set of "culture wars."[5]

As in the United Kingdom, however, activists were not only responding to these painful political developments, fighting fires as they arose, but also drawing on histories of activism, and imagining and building futures beyond the violence of the present. It is these activisms that this edited collection draws to the fore. How did feminist and queer organizations of the 1980s simultaneously resist immediate threats, and establish theory, organizations, and structures that would support their communities in the years to come? How can we draw from these histories to understand how to resist and build in the wake of a recharged far-right movement across both contexts?

This collection brings together chapters that set out some of the sites, causes and organizations that activists used to both resist the emergencies of the present and forge forward in creating lasting social change in the 1980s. The book emerged from a need the editors identified as teachers: our students, often activists themselves, look to the past to explain and inspire their worlds, and have increasingly sought to explore beyond the better-known historical terrain of the period. It also emerged from our interests as researchers. As historians of Britain (Crook) and the United States (Jeffries), we wanted to bring scholars and histories of British and American activisms together: not to compare, but to position alongside one another and to see what intellectual synergies might emerge. Informal conversations had highlighted points of transatlantic convergence and difference in the activist histories we worked on. What sort of productive energies, we wondered, would be revealed if we brought work from the United States and the United Kingdom together, and what might be illuminated if we introduced American and British audiences to more fine-grained activist histories of the period in each other's areas?

The second reason for our dual focus was grounded in the shared politics of the period. Feminist and queer activists faced political opponents ideologically allied with one another. Ronald Reagan and Margaret Thatcher shared a personal and political rapport: "Mr. President, the natural bond of interest between our two countries is strengthened by the common approach which you and I have to our national problems," Thatcher told Reagan in 1981. "If we are to succeed in the battle of ideas, if we are to hold fast and extend the frontiers of freedom," she urged, "we must first proclaim the truth that makes men free. We must have the courage to reassert our traditional values and the resolve to prevail against those who deny our ideals and threaten our way of life."[6]

This volume amplifies the voices of those on the other side of the "battle of ideas"; those who challenged "traditional values"; those who dreamed of new ways of living. The "frontiers of freedom" that activists pushed were a stark contrast to Thatcher's conservative frontiers: they centered on liberation and radical change as they sought to build better worlds. This collection seeks to shine a light on some of the locations and mechanisms of liberation campaigns in this epochal context. The chapters in *Resist, Organize, Build* tell the story of an era wherein—as the title of this volume suggests—queer and feminist movements on both sides of the Atlantic were resisting the historical inequalities exacerbated by Reagan and Thatcher, building communities of immediate survival and protest, but also nurturing ideas and organizations that would outlast the specific conditions of that period.

This volume positions scholarship on feminism alongside scholarship on queer activism. Putting it together, we asked: what if we took an expansive view of activism and looked at women's and queer liberation campaigns alongside another? As this volume shows, considering feminist and queer organizing alongside one another highlights shared trajectories, ideas, and aims, but also reveals tensions.[7]

These chapters demonstrate the importance of a close attention to the debates and discussions that arose around race, solidarity, and coalitional organizations in the 1980s: debates that have implications in the present.[8] In the US context, Julie R. Enszer's chapter describes the history—and present—of Aunt Lute Books, a "multicultural, feminist publisher" that has been an important site of feminist organizing since the 1980s and remains so today, and the lesbian-feminist publisher Spinsters Ink, who together published Gloria Anzaldúa's critical Chicanx feminist text *Borderlands/La Frontera* in 1987.[9] Jade Bentil's chapter explores areas where Black and Asian women worked together to resist Thatcher's government in the United Kingdom. The beginning of the Black Women's Movement after 1979, Bentil says, "symbolized a historical moment in which Black feminists made political alliances with Asian feminists to reflect the everyday struggles of women of color and their collaborative efforts to confront and destroy the material sources of their deprivation."[10] These alliances worked across, but were made vulnerable by, the different experiences of the women within them. "Endeavoring to fashion a collective analysis of the ways in which women of color navigated society became increasingly fraught due to the differing social locations that the majority of Black and Asian women occupied within Britain,"

Bentil writes.[11] While foregrounding areas of collaboration, Bentil focuses on the political activity and organizing of women of African, African Caribbean, and African American descent in Britain. In her expansive chapter, she explores the ways that the Black Women's Movement confronted racism in white feminism, challenged police violence, and established sites for community organizing. Bentil's chapter demonstrates the imperative for historians to turn to Black women's organizing when seeking to understand resistance to Thatcher's government.

Another important contribution of the chapters in this volume is the historicization of the concept of intersectionality, as an embodiment and as an organizing principle, for Black feminist activists.[12] Kimberlé Crenshaw's pivotal essay "Demarginalizing the Intersection of Race and Sex: A Black Feminist Critique of Antidiscrimination Doctrine, Feminist Theory and Antiracist Politics" was published in 1989, at the end of the decade covered in this text.[13] Bentil's and Taous Dahmani's essays, in particular, show how UK-based Black feminist activists "theorized" intersectionality in the decade leading up to Crenshaw's US publication.[14] Bentil describes how the "Black socialist feminists in BBWG analyzed their marginalization as "intersecting," contributing to a transnational Black feminist practice that laid the foundations for Kimberlé Crenshaw's coining of "intersectionality" as a theoretical framework in 1989."[15] Dahmani shows how the Black feminist photography magazine *Polareyes* was an important "forerunner to intersectionality, in the way that it simultaneously addressed oppressions related to gender, race, sexual orientation and abilities."[16] These chapters contribute toward the historicization of this crucial term, and to our understanding of the legacy of women's thought and action from this period.[17]

In some instances—like the feminist presses Spinsters Ink and Aunt Lute Books described by Julie R. Enszer and the existence of groups like Gay Student Services historicized by Michael S. Hevel and Charles J. Thompson—the structures that were built in this period of emergency have lasted, despite the constant threat to such grassroots organizations under the growing threat of neoliberalism and institutionalized conservatism of the late twentieth and early twentieth centuries.[18] Some authors in this volume also acknowledge that, while certain tangible structures built in this period have since disbanded, the ideas and "theorization" of this period of feminist and queer activism have endured: this is put forward in Bentil's and in Tamar Holoshitz's chapters on the Black Women's Movement in Britain and on American reproductive rights advocacy, respectively.¹⁹ Our indebtedness to the period is clear from the chapters in this volume, which show how the period was not only one of immediate "fire-fighting," but also of building lasting structures of resistance and the formulation of influential feminist, queer, and anti-racist thought that continues to resonate with a new generation of activists today.²⁰

History and Contexts

The activisms this collection explores emerged from the productive, painful tumult of the 1960s and 1970s. The British Women's Liberation Movement (WLM) was influenced, both in its ideas and its organization, by the women's movements of the United States. Both sets of movements took inspiration from the global radicalism of 1968, and the Black Power movement and the civil rights movement. Both sets of women's movements stressed grassroots organization and undertook radical critiques of the social and political oppression of women. As in the United States, British feminists engaged in consciousness-raising, drawing on their personal experiences to derive political arguments—"the personal is political," as the maxim popularized by American Carol Hanisch went.²¹ But the emphasis on personal experience was also a weakness for the movement: as Black women and other women of color would point out, the British WLM privileged white experiences and often failed to take account of the systemic racism faced by Black women. However, Black women and other women of color played a formative role in many of its campaigns and intellectual work. They would form important autonomous organizations in the 1970s and into the 1980s. Southall Black Sisters was founded in 1979, setting up the Southall Black Women's Centre in 1983, and the Organisation of Women of Asian and African Descent (OWAAD) was established in 1978. Although OWAAD dissolved in 1982, the organization had an enduring and important legacy. Any chronology of women's struggle for liberation, then, needs to consider the 1980s: as chapters in this collection by Bentil, Dahmani, and Turner show, women's demands for resistance and revolution had not dissipated in these later years, but were being led by Black women and other women of color. We suggest that the 1980s should be seen as a longer period than one demarked by decade's beginnings and endings, and by the entrance and retreat of political leaders: we argue that to understand the grassroots activism of this period we need to encompass the late 1970s and look forward to the early 1990s.

The experience of being gay in the 1980s in Britain had been transformed—at least for some—by the earlier visibility, activism, and agitation of the gay liberation movement. The Gay Liberation Front—active between 1970 and 1973—was in part inspired by the Stonewall uprising in New York, highlighting the entanglements of British and American liberationist histories. The first Pride march in England was held in July 1972, just five years after the passage of the Sexual Offences Act 1967, which decriminalized consensual homosexual acts in private between men in England and Wales. The Sexual Offences Act 1967 did not bring male homosexuality onto an even keel with heterosexuality across Britain, however; the age of consent remained unequal. Moreover, Scotland waited until 1980 to decriminalize homosexuality, and Northern Ireland followed in 1982. In its approach to homosexuality, the United Kingdom was not united: the four nations have their own histories.[22]

Legislative homophobia proved to be a major lightning-rod for gay and lesbian protest in Britain in the 1980s: Section 28, while not a focus of a chapter in this collection, formed the backdrop for some of the most memorable protests of the period. Other causes and experiences have been represented on film: in 2014, the film *Pride* brought attention to the interaction between gay liberation activists in London and the struggle of Welsh miners against Thatcher's pit closures,[23] while the cruelties of AIDs in this period have been depicted in recent films including *120 Beats Per Minute* (2017), *Dallas Buyers Club* (2013), and *How to Survive a Plague* (2012), and most recently in the BBC series *It's a Sin* (2021). Other activist experiences have been less well documented: one of the aims of this collection is to highlight these and to place their significance on the historical record.

Despite being portrayed in some historiographies as a period "between the waves," the 1980s were also a time of constant political agitation from queer and feminist organizers in the United States.[24] The chapters in this book show that this was a period in which earlier won rights were defended, in which new groups mobilized over fresh attacks from the right, and in which queer and feminist organizations and theories developed that would influence activisms of the future. Feminist wave theory posits that the 1960s and 1970s saw what was called a "second wave" of American feminism emerge over a wide range of gender equality issues, which then honed in on securing legal reproductive rights. According to this chronology, "second wave" feminist activism died down or descended into infighting in the 1980s as a result of the rise of the New Right, and was subsequently followed by a youth-centered "third wave" that emerged in the early 1990s.[25] This timeline skips past the 1980s as a time of intense and productive progressive political movements, and fails to include explicitly feminist work as a part of the AIDS activism of this era. In fact, this timeline partly inspired us to organize this very collection—both of us frequently had students, in American and British history, respectively, request further reading specifically portraying and analyzing the activism of this period in response to the renewed attacks on feminist and gay liberation goals under Reagan and Thatcher.

Some of the activism that began in this period has been well chronicled by historians, in particular the AIDS activist movement in the United States. Groups such as Gay Men's Health Crisis and ACT UP fought for the Reagan administration to finally publicly recognize the virus, for the inclusion of women's symptoms in the Centers for Disease Control's official definition of illnesses related to the virus, and for research into antiretroviral drugs.[26] In addition to these moves at the national level, AIDS activists across the country built a wide-ranging, inclusive set of grassroots health care and community support networks, which helped center pleasure in safer sex, included lesbian sex practices in the understanding of how AIDS was transmitted, created HIV education, provided support for incarcerated people with HIV/AIDS, campaigned against dehumanizing portrayals of people with AIDS in art and in the media, and documented the experiences of AIDS activists through art, using emerging home video technologies to record and archive their fight, and the lives that were lost, amongst many other actions.[27] In this volume, Katie Batza's chapter on the early response to AIDS in St. Louis, Missouri, shows how "the history of AIDS in the Heartland region challenges many of the paradigms about the epidemic put forth by the dominant historical narrative that focuses on the coastal cities like New York and San Francisco," and that organizations in the region "emerged as some of the most transformational sites of activism as they provided desperately needed services while simultaneously challenging people largely unaffected by the HIV/AIDS epidemic to engage and invest in the epidemic morally, spiritually, and financially."[28]

American activists in the 1980s reached across movements—many women involved in AIDS activist groups had been active in other feminist and queer organizations.[29] An earlier major strand of feminist action in the late twentieth century was the welfare rights movement. Black women-led groups fought hard in the decades preceding the Reagan administration's efforts to crack down on welfare, which blamed young Black and Latinx women for American economic decline.[30] These groups underlined the ways that welfare "was organized and funded in unfair and unequal ways and dependent on racial exclusions, ensuring that some of those who were entitled to benefits were not getting them."[31] Further, Black and Indigenous women and other women of color in the United States in the early 1980s established a movement in feminist thought, in which they centralized anti-racist action within their feminism: this was, in fact, the first use of the term "third wave" in the United States.[32] Through their writings, Gloria Anzaldúa, Cherríe Moraga, bell hooks, Barbara Smith, and other thinkers and activists in this era challenged the "white, middle-class, first world feminism" they had encountered in previous years of organizing, and articulated an "anti-racist, women-of-color-led feminism for the coming decade."[33]

Even this brief overview of some of the many activities of queer and feminist organizers shows that this period of political, social, and cultural history should be the focus of further exploration.[34] This is crucial in order to understand the pivotal activist work that was started in this period, as resistance against intensified reactionary forces, and how it influenced the social movements of the decades that followed, including the anti-racist, feminist, and queer movements of today.[35] The chapters that follow shed light on feminist and queer thought and practice in this period, illuminating new facets of national and transnational debates based in the United States and the United Kingdom, and revealing underexplored, localized efforts of activists in both contexts.

Frameworks and Historiographical Context

This collection is structured into sections around four critical themes: student politics and the body politic; anti-racist, anti-imperialist, and anti-borders action; families, reproduction, and health; and grassroots images, speech, and power. It contributes to a vibrant scholarly conversation around activisms in the post-war period.³⁶ In the United Kingdom, one of the most exciting areas of work is that which is uncovering the experiences of Black women and of communities of color in the 1980s. For example, Amelia Francis has used oral history to explore the role of gender in the Black Liberation Front and women in Black radical organizations; Sue Lemos has challenged the hegemonic whiteness of queer histories of 1980s Britain, noting the surge of LGBTQ+ activism by people of color in the early 1980s ("Perhaps 1981 could be characterised as our 'Stonewall' year," she comments); Aleema Gray has developed a political history of the Rastafari community in England; Jessica White has argued for the importance of Black women's centers.³⁷

Outside this volume, historians have charted women's involvement with other campaigns that resisted Thatcher. Natalie Thomlinson and Florence Sutcliffe-Braithwaite have recently pioneered work into the National Women Against Pit Closures movement.³⁸ Others have focused on women's anti-militarism and peace activism.³⁹ While some agitated around national or local injustices, the 1980s were far from a parochial period for protesters, and in Britain and the United States, women protested nuclear weapons and militaristic foreign policies. Though the engagement of US anti-imperialist groups with US foreign policy is not explored in this volume, a number of chapters contend with the politics of borders and global solidarities from the perspective of activists in the United Kingdom. Charlotte Lydia Riley's chapter in this volume explores the WLM's engagement with the UN Decade for Women, arguing that they "both challenged and replicated the global power imbalances between the Global North and Global South, and specifically the position of women within this hierarchy of global power."⁴⁰ Meanwhile, Jade Bentil's chapter shows how the Black Women's Movement's "tireless campaigning against the exploitative use of the contraceptive injection Depo-Provera" in the United Kingdom and globally is just one way that they "demanded global liberation for Black women."⁴¹

The rise of the politics of the New Right has been subject to historiographical interest. As such, there is a rich historiography of the 1980s in Britain that adopts Thatcher and Thatcherism as its lens.⁴² The purpose of *Resist, Organize, Build* is different: it has as its focus grassroots activism. However, it is not the first scholarly endeavor to disentangle the political leadership of the era from broader social and cultural shifts. In 2014, Stephen Brooke argued that "an overemphasis upon Thatcher or overly identifying the 1980s with the person or her associated ideology obscures a richer historical understanding of that decade, flattening out, rather than opening up our historical understanding of the 1980s."[43] More recently, historians have suggested that "Thatcher and Thatcherism were not inevitable, and were not the sole guiding force of or analytic framework through which we should understand the 1980s. There were other, longer, economic, technological, social and cultural trajectories that account for historical phenomena occurring during the decade."[44] This collection is in harmony with this approach and centers activists' social critiques and political activities to understand the period.

A large body of scholarship on social movements in the United States continues to grow. This collection is, therefore, joining a tradition of feminist and queer historical and theoretical scholarship on the activist cultures that have always been a part of the fabric of American life.[45] Laura Briggs's *How All Politics Became Reproductive Politics* demonstrates this, tracing the activism of welfare rights organizers of the 1970s and the impact of restrictions imposed by Reagan's neoliberal agenda, and then following these debates over reproductive labor up to the administration of Donald Trump. Premilla Nadasen's work on feminist, grassroots organizing has recently included a monograph on the organizing of African American domestic workers, *Household Workers Unite*.[46] Other feminist histories have recently explored the decades-long movements of "race women" in the United States, the Black intellectuals whose work spanned from the late nineteenth century through the Black Power organizing of the 1970s.[47] In *Race Women Internationalists*, Imaobong Umoren follows the transnational activism of three of these women as they built global networks across borders and across liberation movements. Our collection has been inspired by these authors' research to show the importance of transnational networks, communications, and collaborations, and to reflect new chronologies in the history of activism in the twentieth century.

Queer historical studies of the late twentieth century have also set the stage for this collection. There has been a move within queer histories of the United States to focus on activist interactions with the state.[48] The collection *Beyond the Politics of the Closet*, edited by Jonathan Bell, has continued this intervention, which traces the intertwined histories of gay rights movements and American politics since the 1970s, including local housing and health care politics and an important focus on the impact of the AIDS crisis on "racial divisions within sexual minority activism."[49] Scholars, activists, and artists are also undertaking exciting new interdisciplinary research on queer activist histories of the late twentieth-century United States both inside and outside of the academy. Che Gossett, for instance, connects grassroots histories of AIDS activism with ongoing grassroots activism in their writing, and the activist and filmmaker Tourmaline makes films and other artworks that delve into Black trans and queer American histories.[50]

Queer British history has also flourished. Recent work, including Brian Lewis's *Queer British History: New Approaches and Perspectives*, has demonstrated the richness of the modern field.[51] Historians have turned to broad and more bounded histories as a means of exploring LGBTQ+ pasts: Rebecca Jennings has set out a lesbian history of Britain, while Alison Oram has explored women's cross-dressing in modern British press and popular culture, and Chris O'Rourke has argued for the possibilities for queerness within cross-dressing films.[52] Other histories of queer Britain have asserted the importance of place, space, and locality: Matt Houlbrook has explored the relationship between London and its queer communities.[53] Our edited collection is attentive to the politics of place while seeking to identify connections and divergences among groups and moments across geographical locations.

Arguments, Terminology, and Structure of this Volume

Our framework and choice of language—of a "long 1980s"—acknowledges that the ringing in of a new decade does not beget a new set of historical trends. "The long 1980s" acknowledges that the start and end of a decade does not dictate the start and end of activism. Using a decade as an organizing structure, however, recognizes the trends and aesthetics that are conjured in the public memory when a certain decade is invoked—one might look to Wayne Koestenbaum's essay titled "My 1980s," a remembrance of "AIDS, wild art, and Reagan's America," as an example of this.[54] Though the authors in this collection hone in on the 1980s as a period seen to be "between the waves" in feminist and queer activism, and which saw a unique set of challenges due to the racist, heterosexist governments in both contexts, many of the crises and movements explored here began in the late 1970s and fed into the early 1990s (and beyond): hence our term "the long 1980s." Of course, doing such contemporary history presents its own challenges. As Claire Bond Potter and Renee C. Romano note, recent histories face issues around methodology, approach, and source selection: it "talks back." The chapters in this volume deal with these challenges in different ways, and no singular approach was mandated by the editors.[55]

Some linguistic choices should, however, be acknowledged here. First, the contributors tend to refer to the movements they are discussing using the language and terms preferred by the organizations under discussion and individual authors note their personal approaches to language in their essays. The term "queer" has long occupied a contested position, first used as an insult but later reclaimed as a mode of self-description.[56] We have chosen to use the term "queer" for its expansiveness, whilst acknowledging that the turn toward reclaiming this term happened a little later than the period that some of the chapters cover. We use it in our title in recognition of the work undertaken to reclaim and mobilize the term, taking the position that, as Lewis has argued, "queer" is useful as a "big-tent term" and as a signifier that it "builds on a body of recent scholarship that differs in significant ways from the pioneering gay and lesbian history of the 1970s."[57] Our use of "queer" also attempts to recognize the sexual identities of those involved in this era of activism that are not explicitly covered in the chapters of this book, though were undoubtedly present in this period of activism. The "queer" activism in this book does not highlight much of the important work of those challenging sexual binaries, including bisexual, pansexual, or queer activists not committed to one static sexual identity, which in some ways is reflective of the dominance of the terms "lesbian" and "gay" in organizing of this period.[58] However, while the work of bisexual activists did not arise in the work submitted to this volume, important recognition of activists who were not monosexual has been explored by Steven Angelides and Lilian Faderman, among others.[59]

Transgender and queer activists of color have been central to the fight for sexual and gender liberation.[60] Some of the work in *Resist, Organize, Build* does describe the importance of trans activism within the larger LGBTQ+ struggle. Hevel and Thompson's chapter on the history of Gay Student Services at Texas A&M University describes the way that the organization was "advancing toward greater inclusion" in changing its name ultimately to "Gay, Lesbian, Bisexual and Transgender Aggies" by 1997.[61] Nora Kassner's chapter on queer foster families mentions the way in which Gay and Lesbian Adolescent Social Services in Los Angeles "operated three state-licensed group homes" that each provided care for "between six and twelve queer and trans youth at a time."[62] Flora Dunster's contribution to *Resist, Organize, Build* discusses the themes of the feminist sex wars as they played out in an underground publication, *Lesbians Talk*, which recognizes "lesbian solidarities past" and the work of trans activists of this period, working against reactionary sentiments from the right and from within certain feminisms.[63] While the vastness of trans and feminist resistance in this era across these two contexts could not be captured in this one volume, we hope that these chapters point readers toward further research on trans histories, by such thinkers such as Susan Stryker, C. Riley Snorton, and Che Gossett, and inspire further volumes on the work of trans activists of this era.[64]

Several themes emerged in the authors' submissions to this collection and have fed into how we organized the sections. An important theme that emerges in the stories our authors tell is the importance of student activism in this period in confronting the manifestations of the New Right's homophobia on campus. Two chapters make up this first section. Katherine Rye Jewell's account uses American college radio to examine how queer activists worked both inside of and necessarily against the institutional limits they faced at their universities, while Michael S. Hevel and Charles J. Thompson's chapter explores the fight that a group of activists took on at Texas A&M University in their endeavor to run an official gay student services on campus. These chapters further historicize the recent culture wars on American campuses and illuminate the longer story of student activism. The book then turns to the urgent anti-racist work happening in this period, which connected activists engaged in global liberation struggles. Jade Bentil's chapter uses archival material and oral history interviews with members of the Black Women's Movement to explore how Black women resisted the Thatcher government and challenged conceptions of nationhood in 1980s Britain. Charlotte Lydia Riley's chapter uses the feminist magazine *Spare Rib*'s coverage of the UN Decade for Women conferences to challenge depictions of British feminism as parochial and to examine the extent and limitations of the WLM's engagement with international gender issues. The third theme is that of continued reproductive rights organizing, which has been strongly associated with the preceding decade, and was necessitated by federal and local threats to the gains of these movements. The third section of this volume thus brings together writing on families, reproduction, and bodily health. This includes Nora Kassner's microhistorical account of queer foster parenting activism in 1980s Los Angeles, which shows how queer organizations responded to a spike in homelessness under Reagan, and its impact on LGBTQ+ youth. Kate Turner's chapter sets out how the British Black Women's Movement situated mothering as a political activity and contrasts it to the politics of the family put forward by Thatcherism. The section contains Tamar Holoshitz's chapter on the significance of pro-choice legal activism in the 1980s. Her contribution demonstrates the importance of not portraying the period myopically as one of a series of increasing restrictions on access to abortion, as doing so obscures the work of feminist activists, and highlights ways that reproductive rights activists fighting in the current political climate can learn from the legacy of 1980s reproductive rights activists. Finally, Katie Batza demonstrates the importance of understanding the activist response to AIDS in religious and in rural communities, complementing analyses of AIDS that center on activism in major US cities.

Another key theme of *Resist, Organize, Build* is the ways that grassroots print cultures were used in this period to forge networks, confront the racist and heterosexist mainstream media, and create documentation of the voices of 1980s activists as a legacy for future generations. The fourth section therefore examines the development of grassroots images, speech, and power. Taous Dahmani examines *Polareyes*, a single-issue photography and text magazine produced by a collective of Black women in 1987 as a site of resistance and creativity, while Flora Dunster asserts the complexity of the sex wars in Britain, turning to the book series *Lesbians Talk Issues* to explore the feminist lesbian politics of the 1980s and early 1990s and to trouble the binaries constructed around the positions adopted during the "sex wars." Julie R. Enszer's chapter describes the importance of two queer feminist publishing houses in the proliferation of lesbian feminist work of the period, which enabled such critical theoretical writings as Gloria Anzaldúa's *Borderlands* to gain circulation.

The chapters within this volume highlight not only emergent histories but emergent scholars—many of the authors in these pages are in the early stages of their career, conducting research that will come to be significant contributions to the fields in which they work. It brings together researchers based in Europe and the United States, and those who have had experiences working across these contexts. This is not intended to be an exhaustive collection of the feminist and gay rights activism of this period, but rather a snapshot of some of the exciting work being done in the field. The collection's audience is intended to be scholars, students, and communities interested in queer and feminist histories. It furthers the growing literature on this epoch by elucidating how marginalized communities in the United States and Britain fought for their rights and those of others during a time of renewed conservatism in these nations.

These chapters tell the stories of previously underexplored groups, individuals, and movements of local, national, and transatlantic scales. In and across their various contexts, these activists fought against heightened violence and repression, and put in place alternative structures of community and care across their respective communities. The contributions to this volume depict the challenges and gains that faced activists working from seemingly disparate organizational frames. We hope you will find courage and hope in these historical movements as we forge forward as scholars trying to understand past resistance, and as feminist and queer activists in the present.

Notes

1. Araba Mercer, in *Lesbians Talk Making Black Waves*, eds. Valerie Mason-John and Ann Khambatta (London: Scarlet Press, 1993), 53. This series is discussed in Flora Dunster's chapter in this volume.

2. John D'Emilio and Estelle B. Freedman, *Intimate Matters: A History of Sexuality in America*, 2nd ed. (Chicago: University of Chicago Press, 2012), 345.

3. Laura Briggs, *How All Politics Became Reproductive Politics: From Welfare Reform to Foreclosure to Trump* (Oakland: University of California Press, 2017), 70–71, 73. For more on the history of public discourse surrounding young women in the US culture wars from the 1980s onward, see Charlie Jeffries, *Teenage Dreams: Girlhood Sexualities in the U.S. Culture Wars* (New Brunswick, NJ: Rutgers University Press, 2022).

4. See D'Emilio and Freedman, *Intimate Matters*, 354, and Alexandra M. Lord, *Condom Nation: The U.S. Government's Sex Education Campaign from World War I to the Internet* (Baltimore, MD: Johns Hopkins University Press, 2010), 148.

5. See James Davison Hunter, *Culture Wars: The Struggle to Define America* (New York: Basic Books, 1991), and Andrew Hartman, *A War for the Soul of America: A History of the Culture Wars* (Chicago: University of Chicago Press, 2015).

6. Margaret Thatcher, Remarks Arriving at the White House, 26 February 1981. www.margaretthatcher.org/document/104576

7. See Jade Bentil, "'We were fire-fighting against Thatcher and the system she was putting forward': The Black Women's Movement and the Boundaries of Nationhood in Thatcher's Britain," and Kate Turner, "Thatcherism, the Black Women's Movement and the Politics of Motherhood in Britain," both in this volume.

8. See Nydia A. Swaby, "'Disparate in Voice, Sympathetic in Direction': Gendered Political Blackness and the Politics of Solidarity." *Feminist Review* 108 (2014): 11–25. For more on race in 1980s Britain, see also Rob Waters, *Thinking Black: Britain, 1964–1985* (Oakland: University of California Press, 2018); Kieran Connell, *Black Handsworth: race in 1980s Britain* (Oakland: University of California Press, 2019); Simon Peplow, *Race and riots in Thatcher's Britain* (Manchester: Manchester University Press, 2019); Daniel Renshaw, "The Violent Frontline: space, ethnicity and confronting the state in Edwardian Spitalfields and 1980s Brixton,' *Contemporary British History*, 32 (2018), 231–252.

9. See Julie R. Enszer, "The Business of Feminism Endures: Four Decades of Spinsters Ink and Aunt Lute Books Publishing Lesbian-Feminist Books in the United States," in this volume.

10. Bentil, "We were fire-fighting . . . ," in this volume.

11. Bentil, 'We were fire-fighting. . . ."

12. Argued by Bentil, "We were fire-fighting . . . ," 94–96, and Taous Dahmani, "*Polareyes*: A Magazine by and for Black British Women Photographers as Site of Resistance in London, 1987," 311–312, both in this volume.

13. Kimberlé Crenshaw, "Demarginalizing the Intersection of Race and Sex: A Black Feminist Critique of Antidiscrimination Doctrine, Feminist Theory and Antiracist Politics," *The University of Chicago Legal Forum* 140 (1989).

14. Bentil, "We were fire-fighting. . . ."

15. Bentil, "We were fire-fighting. . . ."

16. Dahmani, "*Polareyes*."

17. See Bentil, "We were fire-fighting. . . ."

18. See Enszer, "The Business of Feminism Endures," and Michael S. Hevel and Charles J. Thompson, "Aggies are *Not* Queers": A History of *Gay Student Services v. Texas A&M University*, 1975–1985," both in this volume.

19. See Bentil, "We were fire-fighting . . ." and Tamar Holoshitz, "A Framework for Choice: The Lasting Influence of 1980s Advocacy on Reproductive Rights in the United States," both in this volume.

20. For more on the impact of Black women's organizing in the 1980s on today's "movements for social justice," see Bentil, "We were fire-fighting. . . ."

21. Carol Hanisch, "The Personal is Political," *Notes from the Second Year: Women's Liberation Major Writings of the Radical Feminists* (New York: Radical Feminism, 1970): 76–78.

22. Exciting work is going on in this field. For example, an AHRC-funded project led by Tom Hulme and Leanne McCormick is examining sexuality in Northern Ireland from the late nineteenth to the mid–twentieth century.

23. Academic work has also drawn attention to solidarities between miners and gay activists, and connections between London and the coalfields during the 1980s. See Diarmaid Kelliher, "Solidarity and Sexuality: Lesbians and Gays Support the Miners 1984–5," *History Workshop Journal* 77.1 (Spring 2014):

240–262, and Diarmaid Kelliher, "Contested Spaces: London and the 1984–5 Miners' Strike," *Twentieth Century British History* 28.4 (December 2017): 595–617.

24. For more on the problems of understanding US feminisms in waves, see Kimberly Springer, "Third Wave Black Feminism?" *Signs* 27 (Summer 2002), and *No Permanent Waves: Recasting Histories of U.S. Feminism*, ed. Nancy Hewitt (New Brunswick, NJ: Rutgers University Press, 2010). The contributors to the collection *No Permanent Waves* made an important intervention into thinking outside of the traditional wave chronology, and how troubling that timeline is critical in understanding the activism of those who have been marginalized within or excluded by those involved in mainstream feminist movements. See, for example, Whitney A. Peoples, "'Under Construction': Identifying Foundations of Hip-Hop Feminism and Exploring Bridges between Black Second Wave and Hip-Hop Feminisms"; Marisela Chávez, "'We Have a Long, Beautiful History': Chicana Feminist Trajectories and Legacies"; and Leela Fernandes, "Unsettling 'Third Wave Feminism': Feminist Waves, Intersectionality, and Identity Politics in Retrospect."

25. An important recent historical study that disputes this characterization of the 1980s is Lorna N. Bracewell's *Why We Lost the Sex Wars: Sexual Freedom in the #MeToo Era* (Minneapolis: University of Minnesota Press, 2021).

26. For more on the work of AIDS activists, see Sarah Schulman, *Let the Record Show: A Political History of ACT UP New York, 1987–1993* (New York: Farrar, Straus, and Giroux, 2021), Ann Cvetkovich, *An Archive of Feelings: Trauma, Sexuality, and Lesbian Public Culture* (Durham, NC: Duke University Press, 2003), and Gina Corea, *The Invisible Epidemic: The Story of Women and AIDS* (New York: Harper Collins, 1992).

27. See Schulman, *Let the Record Show*, Cvetkovich, *An Archive of Feelings*; Corea, *The Invisible Epidemic*; Nancy Goldstein, "Lesbians and the Medical Profession: HIV/AIDS and the Pursuit of Visibility," in *The Gender Politics of HIV/AIDS in Women: Perspectives on the Pandemic in the United States*, eds. Nancy Goldstein and Jennifer L. Manlowe (New York: New York University Press, 1997); Deborah B. Gould, "Life during Wartime: Emotions and the Development of ACT UP," *Mobilization* 7 (2002); Douglas Crimp, *Melancholia and Moralism* (Cambridge, MA: MIT Press, 2002); Alexandra Juhasz, "AIDS Video: To Dream and Dance with the Censor," *EJump Cut: A Review of Contemporary Media* 52 (Summer 2010).

28. See Katie Batza, "Opening DOORWAYS and Closing Others: Tactical Deployments of Respectability, Religion, and Race in the St. Louis Early-AIDS Response," in this volume.

29. Cvetkovich, *An Archive of Feelings*, 157.

30. Briggs, *How All Politics Became Reproductive Politics*, 34–35. See also Premilla Nadasen, *Welfare Warriors: The Welfare Rights Movement in the United States* (New York: Routledge, 2005).

31. Briggs, *How All Politics Became Reproductive Politics*, 35.

32. See Leslie Heywood and Jennifer Drake, "Introduction," *Third Wave Agenda: Being Feminist, Doing Feminism* (Minneapolis: University of Minnesota Press, 1997), cited by Catherine M. Orr, in "Charting the Currents of the Third Wave," *Hypatia* 12.3 (August 1997): 29–45, and Springer, "Third Wave Black Feminism?," 1063.

33. First quote is from Orr, "Charting the Currents," 29–45. Second quote is from Springer, "Third Wave Black Feminism?," 1063.

34. For more on the limits of wave theory and the importance of this period of activism, see Bentil, "We were fire-fighting. . . ." See also Lisa Levenstein, *They Didn't See Us Coming: The Hidden History of Feminism in the Nineties* (New York: Basic Books, 2020), which shows the importance of this kind of historical research in a study of a different decade.

35. For more on the impact of Black women's organizing in the 1980s on today's "movements for social justice," see Bentil, "We were fire-fighting. . . ."

36. The British WLM, for example, has seen its historiography flourish. See Margaretta Jolly, *Sisterhood and After: An Oral History of the Women's Liberation Movement* (Oxford: Oxford University Press, 2019); Eve Setch, "The Face of Metropolitan Feminism: The London Women's Liberation Workshop, 1969–79,' *Twentieth Century British History*, 13.2 (2002): 171–190; Sarah Stoller, "Forging a Politics of Care: Theorizing Household Work in the British Women's Liberation Movement,' *History Workshop Journal* 85 (Spring 2018): 95–119; Sue Bruley, "Consciousness-Raising in Clapham: Women's Liberation as 'Lived Experience' in South London in the 1970s," *Women's History Review* 22:5 (2013): 717–738; Laurel Forster, "Spreading the Word: Feminist Print Cultures and the Women's Liberation Movement," *Women's History Review* 25.5 (2016): 812–831; Sarah Browne, *The Women's Liberation Movement in Scotland* (Manchester: Manchester University Press, 2014); Sue Bruley, "Women's Liberation at the Grass Roots: A View from Some English Towns, c.1968–1990," *Women's History Review* 25.5 (2016): 723–740; Terese Jonsson, "The Narrative Reproduction of White Feminist Racism," *Feminist Review* 113.1 (July 2016): 50–67; Natalie Thomlinson, *Race, Ethnicity and the Women's Movement in England, 1968–1993* (Basingstoke: Palgrave Macmillan, 2016); George Stevenson, *The Women's Liberation Movement and the Politics of Class in Britain* (London & New York: Bloomsbury, 2019).

37. These scholars also represent the ways that historical research in this area is promoted outside the boundaries of traditional journals, and that early career scholars are turning to blogs and podcasts to share their work more expansively and inclusively. See Amelia Francis, "'No Liberation Without Black Women': Gender in the Black Liberation Front," *Women's History Network Blog*, 22 October 2018, womenshistorynetwork.org/no-liberation-without-black-women-gender-in-the-black-liberation-front-by-amelia-francis; Sue Lemos, "'I thanked the ancestors it is not something you can box up neatly': Uncovering stories of

Black and Brown LGBTQ+ activism in post-war Britain." *Queer/Disrupt*, January 15, 2021. www.queerdisrupt.com/index.php/2021/01/15/i-thanked-the-ancestors-it-is-not-something-you-can-box-up-neatly-uncovering-stories-of-black-and-brown-lgbtq-activism-in-post-war-britain; Warwick PG Podcast, "Queer(in)g History," soundcloud.com/user-627299331/queering-history; Aleema Gray, "The Rastafari in Britain: Writing Community-Engaged History," *History Workshop Online* (25 November 2019), www.historyworkshop.org.uk/the-rastafari-in-britain. Also see Derek Bishton, "Aleema Gray on Pioneer Rastafari Filmmaker D Elmina Davis," www.derekbishton.com/aleema-gray-on-pioneer-rastafari-filmmaker-d-elmina-davis. Of course the academic journal article endures—see Jessica White, "Black Women's Groups, Life Narratives, and the Construction of the Self in Late Twentieth-Century Britain," *The Historical Journal* (2021): 1–21.

38. Natalie Thomlinson and Florence Sutcliffe-Braithwaite, "National Women Against Pit Closures: Gender, Trade Unionism, and Community Activism," *Contemporary British History* 32.1 (2018): 78–100.

39. See Jill Liddington, *The Road to Greenham Common: Feminism and Anti-Militarism in Britain since 1820* (Syracuse, NY: Syracuse University Press, 1991); Elaine Titcombe, "Women Activists: Rewriting Greenham's History," *Women's History Review* 22.2 (2013): 310–329.

40. See Charlotte Lydia Riley, "Spiritualists, Ideologues, Pragmatists, Feminists, and Women of All Descriptions: The British Women's Liberation Movement, the UN Decade for Women, and Feminist Transnationalism in *Spare Rib*," in this volume.

41. Bentil, "We were fire-fighting. . . ."

42. See, for example, Robert Saunders and Ben Jackson (eds.), *Making Thatcher's Britain* (Cambridge: Cambridge University Press, 2012).

43. Stephen Brooke, "Living in 'New Times': Historicizing 1980s Britain," *History Compass* 12 (2014): 20–32.

44. Matthew Hilton, Chris Moores and Florence Sutcliffe-Braithwaite, "*New Times* revisited: Britain in the 1980s," *Contemporary British History* 31.2 (2017): 145–165, 146.

45. Including such publications as *Beyond the Politics of the Closet: Gay Rights and the American State Since the 1970s*, ed. Jonathan Bell (Philadelphia: University of Pennsylvania Press, 2020), and Bradford Martin, *The Other Eighties: A Secret History of America in the Age of Reagan* (New York: Hill and Wang, 2011).

46. Premilla Nadasen, *Household Workers Unite: The Untold Story of African American Women Who Built a Movement* (Boston: Beacon Press, 2015).

47. See Brittney C. Cooper, *Beyond Respectability: The Intellectual Thought of Race Women* (Urbana: University of Illinois Press, 2017), and Imaobong D. Umoren, *Race Women Internationalists: Activist-Intellectuals and Global Freedom Struggles* (Oakland: University of California Press, 2018).

48. Work on sexuality and the state has been driven in particular by the work of Margot Canaday, in *The Straight State: Sexuality and Citizenship in Twentieth-Century America* (Princeton, NJ: Princeton University Press, 2009).

49. Bell (ed.), *Beyond the Politics of the Closet*, 10.

50. See Che Gossett and Eva Hayward, "Trans in a Time of HIV/AIDS," in their special issue of *Transgender Studies Quarterly* of the same title: *Transgender Studies Quarterly* 7.4 (November 2020), in particular from 543 on the work of Tourmaline and other artists creating an "anarchival archive." See also Che Gossett, "We Will Not Rest in Peace: AIDS Activism, Black Radicalism, Queer and/or Trans Resistance," in *Queer Necropolitics*, eds. Adi Kuntsman, Jin Haritaworn, and Silvia Posocco (New York: Routledge, 2014), and Che Gossett, "Silhouettes of Defiance: Memorializing Sites of Queer and Trans Resistance in a Time of Neoliberal Inclusivity," in volume 2 of *The Transgender Studies Reader*, eds. Susan Stryker and Aren Aizura (New York: Routledge, 2013), and Tourmaline's films *The Personal Things* (2016) and *Happy Birthday Marsha!* (2018).

51. Brian Lewis, *Queer British History: New Approaches and Perspectives* (Manchester: Manchester University Press, 2013).

52. Alison Oram, *Her Husband was a Woman!: Women's Gender-Crossing in Modern British Popular Culture* (Abingdon: Routledge, 2007); Rebecca Jennings, *A Lesbian History of Britain: Love and Sex between Women since 1500* (Santa Barbara, CA: Greenwood World Publishing, 2007); Chris O'Rourke, "'What a Pretty Man—or Girl!': Male Cross-Dressing Performances in Early British Cinema, 1898–1918," *Gender & History* 32 (2020): 86–107.

53. Matt Houlbrook, *Queer London: Perils and Pleasures in the Sexual Metropolis 1918–1957* (University of Chicago Press, 2005).

54. See Wayne Koestenbaum, "My 1980s," in *My 1980s & Other Essays* (New York: Farrar, Straus and Giroux, 2013). Quote from Wayne Koestenbaum, "Wayne Koestenbaum: My 1980s," *Salon* 24 (August 2013). www.salon.com/2013/08/23/wayne_koestenbaum_my_1980s

55. Claire Bond Potter and Renee C. Romano, *Doing Recent History: On Privacy, Copyright, Video Games, Institutional Review Boards, Activist Scholarship, and History that Talks Back* (Athens & London: University of Georgia Press, 2012).

56. Brian Lewis (ed.), "Introduction," *British Queer History: New Approaches and Perspectives* (Manchester: Manchester University Press, 2013), 1–16, 2.

57. Lewis, "Introduction," 3.

58. See, for example, Cvetkovich's interviews with AIDS activists about sexual fluidity in the movement in *An Archive of Feelings*, from 191, and Lilian Faderman, *The Gay Revolution: The Story of the Struggle* (New York: Simon & Schuster, 2015), xx.

59. See, for example, Steven Angelides, *A History of Bisexuality* (Chicago: University of Chicago Press, 2001) and Faderman, *The Gay Revolution*.

60. See, for example, C. Riley Snorton, *Black on Both Sides: A Racial History of Trans Identity* (Minneapolis: University of Minnesota Press, 2017), 208. See also Scott James, "Queer People of Color Led the L.G.B.T.Q. Charge, but Were Denied the Rewards," *New York Times*, 22 June 2019.

61. Hevel and Thompson, "Aggies are *Not* Queers."

62. Nora Kassner, "Making Queer Families: Foster Family Activism in Los Angeles, 1977–1985," in this volume.

63. Flora Dunster, "*Lesbians Talk*: British Lesbian Politics and the Sex Wars," in this volume.

64. See, for example, Susan Stryker, *Transgender History (Second Edition): The Roots of Today's Revolution* (Berkeley, CA: Seal Press, 2017); Snorton, *Black on Both Sides*; Gossett and Hayward, "Trans in a Time of HIV/AIDS."

Works Cited

Angelides, Steven, *A History of Bisexuality*. Chicago: University of Chicago Press, 2001.

Batza, Katie. "Opening DOORWAYS and Closing Others: Tactical Deployments of Respectability, Religion, and Race in the St. Louis Early-AIDS Response," in *Resist, Organize, Build*, eds. Sarah Crook and Charlie Jeffries. Albany, NY: SUNY Press, 2022.

Bell, Jonathan, ed. *Beyond the Politics of the Closet: Gay Rights and the American State Since the 1970s*. Philadelphia: University of Pennsylvania Press, 2020.

Bentil, Jade. " 'We were fire-fighting against Thatcher and the system she was putting forward': The Black Women's Movement and the Boundaries of Nationhood in Thatcher's Britain," in *Resist, Organize, Build*," in *Resist, Organize, Build*, eds. Sarah Crook and Charlie Jeffries. Albany, NY: SUNY Press, 2022.

Bishton, Derek. "Aleema Gray on Pioneer Rastafari Filmmaker D Elmina Davis." www.derekbishton.com/aleema-gray-on-pioneer-rastafari-filmmaker-d-elmina-davis

Black, Lawrence. "An Enlightening Decade? New Histories of 1970s Britain." *International Labor and Working-Class History* 82 (2012): 174–186.

Bracewell, Lorna N. *Why We Lost the Sex Wars: Sexual Freedom in the #MeToo Era*. Minneapolis: University of Minnesota Press, 2021.

Briggs, Laura. *How All Politics Became Reproductive Politics: From Welfare Reform to Foreclosure to Trump*. Oakland: University of California Press, 2017.

Brooke, Stephen. "Living in 'New Times': Historicizing 1980s Britain." *History Compass* 12 (2014): 20–32.

Browne, Sarah. *The Women's Liberation Movement in Scotland*. Manchester: Manchester University Press, 2014.

Bruley, Sue. "Consciousness-Raising in Clapham: Women's Liberation as 'Lived Experience' in South London in the 1970s." *Women's History Review* 22.5 (2013): 717–738.

Bruley, Sue. "Women's Liberation at the Grass Roots: A View from Some English Towns, c.1968–1990." *Women's History Review* 25.5 (2016): 723–740.

Canaday, Margot. *The Straight State: Sexuality and Citizenship in Twentieth-Century America*. Princeton, NJ: Princeton University Press, 2009.

Connell, Kieran. *Black Handsworth: Race in 1980s Britain*. Berkeley, CA, University of California Press, 2019.

Cooper, Brittney C. *Beyond Respectability: The Intellectual Thought of Race Women*. Urbana: University of Illinois Press, 2017.

Coote, Anna, and Beatrix Campbell. *Sweet Freedom: The Struggle for Women's Liberation*. London: Picador, 1982.

Corea, Gina. *The Invisible Epidemic: The Story of Women and AIDS*. New York: Harper Collins, 1992.

Crenshaw, Kimberlé. "Demarginalizing the Intersection of Race and Sex: A Black Feminist Critique of Antidiscrimination Doctrine, Feminist Theory and Antiracist Politics." *The University of Chicago Legal Forum* 140 (1989).

Crimp, Douglas. *Melancholia and Moralism*. Cambridge, MA: MIT Press, 2002.

Cvetkovich, Ann. *An Archive of Feelings: Trauma, Sexuality, and Lesbian Public Culture*. Durham, NC: Duke University Press, 2003.

D'Emilio, John, and Estelle B. Freedman. *Intimate Matters: A History of Sexuality in America*, 2nd ed. Chicago: University of Chicago Press, 2012.

Dahmani, Taous. "*Polareyes*: A Magazine by and For Black British Women Photographers as Site of Resistance in London, 1987," in *Resist, Organize, Build*, eds. Sarah Crook and Charlie Jeffries. Albany, NY: SUNY Press, 2022.

Dunster, Flora. "Lesbians Talk: British Lesbian Politics and the Sex Wars," in *Resist, Organize, Build*, eds. Sarah Crook and Charlie Jeffries. Albany, NY: SUNY Press, 2022.

Enszer, Julie R. "The Business of Feminism Endures: Four Decades of Spinsters Ink and Aunt Lute Books Publishing Lesbian-Feminist Books in the United States," in *Resist, Organize, Build*, eds. Sarah Crook and Charlie Jeffries. Albany, NY: SUNY Press, 2022.

Faderman, Lilian. *The Gay Revolution: The Story of the Struggle*. New York: Simon & Schuster, 2015.

Forster, Laurel. "Spreading the Word: Feminist Print Cultures and the Women's Liberation Movement." *Women's History Review* 25.5: (2016) 812–831.

Francis, Amelia. " 'No Liberation Without Black Women': Gender in the Black Liberation Front." Women's History Network blog, 22 October 2018. https://womenshistorynetwork.org/no-liberation-without-black-women-gender-in-the-black-liberation-front-by-amelia-francis

Goldstein, Nancy. "Lesbians and the Medical Profession: HIV/AIDS and the Pursuit of Visibility," in *The Gender Politics of HIV/AIDS in Women: Perspectives on the Pandemic in the United States*, eds. Nancy Goldstein and Jennifer L. Manlowe. New York: New York University Press, 1997.

Gossett, Che, and Eva Hayward. "Trans in a Time of HIV/AIDS." *Transgender Studies Quarterly* 7.4 (November 2020): 527–553.

Gossett, Che. "Silhouettes of Defiance: Memorializing Sites of Queer and Trans Resistance in a Time of Neoliberal Inclusivity," in *The Transgender Studies Reader*, vol. 2, eds. Susan Stryker and Aren Azuira. New York: Routledge, 2013.

Gossett, Che. "We Will Not Rest in Peace: AIDS Activism, Black Radicalism, Queer and/or Trans Resistance." *Queer Necropolitics*, eds. Adi Kuntsman, Jin Haritaworn, and Silvia Posocco. New York: Routledge, 2014.

Gould, Deborah B. "Life During Wartime: Emotions and the Development of ACT UP." *Mobilization* 7 (2002).

Gray, Aleema. "The Rastafari in Britain: Writing Community-Engaged History." *History Workshop Online*, 25 November 2019. www.historyworkshop.org.uk/the-rastafari-in-britain

Hanisch, Carol. "The Personal is Political." *Notes from the Second Year: Women's Liberation Major Writings of the Radical Feminists*. New York: Radical Feminism, 1970.

Hartman, Andrew. *A War for the Soul of America: A History of the Culture Wars*. Chicago: University of Chicago Press, 2015.

Hevel, Michael S., and Charles J. Thompson. ""Aggies are *Not* Queers": A History of *Gay Student Services v. Texas A&M University, 1975–1985*," in *Resist, Organize, Build*, eds. Sarah Crook and Charlie Jeffries. Albany, NY: SUNY Press, 2022.

Hewitt, Nancy, ed. *No Permanent Waves: Recasting Histories of U.S. Feminism*. New Brunswick, NJ: Rutgers University Press, 2010.

Heywood, Leslie, and Jennifer Drake. "Introduction." *Third Wave Agenda: Being Feminist, Doing Feminism*. Minneapolis: University of Minnesota Press, 1997.

Hilton, Matthew, Chris Moores, and Florence Sutcliffe-Braithwaite. "New Times Revisited: Britain in the 1980s." *Contemporary British History* 31.2 (2017): 145–165, 146.

Holoshitz, Tamar. "A Framework for Choice: The Lasting Influence of 1980s Advocacy on Reproductive Rights in the United States," in *Resist, Organize, Build*, eds. Sarah Crook and Charlie Jeffries. Albany, NY: SUNY Press, 2022.

Houlbrook, Matt. *Queer London: Perils and Pleasures in the Sexual Metropolis 1918–1957*. Chicago: University of Chicago Press, 2005.

Hunter, James Davison. *Culture Wars: The Struggle to Define America*. New York: Basic Books, 1991.

James, Scott. "Queer People of Color Led the L.G.B.T.Q. Charge, but Were Denied the Rewards." *New York Times*, 22 June 2019. www.google.co.uk/books/edition/Beyond_the_Politics_of_the_Closet/6ureDwAAQBAJ?hl=en&gbpv=1&printsec=frontcover

Jeffries, Charlie. *Teenage Dreams: Girlhood Sexualities in the U.S. Culture Wars*. New Brunswick, NJ: Rutgers University Press, 2022.
Jennings, Rebecca. *A Lesbian History of Britain: Love and Sex Between Women Since 1500*. Santa Barbara, CA: Greenwood World Publishing, 2007.
Jolly, Margaretta. *Sisterhood and After: An Oral History of the Women's Liberation Movement*. Oxford: Oxford University Press, 2019.
Jonsson, Terese. "The Narrative Reproduction of White Feminist Racism." *Feminist Review* 113.1 (July 2016): 50–67.
Juhasz, Alexandra. "AIDS Video: To Dream and Dance with the Censor." *EJump Cut: A Review of Contemporary Media* 52 (Summer 2010).
Kassner, Nora. "Making Queer Families: Foster Family Activism in Los Angeles, 1977–1985," in *Resist, Organize, Build*, eds. Sarah Crook and Charlie Jeffries. Albany, NY: SUNY Press, 2022.
Kelliher, Diarmaid. "Contested Spaces: London and the 1984–5 Miners' Strike." *Twentieth Century British History* 28.4 (December 2017): 595–617.
Kelliher, Diarmaid. "Solidarity and Sexuality: Lesbians and Gays Support the Miners 1984–5." *History Workshop Journal* 77.1 (Spring 2014): 240–262.
Koestenbaum, Wayne. "My 1980s." *My 1980s & Other Essays*. New York: Farrar, Straus and Giroux, 2013.
Koestenbaum, Wayne. "Wayne Koestenbaum: My 1980s." *Salon* 24 (August 2013). www.salon.com/2013/08/23/wayne_koestenbaum_my_1980s
Lemos, Sue. "'I thanked the ancestors it is not something you can box up neatly': Uncovering Stories of Black and Brown LGBTQ+ Activism in Post-war Britain." *Queer/Disrupt* 15 January 2021. www.queerdisrupt.com/index.php/2021/01/15/i-thanked-the-ancestors-it-is-not-something-you-can-box-up-neatly-uncovering-stories-of-black-and-brown-lgbtq-activism-in-post-war-britain
Levenstein, Lisa. *They Didn't See Us Coming: The Hidden History of Feminism in the Nineties*. New York: Basic Books, 2020.
Lewis, Brian, ed. "Introduction." *British Queer History: New Approaches and Perspectives*. Manchester: Manchester University Press, 2013.
Liddington, Jill. *The Road to Greenham Common: Feminism and Anti-Militarism in Britain since 1820*. Syracuse, NY: Syracuse University Press, 1991.
Lord, Alexandra M. *Condom Nation: The U.S. Government's Sex Education Campaign from World War I to the Internet*. Baltimore, MD: Johns Hopkins University Press, 2010.
Martin, Bradford. *The Other Eighties: A Secret History of America in the Age of Reagan*. New York: Hill and Wang, 2011.
Mason-John, Valerie, and Ann Khambatta, eds. *Lesbians Talk Making Black Waves*. London: Scarlet Press, 1993.
Nadasen, Premilla. *Household Workers Unite: The Untold Story of African American Women who Built a Movement*. Boston: Beacon Press, 2015.

Nadasen, Premilla. *Welfare Warriors: The Welfare Rights Movement in the United States.* New York: Routledge, 2005.

Oram, Alison. *Her Husband Was a Woman!: Women's Gender-Crossing in Modern British Popular Culture.* Abingdon: Routledge, 2007.

O'Rourke, Chris. "What a Pretty Man—or Girl!': Male Cross-Dressing Performances in Early British Cinema, 1898–1918." *Gender & History* 32 (2020): 86–107.

Orr, Catherine M. "Charting the Currents of the Third Wave." *Hypatia* 12.3 (August 1997): 29–45.

Peplow, Simon. *Race and riots in Thatcher's Britain.* Manchester: Manchester University Press, 2019.

Renshaw, Daniel. "The Violent Frontline: Space, Ethnicity and Confronting the State in Edwardian Spitalfields and 1980s Brixton." *Contemporary British History* 32 (2018): 231–252.

Riley, Charlotte Lydia. "'Spiritualists, ideologues, pragmatists, feminists and women of all descriptions': The British Women's Liberation Movement, the UN Decade For Women and Feminist Transnationalism in *Spare Rib*," in *Resist, Organize, Build*, eds. Sarah Crook and Charlie Jeffries. Albany, NY: SUNY Press, 2022.

Rowbotham, Sheila. *Promise of a Dream: Remembering the Sixties.* London: Verso, 2001.

Rowbotham, Sheila. *Women, Resistance, and Revolution: A History of Women and Revolution in the Modern World.* New York: Pantheon, 1972.

Saunders, Robert, and Ben Jackson, eds. *Making Thatcher's Britain.* Cambridge: Cambridge University Press, 2012.

Setch, Eve. "The Face of Metropolitan Feminism: The London Women's Liberation Workshop, 1969–79." *Twentieth Century British History* 13.2 (2002): 171–190.

Snorton, C. Riley. *Black on Both Sides: A Racial History of Trans Identity.* Minneapolis: University of Minnesota Press, 2017.

Springer, Kimberly. "Third Wave Black Feminism?" *Signs* 27 (Summer 2002): 1059–1082.

Stevenson, George. *The Women's Liberation Movement and the Politics of Class in Britain.* London & New York: Bloomsbury, 2019.

Stoller, Sarah. "Forging a Politics of Care: Theorizing Household Work in the British Women's Liberation Movement." *History Workshop Journal* 85 (Spring 2018): 95–119.

Stryker, Susan. *Transgender History (Second Edition): The Roots of Today's Revolution.* Berkeley, CA: Seal Press, 2017.

Swaby, Nydia A. "'Disparate in Voice, Sympathetic in Direction': Gendered Political Blackness and the Politics of Solidarity." *Feminist Review* 108 (2014): 11–25.

Thatcher, Margaret. Remarks arriving at the White House, 26 February 1981. www.margaretthatcher.org/document/104576
Thomlinson, Natalie, and Florence Sutcliffe-Braithwaite. "National Women Against Pit Closures: Gender, Trade Unionism, and Community Activism." *Contemporary British History* 32.1 (2018): 78–100.
Thomlinson, Natalie. *Race, Ethnicity and the Women's Movement in England, 1968–1993*. Basingstoke: Palgrave Macmillan, 2016.
Titcombe, Elaine. "Women Activists: Rewriting Greenham's History." *Women's History Review* 22.2 (2013): 310–329.
Tourmaline (director). *Happy Birthday Marsha!* Film. 2018.
Tourmaline (director). *The Personal Things*. Film. 2016.
Turner, Kate. "Thatcherism, the Black Women's Movement and the Politics of Motherhood in Britain," in *Resist, Organize, Build*, eds. Sarah Crook and Charlie Jeffries. Albany, NY: SUNY Press, 2022.
Umoren, Imaobong D. *Race Women Internationalists: Activist-Intellectuals and Global Freedom Struggles*. Oakland: University of California Press, 2018.
Waites, Matthew. "Equality at Last? Homosexuality, Heterosexuality and the Age of Consent in the United Kingdom." *Sociology* 37.4 (2003): 637–655.
Warwick PG Podcast, Queer(in)g History. https://soundcloud.com/user-627299331/queering-history
Waters, Rob. *Thinking Black: Britain, 1964–1985*. Oakland: University of California Press, 2018.
White, Jessica. "Black Women's Groups, Life Narratives, and the Construction of the Self in Late Twentieth-Century Britain." *The Historical Journal* (2021): 1–21.

I
Student Politics and the Body Politic

"Aggies are Not Queers"
A History of *Gay Student Services v. Texas A&M University*, 1975–1985

Michael S. Hevel and Charles J. Thompson

As Parents' Weekend approached at Texas A&M University in 1975, Sheri Skinner, a graduate student from Massachusetts, heard about a poster in the student union advertising a meeting to start a campus chapter of a national gay organization. By the next time Skinner was in the union, the signs had already been removed, probably for fear of a parent seeing them. Provided with the relevant information from her friend, Skinner went to the meeting room at the appointed time. An unrelated meeting was taking place. Skinner waited outside the room and soon saw two other women students hanging out in the general vicinity. Skinner asked them, "Are you here for the same reason I'm here?" They were. The three young women noticed a few men also hanging around the room. They asked them, "Are you here for the same reason as us?" It soon became clear that the advertised meeting would not materialize, but the assembled students introduced themselves and decided that Texas A&M needed a group for gay students. "If no one else is going to start one," Skinner remembered the group thinking, "why don't *we* start a group of our own?"[1]

The students' decision to form a group would result in a lawsuit that would drag on for nine years. The case, *Gay Student Services v. Texas A&M University*, would be one of many legal actions between

LGBTQ[2] college students and their institutions over student organization recognition from the early 1970s and late 1990s in the United States. Collectively, these cases represent an important but understudied aspect of the history of LGBTQ college students and gay rights activism.[3] Although LGBTQ students sometimes lost their case in the trial court, including those students at Texas A&M, they won nearly every lawsuit on appeal. These cases comprise one of LGBTQ Americans' first successful claims of their Constitutional rights, becoming important pieces in the puzzle of legal precedents that would help lead the US Supreme Court to strike down anti-gay laws, including sodomy statutes and the so-called Defense of Marriage Act, and find a Constitutional right to gay marriage in the early twenty-first century. Drawing on archival materials, newspaper articles, and interviews, this chapter uses historical methods to reconstruct the events surrounding LGBTQ students' activism and legal action to achieve recognition for their student organization at Texas A&M University in the 1970s and 1980s.

As the longest of these lawsuits, a history of *Gay Student Services* reveals the resolve of LGBTQ college students to claim their rights and establish campus organizations. This history combines with Katherine Rye Jewell's chapter in this volume to illustrate the importance—and the fragility—of aspects of the extracurriculum at college and university campuses in providing connections for LGBTQ people and educating the larger populace about their existence. At Texas A&M, LGBTQ students ensured their group existed despite the presence of extreme institutional hostility for almost a decade. Members were regularly the targets of homophobic students and victims of intransigence of Texas A&M administrators and lawyers. The cost to those LGBTQ students involved in the lawsuit was high, but the benefits to their successors were great. Gay Student Services eventually had a lasting effect on campus and contributed to change in the larger society.

Threatened into Suing, Threatening to Sue

Sheri Skinner and her fellow students would have been hard pressed to choose a less hospitable institution at which to start a LGBTQ student organization. If Texas A&M was not the most conservative campus in the country—if some private, evangelical college could claim that mantle—then it would be hard to imagine another large, public research university more conservative. Located in College Station, ninety miles northwest of Houston, Texas A&M's enrollment had reached 25,000 students by 1975 and would swell to over 35,000 by 1985. Texas A&M was one of six "senior military colleges" in the United States, institutions with the strongest military presence on campus outside the service academies such as West Point. The Corp of Cadets, a student military organization, had an outsized influence over Texas A&M's campus life, and its alumni had an outsized influence over the larger university. They were regular benefactors to the university and often served on its board of regents. Even as late as 1975, many of these men were uncomfortable with the presence of women—who started attending in 1963—and the absence of compulsory military drill—which ended in 1965—on campus, much less recognizing a student organization for those who transgressed heterosexuality. Little wonder then that new students in the early 1970s were told at orientation that at Texas A&M there was "no drugs, no sex, and no homosexuals."[4]

After their initial decision to start a group, Skinner and her fellow students began meeting in private homes and apartments in College Station. Skinner suggested calling the group "Alternative," and the name stuck. At first, they decided that their group should not be a student organization but a community group. This would be more inclusive, welcoming students and local residents of all ages. The nascent group remained evenly divided between men and women, and members "got along real well." "One of the . . . major reason[s] for being was, really, to serve as a family for one another," recalled Skinner, because the members' actual "families were not aware of their being gay, and they were scared to death of going home." The group had no membership restrictions, and a straight young woman with many gay friends became one of Alternative's earliest active members.[5]

Alternative continued its "perfectly happy" existence as a community organization for some time. Group members felt safer meeting in homes than publicly on campus. In these private spaces, according to Skinner, Alternative members knew that they were welcome, they "could just sit there and drink our Cokes and talk, . . . let our hair down and not be afraid." The group started a speakers' bureau that mostly helped Texas A&M faculty find someone to speak to their classes about homosexuality. Alternative members also created "Gay Line," a telephone number staffed most nights of the week that served as referral service for individuals seeking connections to gay-friendly physicians, attorneys, counselors, and religious officials.[6]

Late one night in the spring of 1976, two Texas A&M men active in Alternative were posting flyers advertising Gay Line. They likely chose the dark of night because the use of campus bulletin boards extended only to recognized student organizations. Three large men with shaven heads, members of the Corp of Cadets, noticed the signs and approached the Alternative members. One of the cadets drew a switchblade. Holding the Alternative members at knifepoint, he forced them to remove their signs.[7]

This set in motion the events that would lead Alternative members to seek recognition as a student organization. The Alternative members called the campus police but received a lackluster response. They did not know the names of the cadets who held them at knifepoint, and their description of large white men with short hair who belonged to the Corp of Cadets likely described thousands of Texas A&M students. Having not gotten much help from the campus police, Skinner remembered the members thinking, "Well, it's time to go the [campus] authorities. And they'll protect us. We're students, right?"[8] But before they met with administrators at Texas A&M, they sought out legal advice from a local attorney who had previously worked with LGBTQ clients. More than wanting to know their potential rights, the students wanted to know if there were potential legal ramifications for being publicly involved in an organization that, ostensibly, would suggest their sexual lives violated the Texas law that criminalized gay sex.[9]

Legal advice in hand, Skinner and several other Alternative members met with Dr. John Koldus, vice president of student services, on April 4, 1976. The students explained that they did not need official recognition for their organization, but they wanted permission to use campus bulletin boards. Most Alternative members wished to remain anonymous, and they believed that recognition might create an "uncomfortable" situation at the conservative university. Koldus reiterated that posting on campus bulletin boards extended only to recognized organizations and told them a "partial granting of rights was out of the question." If Alternative members were unwilling to include their names on the application necessary to recognize their organization, "there would be no rights at all." Koldus was convinced that the students would never publicly disclose their sexuality. "He thought our position was that we were so ashamed of ourselves that we wanted to crawl under a rock," Skinner recalled, "and that we would never *dare* go for recognition."[10]

If Koldus believed that, Skinner and her colleagues' actions the next day must have surprised him: they applied for official recognition from

Texas A&M. The students decided to split into two groups. Alternative would retain its name and its community focus, and its student members would create a new group at Texas A&M. The students received help in applying for recognition from Dr. Carolyn Adair, the director of student affairs. She advised the students to register their group as a service organization, which may have contributed to the new group's name, "Gay Student Services," and certainly proved helpful in subsequent legal proceedings. In their application, the students listed the purposes of GSS as providing referral services to students, information to the campus community about gay life, speakers to classes and organizations, and "a forum for the interchange of ideas and constructive solutions to gay people's problems."[11]

The benefits of official recognition were many and quite helpful to college students with limited means. Recognized student organizations could use campus facilities for meetings and events free of charge, advertise on campus through campus bulletin boards and kiosks, include publicity in the All-University Calendar and Student Organization Guide, use a graphic arts service to create and copy posters, access funds from the student activity fee, use space in the Student Programs Office, get budgeting assistance, and receive secretarial support, free banking, and a campus mailbox.[12]

Texas A&M administrators responded to GSS's application by circumventing the normal procedures, and they did so slowly. Bypassing the board that usually reviewed applications for new student organizations, Koldus instructed Adair to forward GSS's application directly to him. He took no immediate action. GSS leaders returned to Koldus's office in May to seek a decision about their application. Koldus said that he was waiting for the Texas A&M president and legal staff's advice. Later that month—and unbeknownst to GSS members—the president told Koldus that they would refuse to offer recognition "until and unless we are ordered by higher authority to do so." Still Koldus did not respond to GSS. Its members again met with Koldus in mid-June and at the end of September to check on their application. While cordial to the students, Koldus refused to be pressed into making a decision about their application, telling the students, "This has become a legal chess game. We have made our move. You have a legal move which would be inappropriate for me to comment on."[13]

Indeed, not until a GSS attorney threatened legal action did Koldus write a letter in GSS rejecting their application to be a recognized student organization in November 1976. Koldus noted a university regulation that required recognized student organizations to have "purposes which are consistent with the philosophy and goals" of Texas A&M. Because gay sex was illegal in Texas, "it would be most inappropriate for a state institution to support a student organization which is likely to incite, promote and result in acts contrary to" state law. Moreover, Koldus rejected the "services" aspect of GSS, telling its leaders that "the university administrative staff and faculty are responsible for providing referral services, educational information, appropriate speakers for classes and a forum for the interchange of ideas."[14]

Sex was the elephant in the room in meetings between LGBTQ students and university administrators. Skinner remembered Dr. Adair subtly suggesting that category of "service" instead of "social" for their group might alleviate a potential association with sex. Skinner's blunt interpretation of this was that "they figure by 'social' you mean you want to roll around on the coffee tables after every meeting and screw to your heart's delight." In fact, this was exactly how Skinner perceived her meetings with Koldus: "He was *convinced* that our purpose in being was for sexual activity. And that at every meeting . . . we got through the business as fast as we can so we could have giant orgies all over everybody's living rooms." Remembering those early meetings, Skinner recalled that Koldus "was of course pleasant, very cordial—but just unbelievably ignorant." However, the GSS leaders did not consider their group a conduit for sex or romance. "Our concern was with the emotional wellbeing and physical safety of the members," Skinner recalled. "Mainly we wanted a safe place for kids to be able to come and just talk, and share their experiences, and find friends."[15]

The concern over sex helped the students realize the importance of delineating the roles of Alternative and GSS. Alternative would coordinate social and political activities. It hosted a number of successful parties at the Unitarian Church. In contrast, GSS would hold close to the service aspect of its name, operating Gay Line and the speakers' bureau. The main aspect overlapping between the two groups was membership, as a majority of Alternative members were Texas A&M students and a majority of GSS members also belonged to Alternative.[16]

On the last day of February 1977, GSS members Michael Minton, Keith Stewart, and Patricia Wooldridge sued Texas A&M and its leaders in federal court for violating their civil rights by refusing to recognize GSS. They were offended by Koldus's insinuation that recognizing their group would contribute to gay sex, with one member telling the student paper, the *Battalion*, "That's like saying every time there's a faculty party because they are all heterosexual they swap wives." The plaintiffs expressed optimism about their chance in court, pointing to numerous other legal victories by LGBTQ student organizations seeking recognition. Stewart believed recognition would help gay people on campus who were afraid to come out of the closet, "I know how it feels because I was in their shoes." Minton, the GSS president, noted, "The primary reason I'm suing is because I do not think there is anything wrong with being gay. And I think it's a travesty for any one society, particularly an institution of higher education, to perpetuate the attitude that gays are sick, unproductive and should try to change." He also predicted the visibility of their lawsuit: "This University, as the bastion of conservatism in the south is going to be a very, very important case for gay rights. It's going to receive a lot of national attention."[17]

The lawsuit immediately grabbed the attention of homophobes on campus and in the state. In early March, residents of Hart Hall unfurled a banner from a window that announced, "Aggies are not queers—beat the hell out of GSSO!" A couple of weeks later, the Texas A&M Board of Regents announced they would "proceed in every legal way" to prevent recognition of GSS, noting that "so-called 'gay' activities run diabolically counter to the traditions and standards of" the institution. That same month, a Republican state senator from Houston introduced a bill that criminalized the approval of gay student organizations by board members at public colleges and universities. Members could be fined up to $500 and jailed up to thirty days. When asked about the rationale for the bill, the representative's administrative assistant responded, "He doesn't like queers!" Koldus told a *Battalion* reporter that the bill "seemed to support A&M's stand" against GSS. So too would a federal district judge in Houston.[18]

Early Trials

Compared to subsequent stages of the lawsuit, the first proved the shortest. Nominated by President Gerald Ford and confirmed by the United States Senate in May 1976, Ross Sterling had not been a federal judge for a year before *Gay Student Services* landed on his docket. At the end of June 1977, the Texas Attorney General, who represented state agencies in litigation, filed a motion to dismiss the lawsuit. Judge Sterling granted the request on November 2, 1977. He provided no legal theory upon which he based the dismissal, noting only that the motion was "meritorious and unopposed." At the end of the month, GSS attorneys filed an appeal to the Fifth Circuit Court of Appeals in New Orleans.[19]

GSS leaders expected the appeal to take three to six months. "I think we have a good case," Michael Minton said to a *Battalion* reporter in March 1978. A Texas A&M attorney told the same reporter that, because the case had been dismissed, GSS had the "burden of moving the case forward." A three-judge panel of the Fifth Circuit did not hear oral arguments until November 27, 1979. Three years to the month that GSS members first filed their lawsuit, in February 1980, the appellate judges determined that they deserved a day in court. Judge Sterling had erred in dismissing the case, the judges decided. However, they did not want their demand for a new trial to be interpreted as an assurance that GSS ultimately deserved a legal victory, writing "we intimate no opinion as to how the case should be decided once the relevant facts have been fully developed."[20]

Following the victory at the Fifth Circuit, a GSS attorney expressed confidence in the overarching legal effort to a *Battalion* reporter, noting victories in recent similar cases. Although GSS's original plaintiffs had graduated, the group would "simply add new plaintiffs." Pressed about the challenges of yet another legal effort in federal court, an Alternative officer told the *Battalion*, "If we've come this far, we're not going to back out now." He believed that Texas A&M's numerous legal maneuverings were an effort to delay and demoralize LGBTQ students, "They're hoping to wear us into the ground until everybody graduates or we run out of money." Exhausting the group of money would be hard, because GSS alumni were providing funds for the lawsuits and the attorneys were working at greatly reduced fees, although legal costs had climbed to over $2,500 (almost $8,000 in 2020). Meanwhile, when asked about the possibility of settling the case in face of legal defeat, Koldus reiterated Texas A&M's entrenched position: "We've taken our stand in terms of our interpretation of the law and we plan to continue our argument against the group." In fact, university officials were so incensed by the Fifth Circuit's decision that they asked the US Supreme Court to overrule it. The Supreme Court refused their appeal in December 1980, ensuring that a trial on the merits would finally be held, almost five years after GSS filed suit.[21]

As the lawsuit meandered through different federal courts—and without a recognized organization to serve LGBTQ students and provide education about their experiences—Texas A&M remained a place hostile toward sexual minorities. GSS members might recognize students at a gay bar in Dallas or Houston who had never told anyone on campus about their sexual orientation. "They're afraid to come out here," a GSS member told the *Battalion* in 1980. GSS and Alternative continued to operate Gay Line, but upward of 90 percent of the calls were pranks. One volunteer for the referral service who had previously lived in other Texas cities said, "I've never been to a place where people are so closed-minded." And just like those who held some of its earliest members at knifepoint, GSS always seemed to face scrutiny from those on campus with military ties. An article about the lawsuit quoted one ROTC member, "Everybody here hates the fags worse than they hate the wags [women members of the Corp of Cadets; women were first allowed to join the Corp in 1974]." But this young man was not completely opposed to recognition: "I don't see anything wrong with recognizing gay students. I think they ought to have to wear little buttons so we can tell who they are and stay away from them."[22]

GSS's next opportunity to claim their right to recognition began at 1:30 p.m. on November 16, 1981, in Judge Sterling's Houston courtroom. Two of GSS's witnesses emphasized that recognizing the group could change attitudes on campus. "Recognition would prove that you aren't dealing with twisted minds and outlaws, and would be a step in the direction of bringing things out in the light," testified Sheri Skinner, who had now graduated from Texas A&M. A University of Houston sociologist and former Kinsey Institute researcher claimed that GSS recognition could lead to an "attitude of liberalization" among students. Texas A&M's witnesses argued that recognition would increase gay sex and its negative consequences. A physician with the state's department of public health suggested that sexually transmitted diseases would increase, as gay men had higher rates than their share of the population. He had to admit, however, that these rates among lesbians were lower than among heterosexuals. Dr. Paul Cameron, a faculty member at the University of Nebraska who would be expelled two years later from the American Psychological Association for not cooperating with an ethics investigation, provided more fiery testimony. Homosexuality "is an appetite which . . . results in adverse social and personal consequences," he told the court, "and appetites are acquired." If recognized, GSS "would recruit others with the same (homosexual) appetite."[23]

Attorneys for both sides expected a decision about a month after the four-day trial, but Judge Sterling did not issue his opinion until the end of May 1982. As he had in 1977, Sterling sided with A&M. He used testimony from those involved with GSS, who had said the group was not designed to promote political activism but was a typical student group, to classify GSS as a social rather than a service organization. This made it more like fraternities and sororities in his view, which Texas A&M had also refused to recognize. Therefore, GSS members were not being treated any differently than students in similar types of organizations. GSS's legal team was baffled by the ruling. "We think the trial went just fine," said one attorney, "but we think the judge overlooked the facts." An attorney for Texas A&M expressed "prevailing relief" at the ruling, noting "A major hurdle has been accomplished."[24]

GSS quickly appealed the court's decision, and the trial loss reemphasized to GSS leaders the importance of being a service rather than social organization. Having not been a recognized organization for five years, of course, made it difficult for the organization to function. James Kaster, a sophomore who was responsible for GSS's activities at the time, recalled, "So it was my goal to look like and function like a campus organization, because as a service organization we better do it." The primary service that remained was Gay Line. To this, GSS reinvigorated its speakers' bureau and added a roommate service for LGBTQ students. GSS members also envisioned creating a resource library and funding a scholarship, but, with no access to funds for student organizations, money was scarce. Kaster used almost $300 (the equivalent of nearly $800 in 2019) to pay GSS expenses during his leadership.[25] As time would tell, the Fifth Circuit Court of Appeals paid close attention to the nature of GSS.

The Second Appeal

The second appeal effort occupied almost the entirety of 1983. Attorneys filed legal briefs in early February and delivered oral arguments before a three-judge panel of the Fifth Circuit in late November. Both sides were aided by new allies. Dallas Doctors Against AIDS hired attorneys to write an amicus brief in support of Texas A&M, arguing that recognizing

GSS would create a public health issue on campus because of "the direct connection between homosexual activity and increased . . . incidences of dangerous transmissible diseases." Although the group's name implied professional familiarity with the disease, none of the members had done research on AIDS. Most had probably never cared for an AIDS patient. The Texas Human Rights Foundation, a group focused on ending discrimination based on sexual orientation, helped GSS meet its legal costs and plan its appeal. "For the University to recognize other groups . . . and to deny gay students the right to have their own . . . organization flies in the face of other court decisions," said Robert Schwab, an attorney for the group. "It also defies reason." Schwab would die from AIDS-related causes two weeks after oral arguments in the case.[26]

As GSS members anticipated the Fifth Circuit's decision, they realized the need for a leader to be the public face of the group, win or lose. GSS members approached Marco Roberts, who had recently joined the group. GSS officers, its president, vice president, and secretary, were usually the only members of the group publicly out, and they knew that, should they ever win their lawsuit against A&M, their names would have to be included on the recognition paperwork. In an era before the internet and social media, those students who came out on campus had lower risk that this news would travel to their hometowns. However, with the media storm that would follow the appellate decision, Roberts knew that his anonymity would disappear. He went home and came out to his parents. His mother was heartbroken, and they did not speak for a year. "In a campus of 38,000 people, and a metro of around 90,000, I was 'the gay,' with all the consequences you might imagine that entailed," Roberts later remembered. "I promise you, no one fought me for that limelight."[27]

The limelight was slow to come, as nearly a year passed after oral arguments before the Fifth Circuit issued its ruling in August 1984. The appellate judges began their ruling by reviewing the same facts as the district court but reaching a different conclusion. The appellate judges considered the trial court's finding that GSS was a fraternal or social group "clearly erroneous." The finding was at odds with the group's stated purpose, Dr. Koldus's denial of recognition centered on the homosexual character of the group, and the Texas A&M Board of Regents had passed an anti-gay policy position soon after GSS members had filed their lawsuit. The appellate judges believed Judge Sterling had taken GSS members' testimony out of context to compare them to fraternities and sororities.

The judges concluded that it was "clear from the facts" that Texas A&M refused to recognize GSS because of its focus on homosexuality.[28]

Having determined that Texas A&M officials denied GSS recognition because of the "content of its message," the judges needed to determine if this denial violated its members' "rights under the First Amendment." The judges compared the facts from Texas A&M with those before the Supreme Court in *Healy v. James*, which had found a Connecticut college's refusal to recognize a campus chapter of Students for a Democratic Society violated the First Amendment. The benefits of recognition were similar and the justification for denial was similar in both cases: an organization antithetical to the institution's values. In *Healy*, the Supreme Court noted there was "no doubt that denial of official recognition, without justification, to college organizations burdens or abridges" freedom of association under the First Amendment; the institution had a "heavy burden" of justifying its action. The judges turned their attention to whether Texas A&M's reasons for denying recognition met such a burden. They noted that Dr. Koldus's letter that denied recognition to GSS for being incongruent "with the philosophy and goals" of the institution was "clearly forbidden by *Healy*." The appellate judges pointed out that a recognized religious group on campus had used campus bulletin boards to display large posters of chained hands with the caption, "Homosexuality—Not so Gay." "Therefore," they wrote, it "appears that TAMU did not object to the presentation of negative ideas about homosexuality by its recognized student groups." Since Texas A&M "opened its forum to other similar student groups, . . . it may not close the forum to GSS."[29]

GSS members celebrated the legal victory. "After eight years of holding out for acceptance and recognition, we're very, very happy," said Glynn Brown, the group's vice president. "This is a giant step for the Bryan-College Station gay community and a real step forward in civil rights." The group and its attorneys held a press conference that Saturday at the Ramada Inn, where Marco Roberts announced in front of television cameras GSS's plans to apply for recognition within the next week. "At this point, we're elated about the decision rendered," said Roberts. "We are even more pleased that the decision was unanimous."[30]

Others at Texas A&M were less celebratory. The *Battalion* polled one hundred people in the library, and 55 percent disagreed with the ruling. This percentage represented a majority but by no means suggested a universal disdain on campus toward recognizing GSS, with 40 percent of respondents agreeing with the appeals court. But Texas A&M leaders' reactions seemed to universally align with the slight majority. The student body president told the paper, "I don't see the need for . . . any type of group based on sexual orientation." Those with even more authority agreed with him. The Board of Regents instructed their legal staff to prepare an appeal. As one local reporter observed, "If Aggies are nothing else, they are stubborn when they feel a principle is at stake. It always has been an A&M tradition to fight each game and each battle to the bitter end."[31]

GSS, Texas A&M, and the US Supreme Court

The bitter end in this instance would be the United States Supreme Court. The Texas Attorney General had been representing Texas A&M in the case, so the board would either need his approval to appeal or his permission to pursue on appeal on their own. The *Battalion* editorial board criticized the appeal effort, writing, "The amount of money wasted on this fight is immeasurable. The university administration needs to realize that this is not a question of approving homosexual behavior; it is a matter of basic civil liberties." Not surprisingly, GSS leaders agreed with the editors—"I think it will be damaging to the University in the long-run," said Marco Roberts—but so too did the Student Senate, passing a resolution in favor of recognition, but only by one vote. More significantly, Attorney General Jim Mattox agreed with the *Battalion*. He refused to appeal the ruling, but eventually agreed to let Texas A&M pursue an appeal if no state funds were used for attorney fees and any potential damages. Texas A&M officials jumped at the chance. The Board of Trustees expressed confidence that they could easily raise the money for the appeal, and they hired a Houston firm where their vice chairman was a senior partner. "I'm just shocked that they'll go to such lengths to keep us off campus," Roberts said.[32]

GSS members now stared down an even longer path on their legal journey. Their attorneys advised them that, if the Supreme Court agreed to hear the appeal, it would not occur for at least another year, drawing their eight-year legal battle into its ninth year. The potential silver lining for GSS was that a Supreme Court victory would set a national precedent about the rights of gay student organizations. "We waited eight years," Roberts acquiesced. "I don't think it will hurt to wait eight more months." Texas A&M's general counsel claimed that legitimate, unresolved legal questions were at stake. "Our argument is that official recognition is not protected by the First Amendment," he said.[33]

By 1984, multiple federal courts had concluded otherwise about LGBTQ student organizations—including the Fourth Circuit Court of Appeals in 1976 (*Gay Alliance of Students v. Matthews*) and the Eighth Circuit in 1977 (*Gay Lib. v. University of Missouri*)—but the Supreme Court had not considered the issue. On April 1, 1985, the Supreme Court announced it would not hear Texas A&M's appeal, effectively endorsing the Fifth Circuit's ruling. "It's fantastic," Marco Roberts told the *Battalion*. An attorney for GSS described the decision as "long overdue." But Texas A&M leaders were not ready to accept such a verdict and imagined a frightening future for their campus. "It opens questions of how far administrators can go in regulating student conduct," worried Ted Hajovsky, Texas A&M's general counsel. "If, say, an animal-sacrifice group applies for recognition, does this mean we're not able to probe into those activities?" When pressed by reporters, Hajovsky admitted that A&M had not received applications for such groups nor was he aware of universities that recognized gay groups experiencing similar requests.[34]

"Will A&M finally let gay issue die?" a *Battalion* editorial board headline asked the day after the Supreme Court's denial. "Have the powers-that-be here finally . . . accepted that they can't discriminate at will against people whose politics, or sexual preferences, they don't like?" The answer was no. Just as soon as the Supreme Court refused to hear their appeal, Texas A&M attorneys began legal maneuverings to seek a rehearing from the highest court. It was a long shot—one Texas A&M attorney described the odds as "about 100 to one against"—but the institution's leaders "refuse[d] to drop the case until the last appeal has been exhausted." They did concede, however, that the university would, if it had to, accept legal defeat. "A&M has a history of being good soldiers," Hajovsky said, "and like good soldiers, we will comply."[35]

And they did. On May 20, 1985, the Supreme Court denied Texas A&M's request to rehear their case against GSS. Judge Ross Sterling, who had twice ruled against GSS's recognition, issued an injunction that ordered A&M to recognize the group. "We're obviously all very happy that it (the case) is finally coming to an end," Marco Roberts told reporters. Ted Hajovsky admitted defeat, "I think we've exhausted our legal remedies." Campus administrators struck a similar tone. "The Supreme Court made a decision and the University will abide by it,"

John Koldus said. The only thing that stood between GSS and recognition was paperwork. On June 6, 1985, Texas A&M officially recognized Gay Student Services—3,349 days after the group first submitted its application.[36]

An Enduring Legacy

GSS would have an enduring influence on Texas A&M. Over the next decade, GSS members would change the name of their organization—advancing toward greater inclusion—several times, eventually to Gay, Lesbian, Bisexual, and Transgender Aggies in 1997. The group remained active for decades, being named Texas A&M's student organization of the year in 2010. The existence of the organization on campus contributed to major institutional change toward sexual minorities. In 1988, Texas A&M hired an out lesbian to lead its newly created women's studies program, and an LGBTQ literature course began five years later. In 1997, the first Texas A&M employee was hired whose primary job responsibility was to serve the needs of LGBTQ students, which culminated eleven years later when Texas A&M leaders established the GLBT Resource Center.[37]

But even as GSS leaders and their successors slowly made strides to make the institution less hostile, Texas A&M remained a hard place to not be straight. Less than a year after its recognition, GSS had to establish "Pink Panther Patrols" to stop anti-gay students from removing its flyers from campus bulletin boards.[38] In 1991, the Texas A&M president reversed his earlier approval to add sexual orientation to the institution's nondiscrimination policy. As LGBTQ student leaders lobbied for protection enshrined in campus policy, homophobic students flooded their referral hotline. A representative message captured the vitriol still present on campus: "You all suck way too much dick, you buttfuckers. . . . Fucking fags, I'd like to kick all your asses." Texas A&M would not add sexual orientation to its nondiscrimination policy for another nine years, and homophobia never completely subsided. In 2014, some students complained that the GLBT Resource Center planned a ceremony to honor the accomplishments of graduating LGBTQ students. "This special Texas A&M ceremony essentially promotes and celebrates dangerous and risky sexual activity that can seriously jeopardize a person's well-being," claimed a leader of a conservative group on campus.[39]

Such criticism of even modest institutional support for LGBTQ students had overtones of the hostility during GSS's legal battle that started almost four decades earlier. But the pervasiveness of the hostility had dissipated over time. The existence of an LGBTQ student organization and the perseverance of its members played no small part in this change. Perhaps the best example of this was a symposium hosted by Texas A&M to recognize the twenty-fifth anniversary of GSS's legal victory in 2010. The university president opened the symposium. Attendees, including some GSS alumni who had shepherded the group through its long lawsuit, considered the history and future of LGBTQ issues in higher education. What would Riley Brian, the current president of GLBT Aggies, like to say to those alumni who carried on a legal fight against their alma mater for almost a decade, asked a reporter for an LGBTQ paper in Houston. "I would tell them thank you for not giving up," Brian replied. "Without them and their hard work, who knows how much longer it would have been for GLBT people to have the right to form organizations to meet on campuses around the country."[40]

Notes

1. "Interviews with Sheri Skinner" audio cassette, December 9, 1984, Kevin Bailey Collection, Cushing Library, University Libraries, Texas A&M University, College Station, Texas (hereafter cited as "Cushing Library"); Eric Rieder, "Gays at A&M Fear AIDS Will Be Used to Attack Legal Rights Won," *Houston Post*, August 14, 1983. Most of the sources used in this chapter come from newspaper articles first identified in the LGBTQ Archive in the Cushing Library.

2. We use the LGBTQ acronym to capture the broad continuum on which people who joined Gay Student Services might have identified, today or in the past. The archival record suggests that members of Gay Student Services almost exclusively used "gay" and "lesbian" to refer to themselves during the lawsuit. Although today scholars increasingly use "queer" as an encompassing and emancipatory label for LGBTQ people, we resist this because there is nothing in the record that suggests GSS members ever used this label to refer to themselves. Quite the opposite in fact, for the archival record does contain instances of those most hostile to GSS labeling its members "queers." For an excellent rationale for labeling previous generations of LGBTQ people as queer in contemporary scholarship, see Brittney L. Beck, "'A Different Kind of Activism': The University Committee on Sexism and Homophobia, 1981–1992,"

American Educational Research Journal 56.4 (2019): 1356–1358. https://doi.org/10.3102/0002831218818784

3. As historians have begun to reconstruct the experiences of LGBTQ college students over the past fifteen years, two important strands of scholarship have emerged. First, historians have revealed college presidents and deans of students' efforts—often in coordination with police—to "purge" their campuses of gay students from the 1920s through the 1950s. See Patrick Dilley, "20th Century Postsecondary Practices and Policies to Control Gay Students," *Review of Higher Education* 25 (2002): 409–431; Nicholas L. Syrett, "The Boys of Beaver Meadow: A Homosexual Community at 1920s Dartmouth College," *American Studies* 48 (2007): 9–18; William Wright, *Harvard's Secret Court: The Savage 1920 Purge of Campus Homosexuals* (New York: St. Martin's Press, 2005); Margaret A. Nash and Jennifer A. Silverman, "'An Indelible Mark': Gay Purges in Higher Education in the 1940s," *History of Education Quarterly* 55 (2015): 441–459. Women students could also be expelled for lesbianism, though the historical record has yet to uncover similar proactive administrative purges of lesbians. See Anne MacKay, ed., *Wolf Girls at Vassar: Lesbian and Gay Experiences 1930–1990* (New York: St. Martin's Press, 1992), 65; Kelly C. Sartorius, *Deans of Women and the Feminist Movement: Emily Taylor's Activism* (New York: Palgrave Macmillan, 2014). Second, historians have explored the creation and contributions of early gay student organizations. Scholars have demonstrated how these organizations, in spite of appalling homophobia, improved the campus climate for gay and lesbians beginning in the 1970s. See Brett Beemyn, "The Silence Is Broken: A History of the First Lesbian, Gay, and Bisexual College Student Groups," *Journal of the History of Sexuality* 12.2 (2003): 205–223; Jessica Clawson, "Coming Out of the Campus Closet: The Emerging Visibility of Queer Students at the University of Florida, 1970–1982," *Educational Studies* 50 (2014): 209–230; Patrick Dilley, *Queer Man on Campus: A History of Non-Heterosexual College Men, 1945–2000* (New York: RoutledgeFarmer, 2002); Patrick Dilley, *Gay Liberation to Campus Assimilation: Early Non-Heterosexual Student Organizing at Midwestern Universities* (New York: Palgrave Macmillan, 2019); T. Evan Faulkenbury and Aaron Hayworth, "The Carolina Gay Association, Oral History, and Coming Out at the University of North Carolina," *The Oral History Review* 43.1 (2016): 115–137; David Nichols and Morris J. Kafka-Hozschlag, "The Rutgers University Lesbian/Gay Alliance, 1969–1989: The First Twenty Years," *The Journal of the Rutgers University Libraries* 51.2 (1989): 55–95; David A. Reichard, "Behind the Scenes at the Gayzette: The Gay Student Union and Queer World Making at UCLA in the 1970s," *The Oral History Review* 43.1 (2016): 98–114. Gay student organization struggle-for-recognition lawsuits represent the missing historical link between higher education administrators' persecution of gay students and the accomplishments of gay student organizations. The first histories of these struggle-for-recognition lawsuits focused on unreported cases at individual campuses in California and

Kansas in the early 1970s, rather than major cases like *Gay Student Services*. See David A. Reichard, "'We Can't Hide and They Are Wrong': The Society for Homosexual Freedom and the Struggle for Recognition at Sacramento State College, 1969–1971," *Law and History Review* 28.3 (2010): 630–674; Beth Bailey, *Sex in the Heartland* (Cambridge, MA: Harvard University Press, 1999), 178–183. Timothy Reese Cain and Michael S. Hevel's "'Gay People Pay Activity Fees Too': The Committee on Gay Education's Pioneering Legal Victories at the University of Georgia," *Review of Higher Education* 45.1 (2021): 61–91. offers a history of the events surrounding the lawsuit that resulted in the first published judicial decision. For a full historiographic treatment of LGBTQ people in higher education, see Karen L. Graves, "The History of Lesbian, Gay, Bisexual, Transgender, Queer Issues in Higher Education," in *Higher Education: Handbook of Theory and Research*, ed. Michael B. Paulsen, vol. 33 (Springer, 2018), 127–173.

From the late nineteenth century through most of the twentieth, police officers arrested suspected gays and lesbians and regularly raided those places where they assembled in the United States, especially gay bars. Judges imposed penalties, including imprisonment, on those whom the police arrested. In contrast, gay college students' lawsuits helped establish a trend of gay and lesbian Americans using the courts to advance their rights rather than be victims of the legal system. On LGBTQ people being persecuted through the legal system, see generally, George Chauncey, *Gay New York: Gender, Urban Culture, and the Making of the Gay Male World* (New York: Basic Books, 1994); Marc Stein, *City of Sisterly and Brotherly Loves: Lesbian and Gay Philadelphia, 1945–1972* (Chicago: University of Chicago Press, 2000).

4. Henry C. Dethloff, *A Centennial History of Texas A&M University, 1876–1976*, vol. 2 (College Station: Texas A&M University Press, 1975), 563–564, 568–571; Michael Haederle, "A&M Loses Long Battle to Ban Gay Group," *Houston Post*, April 2, 1985; Mark Eastman, "*Gay Student Services vs. Texas A&M University*: The Story of the Students Behind the Fight," *Montrose Star*, April 23, 2010.

5. "Interviews with Sheri Skinner," Cushing Library.
6. "Interviews with Sheri Skinner," Cushing Library.
7. "Interviews with Sheri Skinner," Cushing Library.
8. "Interviews with Sheri Skinner," Cushing Library.
9. "Interviews with Sheri Skinner," Cushing Library.
10. "Interviews with Sheri Skinner," Cushing Library.
11. "Interviews with Sheri Skinner," Cushing Library; *Gay Student Services v. Texas A&M University*, 737 F.2d 1317, 1320 (5th Cir. 1984).
12. *Gay Student Services*, 737 F.2d at 1320.
13. *Gay Student Services*, 737 F.2d at 1320; "M. Minton and S. Skinner meeting with Dr. Koldus," June 18, 1976, "M. Garrett and C. George meeting with Dr. Koldus," September 21, 1976, Lesbian, Gay, Bisexual, Transgender,

and Queer Archive (hereafter cited as "LGBTQ Archive"), Box 2: Chronology, Cushing Library.

14. *Gay Student Services*, 737 F.2d at 1320; Glenna Whitley, "Gay Service Organization Sues A&M," *Texas A&M Battalion*, March 1, 1977.

15. "Interviews with Sheri Skinner," Cushing Library.

16. "Interviews with Sheri Skinner," Cushing Library.

17. Whitley, "Gay Service Organization Sues A&M."

18. "Strong Feelings Expressed," *Texas A&M Battalion*, March 3, 1977; Lee Roy Leschper, "Regents Call Gays 'Diabolic'; Decide to Fight Suit," *Texas A&M Battalion*, March 22, 1977; Glenna Whitley, "Bill Could Prohibit Regents' Approval of Gay Groups," *Texas A&M Battalion*, March 11, 1977.

19. *Gay Student Services v. Texas A&M University*, 612 F.2d 160, 163 (5th Cir. 1980); Greg Propps, "GSSO Suit to Be Heard in New Orleans Court," *Texas A&M Battalion*, March 8, 1978.

20. Propps; "Gays' Lawsuit near Settlement," *Bryan Eagle*, May 18, 1978; "In Town," *Newview*, December 1979; *Gay Student Services*, 612 F.2d at 166.

21. Jan Evans, "Gay Group to Sue University Again," *Texas A&M Battalion*, February 26, 1980; "Judge Must Hear Aggie Homosexuals," *Dallas Morning News*, February 21, 1980; Liz Newlin, "GSSO Case to Go Back to Federal Court," *Texas A&M Battalion*, December 9, 1980; "Supreme Court May Get A&M Gay Rights Case," *Bryan Eagle*, November 12, 1980.

22. Robin Thompson, "Gay-Line Referral Service Gets Mostly Prank Calls," *Texas A&M Battalion*, March 1, 1979; "A&M Gays Want Tradition, Change," *Bryan Eagle*, December 16, 1980.

23. Denise Richter, "GSSO-A&M Testimony Begins Sociologist to Testify Today," *Texas A&M Battalion*, November 17, 1981; Denise Richter, "Final GSSO Witnesses to Be Heard Today," *Texas A&M Battalion*, November 18, 1981; Denise Richter, "Testimony to End Today in GSSO-A&M Case," *Texas A&M Battalion*, November 19, 1981; Denise Richter, "GSSO Suit Decision Expected in 30 Days," *Texas A&M Battalion*, November 20, 1981.

24. Richter, "GSSO Suit Decision Expected in 30 Days"; *Gay Student Services*, 737 F.2d at 1319; Rebecca Zimmerman, "GSSO Suit Againt Texas A&M Dismissed," *Texas A&M Battalion*, May 26, 1982.

25. "Interviews with James Kaster" audio cassette, September 30, 1984, Kevin Bailey Collection, Cushing Library. Kaster has recently published a memoir that covers his involvement and activism in GSS. See James H. Kaster, *Faggots Fight* (self-pub., 2020).

26. Kim Schmidt, "Gay Student Services Continues Battle for Recognition," *Texas A&M Battalion*, February 3, 1983; Elaine Engstrom, "GSS Case Ruling Expected Soon," *Texas A&M Battalion*, November 18, 1983; Fritz Lanham, "Group of Doctors Opposes Recognition of Gay Group," *Bryan Eagle*, August 3, 1983; Schmidt, "Gay Student Services Continues Battle for Recognition."

27. Marco Roberts interview with the first author, May 21, 2017; Michael Crawford, "GSS President: Bad Feelings Caused by Misinformation," *Texas A&M Battalion*, October 8, 1984; Marco Roberts, "30 Years after a Gay Rights Ruling Changed A&M, One of the Case's Chief Advocates Examines the Impact," *Texas A&M Battalion*, March 31, 2015.

28. *Gay Student Services*, 737 F.2d at 1321–1324.

29. *Gay Student Services*, 737 F.2d at 1327–1331.

30. Daniel Puckett, "Court Says A&M Must Recognize Gay Group," *Bryan Eagle*, August 4, 1984; Mark Banks, "Gay Group to Seek A&M Recognition," *Bryan Eagle*, August 5, 1984; Kari Fluegel, "GSS Will Apply for Recognition," *Texas A&M Battalion*, August 7, 1984.

31. Kari Fluegel, "Most Aggies Dislike Court's GSS Decision," *Texas A&M Battalion*, August 8, 1984; Daniel Puckett, "GSS Ahead, but Game's Not Over," *Bryan Eagle*, August 9, 1984; Daniel Puckett, "Regents Ask for Appeal in Gay Recognition Ruling," *Bryan Eagle*, September 25, 1984.

32. "University Should Give in to Liberty," *Texas A&M Battalion*, September 26, 1984; Kari Fluegel, "GSS Supporters Criticize Decision to Appeal Court Ruling," *Texas A&M Battalion*, September 27, 1984; Sarah Oates, "GSS Resolution Passed," *Texas A&M Battalion*, October 18, 1984; Daniel Puckett, "Mattox Won't Appeal Gay Suit Decision," *Bryan Eagle*, October 3, 1984; Daniel Puckett, "A&M to Continue Legal Battle against Gay Group," *Bryan Eagle*, October 26, 1984.

33. Puckett, "A&M to Continue Legal Battle against Gay Group"; Fluegel, "GSS Supporters Criticize Decision to Appeal Court Ruling."

34. Daniel Puckett, "Court Decides Gay Group Must Get Recognition," *Bryan Eagle*, April 2, 1985.

35. "Will A&M Finally Let Gay Issue Die?," *Texas A&M Battalion*, April 2, 1985; Puckett, "Court Decides Gay Group Must Get Recognition."

36. Daniel Puckett, "A&M, GSS Battle Apparently Over," *Bryan Eagle*, May 22, 1985; Karen Bloch, "A&M Won't Fight Final GSS Ruling," *Texas A&M Battalion*, May 29, 1985; "Texas A&M Grants GSS Official Recognition," *Texas A&M Battalion*, June 13, 1985.

37. "GLBT History at TAMU Timeline," 2013–2014, LGBTQ Archive, Cushing Library.

38. "GLBT History at TAMU Timeline," LGBTQ Archive, Cushing Library.

39. "Chronology of Events Relating to the Discrimination and Harassment Policies and Statements at Texas A&M University," "Phone Messages (transcript from tape) on Gay and Lesbian Student Services Hot-line," March 1991, Box 1, Texas A&M University Student Senate Petition Files, Cushing Library; Allen Reed, "GLBT Event Draws Backlash," *Bryan Eagle*, April 16, 2014.

40. Eastman, "Gay Student Services."

Works Cited

Archival Sources and Interviews

Kevin Bailey Collection, 1976–1990. 02/C000068. Cushing Library, University Libraries, Texas A&M University, College Station, TX.
LGBTQ Archive—Chronology, 189–201. 02/C000135. Cushing Library, University Libraries, Texas A&M University, College Station, TX.
Roberts, Marco. Interview by Michael Hevel, May 21, 2017. Author's Personal Collection.

Newspapers

Bryan Eagle
Dallas Morning News
Houston Post
Montrose Star
Newview
Texas A&M Battalion

Secondary Sources

Bailey, Beth. *Sex in the Heartland*. Cambridge, MA: Harvard University Press, 1999.
Beck, Brittney L. "'A Different Kind of Activism': The University Committee on Sexism and Homophobia, 1981–1992." *American Educational Research Journal* 56.4 (2019): 1353–1379. https://doi.org/10.3102/0002831218818784
Beemyn, Brett. "The Silence Is Broken: A History of the First Lesbian, Gay, and Bisexual College Student Groups." *Journal of the History of Sexuality* 12.2 (2003): 205–223.
Cain, Timothy Reese, and Michael S. Hevel. "'Gay People Pay Activity Fees Too': The Committee on Gay Education's Pioneering Legal Victories at the University of Georgia." *Review of Higher Education* 45.1 (2021): 61–91.
Chauncey, George. *Gay New York: Gender, Urban Culture, and the Making of the Gay Male World*. New York: Basic Books, 1994.
Clawson, Jessica. "Coming Out of the Campus Closet: The Emerging Visibility of Queer Students at the University of Florida, 1970–1982." *Educational Studies* 50 (2014): 209–230.
Dethloff, Henry C. *A Centennial History of Texas A&M University, 1876–1976*. Vol. 2. College Station: Texas A&M University Press, 1975.

Dilley, Patrick. "20th Century Postsecondary Practices and Policies to Control Gay Students." *Review of Higher Education* 25 (2002): 409–431.

Dilley, Patrick. *Gay Liberation to Campus Assimilation: Early Non-Heterosexual Student Organizing at Midwestern Universities*. New York: Palgrave Macmillan, 2019.

Dilley, Patrick. *Queer Man on Campus: A History of Non-Heterosexual College Men, 1945–2000*. New York: RoutledgeFarmer, 2002.

Faulkenbury, T. Evan, and Aaron Hayworth. "The Carolina Gay Association, Oral History, and Coming Out at the University of North Carolina." *The Oral History Review* 43.1 (2016): 115–137.

Graves, Karen L. "The History of Lesbian, Gay, Bisexual, Transgender, Queer Issues in Higher Education," in *Higher Education: Handbook of Theory and Research*, ed. Michael B. Paulsen. New York: Springer, 2018. 127–173.

Kaster, James H. *Faggots Fight*. Self-published, 2020.

MacKay, Anne, ed. *Wolf Girls at Vassar: Lesbian and Gay Experiences 1930–1990*. New York: St. Martin's Press, 1992.

Nash, Margaret A., and Jennifer A. Silverman,. "'An Indelible Mark': Gay Purges in Higher Education in the 1940s." *History of Education Quarterly* 55 (2015): 441–459.

Nichols, David, and Morris J. Kafka-Hozschlag. "The Rutgers University Lesbian/Gay Alliance, 1969–1989: The First Twenty Years." *The Journal of the Rutgers University Libraries* 51.2 (1989): 55–95.

Reichard, David A. "Behind the Scenes at the Gayzette: The Gay Student Union and Queer World Making at UCLA in the 1970s." *The Oral History Review* 43.1 (2016): 98–114.

Reichard, David A. "'We Can't Hide and They Are Wrong': The Society for Homosexual Freedom and the Struggle for Recognition at Sacramento State College, 1969–1971." *Law and History Review* 28.3 (2010): 630–674.

Sartorius, Kelly C. *Deans of Women and the Feminist Movement: Emily Taylor's Activism*. New York: Palgrave Macmillan, 2014.

Stein, Marc. *City of Sisterly and Brotherly Loves: Lesbian and Gay Philadelphia, 1945–1972*. Chicago: University of Chicago Press, 2000.

Syrett, Nicholas L. "The Boys of Beaver Meadow: A Homosexual Community at 1920s Dartmouth College." *American Studies* 48 (2007): 9–18.

Wright, William. *Harvard's Secret Court: The Savage 1920 Purge of Campus Homosexuals*. New York: St. Martin's Press, 2005.

"Specialty" Listening

Creating Space for Queer Programming on American College Radio in the Long 1980s

KATHERINE RYE JEWELL

Throughout the long 1980s, noncommercial educational FM radio, occupying signals between 88.9 and 91.9, provided a vital outlet for activist communities for the discussion of issues, challenges, and solidarity-building. Stations such as those affiliated with the progressive Pacifica Foundation, as well as community and college stations, participated in a long tradition of airing progressive programming on radio.[1] These spaces complemented activist strategies to upend negative media depictions of queer people, a movement that accelerated in the 1970s, only to confront rising regulatory action and right-wing activism in the 1980s.[2] On first glance, it seems the confrontation of queer radio programming and culture war hawks conforms to national narratives about post–sexual revolution backlash and the rising culture wars. But exploring institutional limits on college stations at the local level reveals a complicated history beyond national culture-wars politics and media censorship.[3] Activist groups sought to use FCC-licensed educational, noncommercial airwaves, the "left of the dial" in terms of its location on the FM spectrum and these stations' reputation for progressive politics and freedom in programming, to reach listeners in the 1970s. But institutional politics and priorities shaped debates regarding their entry into radio, yielding governance structures that allowed license owners—the institutions themselves—a way to circumvent the image of censorship. These levers are revealed by the case studies in this chapter. At institutions wary of association with such groups, a coded language emerged. Rather than attacking the progressive radio content directly, they could leverage license-holder control and pedagogical functions to limit broadcasts they deemed as damaging to institutional culture and reputation.

Local institutional contexts are essential to understanding the emergence of queer media activism and representation in the 1970s and 1980s. Shows dedicated to conversations within these communities, often referred to as gay programming, were few but increasing in number across stations and many types of institutions during these years. While stations provided crucial space for queer communities, noncommercial, educational radio was not immune from the capitalist media context in which it emerged. Control of outlets of mass communication are, as Nicholas Garnham explained, "matter[s] of central political concern" and not limited to for-profit media corporations.[4] For institutions of higher education, public service and pedagogical goals proved as powerful as market-based tools of program selection and audience appeal to limit progressive content. A focus on institutional environments and their media expands traditional narratives about representation of sexual identities dominated by culture war battles, deregulation and market-based decision making.[5]

Institutions and the radio stations they owned were often located in metropolitan radio markets and reaching listeners outside of campus communities. Together, they reveal more than political relevance of media representation of sexual minorities. The selected stations in this chapter demonstrate the complex dynamics that shaped the most common form of explicitly queer broadcasting before the 1990s. Rising national exposure and commercial success for queer expression, evolving questions about identity, and the need for locally grounded media to anchor communities shaped program development across institutions and radio markets. These programs linked listeners to supportive networks, communities, and activists while also securing hard-won space and visibility (or at least audibility) on public airwaves.

DJs—college and university students as well as community members—navigated institutional politics and community contexts to create space for alternative voices and augment the work of local activists.[6] Students and community DJs leveraged the protections of educational, noncommercial licenses and, notably, college radio's emerging collective reputation as "alternative" radio, to secure airtime.[7] Exploring the institutional dynamics that structured these shows reveals the coded rhetorical tools used to silence queer voices on the airwaves.

WGTB

WGTB-FM at Georgetown University in the 1970s offers a revealing case to explore the dynamics that shaped and limited activist programming in local context. Located in Washington, DC, a large, metropolitan radio market, Georgetown's signal nevertheless was one of only a few college stations that offered progressive programming. Its license owner, a Jesuit institution, valued public service but posed limits to the programs offered, though not always in overt terms.

In 1971, WGTB's support for alternative voices increased, much to the horror of university leaders and some members of the student body. The FCC's definition of "educational" was broad; stations hosted programs with topics spanning heart disease, debates regarding community investment, or campus lectures and events. WGTB's leftist politics, fostered by a general manager committed to radical radio, pushed the boundaries of programming beyond narrowly defined educational content. WGTB's FM signal prided itself on playing "the progressive type of music" that defied top-forty conventions in both style and musicality. But WGTB's politics took an additional, progressive step.[8]

By the 1970s, many universities had launched FM broadcasting. Previously, most student-run stations were AM carrier-current that catered to campus residents who could access wired signals in dorms or cafeterias. But FM signals reached commuter students and community listeners, acting as an aural institutional "front door" and fulfilling public service commitments by providing educational programming to non–university affiliated listeners.[9] At Georgetown, while its AM suffered from a continual lack of staff, the FM station offered a prominent institutional voice and advertised the Jesuit school's interest in public education, welfare, and civic affairs. In 1971, the FM station closed for eight months for reorganization at the administration's request, after a technical issue arose. Administrators brought in professional help and reopened WGTB, providing it with funding and support.

Other student organizations were not so fortunate in the kind of sanction and funding WGTB received. In February 1973, students' petition to form a gay organization failed. The director of student activities defended the administration's denial, citing Georgetown's "tradition of Christian virtues and ideals." As such, she continued, "We believe that the recognition of any homosexual group is completely inconsistent with the ideals and stated policy of the University." The organized students thus could not access financing or request facilities for events, including group meetings. Students identified a public relations mission for their group: to discuss "the cultural and social nature of homosexuality in America," and they demanded university recognition of their existence.[10] A month later, the administration vetoed the organization's appeal. The university allowed students to post signs but denied funding and official sanction.[11]

With programming freedom, unlike the student group, the FM station staff performed this public relations function, even if not explicitly linked to any student organization or directed to students on campus. Its poetry readings and feminist-lesbian shows provided public discussions and dissemination of ideas where the university would not, and the station gained a reputation for radical politics and administrative scrutiny. The station hosted *Friends*, a historic program for the gay community, and a feminist-themed program, *Sophie's Parlor*, that played music by women.

WGTB did not escape administrative scrutiny, however. With its position on the public airwaves, the station was obligated to serve both campus listeners and the wider community, complicating administrators' desire to limit what the station programmed. By 1975, continual complaints about the station led administrators to consider selling the FM property. Administrators and some students demanded that WGTB balance community commitments with service to Georgetown, such as broadcasting news or sporting events. The station also suffered from a dearth of FCC-licensed student DJs and turned to community members for staffing and programing.[12] In essence, WGTB's politics clashed with those of the majority of Georgetown students and administrators. As the station's license neared renewal in 1975, administrators attempted to limit the station's "controversial programming." Administrators targeted General Manger Kenneth K. Sleeman, originally tasked with cleaning up the station and instituting professional standards, claiming he ran WGTB as an "outrageous" example of "radical, left-wing collective" radio management.[13] Georgetown's administration fired Sleeman and replaced him, hoping the new GM would offer "creative, quality, and in depth" programming while also continuing to reach a diverse audience in line with educational license requirements.[14]

Sleeman fought the firing as well as the criticism that the station had only a "tenuous connection" with Georgetown. He denied interest in fostering a cultural revolution. Instead, he explained, "we are trying to present a wide spectrum of sometimes controversial, sometimes shocking viewpoints not broadcast over traditional media."[15] In other words, WGTB simply fulfilled the purpose of noncommercial, educational radio, which could support media that lacked broad commercial appeal that was profitable to private corporations. Sleeman's defense did not quell criticism, particularly because he refused to broadcast basketball games and aired Washington Free Clinic public service announcements. Denying one broadcast and allowing the other confirmed to critics that WGTB did not serve the campus.[16]

Administrators charged that the clinic PSAs violated the station's mission and relationship with the institution. The clinic, which provided referrals for abortion and family planning services, proved "contrary to the stated goals and purpose of the university," a Georgetown administrator claimed, echoing statements about the proposed Gay Alliance in 1973. Station staffers felt "ordered" to cease broadcasting the PSA. The public relations director denied that Georgetown banned the PSAs, but the clinic considered filing an FCC complaint for discrimination. Sleeman called the administration's actions an "overreaction" and "highly unethical," considering that the clinic provided health services to impoverished city residents.[17]

After Sleeman's dismissal, Georgetown investigated WGTB's use of "sensitive language." Administrators cited Sleeman's failure to adequately control the station and the clinic controversy. Although the source of complaints remains unclear, the administration suggested that the FCC "currently is investigating" on-air language, which justified Sleeman's removal. Supposedly, Sleeman committed "'repeated failures to exercise proper control over the operation of the station in conformity with the duties delegated to you by the University as a licensee.'"[18]

WGTB's troubles amounted to more than ignoring Hoya basketball games, a PSA, and occasionally airing dirty words. Georgetown leveraged institutional values and culture, as well as public and university service, to prevent the broadcast of similar voices that led to alumni complaints or a public image out of keeping with strict Jesuit traditions. The acting general manager banned any material with "sensitive language." Unless a DJ requested exemption, no content would be aired that required a disclaimer.[19] This strike at "alternative" radio targeted more than freeform programming and a few indecent songs; it limited media that had given voice to people and communities decidedly out of mainstream gender relations and heteronormativity. The question regarding who decided the nature of Georgetown's public service masked deeper political and cultural tensions.

In February 1976, a poetry reading by William S. Burroughs and Allen Ginsberg caused more campus commotion over WGTB, revealing simmering divisions on campus. Although the station had previously aired readings by Ginsberg and Burroughs, the broadcast's timing during hours when children could potentially be listening—once again levering the "protection" of children against the gay community—led overseers to take action. A review panel suspended two staffers for airing the tape of a locally performed reading on a Friday morning. The FCC queried whether the station aired content with "such expressions as 'ass' with reference to the human buttocks, 'f—ing, 'shitty,' and 'tits.'"[20] Although the students received permission to tape the show "on the grounds of Burroughs name as a recognized published poet with 'obvious socially redeeming value,'" children might be listening during morning hours.[21]

Timing issues aside, what was at stake, the newspaper suggested, was the fate of "alternative radio" in Washington, DC. At WGTB, a reporter explained, "the news is strange, and they never play any Springsteen," but it offered a "serious and significant attempt" at quality programming unlike anywhere else on the AM or FM spectrum. WGTB, the reporter insisted, "is a University service to students both as listeners and as potential staffers."[22] As one of few college or community stations in Washington, DC, Georgetown's internal dynamics shaped area media by limiting access to alternative voices.

Georgetown's troubles existed in a larger context of federal regulatory and local institutional limits to alternative radio. Georgetown was not alone in receiving scrutiny, and administrators looked to events on other campuses to determine policy. New FCC requirements regarding license-holder control provided administrators with the leverage to force WGTB's compliance. As a case regarding obscenity at the University of Pennsylvania's student-run station WXPN prompted the FCC to encourage greater administrative control at university-owned stations, WXPN's license revocation grabbed headlines and attention. It also provided justification to Georgetown administrators to assert tighter control of their own station.[23] As a WGTB review board member suggested, the "problem is not so much with the sensitive language—that's symptomatic; what the FCC is interested in is whether the licensee, in other words the University, can exercise any control over the station."²⁴ With Sleeman's dismissal still under review, the administration presented WGTB's programming and management as part of a larger problem: the station pushed "decency" boundaries, but more so, it defied university attempts at control and directed programming out of line with its public image, a matter clearly under the purview of the administration, not students running the station.

The next month, Georgetown again closed the station for reorganization. "Enraged" staffers organized a rally. They demanded immediate resumption of broadcasting, staff, format, and "the creation of a binding agreement" between Georgetown and an independent advocacy group, the Committee to Save Alternative Radio. Review Board member Fr. James Walsh rejected these demands and tried to calm concerns. He "envisioned no format changes, just a change in quality that would result from a stronger sense of professionalism and an elimination of lapses in broadcasting judgment." In his view, these staffers claimed unwarranted station ownership. Georgetown, not the staff, he reminded them, held the license. The sides entrenched, language grew heated, "with epithets like 'fascists' or 'commie creeps' not uncommon," as one reporter noted.²⁵

Former staffer and program director Ken Rothchild named the station's "outspoken-ism" as the central issue. Rothchild, a former host of *Friends*, a program for the local gay community, admitted he pushed boundaries. "I talked about giving a blowjob on the air," he later remembered. The show focused on music and entertainment, hosting guests from John Waters to Cheech and Chong. While divisions between the more politically news-oriented staffers and those interested in music percolated at the station, all understood that the station offered a strong voice. Another *Friends* host, Bruce Pennington, reflected that his show "provid[ed] an identity for people who were still trying to find one."²⁶ Students worried about the effects of the administration's actions. "What you'll have," Rothchild continued, "is a liberal radio station that will be more of a national public radio station," if the administration had its way. In Fr. Walsh's view, the station could address political and social controversies within limits established by university culture. He envisioned discussions "on a philosophical and ideological basis," naming "homosexuality, the situation in Portugal, and abortion as the type of issues that should be addressed in this manner."²⁷ Queer programming, other than academic discussion, did not meet his definition, although he avoided explicitly saying so.

By the mid-1970s, college radio's supporters envisioned its potential extension beyond institutional boundaries. Instead of limiting college radio to students as a "sandbox" for musical fun, many students did embrace public service programming. Freeform radio could, in their view, "provide a forum for 'leftist' stands on news items, women's liberation, and homosexual rights." And with student governance's decreasing funding, WGTB petitioned the community for support, garnering $32,000 in donations over a few years. Even staffers who did not fit the political profile felt obliged to these listeners.[28]

WGTB was a publicly licensed station, but the institutional dynamics of its license holder shaped the language regarding its programming. The student newspaper, *The Hoya*, aired controversies over content, particularly WGTB content aimed at queer audiences. Numerous students and campus leaders weighed in on the matter. Some letter writers defended station content as upholding Jesuit pedagogical traditions by allowing "all perspectives" to be "openly manifested," or as protected free speech. Faculty tasked with the station's overhaul argued that a small group of staffers had seized the station to broadcast to a select community and considered the signal "theirs." Fr. Walsh said this "obdurate minority" resisted until the university had no choice but to close and reorganize the station.[29]

Although the Student Senate allowed community groups to maintain a place at WGTB, it obligated the station to serve students first. Some 78 percent of students polled agreed with this requirement, with only one-third supporting programming that appealed to the community. Many students outside of WGTB did not see the point of community engagement. WGTB did not "reflect the listening desires of Georgetown students," musically or politically, in one student's words. Another student never listened "because they're a bunch of wacked-out people down there." While one radical Jesuit decried the station's closure, calling it "another illustration to me that a sex-based morality leads to all sorts of distortions," by and large the campus shrugged its shoulders regarding WGTB's troubles.[30]

But the institution's mission of public service also created opportunities. A poll revealed "that small groups favored some air time for programs for Gays, Blacks, and women." The station's public license required consideration of community needs in programming. Although DJs at Georgetown pushed the limits of institutional and regulatory boundaries, their experiences suggest how local broadcasters across the nation justified their expansion of programming to underserved listeners. Many could do so because a majority of students tended not to tune in to these FM signals. Perhaps most telling, the student newspaper buried news regarding community staffers in a middle section, suggesting that most students cared little about the station.[31]

Ultimately, Georgetown's administration used pedagogical reasons to close WGTB for good in 1979, ending years of vitriol regarding the station. They argued that because the station existed without connection to any communications or training program on campus, offering students hands-on, laboratory experience in managing a radio station, it was not needed. The administration used these pedagogical reasons to paper over the cultural divisions that prompted them to give up the FM outlet. WGTB "worked in a vacuum with no department of communication arts and no curricula in radio or television . . . as an academic base," the administration explained. The university relinquished the asset to the University of the District of Columbia.[32]

Gaybreak for WRSU

At other institutions, student groups and community activists envisioned using student-run stations to provide space for those without mainstream media exposure. But even at universities not operating within a Jesuit campus culture and mission, limits emerged. In 1979, at Rutgers, a Gay Alliance organized to create conversation between gay and straight students and struggled for recognition and funding, similar to what Georgetown's students faced. To address bias and hostility toward gays on campus, organizers looked to WRSU on campus to host a radio show. Radio stations on college campuses in the 1970s often had ample time to fill, with few applicants. They also had strong ties to progressive radio, specifically the Pacifica Foundation stations, who provided professional staffers to guide students. Their support for socially and politically progressive causes, alongside the tradition of community radio allowing diverse voices to have access to the airwaves, created an opportunity for students seeking to influence campus culture while also providing a needed community service. Alliance leaders hoped to shift attitudes on campus in response to an incident in the previous academic year in which a fraternity conducted an "effigy-hanging of the image of a homosexual." Violent statements accompanied the image. In looking to the radio station, the Alliance drew inspiration from feminist consciousness-raising groups to confront isolation and to support individuals in crisis.[33]

WRSU debuted *Gaybreak* in December 1979, New Jersey's first radio show to focus on the gay community, according to local reporting. In a magazine format, Gay Alliance member Sean McKeon offered a thirty-minute show broadcasting local groups such as Dignity Metro, a group for gay Catholics, and interviews with literature scholars and local activists. McKeon, a communications major and Rutgers senior, proposed the show to dubious station staffers. But his audition tape convinced them to give him airtime. Although the show lasted only half an hour in a weekly schedule, McKeon declared it a success. He hoped *Gaybreak* would "fill a large communications gap for gays in the state" and reach a straight audience in ways that would confront discrimination. Thirty minutes was a paltry amount of time, but McKeon knew it was important to carve out this space, particularly given the unsupportive nature of Rutgers' student government toward the Gay Alliance. The show thus served two purposes. It created a reputation for quality programming and reached outside the gay community. McKeon explained, "We hope to reach not only the people who are 'out' and who are secure in their sexuality but also those who aren't so secure and need some encouragement."[34]

Gaybreak did not cause the kind of administrative interference as that seen at Georgetown, and WRSU's educational license provided defense against critics. One community member castigated the "new homosexual radio station" at Rutgers as evidence of a nefarious plot to use tax dollars to create a new "Sodom and Gomorrah." A former manager of WRSU responded to the *Central New Jersey Home News* to confront this bigoted interpretation. *Gaybreak*, he noted, aired for only thirty minutes per week, a fact that "hardly makes us a 'homosexual radio station,'" as the complaint charged. Instead, WRSU's manager defended the station as fulfilling the "federal mandates" of its educational license by serving the community. He pointed to WRSU's "numerous hours of ethnic and specialty programming . . . aimed at the black community, the Indian, Greek and other ethnic groups." Furthermore, WRSU received no tax funding; student fees financed it.[35]

But WRSU's position within Rutgers demonstrated how college stations often had little influence on campus culture and how alternative programming had trouble breaking into popular timeslots or garnering attention beyond alternative media. A majority of Rutgers students tended to ignore the station, as had happened at Georgetown, given WRSU's specialty programming and non-mainstream music.[36] Administrators eventually noticed its lack of pedagogical function and programming that put the university in a light they considered counter to institutional public image. In 1985, the administration attempted to exert control over the station's programming, particularly its more cutting-edge music. Because Rutgers was a public institution, the station's educational function took on added weight compared to Georgetown, where Jesuit tradition served as the key check on content alongside license requirements.

Activists also relied consistently on music, letting artists and musicians carry the message that would facilitate community building. Student groups successfully secured airtime, though groups competed with one another for space and coverage. Yet their presence on stations' schedules helped define alternative, noncommercial radio. College radio stations increasingly identified as defying mainstream culture in the 1980s, actively opposing commercial appeal. For activists, this offered a different kind of limitation than recalcitrant university administrators or inhospitable institutional missions and values.

Beyond securing visibility for shows from queer perspectives, activism and outreach continued locally behind the scenes or targeted vulnerable populations with public service outreach. Network and individual intervention defined the work that DJs and connected activist groups performed via radio shows. Many college radio stations operated with public service in mind, as dictated by their educational licenses. Stations such as KALX at Berkeley conducted sexual health awareness campaigns that blended education with music, such as its 1991 "Condom Countdown" that featured such songs as "Go See the Doctor" by Kool Moe Dee and "Condom Sense" by Magnetic Force.[37] Commercial progressive stations that formed in the 1990s took their cue from these activities. Stephen Mindich, founder and owner of alternative press outlet the *Boston Phoenix*, owned WFNX-FM, which launched a new show in the city in 1992. The show, *One in Ten*, featured "issues and events in the gay and lesbian community," and lasted three-and-a-half hours on Monday nights. The first show featured the Names Memorial Quilt Project and featured comedian and artist Lea DeLaria.[38]

In more conservative areas, college radio linked activists and individuals while giving voice to a diverse queer community. The 1992 launch of the program *Out of the Closet* at WRVU at Vanderbilt University in Nashville, the so-called Buckle of the Bible Belt, exemplified this function. Ron Slomowicz, an engineering student from Orlando, Florida, versed in that city's club scene, had watched *Pump up the Volume*, a movie starring Christian Slater as a radio DJ. The movie convinced him that radio could be a medium to "infect people's minds" with new ideas, as he explained. After attending a Gay and Lesbian Student Conference, where he learned of resources in queer radio, he started his own show. He constructed a character—DJ Ron—who hosted local activists, drag performers, and musicians. He aired the nationally syndicated gay news program, *This Way Out*, which had launched in 1988 in Los Angeles to confront damaging stereotypes amidst the AIDS epidemic.[39]

Out of the Closet openly defied dominant campus culture. Vanderbilt's LAMBDA organization hosted secret meetings to provide a safe space. For a student who was out at school but not at home, other students revealed their homosexuality in their local newspapers, leading to one student's parents disowning him. Slomowicz also experienced hostility for being out on campus. Nevertheless, despite facing some "right-wing nonsense" his first semester, as he put it, he created meaningful links with the Nashville queer and activist community. *Out of the Closet* featured political and community organizations and transgender advocates, and showcased Pride events. DJ Ron interviewed Nashville HIV-activist Mark Middleton, who created the character Bianca Page as a drag performance. DJ Ron coordinated events with local gay and dance clubs such as The Underground, a "straight" club, whose owners welcomed all. The clubs hosted fundraisers, handed out free condoms, and promoted safe sex. Before the Internet, DJ Ron's radio show gave listeners access to that network, listeners who might otherwise not be knowledgeable about Nashville's queer community and institutions.

On campus, DJ Ron maintained active involvement with LAMBDA and helped to build a more welcoming, although not universally so, atmosphere. The arts and philosophy dorm on campus, where Ron resided as a student, hosted an annual "cross dress fest," which he leveraged to host a Drag Show on Vanderbilt's campus. Although WRVU did not reflect the dominant culture of Vanderbilt's conservative culture, its presence provided an outlet for students who did not fit into the fraternity- and sorority-dominated activities, and it connected students to the larger Nashville community. Ron's radio show acted as a clearinghouse of local information—but, importantly, it also served individual functions.

Out of the Closet aided listeners on a personal level. As DJ Ron explained, in the era of Walkmen, kids could listen to his show on headphones, privately accessing gay culture unbeknownst to parents or friends. And occasionally the show provided direct support: in May 1993, the show's first year, a young man called in during a broadcast. He said he was gay, his parents did not know, and he was going to take his own life. Slomowicz had immediate access to a suicide hotline, which he contacted to reach out to the boy in crisis. DJ Ron, a young student himself, had already amassed the resources and connections to provide this lifeline. That November, while DJ Ron was doing a fun show during the Thanksgiving weekend, the boy's father called. His son had come out and admitted he had contemplated ending his life. "You talked him down," the boy's father said. While he "still didn't get the gay thing," he credited DJ Ron and his show with saving his son's life. This story exemplifies the personal nature of radio and the ongoing importance of space on the airwaves for queer and feminist voices. Censorship continued to be a problem in the 1990s. FCC restrictions on language grew vague after the 1978 *FCC v. Pacifica* decision and FCC fines in 1986. For shows that centered on sexuality, this had a chilling effect. DJ Ron reported even avoiding musical content with explicit drug references to avoid trouble, let alone content with sexual themes. But activists continually sought airtime, even if limited or late-night, and they navigated the limits placed on shows by individual station managers, institutions and administrations, or the local community.[40]

Conclusion

Activist groups continued to seek outlets for individual service and local networking. Music grounded community events and defined and channeled identity and expression. Shows on noncommercial and college radio continued to perform important outreach. They provided room for diverse queer and feminist representations, speaking to a multiplicity of experiences and complicating any simple construction of "gay" or "women's" media or diminishing the need for ongoing work. As activist radio since the 1970s demonstrates, programmers consistently faced institutional priorities and dynamics, sometimes clearly leveraged against particular programming, though more often softened by pedagogical goals or public service than any political concern regarding content. Administrators had access to language to encode intentions to limit activist programming or minority voices who appealed beyond campus listeners.

Activists thus faced limits even on alternative, noncommercial airwaves in securing visibility. The tools that administrators wielded demonstrate the importance of considering institutional contexts to understand the limits non-mainstream voices faced in securing access beyond narrow conceptions of censorship or political backlash.

But the shows also anchored and expanded discussions about the role that music and culture could play in shaping cultural attitudes and creating new civic spaces. Institutions could silence stations, whether by implementing more administrative oversight, airing professional staff rather than community volunteers, or selling stations outright, while denying censorship. Still, many shows survived to continue to provide individual service and musical innovation. As with college radio more generally, although some stations such as WRVU went off the air, most continue even as the media landscape transforms.[41] The internet opened up new avenues for organizing to complement and expand, via laptops and smartphones and linking audiences with new communities and musical sounds to serve as soundtracks for life—even as the need for visibility and outreach has remained consistent. The low-power FM movement gave rise to new community-oriented stations in cities from San Francisco to Louisville and Nashville.[42] Still, questions regarding the power of institutions, whether they are internet providers, social media platforms, or universities and colleges, continually structure questions of access and representation of underserved communities and voices.

Notes

1. Phylis W. Johnson and Michael C. Keith, *Queer Airwaves: The Story of Gay and Lesbian Broadcasting* (Routledge, 2014), 28. Indeed, "centralized regulation did not seriously impede the development of radio programs targeting the lesbian and gay subculture and was, therefore, probably a better regime than decentralized state and local regulation," as local censorship occurred more frequently than FCC action against sexually or otherwise explicit content. William N. Eskridge Jr., "Challenging the Apartheid of the Closet: Establishing Conditions for Lesbian and Gay Intimacy, Nomos, and Citizenship, 1961–1981" 25 (n.d.): 900.

2. Several scholars confront "invisibility" of queer representation and securing space in media as a means to transport messages and enhance civic engagement, particularly regarding the depiction of queer women, or to map and reflect emerging conversations regarding feminism. Elke Zobl and Ricarda Drüeke, *Feminist Media: Participatory Spaces, Networks and Cultural Citizenship* (Bielefeld,

Germany: Transcript Verlag, 2012); Susan Driver, *Queer Girls and Popular Culture: Reading, Resisting, and Creating Media* (New York: Peter Lang, 2007).

3. The FCC's KPFK ruling created a significant gray area in regulating on-air content, and many stations exerted extreme caution in what they broadcast, but nevertheless the FCC allowed some limits to its decision. Dennis McDougal, "Obscenities after Midnight," *The Press Democrat*, November 25, 1987. For analysis of the culture wars, see Andrew Hartman, *A War for the Soul of America: A History of the Culture Wars* (Chicago: University of Chicago Press, 2015).

4. Nicholas Garnham, *Capitalism and Communication: Global Culture and the Economics of Information* (Thousand Oaks, CA: Sage, 1990), 65, 160.

5. Christopher P. Loss, *Between Citizens and the State: The Politics of American Higher Education in the 20th Century* (Princeton, NJ: Princeton University Press, 2012).

6. In this volume, see Hevel and Thompson, "Aggies are *Not* Queers: A History of *Gay Student Services v. Texas A&M University*, 1975–1985."

7. See Nicholas Rubin, "Signing On: U.S. College Rock Radio and the Popular Music Industry, 1977–1983" (PhD dissertation, University of Virginia, Charlottesville, Virginia, 2010); Samuel J. Sauls, *The Culture of American College Radio* (Ames: Iowa State University Press, 2000).

8. Dave Pierce, *Riding on the Ether Express: A Memoir of 1960s Los Angeles, the Rise of Freeform Underground Radio, and the Legendary KPPC-FM* (Lafayette, LA: Center for Louisiana Studies, University of Louisiana at Lafayette, 2008); Eric Weisbard, *Top 40 Democracy: The Rival Mainstreams of American Music* (Chicago: University of Chicago Press, 2014), 79.

9. Mike Basile, "WGTB Adds AM Format To Broadcast," *The Hoya*, February 9, 1973, p. 1. https://repository.library.georgetown.edu/handle/10822/555408

10. "University Denies Permission for Homosexuals to Organize," *Hoya*, February 9, 1973, p. 1.

11. Mark Von Hagen, "Ryan Rejects Appeal of Gays to Organize; Court Case Possible" *The Hoya*, March 2, 1973, p. 1. https://repository.library.georgetown.edu/handle/10822/555411

12. "Keep GTB at GU" Georgetown University, *The Hoya*, November 7, 1975, p. 6. https://repository.library.georgetown.edu/handle/10822/554964

13. Guy Raz, *Washington City Paper*, January 29, 1999. www.dcrtv.com/plus/wgtb.html

14. Michael A. Byrnes, "New WGTB Station Manager Announced," Press Release, ca. 1975, Georgetown University Archives, Booth Family Center for Special Collections, Lauinger Library, Georgetown University, Washington, DC; "Radio Free Georgetown," NPR.org. www.npr.org/templates/story/story.php?storyId=3424001

15. Kenneth K. Sleeman, "rostrum" *The Hoya*, November 14, 1975, p. 6. https://repository.library.georgetown.edu/handle/10822/554965

16. Ted J. Sudol, "GU FM Radio Staffers Balk at Broadcasting Hoya B-Ball." *The Hoya*, November 21, 1975, p. 1. https://repository.library.georgetown.edu/handle/10822/554966

17. Mark McAdams, "Henle Won't Bar GTB Ad; Sleeman Cries Censorship," *The Hoya*, December 5, 1975, pp. 1, 5. https://repository.library.georgetown.edu/handle/10822/554967

18. Wayne Saitta, "GTB License Under Investigation, FCC Considers Sensitive Language," *The Hoya*, December 12, 1975, p. 3. https://repository.library.georgetown.edu/handle/10822/554968

19. Jim Colaprico, "Sleeman Barred from Station, Claims Wholesale Censorship," p. 1; Wayne Saitta, "SAC Proposes Return of GU's AM Carrier" *The Hoya*, January 16, 1976, p. 2. https://repository.library.georgetown.edu/handle/10822/554969

20. Barry Wiegand and Margaret Henry, "WGTB Investigated Again after Obscenity Complaint," *The Hoya*, February 27, 1976, p. 3. https://repository.library.georgetown.edu/handle/10822/554975

21. "GTB Review Panel Confirms Suspension of Two Staffers," *The Hoya*, February 19, 1976, p. 3. https://repository.library.georgetown.edu/handle/10822/554974

22. Steve Mathias, "Mary Parish, A Viable Alternative?" *The Hoya*, Feburary 19, 1976, p. 7.

23. P.H. Wiest, "WXPN Status Affects Station at Georgetown," *The Daily Pennsylvanian* 92.35, April 5, 1976.

24. Ted Sudol, "Parish Restricts Editorial Policy," *The Hoya*, December 12, 1975, p. 1.

25. Barry Wiegand, "Biggest Controversy Since Ryan" *The Hoya*, March 17, 1976, p. 2. https://repository.library.georgetown.edu/handle/10822/554976

26. Guy Raz, January 29, 1999.

27. Jim Colaprico, "WGTB Future Format Unsure after Review Board Shutdown," *The Hoya*, March 17, 1976, p. 3.

28. Barry Wiegand, "Biggest Controversy Since Ryan," 2.

29. "WGTB Closing" and "More WGTB" letters to the editor *The Hoya*, March 26, 1976, p. 17. https://repository.library.georgetown.edu/handle/10822/554978

30. "WGTB Closing" and "More WGTB."

31. Cary Fulbright, "Senate GTB Group Says Keep Community Staff" *The Hoya*, April 23, 1976, p. 3. https://repository.library.georgetown.edu/handle/10822/554982

32. Students resumed broadcasting under new call letters in 1982, and they secured the letters WGTB in 1985. "About," WGTB | Georgetown Radio, August 3, 2010. http://georgetownradio.com/about

33. Phyllis Messinger, "Cook's Gays Lack Funds, Recognition," *The Central New Jersey Home News*, December 24, 1979. At Georgetown University, a campus-based Nazi group organized a protest as the GPGU organized an appeal to their charter's revocation. Lorenzo Ascoli, "Georgetown Nazi Organizes Demonstration," *The Hoya*, February 15, 1979. https://repository.library.georgetown.edu/handle/10822/555052

34. Ann Ledesma, "'Gaybreak' First Show of Its Kind in the State," *The Central New Jersey Home News*, December 1, 1979.

35. "Acting against Word of God," *The Central New Jersey Home News*, January 16, 1980, sec. Letters; "Accusation Was Thoughtless"; *The Central New Jersey Home News*, January 31, 1980, sec. Letters.

36. "Students OK Fees; WRSU Stays on Air," *The Central New Jersey Home News*, April 26, 1985.

37. "KALX Condom Countdown," *Los Angeles Times*, December 29, 1991.

38. "WZBC Lea DeLaria and Boston Format Gay Progs." *Boston Globe*, October 2, 1992.

39. Ron Slomowicz, Skype interview, January 30, 2017, author's personal collection; "About TWO—This Way Out." http://thiswayout.org/about-two

40. Slomowicz, Skype interview.

41. Katherine Rye Jewell, "Perspective | Why Musical Innovation Will Continue, Even as Local Radio Disappears," *Washington Post*, November 15, 2017. www.washingtonpost.com/news/made-by-history/wp/2017/11/15/why-musical-innovation-will-continue-even-as-local-radio-disappears

42. Christina Dunbar-Hester, *Low Power to the People: Pirates, Protest, and Politics in FM Radio Activism* (Cambridge, MA: MIT Press, 2014); Nina Huntemann, "A Promise Diminished: The Politics of Low-Power Radio," in *Communities of the Air*, ed. Susan Merrill Squier, Radio Century, Radio Culture (Durham, NC: Duke University Press, 2003), 76–90; "WRVU Group Granted Low-Power FM License," *Nashville Scene*, December 4, 2014. www.nashvillescene.com/nashvillecream/archives/2014/12/04/wrvu-group-granted-low-power-fm-license

Works Cited

ARCHIVAL SOURCES AND INTERVIEWS

Boston Women's Community Radio Records, 1972–1993 (inclusive), 1980–1989 (bulk). MC 710 or T-317. Schlesinger Library, Radcliffe Institute, Harvard University, Cambridge, Massachusetts. https://id.lib.harvard.edu/ead/sch01379/catalog

Hughes, Dave. Phone. January 6, 2019. Author's Personal Collection

Something About the Women Radio Show Records, Digital Collections and Archives, Tufts University Library, Tufts University, Medford, Massachusetts

Phoenix Women Take Back the Night and Women's Words Radio Show Collection, Photos and Documents (MS 243), Library and Archives, Arizona Historical Society, Central Arizona Division, Tempe, Arizona

Slomowicz, Ron. Skype, January 30, 2017. Author's Personal Collection.

"The Book," held by WMBR at Massachusetts Institute of Technology, Cambridge, Massachusetts

WGTB Files in Georgetown University Archives, Booth Family Center for Special Collections Lauinger Library, Georgetown University, Washington, DC

NEWSPAPERS

The Boston Globe
The Central New Jersey Home News
The Daily Pennsylvanian (University of Pennsylvania)
The Hoya digital archives, Digital Georgetown, Georgetown University Libraries, https://repository.library.georgetown.edu
The Los Angeles Times
The New York Times
The Philadelphia Enquirer
The Washington Post

SECONDARY SOURCES

Andersen, Mark, and Mark Jenkins. *Dance of Days: Two Decades of Punk in the Nation's Capital*. New York: Akashic Books, 2009.

Barnouw, Erik. *A Tower in Babel: A History of Broadcasting in the United States, to 1933*. New York: Oxford University Press, 1966.

Byerly, Carolyn M., and Karen Ross. *Women and Media: A Critical Introduction*. John Wiley & Sons, 2008.

Chastagner, Claude. "The Parents' Music Resource Center: From Information to Censorship." *Popular Music* 18.2 (1999): 179–192.

Copeland, Stacey. "Broadcasting Queer Feminisms: Lesbian and Queer Women Programming in Transnational, Local, and Community Radio." *Journal of Radio & Audio Media* 25.2 (July 3, 2018): 209–223. https://doi.org/10.1080/19376529.2018.1482899

Creekmur, Corey K, and Alexander Doty. *Out in Culture: Gay, Lesbian, and Queer Essays on Popular Culture*. Durham, NC: Duke University Press, 1995.

DeShazor, Brian. "Queer Radio History: Pacifica Radio." *Journal of Radio & Audio Media* 25.2 (July 3, 2018): 253–265. https://doi.org/10.1080/19376529.2018.1481246

Douglas, Susan J. *Listening in: Radio and the American Imagination*. Minneapolis: University of Minnesota Press, 2004.

Driver, Susan. *Queer Girls and Popular Culture: Reading, Resisting, and Creating Media*. New York: Peter Lang, 2007.

Eskridge, William N. *Gaylaw: Challenging the Apartheid of the Closet*. Cambridge, MA: Harvard University Press, 2009.

Fisher, Marc. *Something in the Air: Radio, Rock, and the Revolution That Shaped a Generation*. New York: Random House, 2007.

Foege, Alec. *Right of the Dial: The Rise of Clear Channel and the Fall of Commercial Radio*. New York: Faber and Faber, 2008.

Gandy, Oscar H., and Nicholas Garnham. "Political Economy and Cultural Studies: Reconciliation or Divorce?" *Critical Studies in Mass Communication* 12.1 (March 1995): 60–71. https://doi.org/10.1080/15295039509366919

Garnham, Nicholas. *Capitalism and Communication: Global Culture and the Economics of Information*. Thousand Oaks, CA: Sage, 1990.

Gastman, Roger, and Corcoran Gallery of Art. *Pump Me Up: DC Subculture of the 1980s*. Los Angeles: R. Rock Enterprises, 2013.

Goldberg, Suzanne B. *Sexuality and Equality Law*. New York: Routledge, 2017.

Gracyk, Theodore. *I Wanna Be Me: Rock Music and the Politics of Identity*. Philadelphia: Temple University Press, 2001.

Hartman, Andrew. *A War for the Soul of America: A History of the Culture Wars*. Chicago: University of Chicago Press, 2015.

Hilliard, Robert L., and Michael C. Keith. *Dirty Discourse: Sex and Indecency in Broadcasting*. New York: John Wiley & Sons, 2008.

Johnson, Phylis W., and Michael C. Keith. *Queer Airwaves: The Story of Gay and Lesbian Broadcasting: The Story of Gay and Lesbian Broadcasting*. New York: Routledge, 2014.

Eskridge, William N. Jr. "Challenging the Apartheid of the Closet: Establishing Conditions for Lesbian and Gay Intimacy, Nomos, and Citizenship, 1961–1981." *Hofstra Law* Review 25: 155.

Kerrigan, Páraic, and Anne O'Brien. "'Openness through Sound': Dualcasting on Irish LGBT Radio." *Journal of Radio & Audio Media* 25.2 (July 3, 2018): 224–239. https://doi.org/10.1080/19376529.2018.1477779

Krieger, Susan. *Hip Capitalism*. New York: Sage Publications, 1979.

Kruse, Holly. *Site and Sound: Understanding Independent Music Scenes*. P. Lang, 2003.

Kruse, Holly. "Subcultural Identity in Alternative Music Culture." *Popular Music* 12.1 (1993): 33–41.

Lasar, Matthew. *Pacifica Radio: The Rise of an Alternative Network*. Philadelphia: Temple University Press, 2000.

Linfoot, Matthew. "Queer in Your Ear: Connecting Space, Community, and Identity in LGBT BBC Radio Programs, 1992–2000." *Journal of Radio & Audio Media* 25.2 (July 3, 2018): 195–208. https://doi.org/10.1080/19376529.2018.1473402

Loss, Christopher P. *Between Citizens and the State: The Politics of American Higher Education in the 20th Century*. Princeton, NJ: Princeton University Press, 2012.

Motavalli, Jim, and Michael Fedorka. "Liberated Radio—A Do-It-Yourself Guide." *The Radical Teacher* 13 (1979): 23–27.

Pierce, Dave. *Riding on the Ether Express: A Memoir of 1960s Los Angeles, the Rise of Freeform Underground Radio, and the Legendary KPPC-FM*. Lafayette, LA: Center for Louisiana Studies, University of Louisiana at Lafayette, 2008.

Rapping, Elayne. *Media-Tions: Forays into the Culture and Gender Wars*. Boston: South End Press, 1994.

Rubin, Nicholas. "Signing On: U.S. College Rock Radio and the Popular Music Industry, 1977–1983." PhD dissertation, University of Virginia, Charlottesville, Virginia, 2010.

Sauls, Samuel J. *The Culture of American College Radio*. Ames: Iowa State University Press, 2000.

Schulman, Bruce J. *The Seventies: The Great Shift in American Culture, Society, and Politics*. Cambridge, MA: Da Capo Press, 2002.

Slotten, Hugh Richard. *Radio's Hidden Voice: The Origins of Public Broadcasting in the United States*. Urbana: University of Illinois Press, 2009.

Sterling, Christopher H., and Michael C. Keith. *Sounds of Change: A History of FM Broadcasting in America*. Chapel Hill: University of North Carolina Press, 2008.

Stoller, Tony. "Local Radio—A Different Sort of Animal." *Journal of Radio & Audio Media* 25.2 (July 3, 2018): 311–320. https://doi.org/10.1080/19376 529.2018.1478636

Walker, Jesse. *Rebels on the Air: An Alternative History of Radio in America*. New York: New York University Press, 2001.

Winfield, Betty Houchin, and Sandra Davidson. *Bleep! Censoring Rock and Rap Music*. Westport, CT: Greenwood Press, 1999.

Zobl, Elke, and Ricarda Drüeke. *Feminist Media: Participatory Spaces, Networks and Cultural Citizenship*. Bielefeld, Germany: Verlag, 2012.

II
Anti-Racist, Anti-Imperialist, Anti-Borders Action

"We were fire-fighting against Thatcher and the system she was putting forward"

The Black Women's Movement and the Boundaries of Nationhood in Thatcher's Britain

JADE BENTIL

Introduction

When three hundred Black women gathered at the Abeng Centre in Brixton on March 18, 1979, for the inaugural National Black Women's Conference, they were aware that the event marked the historic beginning of the Black Women's Movement (BWM) in Britain.[1] Brought together by the Organisation of Women of Asian and African Descent (OWAAD), the conference represented the emergence of a visible Black feminist political agenda. Black women travelled across the country to articulate a collective politics that sought to confront their experiences of racist, sexist, and classist oppression. As Black feminists gave rousing speeches throughout the day-long conference, at the heart of their analyses was a critique of the imperial foundations of the British nation, the coercive nature of the state and its effects on marginalized communities. By constructing a Black feminist analysis that was anti-imperialist in praxis and that sought to establish links with Black liberation movements throughout the African diaspora, Black women in Britain built on a political tradition of activism that was at the heart of their historical experiences of resistance under slavery, under colonialism and under neocolonialism.[2] Black feminist activist Ama Gueye recalls her feelings of euphoria upon meeting fellow politically engaged Black women; the conference served as an "empowering" testament to the fact that in a nation that sought to suppress their voices, Black women in Britain had the power to tell their "own stories."[3]

Less than two months after OWAAD's inaugural conference Margaret Thatcher came to power. This election result held both symbolic meaning and material consequences for Black people in Britain; whilst Black feminists understood Britain to be a nation-state constituted through ongoing colonial violence, Thatcher's victory constituted a fresh affront. In 1978, Thatcher had distinguished herself as a politician who was eager to reinforce the terms of British national membership and expand the architecture of Black negation. In a television interview, she emphasized that "the British people" were becoming increasingly "afraid" that the country was being "swamped by people of a different culture."[4] Integral to her electoral victory was Thatcher's ability to position herself as a candidate willing to do what was necessary to restore a sense of national prestige to a Britain that was experiencing a "crisis in hegemony" due to a deepening recession and the ongoing disintegration of empire.[5] As the political climate of the country lurched to the right, fascist groups such as the National Front also gained momentum in the late 1970s. This entanglement of state racism and white vigilante terror extended the crisis that had been produced around Black life for more than four hundred years.

Black women's groups campaigned against the socially corrosive policies of the Conservative government. They argued that its right-wing political mandate was "responsible for some of the most vicious attacks that the Black community has had to deal with for many years."[6] Organizing around a plethora of issues such as inequities in education, immigration, healthcare, police brutality and austerity measures, the BWM marked a radical period of sustained political dissent in Thatcher's Britain. Black feminist activist Suzanne Scafe highlights that as they were "completely excluded from access to power," Black women's groups in Britain were "organically structured" to resist "mainstream dominance."[7] Analyzing the BWM as a key site of open rebellion toward state-sanctioned brutality against the enslaved, the colonized and the nominally free during the Thatcher years is thus at the heart of my endeavor to recover the enduring significance of Black women's revolutionary struggle for Black freedom.

The limited scholarship available on the BWM has primarily sought to illustrate the divisions that emerged within the movement during the early to mid-1980s. Feminist scholars such as Heidi Safia Mirza, Natalie Thomlinson and Julia Sudbury provide in-depth analysis of the overarching contours of the BWM, with a particular focus on the issues of lesbianism and Afro-Asian unity as being the main points of contention that lead to the demise of OWAAD in 1983.[8] These studies have been fundamental in demonstrating that a focus on Black women's activism crucially complicates the dominant historiography of feminist organizing, which has traditionally charted the activism of white middle-class women in the Women's Liberation movement (WLM) from the late 1960s to the late 1970s. Such scholarship on Black feminist activism problematizes the parameters of "Second Wave feminism" as a historical framing device: not only were Black women active within radical Black organizing spaces from the late 1960s to the late 1980s but also such hegemonic periodization renders invisible Black women's activism as an autonomous political movement with its own historical dimensions, critiques of global power relations and a multitude of urgent demands. Studies by Tracy Fisher and Ranu Samantrai have also provided invaluable analysis within the historiography of Black feminism in Britain, as they have begun to analyse the significance of the BWM within the wider context of Thatcher's premiership.[9] Such work has considered how the right-wing political terrain of the late 1970s and 1980s influenced Black women's political organizing. This chapter builds on the scholarship of Mirza, Sudbury, Thomlinson, Fisher, and Samantrai to add further insight into how the BWM was shaped by the political landscape of the Thatcher years and how its radical vision exceeded the context of this enclosure.

Utilising oral history interviews that I conducted with women at the helm of the movement, I examine how Black feminists navigated the entanglement of race, gender, class and nation during the Thatcher years. In doing so, this work historicizes the BWM's contribution to the development of Black feminist thought and the Black radical tradition. I argue that the intersection of race, gender, class, and imperialism in Britain placed Black women outside the boundaries of what constituted the nation and rendered their lives disposable within the context of the British national project. In organizing against white supremacy, misogyny, capitalism, and neocolonialism, Black women activists utilized their structural position as "noncitizens" to expose the matrix of violence that undergirded the British nation-state. In their endeavor to create expansive forms of community and imagine alternative modes of social life, Black feminists staged a decade-long rebellion that grappled with and resisted against the desire for inclusion within the fabric of the nation-state. By investigating the nuances of the BWM, this chapter calls to attention the historical importance of Black feminist activism in Britain and the contemporary significance of their resistance within the ongoing struggle for global Black liberation.

It is important to note that within the BWM, the term "Black" was often used to describe people of African, African Caribbean, and South Asian descent in Britain as a "politics of solidarity" against the racist British state.[10] Whilst various Black women's groups employed the idea of Blackness as a political identity, in this work, I center gendered experiences of Blackness in Britain within the context of the African diaspora. I interrogate how anti-Black racism, gender, class, and the conceptualization of nation intersect. The complexities of these intersections demand that distinctions be made between different racialized and ethnic groups in Britain, and that attention be paid to the nuances of self-understandings. Throughout this chapter, therefore, I use the term "Black" to denote women of African, African Caribbean, and African American descent in Britain and primarily focus on their activism in the BWM. Inevitably, in some of the primary sources such as Black feminist newsletters, the term "Black" is at times used as an umbrella term for women of color in Britain. This usage was often dependent on whether a particular group was organizing under the premise of Afro-Asian unity and is reflective of the lack of consensus throughout the BWM as to whether Blackness as a political identity could effectively represent the specific forms of racialized and gendered violence that Black and Asian women were experiencing. This work focuses on the activism of groups such as OWAAD, Brixton Black Women's Group (BBWG) and East London Black Women's Organization (ELBWO). As each of these collectives primarily consisted of African and African Caribbean membership, the usage of the term "Black" within primary sources relating to these groups generally reflects the political concerns of African diasporic women in Britain. In my analysis of the coalitional activism of Black and Asian feminists, I will use the terms "women of color" or "feminists of color."

Whilst the BWM politically mobilized Black women on a national scale, unfortunately, records of many Black women's organizations of the 1970s and 1980s have been lost due to a failure to maintain archival materials.[11] As primary sources relating to London-based Black women's groups have been preserved within Stella Dadzie's organizational papers at the Black Cultural Archives (BCA), the majority of information about the BWM has been ascertained through these documents. Sudbury has noted that despite the lack of records relating to Black women's groups outside of London, we must "treat with caution the many accounts which imply that black women's activism only occurred in London-based groups."[12] Yet whilst recognizing that "one of the critiques that arises a lot" about the BWM is that it was "very London-centric,"[13] and acknowledging that "it was a failing and it was a pity," Stella Dadzie emphasizes that "the very nature of what was happening at the time . . . was happening in London because that was where the biggest Black communities were."[14] Taking into account such limitations, I focus primarily on London-based Black women's groups and activists. Nonetheless, this work contributes to a wider historical interrogation of Black women's activism on a national scale.

Pushed to the Margins:
The Origins of Black Feminist Organizing in Britain

To critically understand the revolutionary vision of the BWM, it is important to contextualize the roots of Black women's activism in Britain. Black women had long been politically active, particularly within the Black Power Movement in the 1960s. Black liberation activists within the movement drew upon political discourses at the center of anticolonial struggles being staged throughout the African diaspora to articulate their experiences of surviving white racial terror in postwar Britain.[15] Black women activists, many of whom were born in or migrated to Britain during their early childhoods, were instrumental in groups such as the Black Panthers and the Black Liberation Front. Developing a Marxist analysis of their status as "second-class" citizens in Britain, Black women drew upon diasporic legacies of Black resistance, in which Black women's "survival" has historically depended on their "militant responses to tyranny."[16] Yet, Black women encountered misogynoir within the movement from Black men activists, as they were relegated to completing "backroom jobs," such as typing and cooking, within Black liberation spaces.[17] "It was a struggle," Black feminist activist Melba Wilson emphasizes, "to get Black women's voices to be heard in that context . . . they were on the pickets for sure, but they were expected to follow, not lead!"[18]

Black women's experiences of marginalization were endemic across the sphere of leftist political organizing, as Black feminists involved in the WLM in Britain were likewise ostracized. Summarizing the sentiments of Black women activists from the 1982 National Black Women's Conference, Hazel V. Carby argues that white feminists historically had "very little idea of what the implications of white womanhood" were for "Black womanhood."[19] OWAAD co-founder Beverley Bryan vividly remembers the WLM being grounded in "bourgeois" political concerns that fundamentally overlooked Black women's lives.[20] "We very much saw ourselves as working-class women," she remembers, "and we felt that the movement of the seventies was centered on white middle-class women with a lot of time on their hands!"[21] Whilst Black feminists sought to challenge the positionalities of Black women in Britain by emphasizing the matrix of oppression that they encountered, their narratives were rendered invisible within the context of white feminism. These experiences of being pushed to the margins of leftist organizing became the impetus for Black women to create their own autonomous spaces and position their experiences of Black womanhood at the center of their activism and theorizations.

Brixton Black Women's Group, OWAAD and the Genesis of Black Socialist Feminism

Brixton Black Women's Group (BBWG), formed in 1973 primarily by women of African Caribbean and African descent, was the first documented Black women's group in Britain and significantly, the first iteration of a decidedly Black feminist collective consciousness. BBWG member Gail Lewis emphasizes that for the organization, reclaiming feminism as Black working-class women was central to their political project. "We wanted to be a counter," Lewis explains, "to the idea that feminism was only represented by white women."[22] Joining BBWG in the late 1970s, Lewis recalls that part of this process of reclamation involved functioning as a "collective" and structuring the group around a non-hierarchical vision of solidarity and liberation.[23] Associational praxis as a process of development of consciousness and collaboration was thus a core dimension of their politics. In a 1981 edition of their newsletter, *Speak Out*, the group underscored that "to be Black and feminist" fundamentally "adds a very different dimension to feminism and involves our coming to terms with the specific implications of such a position."[24]

Through weekly communal study, BBWG consumed a wide range of historical, sociological and political literature, an enriching process that in emphasizing how racism, sexism and capitalism interconnected, helped members to develop an analysis of their positionality within and beyond the nation. "We read Marx," Wilson relates, "and tried to make sense of it as Black women."[25] In utilizing this process of political education to form a structural understanding of their lived experiences, BBWG members came to form their own political analysis, which they termed Black socialist feminism. Reflecting later on the radical contours of their analysis, Lewis laid out the group's primary political aims, proclaiming that "from a position of Black socialist feminism; our central concerns are the Black liberation struggle, the anti-imperialist struggle, and the struggle against capitalism."[26]

Community-based initiatives were at the core of BBWG's Black socialist feminist activism. BBWG established a wide-ranging network of kinship and coalitional organizing, including their offshoot Mary Seacole Group, where they worked alongside Black single mothers to foster communal modes of mothering and caregiving, and the West Indian Parents Action Group, in which they sought to target racial discrimination in education.[27] Employing their Black socialist feminism as praxis, BBWG sought to expose the ways in which Black communities were systematically underserved and how the state continued to limit the life opportunities of working-class Black women and children. Thus, whilst Natalie Thomlinson argues that due to its association with white women, a "specifically 'feminist' politics never entirely superseded older forms of Black women's organization" within the BWM, by engaging the politics of race, gender, and class from the site of Black womanhood, Black women in BBWG not only deconstructed white feminism, but, through the prism of Black socialist feminism, radically reenvisioned the entire idea of a politics of liberation from their liminal space outside the parameters of "nation."[28] BBWG member Scafe recollects that the "defining aspect" of Black women's socialist feminism was that it "articulated the lives of women who were not exceptional."[27] Black socialist feminism "was about harnessing those energies in the ordinary and the everyday" and including that within a "feminist politics."[29]

BBWG provided a groundbreaking blueprint for Black women activists, and as the late 1970s approached, the number of Black women's groups in Britain grew exponentially. The formation of Manchester Black Women's Co-op and Liverpool Black Sisters reflect the increasing critical mass of Black women's organizations dedicated to providing service provision for Black communities throughout the country. As BBWG, alongside Black women from the African Students' Union, ZANU Women's League, the Ethiopian Women's Study Group, the Eritrean Women's Study Group and the Black Women's Alliance of South Africa formed the Organization of Women of Africa and African Descent at Warwick University in 1978, links between Black feminists throughout Britain began to flourish.

Having already been a member of the North London organization United Black Women's Action Group, OWAAD co-founder Stella Dadzie recollects that at the core of the organization's political mission was a desire to function as an "umbrella organization" that gave Black women "a collective force" in Britain.[30] As they began to envisage what a politically mobilized movement of Black women could look like, however, Dadzie recalls an Asian feminist by the name of Hansa "turning up" to one of OWAAD's initial meetings in "motorbike leathers," and asking the crucial question: "what about the Asian women . . . where are we in this?"[31] Once Asian women emphasized the significance of being included in OWAAD, the premise of Afro-Asian unity in the BWM developed organically, as Dadzie explains that "although Asian women may have experienced racism in a different way," it was "still the same racist state" that women of color were being subjected to in Britain.[32]

Renaming OWAAD as the Organisation of Women of Asian and African Descent, Black and Asian women attempted to develop a politics of solidarity around their experiences of oppression in Britain. The formation of OWAAD was thus instrumental in renegotiating the terms of what a feminist movement could look like and who could hold the state to account within the public space. As several Black and Asian women's groups emerged around the country following the First National Black Women's conference in 1979, the inception of the BWM symbolized a historical moment in which Black feminists made political alliances with Asian feminists to confront the everyday struggles of women of color and destroy the material sources of their deprivation. As she co-founded East London Black Women's Organisation (ELBWO) in 1979 following the event, Gueye encapsulates the importance of OWAAD, as she fondly reflects on the unprecedented nature of the First National Black Women's Conference: "That conference, that conference that conference!" she says wistfully.[33] "That conference was a catalyst! And it really helped to embolden my making a statement about me being a feminist!"[34]

The Rise of the Right: Thatcher and Black Socialist Feminist Resistance

The genesis of the BWM came at what Lewis terms as a "very troubled and troubling" time in the late 1970s; the rise of the fascist National Front, sustained attacks on Black communities at the hands of the police, and the political ascent of the Conservative party under Thatcher meant that "things were moving really fast and really deeply to the right."[35] Writing a year after Thatcher's first electoral victory, Stuart Hall argued that Thatcherism represented "something qualitatively new in British politics."[36] In his framing of Thatcherism primarily as an "economic and political project," Hall stressed that it constituted "a radical political force, capable of setting new terms to the political struggle, and effectively condensing a wide range of social and political issues and themes under the . . . banner of the radical Right."[37] Having mapped the trajectory of Thatcherism over the course of the 1970s and the 1980s, however, Hall's analysis had changed significantly by 1989. Highlighting the incursion that Thatcherite politics had made within the sociopolitical landscape of the late twentieth century, Hall asserted that racial essentialism was central to Thatcher's electoral victories. Through traditional, right-wing conceptions of "British values," Thatcherism found its basis within a larger white supremacist project and was "*in defense* of a certain definition of Englishness."[38]

Under the guise of reforming a Britain that had lost its white ethnocultural center, Thatcher's government immediately foregrounded issues such as increasing police powers, stemming the migration of Black and Asian people and the necessity of cuts in public expenditure. Publishing their White Paper on Immigration and Nationality in 1979, the Conservatives sought to reconfigure both the concept and legal status of British nationality around the notion of "partiality," whereby British citizenship could only be obtained by having had a grandparent born in the United Kingdom.[39] The British Nationality Act of 1981 codified the government's anti-Black political mandate into law; African and African Caribbean who had been positioned as "British citizens" under the previous Nationality Act were now being detained in increasing numbers, threatened with deportation and prevented from entering the country after taking trips abroad.[40] The shifting categorization of citizenship is indicative of the processes through which British national identity is both racialized and gendered; whilst white women were increasingly centered within a narrative of Britain that Ina Zweiniger-Bargielowska argues "told a story of vulnerability and decline," the lives of Black women migrants were instrumentalized as the foils against which the parameters of citizenship, and indeed nation, were defined.[41] "Thatcher was able to direct attention toward national identity," Samantrai underscores, "both as the wounded heart of a people in crisis and an inner strength awaiting recovery."[42]

As the government appropriated a vast range of the far-right National Front's rhetoric, Black women activists continued to develop a critique of Britain as a white supremacist nation that maintained its power through the systematic domination of communities of color.[43] The growing political analysis of the BWM is particularly evident within a 1979 issue of *Speak Out*, as BBWG members argued that the government's immigration controls constituted "yet another attack on women's rights."[44] Thus, as Black women "bore the brunt" of severe cuts across the arena of the British public sphere, such as welfare benefits, childcare facilities and social services, Bryan, Dadzie, and Scafe argue that it was "no coincidence" that "a strong, vibrant, militant movement of Black women emerged."[45]

As they critiqued the "ruthlessness" of the Thatcher government and contested the rise of fascism, the first issue of OWAAD's Black feminist journal *FOWAAD!* demonstrates that Black socialist feminists politically mobilized against the specific ways in which the state played "an important role in legitimizing the various dimensions" of Black women's subjection.[46] Whilst Thatcher would declare in 1982 that "the battle for women's rights" in Britain had "largely been won," Dadzie recalls that under her successive governments, there were "certainly many examples of policies that really impacted on Black communities in general and Black women in particular."[47] "I don't think you would have had someone turn up to an OWAAD meeting," she muses, "and announce themselves a friend of Thatcher . . . my personal view of her was that she was a Tory and I was not impressed."[48] Black socialist feminists campaigned against racism, misogyny and classism within state policies through a range of mediums such as public meetings, direct action, newsletters, poetry, theatre productions, sloganeering, and community activism. By targeting a range of areas from housing, employment and education to immigration abuses alongside Asian women, Black women found themselves at the center of the Black resistance to state repression in Thatcher's Britain.

By 1981, Black socialist feminists would find themselves on the frontlines of Black rebellion; uprisings arose across the country as a result of the systematic criminalization of Black communities at the hands of the police force. Recounting the memory of Black people taking to the streets in Brixton, Scafe recalls "explicit police brutality" against Black people as constituting "a situation of war" in early 1980s Britain.[49] In the wake of the uprisings, OWAAD organized against police violence and lent support to Black mothers whose children had been arrested or lost to state-mandated violence. This constituted a form of revolutionary love that reflected what Bryan labels as a "highly charged," "hard-core" political era of Black feminist activism in Britain.[50] In challenging the ways in which the British nation-state sustained itself through the brutality directed toward Black communities, Black women activists sought to defy the logics of expendability that have structured Black life throughout the longue durée of racial slavery.

In their endeavors to organize against state violence, Black socialist feminists also cultivated an anti-imperialist analysis in which they linked their struggles in Britain to anticolonial movements being waged throughout the world. Lewis notes that Black women activists "were trying to articulate a politics that could deepen Black liberationist struggle by injecting into that, a feminist sensibility."[51] Black socialist feminists "could see the links" between "the ways in which the British state as an imperial state was also involved in coercive acts in aspects of its rule."[52] As they continued to be involved in anti-policing and anti-deportation activisms, Black women organizers also supported feminists mobilizing against apartheid and white colonial rule in South Africa and Zimbabwe.[53] In the first issue of their 1979 newsletter, *Speak Out*, BBWG members foreground the "international" dimensions of their activism; the group proclaim that "in Africa and everywhere," Black women were "fighting to build a new socialist society" and as such, the BWM constituted an "important part of the movement throughout the world for change and the destruction of capitalism."[54] As they formed critical networks of solidarity beyond their location in Britain, the BWM's Black socialist feminism distinguished itself as a radical vision of freedom, as it fundamentally transcended the boundaries of the nation. Reflecting the "many voices" of Black women in Britain, Black socialist feminists developed a vision of liberation that sought not to reinscribe the rationale of borders and instead conceived of a connected, global revolution of poor and working-class women of color. Black women's liberation in Britain was irrevocably tied to the freedom dreams and struggles of their "sisters in Asia, Africa, The Americas and the Caribbean."[55]

Black Socialist Feminists in Britain and the Development of Intersectionality

At the core of Black women's Black socialist feminist thought in the BWM was an understanding of what Lewis terms the "irreducible intersectionality" of Black women's lives in Britain.[56] Thomlinson notes that Black women activists' theorizations in the BWM "foreshadowed many contemporary theoretical developments around the politics of intersectionality."[57] In their 1981 *Speak Out* newsletter, BBWG members emphasized that "the status of black women" placed them at "the intersection of all forms of subjugation in society" and that it was by understanding that their "struggle" was "part and parcel of the greater struggle for the liberation of all" Black people from "all forms of oppression, that black feminism [wa]s defined" for them.[58] Such analysis formed part of a wider Black feminist tradition, in which Black women throughout history have drawn upon a range of terms and frameworks to understand themselves in relation to their communities and in relation to the world. In their groundbreaking 1977 statement, the Boston-based Combahee River Collective provided a new grammar in which Black women could understand the matrix of oppression that they faced in America by describing the "interlocking" nature of their subjection as poor, Black lesbian socialist feminists.[59] Four years later, Black socialist feminists in BBWG analyzed their marginalization as "intersecting," contributing to a transnational Black feminist practice that laid the foundations for Kimberlé Crenshaw's coining of "intersectionality" as a theoretical framework in 1989.[60]

An analysis of the intersectional nature of domination in Black women's lives is particularly evident within Black women's groups' tireless campaigning against the exploitative use of the contraceptive injection Depo-Provera in the late 1970s and early 1980s. Black women were routinely denied the autonomous right to have children through systematic sterilization abuses at the hands of doctors who felt that they "bred too much."[61] Such brutalization of Black women's bodies is symptomatic of how the technologies of nation not only rendered Black women's lives as expendable but also completely subject to arbitrary white patriarchal control. Using an array of media, such as publishing numerous pamphlets, as well as hosting community meetings to raise awareness about Black women's right of consent, the BWM sought to uproot the anti-Black misogyny that was endemic to the healthcare system in Britain.

In challenging the choice-based rhetoric of "a woman's right to choose" and making visible the insidious forms of reproductive regulation that they were forced to navigate, the BWM fought to create the conditions for a future in which Black women had reproductive freedom. Drawing links between the reproductive injustice that Black women experienced in Britain and the ways in which Black women throughout the diaspora were "being used as guinea pigs in 'the field of medical research'" by Western governments and pharmaceutical companies alike, the BWM demanded global liberation for Black women. Black socialist feminists not only declared that Black women had the right to exist but also that they had the right to do so completely free from the forces of white hegemony, under which Black women's bodies had historically been commodified to expand and sustain the world-making machinery of slavery and colonialism. Scafe summarizes the historical significance of the contribution that Black women in Britain made to Black feminist theory:

> The BWM in the early 1980s did intersectionality, you know, *we did that*. Sometimes, when I come across intersectionality as a kind of theoretical position that is presented as so crucially new, I feel slightly taken aback by the sense that it's being presented as something that's kind of revolutionised politics, when I think we did that by virtue of who were as Black feminists in Britain . . . We understood the felt and lived intersection of race, class, gender, culture and sexuality. And so, we lived intersectionality.[62]

The Personal is Political: Challenging White Bourgeois Feminism

Black socialist feminists shaped their revolutionary activism around a rich "cauldron" of political concerns that affected Black women's lives, both in Thatcher's Britain and in the wider context of the African diaspora.[63] Within this highly charged political period, however, the differing identity oriented, "personal" aspects of their lives as Black women were relatively unexplored within their theoretical framework of Black socialist feminism. As the urgency of the British sociopolitical terrain meant that Black women's activism was focused on resisting state-sanctioned violence, multifaceted fault lines emerged within the BWM in the early to mid-1980s due to a "failure to acknowledge the personal."[64]

Within the BWM, Black women activists fashioned their Black socialist feminist politics around community-centered campaigns that sought to contest the corrosive sociopolitical climate of the Thatcher era. Conversely, white middle-class feminists in the WLM primarily foregrounded the ways in which the "personal" aspects of their lives constituted political issues, thus employing consciousness-raising as a key tool through which they could achieve gender equality with white middle-class men. Yet, for Black women, who experienced what BBWG termed as the intersection of "racist oppression, sexist oppression" and "economic exploitation," being able to centralize the personal facets of their lives seemed to be a "luxury" that, unlike classed white women, many felt they could not afford to indulge in.[65] Bryan emphasizes that for Black women activists in the Thatcher years, "there was an urgency about what was happening to Black people."[66] "At that time," she relays emphatically, "Black lives did not matter . . . So we saw that as number one. Our main concern was community defence." Positioned as expendable within the WLM and British society at large, Gueye recollects that "the realities" of being a Black woman in Britain in "those days" meant that Black socialist feminists were "fire-fighting a lot of the time."[67] Within such a flurry of political activity, in which Black women activists were relentlessly organizing "against Thatcher and her government and the system she was putting forward," Gueye recalls that white feminists would often tell Black women that they were "so strong":

> And the thing is, at the time, we had to be strong. So we didn't let them know about the weaknesses . . . We didn't let them know that we were having a hard time at work, and an even harder time at home, or that when we went to the doctor, we weren't getting what we needed, or when we went to the police station, we weren't getting the attention that we needed . . . all of that! We got tired of having to explain to them that our positions were different![68]

In a 1990 interview, "Talking Personal, Talking Political" for the feminist journal *Trouble and Strife*, Black socialist feminists from BBWG likewise reflect on the question of "the personal" within the BWM. In the interview, Lewis recollects that whilst Black women activists would strategically organize alongside white feminists around issues such as reproductive rights and therefore, were not "necessarily fighting against each other," the relationship between the BWM and white women's organizations was "tense."[69] Organizing from a position in which they were subjected to anti-Black misogyny within the WLM and tyranny from the British state, many Black women activists felt that the politics of the personal misdirected critical attention away from the death-dealing machinery of state racism and thus, was rooted in the hegemonic principles of white feminism.

Whilst many Black women activists associated a focus on "the personal" with the "petit bourgeois" methods of the WLM, for some Black socialist feminists, consciousness-raising had the potential to be an important political tool for Black women seeking to understand the significance of their personal lived experiences.[70] Wilson highlights that within BBWG, she continually stressed that the group needed to cultivate a greater understanding of how their personal lives as Black women were inherently political.[71] She explains that her emphasis on the personal was rooted within her own lived experiences; upon marrying a white British man and moving from California to London in 1977, she wanted "to put a bit more context" to who she was "as a Black woman and particularly, as a Black woman in an interracial relationship."[72] "I wanted to be in a group," she explains, "that had a consciousness raising aspect to it. I found BWG, which was not that group!"[73] Although she details that as BBWG was a "very political women's group," she was "able to grow politically" within the collective, she ultimately felt that members "had to leave a little too much at the door" as "there was certainly no space, nor time, nor inclination from some of the women for that kind of thing."[74]

Such a lack of focus on the realm of the personal is particularly evident within BBWG newsletters; issues of *Speak Out* published between 1979 and 1981 detail local campaigns against "racism and fascism" and the theoretical dimensions of Black socialist feminism, yet, do not contain a further analysis of how the "private" spheres of Black women's lives could be politicized.[75] Lewis highlights that as BBWG had "a wealth of information and something to offer," she felt that consciousness-raising would be a misuse of the collective's resources and limit the scope of its internationalist, socialist politics.[76] "There was an Irish war going on, there was Palestine, there was Southern Africa, there was class struggle in Britain . . . I wanted to foreground all that stuff," she emphasizes.[77] Fisher argues that the prioritization of political campaigning within the BWM thus produced many "silences" within Black women activists' feminist critique.[78] "The struggle for Black women to define themselves within the context of battles against racism, imperialism" and misogynoir left little space within the movement to meaningfully approach the embedded politics of identity.[79]

As the BWM grew into a formidable political force, the movement began to tentatively address the importance of the politics of identity. OWAAD held a variety of workshops at their annual National Conferences between 1980 and 1982 to raise awareness of issues that straddled the binary between community politics and the personal. Addressing topics such as the importance of Afro-Asian unity, Dadzie highlights that OWAAD's workshops functioned as consciousness-raising exercises and that "a rich mixture" of discussions around identity were also taking place at a local level in Black women's groups.[80] Within the BWM at large, however, Gueye notes that Black women's activism was still firmly rooted within combatting racism, misogyny and imperialism, from a "national standpoint" as well as "globally."[81] She stresses that "one of the most frustrating things" for her was that Black feminists did not have the "benefit" of being able to "translate" their political campaigning into discussions on the political nature of their private lives."[82] The relegation of the politics of the personal is representative of the constraints that "fire-fighting" placed on Black women's time and resources. Bryan and colleagues reveal that as "state harassment reached a new peak in 1981," the pervasiveness of anti-Black racism in Britain predominantly shaped the movement around a specific agenda of political concerns, as "Black women were active around nearly every major community issue."[83]

Emerging Divisions:
Afro-Asian Unity and the Struggle for Black Liberation

As Black socialist feminists emphasized the centrality of political campaigning to achieving their emancipatory aims, complex interpersonal fault lines emerged within the movement; the "consensus" that held the

BWM together through the umbrella ethos of OWAAD began to break down.[84] Whilst in theory, feminists of color in OWAAD endeavored to reflect the heterogeneous political concerns of Black and Asian women, in practice, their politics of solidarity "depended on who was having the loudest voice at a particular moment," a reality that Wilson determines was the organization's ultimate "undoing."[85] Although the organization was confronting "so many important issues of the diaspora" as well as "Black British issues and Asian issues too," Wilson surmises that feminists of color had not "devoted enough time to understanding" how their "differences" could also "contribute" to their "strength."[86] Critiquing the central premise of Afro-Asian unity in OWAAD, Thomlinson argues that as African Caribbean women made up the majority of the group, the organization "could not always adequately cater for the specific needs of Asian women."[87]

Conversely, Bryan emphasizes that although Asian feminists accused Black women of "behaving like men" by shaping OWAAD's political direction around an "exclusionary" agenda, Black women activists "wanted to be inclusive" and thus, made active attempts to share the political platform.[88] Yet, for Gueye, the differing positionalities of Black and Asian women in Britain made organizing around a politics of solidarity increasingly difficult. "We were suspicious of each other," she recollects, "because a lot of the Asian women who were part of the vanguard were educated women . . . who some of us saw as being in a privileged position."[89] Such schisms are therefore demonstrative of the difficulties that women of color encountered in attempting to fashion a political unity under the conditions of white supremacy and anti-Black racism. Endeavoring to fashion a collective analysis of the ways in which women of color navigated society became increasingly fraught due to the differing social locations that the majority of Black and Asian women occupied within Britain. As some feminists of color felt that it was "divisive" to acknowledge the disparities within their experiences of racialized misogyny, what Sudbury terms as a "politics of location" that could more profoundly address the ways in which Black and Asian women were positioned hierarchically within British society never fully came to fruition within the movement.[90] "There just wasn't enough glue to knit it altogether," Wilson reflects wistfully. "We couldn't prevent those differences from becoming divisions."[91]

Discussions within the BWM surrounding the role of "the personal" were also shaped by the larger political dynamics of the Black Nationalist Movement and Black communities in London. In a retrospective

1990 interview on the BWM, BBWG organizer Olive Gallimore notes that Black socialist feminists had traditionally received ire from men in the Black nationalist movement, who "had become quite entrenched in their own sexism and domination of women."[92] Wilson likewise relates that Black socialist feminists encountered misogynoir from Black male activists, who would argue that "any respectable Black woman is not going to be meeting every Sunday afternoon. She's going to be at home cooking Sunday dinner or at Church."[93] Through its association with white women in the WLM, "consciousness-raising was a dirty term at that time," and thus the idea of a specifically Black feminist politics that illuminated the schisms of gender within Black women's lives was framed by Black nationalist men as an elitist pursuit that directed attention away from "real" Black struggles in Thatcher's Britain.[94] In their 1983 editorial, *On Black Women Organising*, BBWG members note that a "popular" way in which Black men undermined Black socialist feminists was through levelling the "accusation" that the BWM consisted of "dominant, middle-class bourgeois women," who were "isolated from women on the street" and therefore, could not truly represent the concerns of working-class Black women.[95] Many Black socialist feminists thus felt that a deeper exploration of "the personal" would serve as confirmation of the misogynistic accusations levelled at them from Black men and consequently, would prevent them from continuing to center their politics within communal forms of restitution. "That's why we couldn't let our guard down," Wilson explains. "We had to be absolutely clear on what it meant to create this thing called a Black socialist feminist movement."[96]

Following the 1981 uprisings, as Black women's groups became involved in the "implosion of community solidarity," such as the Brixton Defence Campaign, the undercurrents of tension between Black nationalist men and Black socialist feminists reached its crescendo.[97] In her 1990 interview, Lewis contends that organizing alongside Black men in the Brixton Defence Campaign presented its own set of issues, as many Black Nationalist men were "separatist, chauvinist people," who Black women activists "did not have much in common with politically."[98] Such complex interpersonal relationships between Black liberation groups are once again illustrative of how the deeply socialized dimensions of race, gender, and class continued to disrupt Black women's organizing; Black nationalist men attempted to exert patriarchal control over Black women in activist spaces, reproducing the power dynamics that were part and parcel of many Black women's interactions with Black men outside of movement spaces. Scafe remembers "feeling a kind of despondency" that the Black socialist feminist politics of the BWM "hadn't really been able to transfer beyond women," as Black feminists were ultimately "back in the same old hierarchies, same old sexisms, same old misogyny."[99] Continuing to center the importance of providing service provision and care for Black communities living in the midst of state violence, a more profound engagement with the politics of identity remained inaccessible to many Black women activists, as the 1983 BBWG editorial notes that "overt feminism . . . seemed sometimes inconsequential, eclipsed by the larger Black struggle" in Tory Britain.[100]

So as to combat the patriarchal violence to which Black men subjected Black women to, Gueye relates that the Black women's group that she co-founded, ELBWO, also allowed men into their organization. Based in Newham, Gueye illustrates the difficulties that Black mothers in the BWM encountered when wanting to attend meetings, as when they attempted to leave "the children at home, the men couldn't cope."[101] To tackle the gendered distribution of labour and the wider intracommunal dimensions of Black social life, ELBWO allowed Black men to have partial membership. This initiative sought to preserve the organization as a safe space for Black women, whilst also inducting Black men into anti-racist activism from a Black feminist orientation. Within the umbrella structure of OWAAD, however, Gueye recounts that ELBWO's inclusivity of Black men was seen by many Black women activists as being detrimental to the wider aims of the BWM; Black women had cultivated their own autonomous spaces, in part, to challenge the anti-Black misogyny that they encountered in the Black Power Movement.[102] Such tensions surrounding the role of Black men in Black women's groups eventually led to ELBWO being ousted from the umbrella auspices of OWAAD, as Gueye recalls that members of the East London group were "seen as the 'renegades' who were 'starting all the trouble'" within the movement.[103] The increasing friction within the BWM illustrates that by 1981, Black socialist feminists were beginning to more overtly establish differing stances on the role of the politics of the personal within Black women's organizing. As ELBWO argued in a 1983 editorial piece, a growing number of Black women activists viewed the lack of focus on the politics of identity within the movement as a "political mistake" that fragmented the collective vision of Black women's organizing.[104] The argument for a Black feminist "politics of difference" that sought to contest the personal aspects of Black women's situation in Britain thus began to rise to the fore within the movement. Mapping the trajectory of the BWM, Thomlinson asserts that in the early to mid-1980s, a "general shift" began to take place, whereby an emergent section of Black women activists started to emphasize the importance of understanding Black women's "subjective experiences," as well as remaining committed to the traditional "political analysis" of Black feminism.[105] "The personal," she argues, "was becoming increasingly political in Black women's circles."[106]

Sexuality and the Politics of Identity: Confronting Lesbophobia within the BWM

As Thatcher sought to consolidate her political mandate by setting her sights on a second term, ideological fault lines continued to materialize within the BWM. While the majority of Black women activists persisted in primarily campaigning against state racism, by 1981, the issues of sexuality and its significance as an axis of Black women's oppression emerged as an increasingly polarizing debate in the movement. As a Black lesbian involved in the BWM Lewis relays that within Black liberation spaces in the 1980s, "lesbianism was not seen as a political issue."[107] "It was seen as something you did privately," she recalls, and BBWG, "like every other Black organization at the time," also "had a notion of the Black community as traditional, as homogenous and unable to deal with difference."[101] She remembers being the "only out lesbian" in BBWG "for a while":

> I was living with a white woman at the time and I felt this enormous split in my life . . . living as a lesbian and with a white woman, yet being involved in anti-racism and Black women's liberation politics. But I did not necessarily want to go into discussion about it because I felt alone.[108]

Lewis's account reveals that the sustained lack of attention within the movement toward "the personal" meant that Black women did not have spaces in which they could fully interrogate the significance of the experiences that had been designated as "private." Without the mechanisms to help them begin to politicize the "personal" facets of their identities and lives as Black women, feelings of isolation grew amongst Black lesbian feminists, disrupting the collective purpose of the BWM, endeavoring as it was to completely uproot all sources of Black women's oppression.

As Black lesbian visibility grew within the wider BWM, however, the importance of including an analysis of Black women's sexuality became a site of contestation. By highlighting how they experienced oppression along the axis of race, gender, class and sexuality, Black lesbian feminists began to emphasize the importance of understanding their experiences as being fundamentally political, particularly within the volatile social climate; the Conservative Government continued to shape their manifesto around a heteronormative agenda of promoting "Victorian Values" and consistently drew upon the symbolism of the white nuclear family as a key mode through which the racial order could be sustained.[109] Yet, by articulating a growing awareness of how their raced, gendered, and classed experiences of lesbophobia shaped their lives, Black lesbians faced pushback within the movement from women who wanted to continue to highlight the political issues that OWAAD had "traditionally" focalized.[110] Dadzie stresses that the perilous sociopolitical terrain, in which Black women were "literally on the front line" and were "literally dying in their own homes as a result of the police coming in," meant that she felt that OWAAD's attention had to remain on "big issues like whether our kids can live, whether we have the right to survive and be."[111] For Black lesbian feminist Linda Bellos, however, OWAAD conferences were typically "homophobic" and "un-inclusive" of women whose identities resided outside heterosexual mores.[112] Such tensions around the visibility of lesbianism in the BWM form part of the wider history of erasure that lesbian women faced within feminist groups in Britain. Amongst white feminists, discussions concerning sexuality came to a head at both the 1974 and 1976 National WLM conferences. In her 1995 essay, "A Vision Back and Forth," Bellos highlights that when white lesbians "fought back" against the discrimination they encountered, "there were ructions" from "white middle-class heterosexual women."[113] Bellos notes that "in the end," the WLM "fell apart as it tried to accommodate the conflict that erupted."[114] Likewise, Black lesbian feminist scholar Valerie Mason-John argues that by refusing to "accept the consignment to second-class status," Black lesbians in OWAAD continued to challenge the organization's refusal to acknowledge the dimensions of racialized lesbophobia.[115]

As many heterosexual Black women activists refused to fully incorporate the critiques of Black lesbians into OWAAD's collective politics,

BBWG members describe OWAAD's final conference as being a "debacle," in which divisions in the movement reached their apex.[116] "We imploded," Gueye emphatically remembers.[117] The issue of homophobia in OWAAD is therefore symptomatic of the ways in which state violence shaped the contours of interpersonal violence, collapsing established notions of a fixed binary between "personal" and "political" issues. The ongoing imposition of white colonial systems of gender and sexuality defined the terms through which many heterosexual Black feminists engaged and disengaged with women whose lives did not adhere to normative codes of social reproduction. As BBWG's 1983 editorial highlights, not only did many Black women activists feel that "sexual activity" was "too sensitive to be discussed publicly," but furthermore, many argued that a focus on lesbianism could become an additional "weapon" that Black men could use to emphasize Black socialist feminists' "lack of seriousness" to the critical political issues affecting Black communities in Thatcher's Britain.[118] Thus, as Fisher contends, the "politics of the period" shaped the structures of Black women's organizations, as well as "their efforts to link theory and practice"; the lesbophobia that Black lesbians experienced throughout British society was reified within Black liberation spaces.[119] Bellos asserts that within both the WLM and the BWM, she "definitely embraced the politics of being a lesbian feminist," and therefore "got fed up with being constantly asked to hide the fact" that she was a lesbian."[120] "I still feel the need to embrace all the things that I am," she declares.[121]

Whilst there were a number of ideological conflicts that led to the demise of OWAAD in 1983, such rifts were also understood as being representative of the practical struggles that Black women organizing have encountered historically. Scafe details that Black socialist feminists' lives were "really defined by the movement" and as a result, their relentless activism eventually took a "huge toll."[122] The myth of the indomitable Black "superwoman" also had devastating effects on the health and mental wellbeing of many Black women activists. Wilson notes that the consensus both within and beyond the movement at the time was that "Black women were so strong . . . Black women could handle anything!"[123] "We couldn't handle every issue!" she exclaims.[124] "We didn't have ways and mechanisms and tools for dealing with it."[125] Continually rebelling against the cycle of anti-Black misogyny eventually led to a period of exhaustion for many Black feminists; ultimately, the labour of fighting on so many fronts was unsustainable. "All that," Gueye summarizes, "is in the melting pot of the personal being political."[126]

On Black Women Organizing: Black Lesbians Speak Out

Assessing the "weaknesses" within the movement, the aftermath of OWAAD's disintegration offered fertile ground for Black socialist feminists to begin to confront issues within the realm of "the personal."[127] As Black women activists began to critically examine the divisions that had led to the organization's demise, BBWG published their post-mortem 1983 article, *On Black Women Organising*. Arguing that whilst Black women still needed "to form strong organisations," BBWG members acknowledge that both personal and political lessons needed to be learnt from the fragmentation of OWAAD.[128] Critiquing lesbophobia in the BWM, BBWG argued in a later 1983 issue of their *Speak Out* newsletter that "traditional resistance" in Black communities should not "prevent" Black socialist feminists "from publicly declaring the need to look at the construction of sexuality and to publicly support lesbian women."[129] As part of the growth in Black socialist feminist thought, the group Sisters in Study emerged out of BBWG in the mid-1980s. "This group not only dealt with study," Wilson explains, "but with our personal interaction with each other and this was now an equal part of our agenda."[130] In their 1988 article for the trailblazing Black feminist anthology *Charting the Journey*, Sisters in Study reflect the political growth within the BWM; the group stress that challenging homophobia in both Black communities and wider British society is the "only acceptable set of circumstances which could enable Black lesbians to be part of their communities on their terms—with no apologies."[131]

The metamorphosis of the BWM was further reflected through the first Black Lesbian Feminist Conference in Britain, titled "We Are Here," in London in 1984. As an organizer of the conference, Bellos asserts that the title of the event sought to challenge how Black lesbians "have been erased from history."[132] As two hundred Black and Asian feminists declared that they "must carve out a space" for themselves on "their own terms," the conference was also significant in reinforcing the importance of solidarity amongst women of color.[124] Building on the ground-breaking success of the conference, Bellos co-facilitated the first Black Lesbian Conference in Britain, "Zami I," in 1985. Detailing the "oppression, discrimination and harassment" that Black lesbians were forced to navigate, they contested their isolation and invisibility within both the BWM and the WLM.[133] In doing so, Black lesbian activists were instrumental in radicalizing the Black socialist feminist politics of the BWM. Cultivating their own spaces, as well as broadening the scope and vision of existing Black women's groups, Black lesbian feminists made possible a politics of identity that refused to reproduce the false dichotomy between public and private life. Using collective political education as a resource to deepen the intersectional analysis that lay at the heart of Black women's organizing, Black lesbian feminists resisted the heteropatriarchal formations that structured interpersonal relationships, as well as state-mandated violence. In their refusal to be silent and accept the depoliticization of their identities, Black lesbians were critical in expanding the revolutionary potential of the movement; a radically different set of social arrangements were possible. Reflecting on the significance of Black lesbian visibility in the landmark Black lesbian feminist roundtable discussion in the 1984 Black feminist edition of *Feminist Review*, "Many Voices, One Chant," Lewis emphasizes the importance of being able to embody her Marxism, feminism and lesbianism "in a Black situation."[134] "That is when I feel really good about it . . . it is about being whole," she asserts.[135]

The Advent of the Greater London Council: The BWM and State Funding

As the radical vision of the BWM evolved throughout the 1980s, the wider political landscape in Britain continued to produce perilous conditions around Black women's lives. In response to the Conservative government's cuts in public expenditure and the increasing centralization of governmental control, Labor-led left-wing city councils began to offer funding to a variety of social justice organizations to stem the tide of the so-called Thatcher Revolution. As they became amongst the primary beneficiaries of such schemes, the debate concerning whether Black women's groups should accept state funding for their community-based activism became a site of contention within the movement.

Prior to the 1980s, discussions around the role of state funding in achieving Black socialist feminists' aims of social change had proven to be fraught with tension within the BWM. Black women activists were deeply invested within community engagement, prioritizing such schemes as a key mode through which Black communities could begin to target the systemic inequities that they experienced. The importance of providing community resources was at the forefront of BBWG's Black socialist feminist politics in the late 1970s, as they squatted a house in

Stockwell Green, which would eventually become their Black Women's Centre. In her 1988 article, *Brixton Black Women's Centre: Organizing on Child Sexual Abuse*, BBWG activist Marlene T. Bogle highlights that the group's members envisioned the center as a new site for their weekly meeting place, as well as offering a "base" in which they could support Black women encountering issues such as "isolation, poverty, racism, sexism and class oppression."[136] Before opening, however, BBWG activists recognized that in order to offer such services, obtaining funding for the center would be critical. Taking place concurrently, following Thatcher's 1979 rise to power, the Labor-run London council of Lambeth appointed a Black candidate, Herman Ouseley, as one of the country's first race relations advisers. As white violence continued to be waged against Black communities, Lambeth Council, under Ouseley's guidance, began to offer Inner City Partnership grants to support various community groups.

The argument regarding whether a Black socialist feminist organization such as BBWG should accept funding from the state proved to be a controversial one. Whilst a left-wing council was offering the funding, such a scheme still formed part of the British national project that Black women activists had shaped their entire politics of resistance in opposition to. Lewis notes that for some women in BBWG, there were many "contradictions" inherent within a Black women's organization "that was supposed to be revolutionary, supposed to be about change" and importantly "centrally supposed to be critical of the state in the way in which it controls Black people and working class people" accepting money from a government body.[137] Whilst Lewis was one of the members "opposed to taking the money," Wilson relates that having conducted "a meeting in typical BBWG style," the "majority of the group" voted in favor of accepting funding from Lambeth Council, as they felt that the importance of creating a community hub for Black women ultimately outweighed the "negative implications" of receiving state funding.[138]

Resolving to utilize the funds, the Black Women's Centre opened in September 1980. Although for many BBWG members, complexities remained as to how to evade "dancing to the tune" of the local authorities, as the first of its kind, the center was indicative of the pioneering nature of the BWM; BBWG developed it as a network of support for Black women in the local area. A library specializing in women's literature, a crèche and a craft workshop were amongst the range of facilities that were provided, expanding BBWG's community outreach. In a 1982 newsletter published by the group, *Centre News*, Black socialist feminists underscored the political significance of the center in challenging the effects of "British capitalism," as "Black people" and their "children" experienced the "brunt" of class-based oppression.[139] BBWG were able to directly invest state funding into their local community, making resources that were institutionally denied to Black women accessible and therefore, providing a counter to the widening social inequalities of Thatcher's Britain.

Whilst BBWG were among the first Black women's organizations to receive state funding, in the wake of the 1981 uprisings, such schemes became widespread. In the same year, The Greater London Council (GLC) set up the Ethnic Minorities Committee (EMC) in 1981 and the Women's Committee (WC) in 1982. Dadzie notes that the GLC's funding programmes were a response to the November 1981 Government-commissioned Scarman report.[140] She highlights that the "image of Black youth confronting the police with Molotov cocktails" in both the uprisings and the Notting Hill Carnival of that year fed a "notion of Black rebellion" that "was at the heart" of the white establishment's "paranoia and stems from the slavery days."[141] The need to "contain" Black protest is evident within the report; the study pathologizes young Black people as would-be "criminals," who require "urgent" state attention to prevent racial chaos from becoming an "endemic, ineradicable disease" threatening "the very survival" of British society.[142] The report placed an emphasis on "community relations" as a mode through which the British national project could be saved and protected against the tide of Black resistance. As the GLC began to support local activisms throughout London, Fisher argues that race and gender were put "on the local and national political agenda like never before."[143] Funding under legislation such as Section 11 of the 1966 Local Government Act was increased exponentially and by 1984, nearly £10 million was jointly available under the EMC and WC.[144] Being incorporated into the GLC's vision of the nation marked a turning point in the BWM; just as BBWG had deliberated prior to 1981, many groups now had to consider the paradoxes that accepting such grants presented with regards to their critiques of the British establishment, whilst also assessing the ability of state funding to facilitate their aims of social transformation.

As grants became available to Black women's groups, the early to mid-1980s witnessed the growth of what Sudbury terms as a "funded Black women's infrastructure" in Britain.[145] Intersecting with the 1983 demise of OWAAD, Black women's groups began to invest more directly in the specific needs of their local communities. Having decided to obtain a grant from the GLC, a 1983 ELBWO newsletter noted that the group felt that due to the historical economic exploitation of Black women, there was no "contradiction" in accepting grants from the state, as the money that the GLC gave out rightfully belonged to them.[146] Receiving funding to set up their own center in 1985, Gueye emphasizes that such a community resource was instrumental in giving Black feminists in Newham a place to "meet" and "strategize," as well as allowing ELBWO to become "a force to be reckoned with," as they maintained regular correspondence with local authorities.[147] Carving out a space in which they could influence local policy, ELBWO's metamorphosis from a grassroots organization to an influential state-funded charity is representative of how numerous Black feminist groups maneuvered themselves into consultant positions to voice the needs of Black women in Britain. Such political tactics marked a change in the direction of the BWM. Whilst a politics of dissent, in which Black women activists resisted the dominance of state institutions, had been central to the BWM in the early 1980s, a politics of representation, in which the importance of Black women being visible in local governance, became a primary focus of a number of Black feminists within the movement by the mid-1980s.

A Site of Contention: Black Socialist Feminist Pushbacks against State Funding

Whilst many Black women's groups utilized GLC funding to finance a host of community projects, there remained a lack of consensus throughout the BWM as to whether state-endorsed activism could fulfill the Black socialist feminist vision of Black liberation. Describing the state's funding methods as "insidious," Bryan and colleagues argue that the mid-1980s saw the proliferation of "policies of subsidised revolution," the effects of which neutralized the militancy of Black radical activism, as "political mobilisation" came "to be seen as a salaried activity."[148] Reflecting upon their 1985 critique, Dadzie argues that it was a "classic Marxist analysis, because once you have a stake in the system, you are less critical of it."[149] Noting that "a lot of the problems" facing Black communities were "institutionalised and historical and could not be resolved with a little bit of funding here or a grant there," Dadzie's assessment demonstrates how grant-aided activism could be harnessed by the British establishment to obscure the ongoing brutality of state-sanctioned misogynoir.[150] This significance of Dadzie's analysis was reflected within the events of the mid-1980s—in September 1985, Cherry Groce, a Black woman from Brixton, was shot and subsequently paralyzed by police who raided her house in search of one of her children. As another wave of Black rebellion reverberated across the country and Black women's groups campaigned against the extrajudicial shooting, the police shooting of Groce reinforced the continued prevalence of state-sanctioned violence against Black women. Government-funded schemes had sought to ingratiate Black women within the public arena of the nation as a form of pacification in the face of ongoing Black revolt. These signifiers of national recognition created new modalities of gratuitous violence that were amenable to the project of "diversity and inclusion" and ultimately, expanded the infrastructure of state racism.

As funded community activism reached its peak in the mid-1980s, many Black socialist feminists formed a critique of the political direction of the BWM and leftist organizations at large. Noting that the advent of GLC funding had served to transform the voluntary sector into a professional job market, a growing number of Black women activists were critical of how socioeconomic capital could be leveraged from the state-mandated "equal opportunities agenda." Bryan's testimony is representative of such criticism, as she argues that the mass funding of community projects created "a whole edifice of equal opportunity purveyors" in Britain, and a "race relations industry" that was "self-perpetuating and continued to market its own kind of roles and functions for over twenty years."[151] Bryan's account illustrates the difficulties that radical political movements encounter when faced with a dominant, resourced regime.[152] As "diversity" positions centering the issues of race and gender in Britain became salaried, many Black leftist organizations and activists were co-opted into mainstream politics, distorting the counter-hegemonic roots that such occupations grew out of. Summarizing the literature on the politics of Black liberation movements in the 1980s, Sudbury notes that the rise of grant activism has been widely regarded a "turning point" for Black liberation groups in Britain.[153] Critics of state-funded initiatives argued that "black struggle" had been "transformed into a "professional ethnic community" run by a state-created, petit-bourgeoisie of "career militants."[154]

The End of a Movement:
The BWM and Thatcherite Neoliberalism

The changing face of the BWM reconfigured the priorities of Black women's groups. Having to regularly produce reports on the development of their Black Women's Centre to Lambeth council, Wilson relates that BBWG had to manage both an "administrative" and "accountability" burden, fundamentally directing time away from their ability to politically organize.[155] The redirection of the movement's political vision can be located within the disappearance of the majority of Black feminist periodicals and newsletters by the mid-1980s; BBWG's fifth and final *Speak Out* newsletter was published in December 1983. Detailing that having to fulfill the terms of being an official charity as well endeavoring to maintain a "clarity of vision about the contradictions of the state," Lewis concludes that the responsibilities of running the center contributed to the "death" of the group in 1986.[156] As a vanguard organization in the development of Black socialist feminism in Britain, BBWG's demise represented a turning point in the BWM. The growing reliance on grant-aided activism meant that ultimately, many organizations lost their political autonomy, precipitating the contraction of the BWM's expansive network.

The demise of BBWG was part of the larger fragmentation of leftist organizations that took place as Thatcher entered her third political term in 1987. The GLC's funding initiatives had been on the receiving end of right-wing attacks for the majority of the 1980s and as such, were at the center of the government's plans to reduce public expenditure.[157] As the Conservative government eventually succeeded in bringing about the end of the GLC in 1986, such a move triggered the dissolution of the organized left in Britain. The end of the GLC had devastating effects on Black women's groups, as Gueye details that whilst ELBWO is still active today, funding for community schemes "dried up" and significantly, "there were less and less spaces for the kind of debate that was informed by the greater masses of people."[158] The lack of funding served to essentially roll back the achievements of the BWM and as community centers were forced to shut down, the fulcrum of Black women's political activity was stunted.

The disintegration of the BWM is therefore demonstrative of the pitfalls within the relationship between Black women's organizations and the state. Being absorbed into the accelerated funding vision of local authorities had the effect of redirecting the BWM's emancipatory vision during its zenith. Due to the transient nature of the funding *modus operandi* of local authorities, grant-aided activism was incapable of facilitating more permanent modes of self-sufficiency for Black communities and, thus, once such an infrastructure was removed, the BWM was left politically susceptible to the dominance of the right. Fisher stresses that neoliberal Thatcherite spending cuts created an "even greater disparity in the uneven distribution" of resources in the late 1980s, "particularly as this access intersected with race, class and gender."[159] As avenues for Black women in Britain to politically mobilize became few and far between, the turn into the final decade of the millennium witnessed the end of the revolutionary BWM. Whilst an extensive network of funded community activism had initially served to target social inequalities experienced by Black women in Britain, the movement's absorption into local governance meant that it became reliant on the same national project that it had originally sought to dismantle.[160] "Trying to wrestle with those contradictions of the state," Lewis contends, "is something that is part of the left's legacy—the history of the left."[161]

The Legacy of the BWM

The BWM was a revolutionary site of resistance to anti-Black racism, misogyny and capitalism in Thatcher's Britain. Organizing from a structural position outside the borders of the nation, Black women disrupted the entire edifice of leftist politics, in which all the women were white and all the Black people were men, thus developing an intersectional theorization of power dynamics that is at the center of movements for social justice today.[162] Summarizing the historical significance of Black women's activism, Wilson describes the BWM as "empowering."[163] "I feel privileged," she emphasizes, "to have been able to have had that experience, and have it continue to inform my worldview."[164] Black women crafted what Gueye describes as "a language" around their experiences of oppression and defiance in Thatcher's Britain, which has since been foundational to the development of discourses around intersectionality.[165] "I think people are more willing to claim the term "Black feminist" than when we started out!" Wilson exclaims.[166] "I feel like that argument has been won because we did the groundwork."[167]

Following the movement, the women I interviewed all went on to have successful careers in a variety of fields, such as academia, mental health activism, healthcare and politics, utilizing their Black socialist feminist analysis to support the next generation of young Black women. The contemporary activism of Black feminists in Britain that has sought to expose the effects of post-2010 Tory austerity measures on marginalized communities is part of what Scafe terms as a "lineage" that connects "the two movements historically."[168]

The Black feminist activists that I was in conversation with throughout my research continue to be critical of the British nation-state. Dadzie stresses that whilst "the politics of the self" are now at the heart of contemporary Black feminist thought, it remains fundamental that Black women critique and challenge the state, as well as organize around issues such as "the use of rape as a political weapon" and the matrix of "poverty and deprivation" that Black women are subjected to across the world.[169] In this call for the continuation of transnational Black feminist solidarities, Dadzie emphasizes that the women who formed the BWM have "thrown down the banner" for younger Black feminists. "We have given them a lot of years of our lives," she declares proudly, "and a lot of energy and I hope a little bit of wisdom along the way."[170]

In mounting a decade-long campaign against the historical domination of Black women by the British state, the BWM is a testament to Black women's role as the "heart" of Black resistance to white supremacy.[171] "We were the ones who challenged the system," Gueye proudly declares. "We were the ones who were not afraid and were courageous enough to do that."[172]

Notes

I would like to thank Dr. Sarah Crook and Dr. Charlie Jeffries for their invaluable support and dedication to seeing my vision for this work come to fruition. My supervisors Dr. Jane Garnett, Dr. Michael Joseph, and Dr. Stephen Tuck—thank you for all your feedback and encouragement throughout the writing of this chapter. My friends Isaac, Saoirse, Lauren, Theophina, and Paula—I will always cherish the many conversations we've had over long brunches, dinners, voice notes, and late-night phone calls where my thinking has been nurtured, supported, and expanded. My amazing family, especially my mum and grandma, thank you for being so invested in seeing me achieve my dreams and always believing in me. This work would not have been possible without the immense contribution of Linda Bellos, Beverley Bryan, Stella Dadzie, Ama Gueye, Gail Lewis, Suzanne Scafe, and Melba Wilson. Each of you took the time to sit down and share your incredible stories with me, and I will forever be grateful. Your freedom dreams have made it possible for me to imagine a radically different world. Thank you.

1. The title of this chapter comes from Ama Gueye, interview transcript (18 May 2017), 8. All further references are from this transcript.
2. Unknown Speaker, *First National Black Women's Conference* (1979).
3. Gueye, interview transcript, 1.
4. Margaret Thatcher, quoted in "Margaret Thatcher Immigration Talk," YouTube. www.youtube.com/watch?v=sHhKI5ijnxQ
5. Tracy Fisher, *What's Left of Blackness?* (Basingstoke: Palgrave Macmillan, 2012), 96.
6. OWAAD, *FOWAAD!*, 1 (1979): 2.
7. Suzanne Scafe, interview transcript (16 May 2017), 2. All further references are from this transcript.
8. Heidi Safia Mirza, *Black British Feminism: A Reader* (London: Routledge, 1997), 1–9; Natalie Thomlinson *Race, Ethnicity and the Women's movement in England, 1968–1993* (Basingstoke: Palgrave Macmillan, 2016), 94–103; Julia Sudbury, "Other Kinds of Dreams," *Black Women's Organisations and the Politics of Transformation* (London: Routledge, 1998), 1–16.
9. Fisher, *What's Left of Blackness?*, 65–122; Ranu Samantrai, *AlterNatives: Black Feminist in the Postimperial Nation* (Stanford, CA: Stanford University Press, 2002), 1–22.
10. Nydia Swaby, "Disparate in voice, Sympathetic in Direction": Gendered Political Blackness and the Politics of Solidarity," *Feminist Review* 108 (2014): 11.
11. Sudbury, "Other Kinds of Dreams," 9.
12. Sudbury, "Other Kinds of Dreams," 9.
13. Stella Dadzie, interview transcript (9 May 2017), 8. All further references are from this transcript.
14. Dadzie, interview transcript, 8.
15. Following the Second World War, Britain experienced a sharp period of economic decline. Intersecting with the contraction of the British empire and the increasing mobilization of anticolonial movements throughout Africa, Asia, and the Caribbean, Britain was in dire need of more labor power to work in the newly formed National Health Service and other national industries. In 1948, the British Nationality Act was passed, marking the creation of citizenship for those who had been positioned as "British subjects" under British colonial rule throughout the world. Extending the exploitation of colonized peoples, Britain called on its new citizens to migrate to Britain and work to rebuild the postwar nation. Once they arrived in the metropole, Black migrants were subjected to low wages, economic deprivation, material dispossession criminalization and

arbitrary white supremacist violence. Further reading: Kennetta Hammond Perry, *London is the Place for Me* (Oxford: Oxford University Press, 2015); Beverley Bryan, Stella Dadzie, and Suzanne Scafe, *The Heart of the Race* (London: Virago Press Ltd., 1986), 17–58.

16. Bryan et al., *Heart of the Race*, 125.

17. "Misogynoir" is a term coined by Moya Bailey and further conceptually expanded by womanist writer Trudy to analyze the ways in which Black women experience racialized misogyny. Further reading: Moya Bailey and Trudy, "On Misogynoir: Citation, Erasure, and Plagiarism," *Feminist Media Studies*, 18.4 (2018); Melba Wilson, interview transcript (10 May 2017), 15. All further references are from this transcript.

18. Wilson, interview transcript, 15.

19. BCA, Dadzie/1/1/10, Hazel V. Carby, *National Black Women's Conference: Notes from Afro-Asian workshop* (1981), 13.

20. Beverley Bryan, interview transcript (7 July 2017), 6. All further references are from this transcript.

21. Bryan, interview transcript, 6.

22. Gail Lewis, interview transcript (3 May 2017), 5. All further references are from this transcript.

23. Lewis, interview transcript, 5; Gail Lewis, quoted in "Talking Personal, Talking Political," Agnes Quashie, *Trouble and Strife*, 19 (1990): 46.

24. Brixton Black Women's Group, *Speak Out* 4 (1981): 2.

25. Wilson, interview transcript, 12.

26. Lewis, "Talking Personal, Talking Political," 49.

27. Bryan, interview transcript, 5; Scafe, interview transcript, 2.

28. Tracy Fisher, *What's Left of Blackness?*, 70.

29. Scafe, interview transcript, 14.

30. Dadzie, interview transcript, 8.

31. Dadzie, interview transcript, 4.

32. Dadzie, interview transcript, 4.

33. Gueye, interview transcript, 4.

34. Gueye, interview transcript, 4.

35. Lewis, interview transcript, 19.

36. Stuart Hall, "Ethnicity: Identity and Difference," *Radical America* 23.4 (1989): 17; Stuart Hall, "Thatcherism—A New Stage," *Marxism Today* 80.2 (1980): 26.

37. Hall, "Thatcherism—a New Stage," 26.

38. Hall, "Ethnicity: Identity and Difference," 17.

39. Floya Anthias, and Nira Yuval-Davis, *Racialized Boundaries: Race, Nation, Gender, Colour and Class and the Anti-racist Struggle* (London: Routledge, 1993), 114.

40. Bryan et al., *Heart of the Race*, 168–169.
41. Ina Zweiniger-Bargielowska, *Women in Twentieth-Century Britain* (Harlow: Longman, 2001), 302.
42. Samantrai, *AlterNatives: Black Feminist in the Postimperial Nation*, 59.
43. Elizabeth Buettner, *Europe after Empire* (Cambridge: Cambridge University Press, 2016), 353; Lewis, interview transcript, 19.
44. BBWG, *Speak Out* 2 (1979): 6.
45. Bryan et al., *Heart of the Race*, 164.
46. OWAAD, *FOWAAD!*, 1 (1979): 1; BBWG, *Speak Out* 4 (1981): 2.
47. Margaret Thatcher, quoted in "My Message to Women of the Nation: Tough," *Outwrite* 15 (1983): 12; Dadzie, interview transcript, 9.
48. Dadzie, interview transcript, 9.
49. Scafe, interview transcript, 8.
50. Bryan, interview transcript, 10.
51. Lewis, interview transcript, 8.
52. Lewis, interview transcript, 11.
53. Lewis, interview transcript, 8.
54. BBWG, *Speak Out* 1: 1–3.
55. Sisters in Study, "From the Inside Looking In: A Reappraisal of *Heart of the Race*." In *Charting the Journey: Writings by Black and Third World Women*, eds. Shabnam Grewal, Jackie Kay, Liliane Landor, Gail Lewis, and Pratibha Parmar. London: Sheba Feminist Publishers, 1988. 91–96; Lewis, interview transcript, 5; BBWG, *Speak Out* 1: 1–3.
56. Lewis, interview transcript, 7.
57. Natalie Thomlinson, "'Second-Wave' Black Feminist Periodicals in Britain." *Women: A Cultural Review* 27.4 (2017): 433.
58. Sudbury, "Other Kinds of Dreams," 96; BBWG, *Speak Out* (1981): 4.
59. Combahee River Collective, *The Combahee River Collective Statement.* http://circuitous.org/scraps/combahee.html
60. Kimberlé Crenshaw, "Demarginalizing the Intersection of Race and Sex: A Black Feminist Critique of Antidiscrimination Doctrine, Feminist Theory and Antiracist Politics," *University of Chicago Legal Forum* (1989).
61. Dadzie, interview transcript, 14.
62. Scafe, interview transcript, 8.
63. Dadzie, interview transcript, 20.
64. BBWG organizer Veronica White, quoted in Fisher, *What's Left of Blackness?*, 86.
65. BBWG, *Speak Out* 4 (1981): 4; Gueye, interview transcript, 8.
66. Bryan, interview transcript, 11.
67. Gueye, interview transcript, 11.
68. Gueye, interview transcript, 11.
69. Gail Lewis, quoted in "Talking Personal, Talking Political," 48.

70. Lewis, interview transcript, 5.
71. Wilson, interview transcript, 2.
72. Wilson, interview transcript, 2.
73. Wilson, interview transcript, 2.
74. Wilson, interview transcript, 3.
75. BBWG, *Speak Out* 1 (1979): 1.
76. Gail Lewis, quoted in "Talking Personal, Talking Political," 47.
77. Gail Lewis, quoted in "Talking Personal, Talking Political," 47.
78. Fisher, *What's Left of Blackness?*, 88.
79. Fisher, *What's Left of Blackness?*, 88.
80. Dadzie, interview transcript, 18.
81. Gueye, interview transcript, 16.
82. Gueye, interview transcript, 16.
83. Bryan et al., *Heart of the Race*, 172.
84. Brixton Black Women's Group, *Editorial: On Black Women Organising* (1983), 4.
85. Wilson, interview transcript, 11.
86. Wilson, interview transcript, 11.
87. Thomlinson, "Periodicals," 12.
88. Bryan, interview transcript, 6.
89. Gueye, interview transcript, 10.
90. Sudbury, "Other Kinds of Dreams," 228.
91. Wilson, interview transcript, 14.
92. Olive Gallimore, quoted in "Talking Personal, Talking Political," 50.
93. Wilson, interview transcript, 9.
94. Wilson, interview transcript, 13.
95. BBWG, *On Black Women Organising*, 6.
96. Wilson, interview transcript, 13.
97. Scafe, interview transcript, 14.
98. Gail Lewis, quoted in "Talking Personal, Talking Political," 50.
99. Scafe, interview transcript, 10.
100. BBWG, *On Black Women Organising*, 6.
101. Gueye, interview transcript, 19.
102. Gueye, interview transcript, 17.
103. Gueye, interview transcript, 19.
104. ELBWO, *Editorial* (1983): 1.
105. Thomlinson, "Periodicals," 8.
106. Thomlinson, "Periodicals," 8.
107. Gail Lewis, "Talking Personal, Talking Political," 47.
108. Lewis, "Talking Personal, Talking Political," 47.
109. Outwrite Collective, *Outwrite* 22 (1984): 15.
110. Dadzie, interview transcript, 13.

111. Dadzie, interview transcript, 13.

112. Linda Bellos, interview transcript (19 April 2017), 12. All further references are from this transcript.

113. Linda Bellos, "A Vision Back and Forth," in *Talking Black: Lesbians of African and Asian Descent Speak Out*, ed. Valerie Mason-John (London: Cassell, 1995), 60.

114. Bellos, "A Vision Back and Forth," 60.

115. Valerie Mason-John, ed. *Talking Black: Lesbians of African and Asian Descent Speak Out* (London: Cassell, 1995), 4.

116. BBWG, *On Black Women Organising*, 1.

117. Gueye, interview transcript, 11.

118. BBWG, *On Black Women Organising*, 1.

119. Fisher, *What's Left of Blackness?*, 78.

120. Bellos, interview transcript, 11.

121. Bellos, interview transcript, 11.

122. Scafe, interview transcript, 10.

123. Wilson, interview transcript, 13.

124. Wilson, interview transcript, 13.

125. Wilson, interview transcript, 13.

126. Gueye, interview transcript, 12.

127. BBWG, *On Black Women Organising*, 1.

128. BBWG, *On Black Women Organising*, 1.

129. BBWG, *Speak Out* 5 (1983): 5.

130. Melba Wilson, quoted in "Talking Personal, Talking Political," 51.

131. Sisters in Study, 95.

132. Bellos, interview transcript, 27.

133. Outwrite Collective, "1st National Black Lesbian Conference," *Outwrite* 40 (1985): 20.

134. Gail Lewis, quoted in "Becoming Visible: Black Lesbian Discussions," Carmen, Gail, Shaila, and Pratibha, *Feminist Review* 17 (1984): 71.

135. Gail Lewis, "Becoming Visible," 71.

136. Marlene T. Bogle, "Brixton Black Women's Centre: Organizing on Child Sexual Abuse," *Feminist Review* 28 (1988): 132.

137. Lewis, interview transcript, 21.

138. Lewis, interview transcript, 21; Wilson, interview transcript, 8.

139. BBWG, *Centre News* 1 (1982): 1.

140. Dadzie, interview transcript, 12.

141. Dadzie, interview transcript, 12.

142. Lord Scarman, quoted in "Q&A: The Scarman Report," *BBC*. http://news.bbc.co.uk/1/hi/programmes/bbc_parliament/3631579.stm

143. Andrew Gamble, "Privatization, Thatcherism, and the British State," *Journal of Law and Society* 16.1 (1988): 1; Fisher, *What's Left of Blackness?*, 99.

144. Fisher, *What's Left of Blackness?*, 99.
145. Sudbury, "Other Kinds of Dreams," 12.
146. ELBWO, Editorial, no. 1 (1983): 2.
147. Gueye, interview transcript, 2.
148. Bryan et al., *Heart of the Race*, 172.
149. Dadzie, interview transcript, 11.
150. Dadzie, interview transcript, 11.
151. Bryan, interview transcript, 7.
152. Bryan, interview transcript, 7.
153. Sudbury, "Other Kinds of Dreams," 12.
154. Sudbury, "Other Kinds of Dreams," 12.
155. Wilson, interview transcript, 14.
156. Lewis, interview transcript, 21.
157. Fisher, *What's Left of Blackness?*, 101.
158. Gueye, interview transcript, 11.
159. Fisher, *What's Left of Blackness?*, 98.
160. Gueye, interview transcript, 21.
161. Lewis, interview transcript, 23.
162. Paraphrase of *All the Women Are White, All the Blacks Are Men, but Some of Us Are Brave: Black Women's Studies*, eds. Akasha Gloria Hull, Barbara Smith, Patricia Bell-Scott (New York: Feminist Press, 1982).
163. Wilson, interview transcript, 19.
164. Wilson, interview transcript, 19.
165. Gueye, interview transcript, 23.
166. Wilson, interview transcript, 18.
167. Wilson, interview transcript, 18.
168. Scafe, interview transcript, 24.
169. Dadzie, interview transcript, 21.
170. Dadzie, interview transcript, 21.
171. Bryan et al., *Heart of the Race*, 1.
172. Gueye, interview transcript, 23.

Works Cited

PRIMARY SOURCES

Oral History Interviews

Bellos, Linda, interviewed 19 April 2017.
Bryan, Beverley, interviewed 7 July 2017.

Dadzie, Stella, interviewed 9 May 2017.
Gueye, Ama, interviewed 18 May 2017.
Lewis, Gail, interviewed 3 May 2017.
Scafe, Suzanne, interviewed 16 May 2017.
Wilson, Melba, interviewed 10 May 2017.

Articles

Black Woman Talk, "Black Woman Talk Collective." *Feminist Review* 17 (1984): 100.
Brixton Black Women's Group and Alice Henry. "Interview: Black Politics ⇆ Black Feminism: Brixton Black Women's Group Talks about Its Part of British Black Feminism." *Off Our Backs* 14.11 (1984): 14–15.
Brixton Black Women's Group. "Black Women Organising." "One Chant: Black Feminist Perspectives." *Feminist Review* 17 (1984): 84–89.
Carmen, Gail, and Shaila Pratibha. "Becoming Visible: Black Lesbian Discussions." *Feminist Review* 17 (1984): 53–72.

London, Black Cultural Archives—Sources Relating to the Black Women's Movement

DADZIE/1/1/1.
DADZIE/1/1/2.
DADZIE/1/1/3.
DADZIE/1/1/4.
DADZIE/1/1/5.
DADZIE/1/1/6.
DADZIE/1/1/10.
DADZIE/1/1/11.
DADZIE/1/1/12.
DADZIE/1/1/14.
DADZIE/1/1/18.
DADZIE/1/1/19.
DADZIE/1/1/21.
DADZIE/1/1/22.
DADZIE/1/1/23.
DADZIE/1/1/24.
DADZIE/1/1/31.
DADZIE/1/1/34.
DADZIE/1/1/38.
DADZIE/1/9.

DADZIE/1/8/1.
DADZIE/1/8/4.
DADZIE/4/12.
DADZIE/6/3.
MUR 11.2.
MUR 305.89.
RC/PC/1/01/F/1.
RC/RF/5/07/U1.

Oral Histories from the Black Cultural Archives

Bryan, Beverley, interviewed by Kwame Phillips, 6 January 2010, BCA, *Oral Histories of the Black Women's Movement: The Heart of the Race*, ORAL/1/31.
Dadzie, Stella, interviewed by Ego Ahiawe, 10 March 2009, BCA, *Oral Histories of the Black Women's Movement: The Heart of the Race*, ORAL/1/1/07.
Gueye, Anna, interviewed by Yepoka Yeebo, 1 March 2009, BCA, *Oral Histories of the Black Women's Movement: The Heart of the Race*, ORAL/1/04.
Jackman, Donna and Carol Leeming, interviewed by Annette Sylvester, 19 March 2009, BCA, *Oral Histories of the Black Women's Movement: The Heart of the Race*, ORAL/1/1/14.
Lewis, Dr Gail, interviewed by Marie Bernard, date unknown, BCA, *Oral Histories of the Black Women's Movement: The Heart of the Race*, ORAL/1/22.
Lockhart, Judith, interviewed by Sheila Ruiz, 2 February 2009, BCA, *Oral Histories of the Black Women's Movement: The Heart of the Race*, ORAL/1/1/05.
Mason-John, Valerie, interviewed by Annette Sylvester, 20 February 2009, BCA, *Oral Histories of the Black Women's Movement: The Heart of the Race*, ORAL/1/02.
Mckenley, Dr. Jan, interviewed by Yepoka Yeebo, 7 May 2009, BCA, *Oral Histories of the Black Women's Movement: The Heart of the Race*, ORAL/1/21.
Otitoju, Femi, interviewed by Yepoka Yeebo, 13 February 2009, BCA, *Oral Histories of the Black Women's Movement: The Heart of the Race*, ORAL/1/10
Pieters, Donna, interviewed by Emma Skeete, date unknown, BCA, *Oral Histories of the Black Women's Movement: The Heart of the Race*, ORAL/1/16.
Tsele, Lindiwe, interviewed by Annette Sylvester, 3 September 2009, BCA, *Oral Histories of the Black Women's Movement: The Heart of the Race*, ORAL/1/23.

Periodicals

Bhavnani, K., "Racist Acts." *Spare Rib* 117 (1982): 24–27.
"Editorial." *We Are Here: Black Women's Magazine*, 1988.
"Editorial." *FOWAAD* 4. Lee and Black, 1985.

"Black Women Together." *Spare Rib* 87 (1979): 42–45.
"Black Women Fighting Back." *Spare Rib* 95 (1980): 49.

Secondary Sources

Books

Anthias, Floya, and Nira Yuval-Davis. *Racialized Boundaries: Race, Nation, Gender, Colour and Class and the Anti-racist Struggle*. London: Routledge, 1993.
Bellos, Linda. "A Vision Back and Forth," in *Talking Black: Lesbians of African and Asian Descent Speak Out*, ed. Valerie Mason-John. London: Cassell, 1995. 52–71.
Bryan, Beverley, Stella Dadzie, and Suzanne Scafe. *The Heart of the Race*. London: Virago Press Ltd., 1986.
Buettner, Elizabeth. *Europe after Empire: Decolonisation, Society and Culture*. Cambridge: Cambridge University Press, 2016.
Carby, Hazel V. *Cultures in Babylon: Black Britain and African American*. London: Verso, 1999.
Carby, Hazel V. "White Women Listen! Black Feminism and the Boundaries of Sisterhood," in *Black British Cultural Studies: A Reader*, eds. Houston A. Baker Jr. and Manthia Diawara. Chicago: University of Chicago Press, 1996. 82–89.
Fisher, Tracey. *What's Left of Blackness: Feminisms, Transracial Solidarities, and the Politics of Belonging in Britain*. Basingstoke: Palgrave Macmillan, 2012.
Goulbourne, Harry. *Ethnicity and Nationalism in Post-Imperial Britain*. New York: Cambridge University Press, 1991.
Goulbourne, Harry. *Race Relations in Britain Since 1945*. Basingstoke: Palgrave Macmillan, 1998.
Jackson, Ben, and Robert Saunders, eds. *Making Thatcher's Britain*. Cambridge: Cambridge University Press, 2012.
Mason-John, Valerie, and Ann Khambatta. *Lesbians Talk Making Black Waves*. London: Scarlett Press, 1993.
Mason-John, Valerie. *Talking Black: Lesbians of African and Asian Descent Speak Out*. London: Cassell, 1995.
Mirza, Heidi Safia. *Black British Feminism: A Reader*. London: Routledge, 1997.
Ngcobo, Lauretta, ed. *Let It Be Told: Essays by Black Women in Britain*. London: Pluto Press, 1987.
Riddell, Peter. *The Thatcher Era And its Legacy*. Oxford: Basil Blackwell Ltd., 1989.
Samantrai, Ranu. *AlterNatives: Black Feminist in the Postimperial Nation*. Stanford, CA: Stanford University Press, 2002.
Samuel, Raphael, ed. *Patriotism: The Making and Unmaking of British National Identity*. London: Routledge, 1989.

Skellington, Richard. *"Race" in Britain Today*. London: Sage Publications, 1992.
Sisters in Study. "From the Inside Looking In: A Reappraisal of *Heart of the Race*," in *Charting the Journey: Writings by Black and Third World Women*, eds. Shabnam Grewal, Jackie Kay, Liliane Landor, Gail Lewis, and Pratibha Parmar. London: Sheba Feminist Publishers, 1988. 91–96.
Sudbury, Julia. *"Other Kinds of Dreams": Black Women's Organisations and the Politics of Transformation*. London: Routledge, 1998.
Thomlinson, Natalie. *Race, Ethnicity and the Women's movement in England, 1968–1993*. Basingstoke: Palgrave Macmillan, 2016.
Vinen, Richard. *Thatcher's Britain The Politics and Social Upheaval of the Thatcher Era*. London: Simon & Schuster UK, 2010.
Williams, Claudette. "We Are a Natural Part of Many Different Struggles: Black Women Organizing," in *Inside Babylon: The Caribbean Diaspora in Britain*, eds. Clive Harris and Winston James. London: Verso, 1993. 153–164.
Yuval-Davis, Nira, and Floya Anthias, eds. *Woman-Nation-State*. Basingstoke: Macmillan Press Ltd., 1989.
Zweiniger-Bargielowska, Ina. *Women in Twentieth-Century Britain*. Harlow: Longman, 2001.

Articles

Amos, Valerie, and Pratibha Parmar. "Challenging Imperial Feminism." *Feminist Review: Many Voices, One Chant: Black Feminist Perspectives* 17 (1984): 3–19.
Bailey, Moya, and Trudy. "On Misogynoir: Citation, Erasure, and Plagiarism." *Feminist Media Studies* 18:4 (2018): 762–768.
Brixton Black Women's Group. "Black Women Organising." *Feminist Review: Many Voices, One Chant: Black Feminist Perspective* 17 (1984): 84–89.
Burin, Yula and Ego Ahaiwe Sowinski. "Sister to Sister: Developing a Black British Feminist Archival Consciousness." *Feminist Review* 108 (2014): 112–119.
Crenshaw, Kimberlé. "Demarginalizing the Intersection of Race and Sex: A Black Feminist Critique of Antidiscrimination Doctrine, Feminist Theory and Antiracist Politics." *University of Chicago Legal Forum* 1 (1989): 139–167.
Francis, Matthew. "Mrs Thatcher's peacock blue sari: Ethnic Minorities, Electoral Politics and the Conservative Party, c. 1974–86." *Contemporary British History* 31:2 (2017): 274–293.
Gamble, Andrew. "Privatization, Thatcherism, and the British State." *Journal of Law and Society* 16. 1 (1988): 1–20.
Garrett, Geoffrey. "The Political Consequences of Thatcherism." *Political Behavior* 14.4 (1992): 361–382.
Gilroy, Paul. "You Can't Fool the Youths . . . Race and Class Formation in the 1980s." *Race & Class* 23:2–3 (1981): 207–222.

Hall, Stuart. "Ethnicity: Identity and Difference." *Radical America* 23.4 (1989): 9–20.
Quashie, Agnes. "Talking Political, Talking Personal," in *Trouble and Strife*, 19 (1990): 44–52.
Thomlinson, Natalie. "Second-Wave" Black Feminist Periodicals in Britain." *Women: A Cultural Review* 27.4 (2017): 432–445.
Thomlinson, Natalie. "The Colour of Feminism: White Feminists and Race in the Women's Liberation Movement." *The Journal of the Historical Association* 97.327 (2012): 453–475.

"Spiritualists, ideologues, pragmatists, feminists, and women of all descriptions"

The British Women's Liberation Movement, the UN Decade For Women, and Feminist Transnationalism in *Spare Rib*

CHARLOTTE LYDIA RILEY

You May Have Made Up The Name Yourself: *Spare Rib* at the United Nations

When the writer Tsehai Berhane-Selassie arrived in Nairobi for the 1985 United Nations Decade for Women conference, she duly went along, with another woman from the *Spare Rib* collective, to collect her press accreditation. However, she found the authorities—represented by one Mr. Hess, a UN official—to be unusually hostile to their request. Hess was dubious about the veracity of the women's claim to be serious journalists, saying "I don't know what *Spare Rib* is . . . You may have made up the name yourself"; he relented only when they produced a copy of the magazine.[1] In this way, Berhane-Selassie was able to obtain her press pass, and duly sent back a report from the conference.[2] But, as the women protested at the time, "if it were a woman in his place, she would have heard of *Spare Rib*."[3]

Spare Rib, the iconic second-wave feminist magazine, the most important publication in the British women's liberation movement

(WLM), grew out of 1960s countercultural underground publishing tradition. Although it started as a publication focused on "women's issues" such as unwanted body hair (albeit with a feminist slant), within a few years the coverage had shifted in a more interesting direction. Soon the magazine covered news, science, law, health, and international issues, with discussion of such topics as reproductive justice, violence against women, and women's labor politics, both at home and overseas.[4] *Spare Rib* was "by far the most famous and longest lasting" of the feminist magazines and newspapers produced in the 1960s, 1970s, and 1980s, and its coverage blended effectively the personal and the domestic with the political and the international.[5]

In this context, Tsehai Berhane-Selassie's report was exactly the sort of thing *Spare Rib*'s readers expected: they were primed to read about the "spiritualists, ideologues, pragmatists, feminists and women of all descriptions" present at the conference, to explore their debates, and to understand their positions.[6] The event in Nairobi was the third in a series of conferences held by the United Nations to try to understand, measure, and improve the global status of women. The first had been organized in Mexico City in 1975, at which point the United Nations had proclaimed the period between 1976 and 1985 the official "Decade for Women." In this period, officials and activists working at and alongside the three official conferences—Mexico City, Copenhagen, and Nairobi—sought to effect real and lasting improvements in the status of women around the world, in the Global North and Global South.[7] The conferences were huge events, with thousands of participants from around the world, which brought many important issues to the world stage; they were also dogged by controversies, riven by disputes, and accused by many of institutionalizing north-south divides.[8] This was reflected in the global news coverage of the first conference. Headlines included "When The Girls Fall Out" (*Daily Express*, 23 June 1975); "Militant Feminists in a Fury" (*Canberra Times*, 25 June 1975 from AP Reuters); "Screaming Women Fight to Be Heard at Conference" (*The Times*, 30 June 1975); and "Women Row in Mexico" (Peggy Simpson, AP, June 1975).[9]

Many delegates and NGOs associated with the conferences felt extremely positive about their experiences, and were optimistic about the effect the Decade for Women would have on gender rights around the world. Leticia Shahani, the secretary-general of the final conference in Nairobi, spoke of a "critical mass" having been reached in support of the global women's movement.[10] But reports presented at the 1985 conference, and at the 1995 follow-up conference in Beijing, showed that, in reality, the overall status of women worldwide and their material conditions had not improved.[11]

This article argues that the *Spare Rib* coverage of the UN Decade for Women conferences, and the wider interactions between the British WLM and the UN work on women's rights and gender equality, shine a new light on the trajectory of British feminist activism in this period of the late 1970s and early 1980s. It is sometimes argued that the WLM had disbanded as a coherent movement after the contentious tenth WLM conference held in Birmingham in 1978.[12] Yet a reading of *Spare Rib* demonstrates that there was in fact still a continuing movement, unified by shared concerns and values, albeit pluralistic and multifaceted in its focus and approach; the UN Decade for Women thus provides an important international context for this continued development of British feminist thought and activism in this period. Further, exploring the connections between the UN Decade for Women and the WLM problematizes the idea that British feminism was inward-looking and parochial.[13] In fact, the women of the British WLM were often engaged with and exercised by international issues, although the extent and quality of their engagement was shaped and framed by British racial and postcolonial politics.[14]

Women's Rights Are Human Rights: The UN Decade for Women

The history of the International Women's Year (IWY) conference, the Decade for Women, and the gradual adoption of feminist concerns by the United Nations, culminating in the adoption of 1975–1985 as a "Decade for Women," is long and somewhat circuitous.[15] The organization Women's International Democratic Federation (WIDF)—which had been founded in Paris in 1945 as an organization committed to anti-fascism, world peace, child welfare, and gender equality—had been lobbying for some time for an International Women's Year, which could be used to showcase pressing issues around gender equality on the world stage. The WIDF, which is often dismissed merely as a communist front but which needs to be taken seriously as an organizational actor in international relations, was an observer organization of the Commission on the Status of Women, and managed to convince the Romanian delegation to propose

1975 as the Year of Women.¹⁶ This proposal was approved and passed on to the UN General Assembly, who in turn approved the request and called for a conference to mark this designated celebratory year.¹⁷ Two women—the Finnish delegate to the General Assembly, Helvi Sipilä, and the British deputy director of the UN Branch for the Promotion of Equality of Men and Women, Margaret K. Bruce, were appointed to organize activities for the sponsored year. The two women worked with NGOs to secure donations from governments and private foundations to enable the conference to take place, and drafted a conference treaty that could be debated, amended, and (hopefully) adopted at the first event.¹⁸

The UN conferences on women—Mexico City in 1975, Copenhagen in 1980, and Nairobi in 1985 (and the follow-up event in Beijing in 1995), and the UN "Decade of Women," which ran from 1975 to 1985—should be seen therefore as central to the creation of a transnational women's rights lobby, and the institutionalization of a gender-based approach to international relations and the international human rights community. In doing so, as Zinsser points out, these mechanisms were building on over a century of transnational organizing for women's rights that could be traced back to the 1840s, when European and North American activists corresponded on issues such as female suffrage.¹⁹ Jocelyn Olcott, in her work, has amplified this sense of a historic trajectory and feminist context for the movement, by amplifying the billing given to the International Women's Conference in 1975 by its organizers: the greatest consciousness-raising movement in history.²⁰

The conferences were huge events, with thousands of participants from around the world, which brought many important issues to the world stage. Perhaps unavoidably, they were also mired in controversy from their beginning. The 1975 conference was initially criticized by Soviet women's groups who wanted to hold their own event in East Berlin to avoid what they saw as Western influence.²¹ More damagingly, the *New York Times* reported the (short-lived) UN proposal that the conference should be devoted to "gender equality," because a conference focusing solely on women's issues would be dismissed and "treated lightly as a ladies' meeting." Although this proposal was not accepted, it is certainly true that the conference was struggling to secure financial support, with one female official ruefully commenting that it was likely to be "the cheapest conference the United Nations has ever held."²² Eventually, Mexico City agreed to host the conference, and it was scheduled for June.

The Women's Conference needs to be understood in the context of the United Nations as an organization that had, in the early 1970s, held a series of conferences on so-called "soft" issues, including the 1972 event on the environment and 1974 conferences on food and population control. These conferences had run parallel NGO events alongside the official program, and this approach was continued at the 1975 women's conference in Mexico City. This was important, both because NGOs had been so influential in creating the context in which this conference could be held, but also in the context of feminist critique of the United Nation's tendency to privilege "experts" and expertise over lived experience. Mexico City prioritized the voices of female experts, but also tried to get to the testimony of "ordinary women." In this context, "political" issues including apartheid, Palestine, and economic inequality sat on the program alongside discussion of domestic labor, sex work, and access to health care.[23] The NGO event showcased the wide variety of women's participation in global civil society—from middle-class voluntarist organizations to radical liberationist groups.[24] It had been designed to showcase debate—Olcott has demonstrated that this was interpreted as a weakness by the global media, who saw it as a sign that women could not agree on key issues affecting them, but argues that the vibrancy of these arguments between women from different backgrounds and different experiences was in fact a testament to the strength and power of the global women's movement: "disunity was, in fact, an achievement of IWY."[25] The conferences at Copenhagen in 1980 and Nairobi in 1985 were likewise driven by passionate, combative debate.[26]

"A Soap Opera in the Sun": The IWY Conferences and *Spare Rib*

The UN women's conferences have been underexplored by historians, and there is certainly room in the field of diplomatic and international history for more "feminist curiosity" about how these institutions, events, and spaces continue to shape power and inequalities.[27] Taking this approach, this chapter examines how the Decade for Women conferences and the United Nations as an institution were represented in the British feminist magazine *Spare Rib*. The chapter focuses on both the conferences themselves and the wider context of coverage of development and international gender issues in the magazine.

This is a productive exercise for a number of reasons. First, *Spare Rib* really was central to the development of British second-wave feminism as well as being a key site of feminist cultural heritage.[28] The magazine was launched in 1972 and ran for twenty years. *Spare Rib* pushed at the traditional structures of magazine publishing, gradually shifting to a less hierarchical editorial policy, a greater focus on news, current affairs, and campaigning, and increasing space provided for readers to contribute to debates through letters and longer editorials. In 1975, the magazine explicitly aligned with a socialist feminist perspective; in 1981, the magazine reiterated its desire to "reflect women's lives in all their diverse situations."[29] *Spare Rib* should be understood as mutually constitutive of the British WLM in the long 1980s, in a wider context that saw a commitment to celebrating and disseminating women's writing, a focus on collective approaches to publishing, and an understanding of the written word as both historically connected to women's activism and as a "potential portal to power."[30] The magazine was as much *shaping* as *shaped by* the women's movement in this period.[31]

Using *Spare Rib* to explore the relationship between the British WLM and the transnational context of the UN Decade for Women is also fruitful because it centers an often overlooked or underemphasized aspect of the WLM: the extent to which it operated within a transnational context. More specifically, it illuminates the ways in which the British WLM explored, understood, and both challenged and replicated the global power imbalances between the Global North and Global South, and specifically the position of women within this hierarchy of global power. In a piece historicizing the WLM published in 2016, Sue Bruley and Laurel Forster defined the women's liberation movement as "the upsurge in feminist activism and other feminist practices, agency and organization in Europe, North America and many other developed countries."[32] But the WLM should be understood within a truly global context, which incorporates the lived experience, theoretical engagement, and political activism of women in "developing" countries too, not least because of Britain's imperial history, and the postcolonial connections between the ex-metropole and the ex-colonies that fundamentally shaped the power imbalance between Global North and Global South.[33] These narratives must also be read in the context of the maternalistic, often deeply patronizing imperial feminism of the nineteenth century, and the empire-tinged internationalism of the interwar years; there is a long history of white British women using spaces within the Global South as sites of political ideology or power, to express a sense of sisterhood or (often) a hierarchical, maternal connection to other women.[34]

In focusing on *Spare Rib*'s presentation of the UN Decade for Women, this chapter examines how popular narratives about the "developing world" worked within the WLM, and argues that women echoed, but also challenged, wider understandings of development, the north-south divide, and global inequality. I argue that the magazine can be used to illustrate a particular, and contingent, British feminist engagement with international and transnational feminist issues. Writers for the magazine were interested in the IWY events from a personal or political (or personal-as-political) perspective, and the topic was situated within a limited but intentional engagement with issues around transnational female solidarity, international political structures, and the way that global inequalities could be shaped not only by gender but also race and (neo)colonialism.[35]

United Nations Notices Women: *Spare Rib* and the Wider World

Despite its image as a British-focused magazine, *Spare Rib* featured sustained coverage of international women's politics: in the early years, this was part of the main news or "news shorts" section of the magazine, in the later 1970s it was grouped specifically under "Foreign News," and by the 1980s there was extensive reporting in the "International News" section. The magazine carried a number of stories about the United Nations as an organization, often with a critical voice, although in the early years this reporting often prioritized the concerns of white, Western, professional women rather than women as a global class. For example, in 1974, the magazine ran a short piece entitled "Some are more equal than others with the UN family!," which covered the concentration of female staff in the nonprofessional and lower ranks of the UN secretariat and noted that the male-female employment ratio at directorial level stood at 37:1.[36] This echoes institutional concerns at the United Nations; in December 1975, the International Women's Year Secretariat sponsored a panel discussion in New York that explored why so few women were employed within the secretariat, and produced a publication based on this event that tried to theorize the underrepresentation of women within the organization and posited some possible approaches to improving this issue.[37] Critiquing the United Nations based on the number of women employed in top jobs—rather than the women affected by policies at a grassroots level—demonstrates a particular approach to internationalist feminist politics, one that prioritizes women with whom some readers of *Spare Rib* might have felt a professional or personal affinity.

Spare Rib actually contained little coverage of the 1975 Mexico City conference or the International Women's Year in general. This perhaps reflects the fact that the British government did not enthusiastically participate in either the conference or IWY. As Helen McCarthy has identified, the conference held little significance for the British state, and the issue of women in the transnational community was deemed "marginal at best" and explicitly not a "priority aim" of British foreign policy.[38] The Foreign and Commonwealth Office (FCO) wanted to engage with the IWY only as a space in which to emphasize existing tenets of British foreign policy, particularly the tensions of Cold War politics and postcolonial struggles for power. As such, their commitment to the event was limited, despite Barbara Castle's efforts to lobby the government to budget more funding to supporting IWY in the United Kingdom than the "paltry sum" of £10,000 that had been initially promised. The government eventually approved funding of £200,000 over three years, although this came from the Ministry for Overseas Development budget rather than the FCO, reflecting both Minister for Overseas Development Judith Hart's personal commitment to the cause and the British government attitude that IWY was less to do with foreign policy or diplomacy, and more a vague sense of engaging with potential partners in the developing world.[39]

The magazine did contain one detailed write-up of the conference, which contained three views—a descriptive and analytical piece by British writer Jenny Rathbone, a piece by Indian journalist Amiya Rao that had initially been printed in the *Hindustan Times*, and an extracted statement by Charlotte Bunch and Frances Doughty, key figures in the American delegation to Mexico City. Rathbone reported that the official conference had been mostly "self-congratulatory," with governments lauding their own countries' achievements in gender equality. Millie Miller, the Labour MP who had headed the British delegation, had apparently "blamed the Latin American and Third World delegates for wrecking the conference" because they "constantly brought up 'political' issues . . . denouncing Zionism, imperialism, racism and every other ism except sexism which was what the conference was supposed to be about"; she later repeated these critiques to the Foreign Office on her return.[40] Rathbone criticized the British delegation for its tendency to "vote in line with the US, abstaining on all politically sensitive issues." And she approvingly quoted the Mexican Women's Liberation Movement, which had critiqued the official conference as a "politically inoffensive and innocuous" event that attempted to "assimilate" radical women into the Western capitalist system.[41]

Amiya Rao's piece also critiqued the bourgeois concerns of the more privileged delegates at Mexico City, stating that

> In this International Women's Year we are talking of equal rights, of equal pay for equal work; we pretend to be perturbed if our husbands do not share with us the kitchen chores; some of us have been toying with the idea of dropping Miss or Mrs and substituting Ms before our names. All these, no doubt, are worthy objectives. But in this vast land of ours what is the proportion of such women demanding equal status to those humble people living below the poverty line whose only demand is a handful of grain and who have to sell their daughters to remain alive?[42]

This critique sits clearly within Jocelyn Olcott's argument that international readings of the conference often focused explicitly on the discussions on sexual politics rather than other political approaches.[43]

The final section was taken from a statement written by Charlotte Bunch and Frances Doughty, entitled "US Feminists and International Women's Year," which had critiqued the fundamental structure of the IWY event in advance of its staging. They pointed out that "most countries, except for the US, Canada and Mexico, will be represented by relatively few women either sent by their governments or who can afford the high cost of coming"—in fact, "we have heard that even West European feminists cannot afford to come in large numbers."[44] This certainly applied to women within the British WLM, who could not afford the airfare to Mexico City.[45]

The British delegation did include several women, partly because the FCO recognized the importance of being *seen* to send female delegates: as well as MPs Millie Miller and Shirley Summerskill, there was Elizabeth Waller, the FCO Woman's Officer; Janet Cockcroft, the British representative on the Commission on the Status of Women; Kay Carmichael, an advisor in the Downing Street Policy Unit; and Teresa Spens, a member of the Ministry for Overseas Development.[46] But ordinary

British women were not represented. In this context, where it appeared to British left-wing feminists that their sisters in the Global South had developed legitimate critiques of the IWY, and that their own presence was not encouraged either by the formal structures of the conference or by their own government, it is unsurprising that the magazine was slow to recognize the potential of the United Nations in gender equality.

The magazine showed more interest in the 1980 and 1985 conferences, with sustained coverage discussing the official UN conference, the NGO events, and the British government responses to the events; the United Nations and the British government again came in for criticism. Jill Nicholls, the feminist filmmaker, was a member of the *Spare Rib* collective between 1974 and 1980. In a piece headlined, with some sarcasm, "United Nations Notices Women," Nicholls described the 1980 Copenhagen conference in dismissive terms as "the time it takes 136 representatives of governments, four observer delegations and several representatives of UN bodies to read out lists of their achievements."[47] The piece was illustrated by images of smiling happy women, captioned "the bright face of woman, looking forward to the future," taken from "official government handouts," emphasizing that the official event was essentially window dressing.[48] Nicholls gave a verbal portrait of the feeling of the official conference, which she dubbed a "frozen spectacle" of "delays, oblique debates and maneuverings," enlivened only by the occasional "spectacular spark" of protestors breaking into the proceedings and making interventions (quoting one woman, for example, screaming about "the women living in their own shit in Armagh jail," and describing anti-nuclear protestors managing to unfurl a banner in the hall).[49] She pushed against the idea that the event had been "politicized" by women from the Global South, arguing both that "an international conference on women cannot be—should not be—entirely separate from the issues of world politics." Instead, she argued, women should rebel "against the idea that for women not to be excluded means that we have to imitate the dreary motions of men's politics." She concluded that "what was lacking at the official conference was a *political* understanding of women's oppression." Because of this, although the plan of action was in theory "quite a radical document, if a bit vague," it did not include any discussion of sexuality, male power, or the necessity or existence of "a movement of women to liberate ourselves."[50]

Nicholls also included in her reporting a short piece entitled "Come on, our side," in which she critiqued the British official response to the Copenhagen conference.[51] In this, she scathingly quoted Kay Coombs, the

Foreign Office representative on the British delegation, saying that there were "no ardent feminists" among the British delegates, and derided the decision by Britain not to sign up to CEDAW at the event.[52] She also repeatedly framed the British delegation as unrepresentative of ordinary British women, or certainly British feminists—putting "'our' delegation" in quotation marks, and quoting Dame Anne Warburton, a member of the British delegation, as never having heard of *Spare Rib* before (unlike a member of the Australian delegation, who actually subscribed to the magazine, as Nicholls discovered when she met her "in the loo").[53] In Britain there had been a little advance publicity of the conference, but Nicholls also acknowledged that "international awareness is low"; Copenhagen could have been an opportunity for women within the British WLM to travel a relatively short distance to attend the conference, but it seems very few were able or willing to make the trip.[54]

Nicholls was also critical of the NGO forum that ran alongside the official conference, although she was open to the idea that this event might be actively trying to subvert the norms of international conferences and that in providing a "creative, imaginary and fun" space for activism, the NGO forum might be a fitting medium to message in an appropriate way. However, she echoed delegates' concerns that the forum was underfunded, and did not, for example, provide a crèche—at a women's conference!—or translation facilities, which limited the involvement of women in predictable ways. Despite these limitations, debate in this space felt dynamic—the forum was attended by 8,000 women and a small number of men, representing "traditional women's organisations, population control agencies, national liberation movements, women's professional organisations, Women's Liberation campaigns and publications, church groups, development organisations, their governments—or simply themselves." For Nicholls, "it was weird to be at a women's conference where feminism was seen as just one perspective among many" (although there were very few avowedly antifeminist voices), and argued that the loose framework of the NGO event was problematic: in comparison, "a Woman's Liberation conference would have at least some structure for reporting back and making announcements." There was a sense, she felt, that this sort of loose organizational structure would simply "keep us where the Big Boys want us—in a shambles on the fringes," and quoted Madhu Kishwar, the pioneer of Indian women's studies, who described the forum as "just the nursery where the children play while the adults get on with their decisions."[55]

Nicholls was also concerned that the focus on the problems faced by women of the Global South was often "voyeuristic," functioning to present them as victims with crises that needed to be solved by their Western sisters, rather than equal partners in a process where all women could "speak out, learn and change." This tension was especially apparent in the discussions on female genital mutilation (FGM), in which Arab and African women had accused Western women of "just launching a new crusade, behaving like missionaries, being patronising, imperialist and interfering."[56] Conversely, some Western women felt they could not speak out about the problems they faced, such as sexism in the workplace, street harassment, or problems accessing childcare, because they were so "trivial" compared to the problems of women in the Global South. This placed a problematic limitation on global sisterhood that was not only felt in one direction, which was resented just as strongly by both sides, one of whom felt their problems had been diminished, the other feeling that their issues had been exoticized and rendered insurmountable without Western help. More structurally, it was clear, by "agreeing not to make decisions, [women] leave others to make decisions for us." The loose and open structure of the NGO forum meant that it was easy to cast it as a feminized space for collaborative discussion, against the formal power structures of the UN conference down the road.[57] There was no mechanism for the women at the NGO conference to mobilize, or weaponize, their concerns.

Mindful of these concerns, in 1984 Erin Stuart wrote for *Spare Rib* calling for women's voluntary organizations to make representations to the British government to be included in the Nairobi conference the following year. The government had ignored NGOs in their submission for the 1980 conference and Stuart was keen that women's groups, especially those representing "a cross-section of age, race, income, occupation or feminism in Britain," should be proactive in lobbying government to do more than merely "gain political mileage for itself" by attending.[58] A further article called for the British government to take the conference more seriously after it became apparent that the British data submission to the United Nations provided a "very skewed" account of women's life in Britain, either refusing to provide information or providing only cursory answers—a section of fifty-four questions including policy, content, employment of women, alternative media, women's organizations, and international cooperation received only three sentences in response.[59]

As highlighted at the beginning of this chapter, it was Tsehai Berhane-Selassie who wrote the long report from Nairobi in 1985, which asked in the headline if the event were merely "A Soap Opera in the Sun"?[60] After eventually obtaining her press pass, Berhane-Selassie attended the UN conference and the NGO forum, as well as several development workshops and local tours intended to explore the lives of Kenyan women. The government conference was again marked by its ponderous decision-making process—first, a whole week dedicated to each government delegation reading out lists of their achievements on women's issues, followed by an eighteen-hour session to try to define the scope of the conference (which did not reach a conclusion).[61] Again, "politicization" was raised as an issue, with delegates split between those who wanted to define women's issues in the broadest possible terms, and those who were still "stuck with the idea that it was to do with caring and welfare"; by the end of the session, the American delegation had threatened to walk out over this conflict.[62]

Berhane-Selassie again critiqued the British government for their approach to the conference, echoing the issues raised by British NGOs, who had presented to the official British delegation a demand for dialogue:

> They emphasised that the British government had done virtually nothing to make the majority of British women aware of the aims and programmes of the Decade . . . pointed at the government's failure to promote women's interests . . . criticised the lack of publicity and media coverage of the Decade "events" including the questionnaire sent by the UN for completion by governments . . . condemned the ineptitude of organising only two meetings (both in the *House of Lords!*) and objected to the fact that the delegates did not properly represent British women in terms of class background, race, or occupational and income levels.[63]

Berhane-Selassie included this coverage of the British NGO frustration with the British official delegation as part of a wider critique of the official conference. She argued that Western governments such as the United States and Britain were "uncomfortable" with the pressure the forum was putting on the formal conference to engage with "the issues of international inequality, imperialism, and the problems of colonialism and war."[64]

In contrast, Berhane-Selassie praised the parallel NGO forum because "women were in almost full control," with "no sign of the differences which had characterised the mid-decade conference in Copenhagen when the crusading zeal of western women to talking about female circumcision had distressed the Africans." In a welcome contrast, the panel on FGM in Nairobi was dominated by African women with direct experience of the practice and of working to combat it.[65] Berhane-Selassie also highlighted the role of the "peace tent"; this was an initiative of the Women's International League for Peace and Freedom (WILPF) to create a space in which women from opposing sides in global political conflicts could come together.[66] Berhane-Selassie emphasized its role as a conceptual space in which women from both sides of the Cold War, for instance, "could further the links being built around the resistance to the arms race." This had been productive, although there had been more "tension" in discussions around the Middle East, and police had to be brought in twice (once after both the panel and audience had already "left in exasperation" at the descent into a row).[67]

Race and migration were also central topics, perhaps especially so because the conference was taking place in the Global South, where "migrants in Europe, along with black women in Europe and the USA raised the issue of racism," and women of color expressed solidarity across national lines—Angela Davis, for example, declaring that she would work with others to try to cancel Third World debt. As Berhane-Selassie argued, "racism was the basis of international inequality" for most of the delegates, although broader issues of international inequalities (exacerbated by problems such as famine) and, of course, male-female inequalities also dominated discussion.[68] She concluded that "the most concrete achievement of the Forum was the exchange of information and, even more important, of addresses and work programmes." The experience left both individuals and organizations "exhilarated." Although the aims and outcomes of the Forum were necessarily limited and partial, this affective response to the meeting should be taken seriously as a meaningful intervention in transnational women's liberation politics.[69] The 1985 conference was a high point of transnational feminist activism, and of British WLM active engagement with these issues.

Development: A Man's World?

This *Spare Rib* coverage of the International Women's Year in 1975 and the subsequent UN Decade for Women should be set within the context of broader transnational critiques of "development" in this period.

These originated in the Global South, and were particularly critical of instruments such as the World Bank/IMF and the use of development programs to instill particular values or promote approaches to economy and government. Much of this critique developed from an explicitly feminist context.[70] *Spare Rib*'s coverage of development as a concept, and ideas about how development programs might have specifically gendered implications, should be understood within this framework.

In 1978, the magazine ran a long piece by Barbara Rogers, a writer and researcher specializing in issues around overseas development, entitled "Development: a man's world."[71] She critiqued the "overwhelming emphasis on men in development," presenting as evidence the responses by officials from the United Nations, WHO, and World Bank when questioned about gender issues. So, for example, the World Bank Head of Planning who dismissed her question about women in development by saying, "I don't think there's anything of much interest to you here . . . we don't have time for any special projects"; the WHO official who was disbelieving when told that official reports on onchocerciasis entirely omitted women, eventually conceding "how amazing! You're right! I've worked on this for years, read that document dozens of times, and never noticed that it's only about men"; the FAO official who said, "there's hardly anything to say [about women] because we don't have the sort of projects that would involve them." As Rogers concluded, "it was exhausting dealing with all these men"; it seems likely that this exposure of the systemic sexism embedded at the heart of the development industry might have shaped readers' engagement with the UN Decade for Women itself.

Rogers was also critical of her own research practices, her limited interaction with women on the ground, and lack of language skills, although she ended on an upbeat note that she was "confident about the possibility of communication between women coming from opposite sides of the world," demonstrating her own engagement with issues around power and inequality within development studies.[72] In 1980, she published a second long piece, "Discrimination in Development," which continued this theme. In 1980, "women [had] been discovered—after a fashion" as gender had become more central to development work; however, Rogers's work critiqued some of the continuing assumptions about women in the "developing world" held by development organizations, such as the equation of matrilineal societies with poverty. She also questioned the common application of "a Western concept of domesticity," with its gendered division of labor, as a panacea for global poverty.[73] In this way, the concerns of the WLM and the concerns of women in both the development sector and in the Global South can be seen to increasingly intersect.

This critique of development programs, and the exploration of gender issues in the politics of development and the Global South was sustained in *Spare Rib* in the 1970s and 1980s. Particular issues that arose as gendered concerns include the Nestlé baby milk controversy, which Tehila Sasson has written on as a key moment in transnational humanitarian campaigning that focused on remaking global markets into an ethical form of capitalism and transforming the image of "third world mothers" from passive recipients of charity into consumers with agency and choices.[74]

The Depo-Provera scandal was also covered in detail from a variety of different perspectives, with articles centering women's experiences and connecting, for example, the cases of women in Salford who had been given Depo-Provera alongside their German Measles jab, women in the East End and Glasgow being pushed to choose the injection for contraception, and women in the Global South who were not informed that the drug was still in the trial stages.[75] This approach highlights the importance of seeing the Depo-Provera scandal as a transnational struggle rather than only an issue affecting women in the Global South.[76] Rather than depicting women in India, for example, as helpless victims to be saved by British campaigners, this constructs women across the world as an oppressed class and reproduction as a site of this oppression.

General questions of family planning and broader debates around women's reproductive rights—in particular, access to abortion—are also covered repeatedly, in both "news" snippets and in longer features. There was a focus on stories about female-led activism in the Global South, which were explicitly political and presented through an anticolonial lens. This includes, for example, a long interview with Nawal el Saadawi conducted by Jill Nicholls in 1979 (and a follow-up piece in 1986); an article about Namibian women active in the South West African People's Association written by Akwe Amosu that begins "how readers receive this article may well depend on which 'side' of the colonising experience they relate to"; a piece by Madi Gray, the anti-apartheid activist, on female militants in Mozambique, Angola, and Guinea-Bissau, which included transcripts of meetings with women freedom fighters and their thoughts on the independence struggle; and an interview by Tsehai Berhane-Selassie with Gertrude Shope, a key figure in the ANC.[77]

"Spiritualists, ideologues, pragmatists, feminists, and women" | 133

International solidarity and more specifically conceptions of transnational sisterhood became a key issue for the magazine in the early 1980s, overlapping with their UN Decade for Women coverage, and shaped by debates about race within the WLM in Britain and a context in which women in the Global South were pushing to make their voices heard. A piece written in March 1983 by writer and broadcaster Roisin Boyd, a member of the *Spare Rib* collective, explored the concept of "Women's International Solidarity." Boyd's writing was shaped by her own experience as an Irish woman, who had written about her annoyance that her own political concerns about British violence and oppression in Ireland were not taken seriously by some of the white, middle-class, English writers on the *Spare Rib* staff.

In her piece, Boyd centered the lived experience and resulting expertise of women in the Global South, asking,

> Who should write about "other" women's struggles particularly those taking place in Third World or colonised countries? . . . Some feminists believe that although they don't have direct experience of being, say a woman living in a Third World country, they can—by virtue of their own political commitment to those struggles, and perhaps their own experiences in those countries—write and explain themselves what is taking place. Other feminists, and I count myself among them, believe that . . . it is the women who are taking part in particular struggles who should—at last—have their voices heard.[78]

She finished by asking, "How can solidarity be expressed if women's struggles in other countries are shown as being completely separate from those taking place in Britain, or that the only link is the fact that we are women!"[79] These questions were at the heart of feminist solidarity projects in the period and represent conversations ongoing at various levels of the British WLM.

Conclusions

In 1985, Tsehai Berhane-Selassie wrote a long piece entitled "International Sisterhood: What's on the agenda?," in which she highlighted the controversies of "development" at the end of the UN Decade for

Women.[80] She argued that, instead of being helped, "women in the Third World have been affected negatively" by development projects over the last four decades and, moreover, "western women working in the donor agencies have been patronising, racist and almost colonialist in their attitudes towards the Third World women." The piece offered an "update" on this relationship, arguing that international sisterhood had a *concrete* meaning for women in the developing world—women's self-help support schemes—and called for women in development agencies and female organizations like the British group "Change," who were often themselves marginalized, to join more effectively with women in the developing world to promote female self-sufficiency. Her concluding argument, that "Third World women" should not be "integrated" into the development process but should instead have their rights reasserted and their ability for self-sufficiency promoted, centered the voices of these women as well as challenging readers to rethink their own attitudes about the relationship between women around the globe.[81]

British feminist campaigning on international issues was not limited, of course, to the three UN conferences, and nor was engagement with the United Nations framed only through the Decade for Women. But the conceptualization of this period as one in which women's concerns and feminist politics could be centered and taken seriously empowered British women to conceive of their gender politics within a global activist framework. The 1983 *Spare Rib* "A to Z of Feminism," which covered a variety of topics relating to everyday feminism, featured "international sisterhood"—"feminism is NOT only relevant to Western women"—but also "imperialism"—"Britain, which no longer ranks as a world power, still lives on its memories of empire . . . clearly it's not compatible with feminism"—as well as topics such as "Ireland" and "Jewish women."[82] In this way, it exhibited a capacious understanding of what it meant to be a *Spare Rib* feminist and how this feminism connected to the wider community of women.

Sometimes British women's attempts at global solidarity or international sisterhood fell short of the mark. White British women, in particular, may well have been broadly sympathetic to these causes, but their understanding of race and empire was often superficial or partial. But it is also clear that many women in the WLM, and in *Spare Rib* as a collective, thought carefully and critically about British feminists' position in a global feminist movement. Women's history in Britain is often considered at a local or national level or, at most, within a transatlantic context, but we need to think critically too about other transnational connections. Interrogating silences about women around the world, as well as moments of connection, is an important step in building a nuanced and historically literate conception of British feminism and the women's liberation movement within a global context. It is also part of the process of claiming feminism as a transnational movement in political thought and action, with real and tangible effects the world over.

Notes

I would like to thank the editors of this volume for their enthusiastic support and careful edits, which made this piece so much better. Thanks also to the peer reviewers for their helpful suggestions. Finally, I'd like to thank Emma Lundin, who presented with me on the conference panel from which this paper was developed, for all her feminist solidarity and support.

    1. Tsehai Berhane-Selassie, "Decade Conference: A Soap Opera in the Sun?," *Spare Rib* 158 (September 1985): 18.

    2. Berhane-Selassie, "Decade Conference," 18.

    3. Berhane-Selassie, "Decade Conference," 18.

    4. Louise Kimpton Nye, "Introduction: Spare Rib—The First Nine Years." www.bl.uk/spare-rib/articles/introduction-spare-rib-the-first-nine-years

    5. Florence Binard, "The British Women's Liberation Movement in the 1970s: Redefining the Personal and the Political," *Revue Française de Civilisation Britannique* 22—Hors série (2017): 11.

    6. Berhane-Selassie, "Decade Conference," 18.

    7. Throughout this chapter, the term "Global South" is preferred to either "developing world" or "third world." Multiple theorists, beginning with Walter Rodney (*How Europe Underdeveloped Africa* [Revised edition. Washington, DC: Howard University Press, 1981]), have problematized the idea of "developed" and "developing" countries, both because it serves to elide the continuing legacies of imperialism and exploitation that have led to inequalities between nations, and because it assumes that all nations are on the same pathway to "development." The term "third world" is used in this chapter only when quoting from historical actors, although many feminists and other activists began to reclaim this term from the 1970s onward, and "third world feminism" has become an important strand in global feminist thought (Ranjoo Seodu Herr, "Reclaiming Third World Feminism: or Why Transnational Feminism Needs Third World Feminism." *Meridians* 12.1 [2014]: 1–30). The term "developing country" or "developing nation" is used, in quotation marks, in this chapter to reflect historical discourse, and occasionally to align with contemporary usage by the United Nations and other

international organizations such as the OECD when talking about these and similar issues. It is worth noting both that there is no single formalized list of which nations fit into the "developed" or "developing" categories, and that the United Nations has stated that "the designations 'developed' and 'developing' are intended for statistical convenience and do not necessarily express a judgment about the stage reached by a particular country or area in the development process" (United Nations Department for Economic and Social Information and Policy Analysis, Statistics Division. New York: United Nations, 1996), ii.

8. Martha Alter Chen, "Engendering World Conferences: The International Women's Movement and the United Nations," *Third World Quarterly* 16.3 (1995): 480; Kristen Ghodsee, "Revisiting the United Nations Decade for Women: Brief Reflections on Feminism, Capitalism and Cold War Politics in the Early Years of the International Women's Movement," *Women's Studies International Forum* 33 (2010): 4.

9. *Women in the United Nations: A United Nations Publication on the Occasion of the International Women's Year Based on a Panel Discussion Sponsored by the International Women's Year Secretariat . . . 9 December 1975* (New York: United Nations, 1977), 40.

10. Leticia Ramos Shahani, "The UN, Women, and Development: The World Conferences on Women," in eds. Arvonne S. Fraser and Irene Tinker, *Developing Power: How Women Transformed International Development* (New York: Feminist Press City University), 26–36.

11. Judith P. Zinsser, "From Mexico to Copenhagen to Nairobi: The United Nations Decade for Women, 1975–1985," *Journal of World History* 13.1 (Spring 2002): 140–143.

12. See, for example, Jeska Rees, "A Look Back at Anger: The Women's Liberation Movement in 1978," *Women's History Review* 19.3 (2010): 337–356.

13. For example, the relevant chapter in Martin Pugh, *Women and the Women's Movement in Britain since 1914* (Basingstoke: Palgrave, 2014), 260–294, includes very little engagement with international issues except for material covering Greenham Common (which is, itself, treated as rooted in British peace activism, rather than a moment connecting British WLM to a global context).

14. See Natalie Thomlinson, "The Colour of Feminism: White Feminists and Race in the Women's Liberation Movement," *History* 97.327 (2012): 453–475 for an exploration of the racial politics within which British WLM was framed; and Valerie Amos and Pratibha Parmar, "Challenging Imperial Feminism," *Feminist Review* 17 (July 1984): 3–19 for a critique of the postcolonial context of British WLM activism.

15. The United Nations' founding charter had set out the "equal rights of men and women" and the need to ensure respect for human rights "without distinction as to race, sex, language or religion." In 1946, the Commission on the Status of Women was established, alongside the Branch for the Advancement

of Women within the Department on Economic and Social Affairs; in 1948, the Declaration of Human Rights had further enshrined women's rights to human rights. But it was not until 1967 that the Declaration on the Elimination of Discrimination Against Women was adopted. This declaration was the precursor to the Convention on the Elimination of Discrimination Against Women (CEDAW), which was adopted by the General Assembly in 1979; in 1981, the Committee on the Elimination of Discrimination Against Women was established and has since been the main mechanism within the United Nations that works in support of women's rights. It has since been ratified by 189 countries, notably not including the United States. CEDAW is a global human rights treaty and, as such, requires the countries that have ratified it to put measures in place to work to eliminate discrimination against women.

16. Celia Donert, "Women's Rights in Cold War Europe: Disentangling Feminist Histories," *Past and Present* 218.8 (January 2013): 180–202.

17. And, as highlighted above, at this first conference the year became a decade.

18. Karen Garner, *Women and Gender in International History: Theory and Practice* (London: Bloomsbury, 2018), 124.

19. Judith P. Zinsser, "From Mexico to Copenhagen to Nairobi: The United Nations Decade for Women, 1975–1985," *Journal of World History* 13.1 (Spring 2002): 165.

20. Jocelyn Olcott, "Cold War Conflicts and Cheap Cabaret: Sexual Politics at the 1975 United Nations International Women's Year Conference," *Gender & History* 22.3 (November 2010): 735; Jocelyn Olcott, *International Women's Year: The Greatest Consciousness-Raising Event in History* (Oxford: Oxford University Press, 2017).

21. Olcott, *International Women's Years*, 44.

22. Kathleen Teltsch, "UN Wants It to Be More Than a 'Ladies' Meeting," *New York Times*, 10 May 1974.

23. Olcott, *International Women's Year*, 8.

24. Lois A. West, "The United Nations Conferences and Feminist Politics," in eds. Mary K. Meyer and Elizabeth Prügl, *Gender Politics in Global Governance* (Oxford: Rowman and Little Publishers, 1999), 178–179.

25. Olcott, *International Women's Year*, 5.

26. West, "The United Nations Conferences and Feminist Politics," 180–192.

27. Cynthia Enloe, *The Curious Feminist: Searching for Women in a New Age of Empire* (London: University of California Press, 2004), 3.

28. Deborah Withers, "Theorising the Women's Liberation Movement as Cultural Heritage," *Women's History Review* 25.5 (2016): 847–862.

29. Kimpton Nye, "Introduction: Spare Rib." www.bl.uk/spare-rib/articles/introduction-spare-rib-the-first-nine-years

30. Laurel Forster, "Spreading the Word: Feminist Print Cultures and the Women's Liberation Movement," *Women's History Review* 25.5 (2016): 812.

31. More research could be done to compare *Spare Rib* with *Ms.* magazine, which was launched in the same year in the United States and occupied a similar conceptual space in the American feminist movement as *Spare Rib* did in the British. There are some striking similarities—both magazines focused on women's personal-as-political stories, both were instrumental in both documenting but also creating the myths around the two feminist movements, and both struggled to reconcile white, middle-class feminism with the concerns of women of color and working-class women, with *Ms.* as well as *Spare Rib* critiqued for its lack of diversity and representation. However, a big contrast between the two publications is their production values and (connected) financial status: *Spare Rib* sat within a British DIY and "zine" culture and perpetually ran out of money (often relying on volunteers and donations), whereas *Ms.* had its first issue as an insert in the *New York* Magazine and was supported by Warner Communications until 1978 when it became a not-for-profit publication until it was bought in 1987 by Fairfax, an Australian media company (it later returned to a feminist nonprofit organization). For more on *Ms.*, see Abigail Pogrebin, "How Do You Spell Ms.," *New York Magazine*, 28 October 2011, https://nymag.com/news/features/ms-magazine-2011-11; Amy Erdman Farrell, "From a Tarantula on a Banana Boat to a Canary in a Mine: 'Ms. Magazine' as a Cautionary Tale in a Neoliberal Age," *Tulsa Studies in Women's Literature* 30.2 (2011): 393–405.

32. Sue Bruley and Laurel Forster, "Historicising the Women's Liberation Movement," *Women's History Review* 25.5 (2016): 697.

33. See, for example, Terese Jonsson, "The Narrative Reproduction of White Feminist Racism," *Feminist Review* 113.1 (July 2016): 50–67, which explores some of the contemporary issues that arise when the colonial history and context to British feminist activism are not acknowledged or interrogated.

34. See, for example, Antoinette Burton, "The White Woman's Burden: British Feminists and the Indian Women, 1865–1915," *Women's Studies International Forum* 13.4 (1990): 295–308; Chieko Ichikawa, "Jane Eyre's Daughters: The Feminist Missions of Mary Carpenter and Josephine Butler in India," *Women's History Review* 23.2 (2014): 220–238.

35. This approach is significantly influenced by Kimberlé Crenshaw, "Demarginalizing the Intersection of Race and Sex: A Black Feminist Critique of Antidiscrimination Doctrine, Feminist Theory and Antiracist Politics," *University of Chicago Legal Forum* (1989): 139–168.

36. "Some Are More Equal than Others with the UN Family!," *Spare Rib* 20 (February 1974): 27.

37. *Women in the United Nations*.

38. Helen McCarthy, *Women of the World*, 308.

39. Helen McCarthy, "The Diplomatic History of Global Women's Rights: The British Foreign Office and International Women's Year, 1975," *Journal of Contemporary History*, 50.4 (2015): 842–843.

40. Jenny Rathbone, "International Women's Year: Three Views," *Spare Rib* 39 (September 1975): 26; McCarthy, "The Diplomatic History of Global Women's Rights," 846.

41. Rathbone, "International Women's Year: Three Views," 26.

42. Amiya Rao, "International Women's Year: Three Views," *Spare Rib* 39 (September 1975): 27.

43. Jocelyn Olcott, "Cold War Conflicts and Cheap Cabaret: Sexual Politics at the 1975 United Nations International Women's Year Conference' *Gender & History* 22.3 (November 2010): 735.

44. Charlotte Bunch and Frances Doughty, "International Women's Year: Three Views," *Spare Rib* 39 (September 1975): 28.

45. This was confirmed by Sally Alexander as an issue that had limited British WLM participation in the Mexico City conference and future UN Decade for Women events, in conversation with the author at the New Directions in the History of the British Women's Liberation Movement: Rethinking 1970s Feminisms conference, All Souls, Oxford, 4 December 2017.

46. McCarthy, "Diplomatic History of Global Women's Rights," 843–844.

47. Jill Nicholls, "United Nations Notices Women," *Spare Rib* 98 (September 1980): 9–16.

48. Nicholls, "United Nations Notices Women," 9.

49. Nicholls, "United Nations Notices Women," 9.

50. Nicholls, "United Nations Notices Women," b9–10.

51. Jill Nicholls, "Come On, Our Side," *Spare Rib* 98 (September 1980): 13.

52. The United Kingdom eventually signed up to CEDAW in July 1981, although it was not ratified until April 1986.

53. Nicholls, "Come On, Our Side," 13.

54. Nicholls, "United Nations Notices Women," 13.

55. Nicholls, "United Nations Notices Women," 9–16.

56. Nicholls, "United Nations Notices Women," 9–16.

57. Nicholls, "United Nations Notices Women," 16.

58. Erin Stuart, "Feminist Link in the UN Chain," *Spare Rib* 148 (November 1984): 10.

59. Georgina Ashworth, "Asking Women but Not Feminists," *Spare Rib* 147 (October 1984): 13–14.

60. Berhane-Selassie, "Decade Conference," 16–21.

61. Berhane-Selassie, "Decade Conference," 21.

62. Berhane-Selassie, "Decade Conference," 21.

63. Berhane-Selassie, "Decade Conference," 21.

64. Berhane-Selassie, "Decade Conference," 21.

65. Berhane-Selassie, "Decade Conference," 16–21.

66. Mary K. Meyer, "WILPF: Organising Women for Peace in the War System," in eds. Mary K Meyer and Elizabeth Prügl, *Gender Politics in Global Governance* (Rowman and Little Publishers, Oxford: 1999), 112.

67. Berhane-Selassie, "Decade Conference," 19.

68. Berhane-Selassie, "Decade Conference," 20.

69. Berhane-Selassie, "Decade Conference," 21.

70. See, for example, John Rapley, "Development Studies and the Post-Development Critique," *Progress in Development Studies* 4.4 (2004): 350–354; Jan Nederveen Pieterse, "After Post-Development," *Third World Quarterly* 21.2 (April 2000): 175–191. For critiques of development from an explicitly feminist perspective, see Margarita Aguinaga, Miriam Lang, Dunia Mokrani, Alejandra Santillana, "Critiques and Alternatives to Development: A Feminist Perspective," in eds. M. Lang and D. Mokrani, *Beyond Development: Alternative Visions from Latin America* (Fundación Rosa Luxemburg, 2013). 41–60.

71. Barbara Rogers, "Development: A Man's World," *Spare Rib* 70 (May 1978): 32–33.

72. Rogers, "Development: A Man's World," 32–33.

73. Barbara Rogers, "Discrimination in Development," *Spare Rib* 100 (November 1980): 45–48.

74. Tehila Sasson, "Milking the Third World? Humanitarianism, Capitalism, and the Moral Economy of the Nestlé Boycott," *American Historical Review* 121.4 (October 2016), 1196–1224; "Third World: Powdered Milk Kills," *Spare Rib* 34 (April 1975): 26; "Powdered Milk Kills: Nestlé Sues Third World Campaigners," *Spare Rib* 36 (June 1975): 20.

75. "Depo Provera: 3rd World Women Not told This Contraceptive Is Trial," *Spare Rib* 42 (January 1976): 22–23; "'Better a Woman Gets Cancer in 30 Years than Pregnant Now.' Depo Provera in Use," *Spare Rib* 69 (April 1978): 28.

76. For more detail on the Depo Provera scandal, see Emily Callaci, "'Injectable Development': Depo-Provera and the Creation of the Global South," *Radical History Review* 131 (2018) 82–104.

77. Akwe Amosu, "Namibian Women Fight for Freedom," *Spare Rib* 135 (October 1983): 49–50; Madi Gray, "Women Militants: Mozambique, Angola and Guinea Bissau," *Spare Rib* 26 (August 1974); Tsehai Berhane-Selassie, "Diamonds Mean Nothing to Us!," *Spare Rib* 163 (February 1986): 36–39.

78. Roisin Boyd, "Women's International Solidarity," *Spare Rib* 128 (March 1983): 18.

79. Boyd, "Women's International Solidarity," 18.

80. Tsehai Berhane-Selassie, "International Sisterhood: What's on the Agenda?," *Spare Rib* 152 (March 1985): 8–9.

81. Berhane-Selassie, "International Sisterhood," 8–9.

82. "A to Z of Feminism," *Spare Rib* 137 (December 1983): 27–30.

Works Cited

Articles

Amos, Valerie, and Pratibha Parmar. "Challenging Imperial Feminism." *Feminist Review* 17 (July 1984): 3–19.

Bruley, Sue, and Laurel Forster. "Historicising the Women's Liberation Movement." *Women's History Review* 25.5 (2016): 697–700.

Burton, Antoinette. "The White Woman's Burden: British Feminists and the Indian Women, 1865–1915." *Women's Studies International Forum* 13.4 (1990): 295–308.

Callaci, Emily. "'Injectable Development': Depo-Provera and the Creation of the Global South." *Radical History Review* 131 (2018): 82–104.

Chen, Martha Alter. "Engendering World Conferences: The International Women's Movement and the United Nations." *Third World Quarterly* 16.3 (1995): 477–493.

Crenshaw, Kimberlé. "Demarginalizing the Intersection of Race and Sex: A Black Feminist Critique of Antidiscrimination Doctrine, Feminist Theory and Antiracist Politics." *University of Chicago Legal Forum* (1989): 139–168.

Donert, Celia. "Women's Rights in Cold War Europe: Disentangling Feminist Histories." *Past and Present* 218.8 (January 2013): 180–202.

Farrell, Amy Erdman. "From a Tarantula on a Banana Boat to a Canary in a Mine: 'Ms. Magazine' as a Cautionary Tale in a Neoliberal Age." *Tulsa Studies in Women's Literature* 30.2 (2011): 393–405.

Forster, Laurel. "Spreading the Word: Feminist Print Cultures and the Women's Liberation Movement." *Women's History Review* 25.5 (2016): 812–831.

Ghodsee, Kristen. "Revisiting the United Nations Decade for Women: Brief Reflections on Feminism, Capitalism and Cold War Politics in the Early Years of the International Women's Movement." *Women's Studies International Forum* 33 (2010): 3–12.

Herr, Ranjoo Seodu. "Reclaiming Third World Feminism: or Why Transnational Feminism Needs Third World Feminism." *Meridians* 12.1 (2014): 1–30.

Ichikawa, Chieko. "Jane Eyre's Daughters: The Feminist Missions of Mary Carpenter and Josephine Butler in India." *Women's History Review* 23.2 (2014): 220–238.

Jonsson, Terese. "The Narrative Reproduction of White Feminist Racism." *Feminist Review* 113.1 (July 2016): 50–67.

McCarthy, Helen. "The Diplomatic History of Global Women's Rights: The British Foreign Office and International Women's Year, 1975." *Journal of Contemporary History* 50.4 (2015): 833–853.

Nederveen Pieterse, Jan. "After Post-Development." *Third World Quarterly* 21.2 (April 2000): 175–191.

Olcott, Jocelyn. "Cold War Conflicts and Cheap Cabaret: Sexual Politics at the 1975 United Nations International Women's Year Conference." *Gender & History* 22.3 (November 2010): 733–754.

Rapley, John. "Development Studies and the Post-development Critique." *Progress in Development Studies* 4.4 (2004): 350–354.

Rees, Jeska. "A Look Back at Anger: The Women's Liberation Movement in 1978." *Women's History Review* 19.3 (2010): 337–356.

Sasson, Tehila. "Milking the Third World? Humanitarianism, Capitalism, and the Moral Economy of the Nestlé Boycott." *American Historical Review* 121.4 (October 2016): 1196–1224.

Thomlinson, Natalie, "The Colour of Feminism: White Feminists and Race in the Women's Liberation Movement." *History* 97.327 (2012): 453–475.

Withers, Deborah, "Theorising the Women's Liberation Movement *as* Cultural Heritage." *Women's History Review* 25.5 (2016): 847–862.

Zinsser, Judith P. "From Mexico to Copenhagen to Nairobi: The United Nations Decade for Women, 1975–1985." *Journal of World History* 13.1 (Spring 2002): 139–168.

Chapters in Edited Collections

Aguinaga, Margarita, Miriam Lang, Dunia Mokrani, and Alejandra Santillana. "Critiques and Alternatives to Development: A Feminist Perspective," in *Beyond Development: Alternative Visions from Latin America*, eds. M. Lang and D. Mokrani. Quito, Ecuador: Fundación Rosa Luxemburg, 2013. 41–60.

Meyer, Mary K. "WILPF: Organising Women for Peace in the War System," in *Gender Politics in Global Governance*, eds. Mary K Meyer and Elizabeth Prügle. Oxford: Rowman and Little Publishers, 1999. 107–121.

Ramos Shahani, Leticia. "The UN, Women, and Development: The World Conferences on Women," in *Developing Power: How Women Transformed International Development*, eds. Arvonne S. Fraser and Irene Tinker. New York: Feminist Press City University, 2004. 26–36.

West, Lois A. "The United Nations Conferences and Feminist Politics," in *Gender Politics in Global Governance*, eds. Mary K. Meyer and Elizabeth Prügl. Oxford: Rowman and Little Publishers, 1999. 177–196.

Books

Enloe, Cynthia. *The Curious Feminist: Searching for Women in a New Age of Empire*. London: University of California Press, 2004.

Fraser, Arvonne S., and Irene Tinker, eds. *Developing Power: How Women Transformed International Development*. New York: Feminist Press City University, 2004.

Garner, Karen. *Women and Gender in International History: Theory and Practice.* London: Bloomsbury, 2018.
McCarthy, Helen. *Women of the World.* London: Bloomsbury, 2014.
Meyer, Mary K., and Elizabeth Prügl, eds. *Gender Politics in Global Governance.* Oxford: Rowman and Little Publishers, 1999.
Olcott, Jocelyn. *International Women's Year: The Greatest Consciousness-Raising Event in History.* Oxford: Oxford University Press, 2017.
Pugh, Martin. *Women and the Women's Movement in Britain since 1914.* Basingstoke: Palgrave, 2014.
Rodney, Walter. *How Europe Underdeveloped Africa.* Revised edition. Washington, DC: Howard University Press, 1981. [Originally published in 1973]
United Nations Department for Economic and Social Information and Policy Analysis, Statistics Division. Standard Country or Area Codes for Statistical Use. New York: United Nations, 1996.

Websites

Binard, Florence. "The British Women's Liberation Movement in the 1970s: Redefining the Personal and the Political," *Revue Française de Civilisation Britannique [Online]*, 22—Hors série 2017. http://journals.openedition.org/rfcb/1688; doi:10.4000/rfcb.1688
Kimpton Nye, Louise. "Introduction: Spare Rib—The First Nine Years." www.bl.uk/spare-rib/articles/introduction-spare-rib-the-first-nine-years
Pogrebin, Abigail. "How Do You Spell Ms.," *New York Magazine*, 28 October 2011. https://nymag.com/news/features/ms-magazine-2011-11

III
Families, Reproduction, and Health

Making Queer Families
Foster Family Activism in Los Angeles, 1977–1985

Nora Kassner

In 1985, Los Angeles County was the heart of an unlikely revolution in queer family life. At the beginning of the 1980s, "queer" and "parent" seemed like oxymorons; queer people regularly lost custody of their children in divorce proceedings, and alternative ways of becoming parents such as adoption were unthinkable.[1] By the end of the decade, queer parents across the county frequently won legal recognition of their families—whether these families had come together by birth, foster care, adoption, or artificial insemination.[2] The increasing recognition of queer families grew from a series of policy shifts across the United States, as queer activists pushed cities, counties, and states to sanction queer parents.

Despite its prominent gayborhood, West Hollywood, Los Angeles County was an improbable place for a queer family revolution to take place. Los Angeles, after all, was the home of another 1980s revolution: the Reagan Revolution. President Reagan considered L.A. his adoptive hometown, and Reaganesque conservatives had taken control of the Los Angeles County Board of Supervisors. Three of the five members of the Board of Supervisors were Republicans, and a fourth—as a former staff member recalls—refused to support "even the most basic things to do with LGBT rights."[3] Despite this conservative climate, in 1985 Los Angeles County created its first legal recognition of queer families by allowing openly lesbian and gay people to become foster parents. This recognition opened doors to many other milestones, including the expansion of queer parenting through adoption, and the start of a new era in queer activism that centered family issues.

The story of queer foster parenting in Los Angeles County emphasizes the role of contingency in the transformation of US family policy in the late twentieth century. To some historians, this was a period of either conservative or neoliberal ascendancy, in which policymakers stripped away basic protections from families and made parenting a class privilege.[4] To others, the story of queer parenting seems a tale of liberation, as queer people made increasingly successful claims to a right to parent.[5] Neither narrative, however, adequately explains changes to the foster system. Foster care in the United States is a system of last resort, both for families and for policymakers. When children in the 1970s and 1980s fell through the widening cracks in the US welfare state—when governments cut assistance for families, or when children ran away from or were removed from unsupportive families—the foster system was often the only government program that remained to take them in.[6] Thus, expansions of foster parenting in this period reflected the new, or increasingly pressing, social problems governments were trying to address. As policymakers grappled with the growth of the foster system, their decisions were often pragmatic and experimental—not the result of any grand plan.

Why did Los Angeles County make the unlikely decision to authorize lesbian and gay foster parenting? The immediate answer is that authorizing queer foster parenting allowed the county to avoid the potential consequences of a lawsuit. The lawsuit, however, is the end of the story, not its beginning. Instead, the decision to authorize queer foster parents began a decade earlier in political wrangling over two critical issues: how cities should address a growing homelessness crisis, and how LGBTQ activists could succeed in winning rights from often hostile governments. Queer foster parenting became a reality in Los Angeles County because multiple pressures converged at the perfect moment. The growth of youth homelessness placed pressure on county officials to find solutions to the homeless "problem." Queer activists built institutions with the capacity to present themselves as this solution. Closeted queer and queer-friendly county employees pushed to change county policies from the inside—all the while terrified they would be found and fired. In 1984, a chance encounter between two children and a police officer in Pasadena made these forces converge, and queer family life in Los Angeles County changed irrevocably.

The Rise of Youth Homelessness

The journey toward gay and lesbian foster parenting in Los Angeles County began with a seemingly unrelated policy decision. In 1977, California Governor Jerry Brown signed into law Assembly Bill 3121, a collection of juvenile justice reforms. One of the reforms redefined what it meant when a teen ran away from home. Before 1977, the state considered running away a criminal act. Officers who found runaway youth arrested them, and the youth usually ended up in juvenile correctional facilities. Under AB 3121, runaway teens became "children [with] personal or family problems" rather than criminals, and the state began to encourage "community responsibility to establish alternative programs" that would support runaways without incarcerating them.[7]

AB 3121 had unintended consequences. Throughout the 1970s, both California and federal officials worried about an apparent rise in youth homelessness. While many blamed rising divorce rates and alcoholism for family instability, economics may offer another explanation. As families grappled with poverty in the wake of the 1973–1975 recession, teens were pushed away from families that could not support them.[8] Although AB 3121 meant that these teens were no longer incarcerated, few of the "alternative programs" promised in the bill were in place. As a result, many teens who once would have been incarcerated began living on the streets. Alarmed by the increased presence of homeless youth, policy-makers became invested in getting teens off the streets. The California legislature developed a mixed approach to curbing youth homelessness, emphasizing both short-term coping measures and long-term solutions. The legislature funded hotlines, emergency shelters, and medical programs to support youth while they were homeless. To end their homelessness, the legislature funded efforts to find permanent living arrangements.[9]

As part of their long-term housing strategy, the California legislature turned, as it often had before, to the foster system. When police officers or service providers identified homeless youth, they worked with county social workers to find foster families.[10] Foster parents received a small stipend from the county to provide for youths' basic needs, and they were responsible for keeping children fed, clothed, enrolled in school, and home at night.[11] There was a problem, however, with making foster care a solution to the homeless youth problem; counties across the state could not find enough foster parents. In 1984, the *Los Angeles Times* reported that there were only 3,100 licensed foster families for over 8,000 foster children in the county, and foster homes "have been lost faster than they have been replaced." Unable to find foster parents, caseworkers resorted to putting beds for foster youth in offices and hallways. The newspapers called it a crisis, and everyone—from high-level administrators to caseworkers to journalists—made it clear that the county needed to find more foster parents.[12]

The desperate need for foster parents became the first factor in the creation of queer foster parenting. In 1977, Assembly Bill 3121 seemed a perfect solution to a problem: the incarceration of youth who had run away from home. After the bill's passage, it quickly became clear that this solution had created two new problems of its own: a large, visible homeless youth population, and an overburdened foster system. Even as policymakers recognized they needed new solutions for these new problems, they were unsure who would provide the solution. In Los Angeles County, the West Hollywood queer community worked to convince the county that they had the right, and the means, to take on this issue. Their activism brought queer foster parenting to the table at the county and developed the infrastructure to act upon its eventual authorization.

A Queer Approach to Youth Homelessness

By 1981, an estimated three thousand runaway homeless youth lived on the streets of West Hollywood alone.[13] There, they came into contact with an organized network of queer activists, who crafted an alternative explanation for youth homelessness. While federal and state officials blamed family instability, queer activists blamed homophobia, arguing that many of the teens were queer youth who had run away from or been thrown out of unsupportive homes. Albert J. Ogle, who served as Youth Director and Interim Director for the Los Angeles Gay and Lesbian Community Services Center from 1983 to 1985, describes the increased visibility of queer "street youth" in the late 1970s and early 1980s. "The boys," Ogle recalls, "were on Santa Monica, the girls were on Sunset . . . Because of homophobia and lack of support in the schools and in the churches and so on, their only way out was to leave. So they'd go to the coasts, they'd go to New York, they'd go to L.A., San Francisco. They'd have no education, no social skills, they would get involved in survival prostitution."[14]

As West Hollywood queer activists developed the narrative that homophobia was behind the rise of queer youth homelessness, their selective depiction of queer youth allowed them to argue that their shared queer identity made them the ideal service providers to care for these youth. By emphasizing queerness, activists rendered other identities—most significantly race—invisible in their account of youth homelessness. While the majority of queer activists who took on queer youth homelessness were white, it is difficult to know much about the youth with whom they sought to work. One summary of queer homeless youth activists had placed in foster care in 1986–1987 lists roughly half of the youth as white and half as "Hispanic." Activists' publicity material and contemporary news coverage, however, routinely emphasized teens' sexuality without mentioning race.[15]

Activists' silence around race and queer youth homelessness reflected a broader trend at the Gay and Lesbian Community Services Center (called "the Center"), the white-dominated organization through which activists initially tackled queer youth homelessness. Founded in 1971, the Center grew out of the Gay Liberation Front's belief that homophobia and oppression were killing queer communities. By creating a space for both physical health services and political organizing, Center founders sought to combat oppression. Providing services, however, required financial support from the state and local governments activists critiqued. As Katie Batza, who writes on AIDS in the US Heartland in this volume, has previously shown, the Center gradually separated social services from political organizing over the course of the 1970s in an effort to win and retain state funding.[16]

Toward the end of the decade, the Center began to craft a social service program targeting queer homeless youth. Board President Terry DeCrescenzo first became aware that youth were running away from home because they were queer in the early 1970s. DeCrescenzo worked at a county juvenile facility, at which many inmates were homeless teens. She noticed that court reports often mentioned that teens had engaged in "chickbutt" (homosexual) activity, and teens also talked in group therapy about their queer desires. As DeCrescenzo became more involved in the Center in the late 1970s, she saw addressing the needs of nonincarcerated queer homeless youth as a natural extension of her professional work.[17] To fund the Center's planned services, DeCrescenzo, Executive Director Steve Schulte, and Youth Director Joe Thompson made a case to the

L.A. County Board of Supervisors that the Center was the best possible organization to take on youth homelessness for the county.[18]

They faced an unfriendly audience. Rob Saltzman, who worked for Supervisor Ed Edelman, remembers that Edelman was the only supervisor willing to meet with openly queer people. As for the other supervisors, "they were just disrespectful. They essentially viewed LGBT people as unprofessional . . . As far as I know, there were not meetings where they sat down with leaders of the community."[19] In order to work around other supervisors' refusal to address queer issues, activists built a close relationship with Supervisor Edelman. Albert Ogle, who became the Center's Youth Director in 1983 and Interim Executive Director in 1985, credits Edelman with enabling the Center to address queer youth homelessness. Edelman, he says, "was the advocate. He would break through for the Center getting established . . . He opened a lot of doors."[20] Edelman found creative ways to work around the resistance of the other supervisors. To pass a policy, three supervisors had to vote for it. Given four of the five supervisors' disregard for queer people, this was not going to happen. Nevertheless, supervisors had latitude to propose policies that affected only their own district, and other supervisors generally supported these policies. Edelman began to propose county funding for the Center as district-specific grants, and the other supervisors "would look the other way and vote for it."[21]

The first county grants paved the way for the Center to begin addressing queer youth homelessness in West Hollywood. At first, activists focused on short-term, ameliorative programs such as providing food, medical care, and a clothes closet.[22] Activists used these programs to demonstrate to the county that the queer community could provide effective services. Albert Ogle remembers that the Board of Supervisors begrudgingly came to accept that, even if these programs were run by queer people, they were working. To supervisors, the Center became "this crucible of innovation . . . Our programs were excellent. We could show that we were delivering . . . So it made them look good."[23]

From the start, Center board members were interested in offering more than just ameliorative programs. They were also invested in creating long-term homes for queer runaways. Terry DeCrescenzo spearheaded these efforts, and her first plan was to place youth with foster families. DeCrescenzo believed that queer foster homes offered youth the best chance of being part of "one big happy family."[24] Queer foster parents, she argued, could effectively replace the nuclear families teens lost when they ran away from or were thrown out of home. At this point, she saw no downsides to this arrangement; DeCrescenzo earnestly believed that queer foster parents and queer foster children needed each other, and their mutual need would allow them to build healthy relationships.[25]

In 1979, DeCrescenzo and the Center began pushing the county to authorize queer foster parents. Attorney Susan McGreivy contacted Supervisor Edelman on behalf of the Center, asking whether L.A. County would consider licensing queer foster parents. Edelman asked the County Counsel, who informed him that the county had no "official opinion per se," but in practice they would not place youth with queer foster parents.[26] The Counsel stated that Los Angeles County had a "high duty of care . . . in making suitable placements of children to foster homes." In 1970, the Counsel explained, Orange County had lost a civil suit after a foster child had been abused in a foster home. Taking an enormous logical leap, the County Counsel implied that placing children with queer foster parents in L.A. County would likely lead to similar incidents of child abuse: "Because the homosexuality of proposed foster parents is a factor that may be considered and because of the risks of liability inherent in placing dependent wards of the juvenile court in homosexual foster care, we continue in our belief that such placement, at best, would be unwise and could lead to almost unlimited liability by the County."[27]

The County Counsel's assumption that queer people would abuse foster children drew upon a newly popular stereotype of the gay pedophile. Although "moral panics" about child abuse had periodically reoccurred since the 1930s, there was no particular association between queer people and pedophilia. As queer movements gained public visibility over the course of the 1970s, however, the gay pedophile stereotype emerged as a conservative counter-discourse to gay liberation. By the time the L.A. County Counsel weighed in on queer foster parents in 1979, medical, psychological, and popular literature codified the idea that most or all queer people, especially gay men, were threats to children.[28] Drawing on this stereotype, the County Counsel reinforced the idea that queer people were inherently unfit to parent. Their assumption stood in direct opposition to activists' belief in the benefits of a queer family. Rather than positive role models for teens who needed to replace the families they had lost, the county perceived queer foster parents as a threat to children.

The resounding opposition from the County Counsel, and the homophobic rationale the county employed, signaled to DeCrescenzo and other Center board members that they were unlikely to win authorization of queer foster parents anytime soon. Instead, they focused their attention on operating group foster homes for queer youth. Ed Boyle, a local activist, had opened a group home serving six youth at a time in 1976, and there was always a long waiting list. After Boyle's group home closed in late 1980 or early 1981, DeCrescenzo led the Center's efforts to create a new home.[29] Unlike in the case of foster homes, L.A. county officials were open to the idea that group home operators could be queer. Officials indicated to the Center that they were in "dire need" of a group home for queer youth, because "few people have been willing to take such children." The county also considered these teens' sexual orientations as a sign that they were "emotionally disabled" and in need of specialized care. Additionally, the county perceived group homes as professional operations, while foster homes were seen as more intimate, familial arrangements.[30] Thus, group homes were a more natural extension of the professional services the Center was already providing through its medical care, food pantry, and clothes closet.[31] DeCrescenzo would go on to leave the Center and found her own organization, Gay and Lesbian Adolescent Social Services (GLASS), which operated three state-licensed group homes, each serving between six and twelve queer and trans youth at a time.[32]

Terry DeCrescenzo believes that group homes served an important function, even if they were not the solution she originally wanted. In retrospect, she sees her conviction that foster homes would create happy families for all queer homeless youth as "my own little fantasy land." For many youth, foster families were the right fit. Others, DeCrescenzo believes, were better suited to group homes than foster families. She describes some of the teens she worked with over the years as "more emotionally damaged and unable to live in a foster home . . . They had to have the professionalism, but professional distance, of staff rather than a loving foster parent. That was a hard lesson for me to learn."[33]

DeCrescenzo's argument in favor of group homes is in sharp contrast to her initial idealism about foster families. In her description, DeCrescenzo uses, but redeploys, the label "emotionally disabled" that the county applied to queer teens. Rather than considering teens "emotionally disabled" because they were gay, DeCrescenzo argues they were "damaged" because they had been "so abused and ignored and diminished by their own parents."[34] Even though she blames the damage on homophobia rather than homosexuality, the use of the term "damaged" to describe teens hints that queer activists may have held stigmatizing views about the homeless youth they served. Additionally, DeCrescenzo's words of caution about seeing foster families as a universal solution for queer youth are striking in comparison to the idealism she and other activists felt in the late 1970s. Throughout the 1970s and into the 1980s, they continued to see queer foster parents as the ideal solution to the queer youth homelessness problem, even if they suspected that the county would not allow them to try their solution anytime soon.

Breaking the Rules

By the early 1980s, queer activists had largely stopped trying to force the county to authorize foster families. Nevertheless, even as activists shifted their attention to group homes, a few queer people became foster parents in L.A. County. In the early 1980s, queer activists learned that some social workers were willing to ignore county policy, license openly queer foster parents, and place children in their care—as long as they were not caught. Albert Ogle remembers that he and other Center staff members discovered that certain social workers were making "under-the-table" placements of foster youth with queer foster parents.[35] It was one of these under-the-table foster arrangements that led to the lawsuit that would eventually change county policy for all queer people who wanted to become foster parents.

It is unclear why some social workers began placing youth with queer foster parents. It is possible they were simply overworked and willing to accept any prospective foster parent they could find. By the 1980s, the youth homelessness crisis, coupled with other pressures such as the recession early in the decade, was making social workers' lives much more difficult. They had more children than ever in their caseloads, and supervisors were pressuring them to find foster parents quickly. The *Los Angeles Times* described one social worker who had over forty children in her caseload and "had not found the time" to look for foster parents for all of them.[36] Overwhelmed by these pressures, social workers may have been willing to place foster children with formally unacceptable foster parents (such as queer people) in order to make progress on their cases.

Another possible explanation is that placing foster children with foster parents was a deliberate choice by social workers who wanted to change county policy. Both DeCrescenzo, who worked for the county in the 1970s and early 1980s, and Rob Saltzman, Supervisor Edelman's staffer, describe the difficulty of being queer or queer-friendly as an

L.A. County employee. When DeCrescenzo was working at the county juvenile facility, her boss repeatedly warned, "if any staff member was ever found to be a homosexual, they'd be fired."[37] Even though Rob Saltzman worked for the only queer-friendly supervisor in the county and addressed queer issues, he also felt he could not be open about his sexuality at work. Saltzman credits his hesitation about coming out to, "in retrospect, my own fear, my unfounded fear of some horrible thing happening if I came out."[38] Even talking to a queer person could be dangerous. After DeCrescenzo came out, she realized her colleagues were afraid to be seen with her. One colleague, a closeted gay psychologist, approached DeCrescenzo one day and said, "Well, I guess I'm out now." When DeCrescenzo asked why, he replied, "Well, because people see me talking to you." DeCrescenzo exclaimed, "Oh, is that the idea? You talk to me, and that's the scarlet letter? Scarlet G, gay, on your shoulder or forehead or something?" Over time, the number of closeted queer county employees DeCrescenzo knew grew, but the homophobic atmosphere of the county did not change.[39]

The presence of these closeted employees within the county suggests that some social workers may have actively disagreed with the County Counsel's belief that queer people were inherently unfit to parent minors. Given the overwhelmingly homophobic environment of the county, in which being gay—or even being seen talking to a gay person—could potentially lead to firing, these social workers would likely not have felt comfortable openly breaking the county's preferred practice of discrimination. Their quiet decisions to do so may have amounted to a subtle rebellion against the county's homophobic climate. At this point, these explanations are purely speculative. Whatever their reasons, by the 1980s some social workers were breaking the county's unofficial ban on queer foster parents. Their decision to do so, coupled with the earlier pressures on the county from the growth of youth homelessness and the development of an activist queer community, created the perfect environment in which one chance encounter forced policy to change.

Changing Foster Policy in Los Angeles County

The chance encounter that changed L.A. County policy occurred one evening in 1984, when two boys decided to go see a movie. As they were walking down the street in Pasadena, a police officer stopped them.

It is unclear why the officer initially stopped the boys; the officer may have suspected the boys of sex work (a common assumption about queer youth), or if the boys were Black or Latinx, the officer's conduct could have been part of a broader pattern of racialized policing. Whatever the reason he stopped them, the officer began questioning the boys. They told the police officer they lived with their foster mother, Rosalee Sorenson. Sorenson was one of the queer people who had benefitted from social workers' quiet decisions to license queer foster parents despite the county's ban. First licensed in 1981, by 1984 Sorenson had cared for sixteen foster children. She reported that most of her foster children called her home "the best place they've ever been in," and she had never had a complaint from her foster children or their social workers. That changed on this particular night, because, after ascertaining that the boys lived with a foster mother, the police officer asked them what she did for a living. The boys responded that she worked for *Frontiers*, a magazine that covered queer news and entertainment, and that—like most queer publications of the era—sold ad space to escort services and phone sex hotlines.[40]

When the police officer heard the boys' response, things spiraled quickly. Drawing upon the familiar stereotype of the gay pedophile, the officer asked them whether they were being sexually assaulted in Sorenson's home. Whether because he knew about *Frontiers'* ad content, or was suspicious of any queer-affirming publication, he also claimed that Sorenson was exposing children to pornography. Although the officer let the boys go home that night, the Department of Social Services began to make the same claims and quickly removed Sorenson's foster children. Within four days, the older boy's social worker began to regret his decision to remove the child. The social worker called his decision "stupid," and said he was willing to put the child back with Sorenson. The younger child's social worker, as well as their supervisors at the county, refused to return the children to Sorenson.[41]

Seeking to have her foster children returned, Rosalee Sorenson worked with the ACLU to prepare a lawsuit against Los Angeles County, alleging that the county had violated California's Unruh Civil Rights Act.[42] Unruh, passed in 1959, guaranteed all California citizens equal treatment in "business establishments," regardless of "race, color, religion, ancestry, or national origin."[43] Beginning in the 1970s, civil rights attorneys expanded Unruh to guarantee equal treatment for queer people. By 1984, courts had ruled that, under Unruh, "homosexuals, as a class, are protected from arbitrary discrimination." They had determined that queer people had a right to frequent bars and restaurants and use public utilities, and that landlords could not refuse to rent to queer people.[44] Sorenson's suit stretched Unruh to new territory. Previous rulings had applied to privately owned businesses and public utilities. Sorenson's suit asked the Los Angeles Superior Court to apply the same standard to Los Angeles County, treating it as a "business establishment" subject to Unruh's purview and to consider providing foster care akin to receiving a service from this "business." If Sorenson and the ACLU won, their case could amount to a nondiscrimination ordinance for Los Angeles County, banning the county from discriminating against queer people.

Perhaps worried about the ramifications of losing the case, the County Counsel chose to settle out of court. For queer activists' almost decade-long fight for the right to care for queer homeless youth, the settlement proved momentous. In its settlement, the county agreed to authorize queer foster parenting.[45] On February 28, 1985, Lola J. Hobbs, Director of the Los Angeles County Department of Children's Services, sent a memo to her staff. She told her staff that, from then on, official county policy would allow any adult to apply for a license to become a foster parent "regardless of . . . sexual orientation."[46] Queer activists had won. To Terry DeCrescenzo, the settlement "was almost like a light switch . . . We worked so hard and so long and then all of a sudden the county was able to change its opinion seemingly very easily."[47] In reality, the fight for open queer foster parenting had taken almost a decade, but Sorenson's threatened suit provided a catalyst that forced the county to authorize queer foster parents.

The Aftermath

Even as queer activists celebrated their victory, the fight for queer foster parenting was not over. Instead, activists worked throughout the 1980s to ensure that L.A. County's settlement carried weight in day-to-day practices. This was not a given; even after the county statute changed to authorize queer foster parenting, a loophole in the memo sent to county foster care social workers meant that authorization on paper was not enough. For the policy to have teeth, the queer activists and queer-friendly social workers who created the environment in which this policy could come into existence had to continue to fight for it.

The loophole in Los Angeles County's new foster policy emerged in Department of Children's Services Director Lola Hobbs's memo to foster care staff. Hobbs wrote:

> Placement of a child with a licensed foster parent will be recommended without regard to prospective foster parent(s) sexual preference if such placement is in the best interests of the child . . . In the assessment of the appropriateness of a foster home for a particular child, the CSW [children's social worker] shall consider *all* social factors, including the foster parent's sexual orientation. The best interests of the child shall be the controlling factor, and all relevant factors must be considered. Sexual preference may not be the sole basis for precluding placement.[48]

The nebulous definition of "the best interests of the child" allowed social workers who did not believe that a queer foster parent was in the child's "best interests" to refuse to place the child with that parent. Although sexual preference could not be the "sole basis" for refusing to place this child, it is easy to imagine that social workers who did not approve of queer foster parents could come up with additional reasons when pressed. Even though a queer person could receive a license to be a foster parent, that did not necessarily mean they would actually receive foster children. Instead, would-be queer foster parents, who earlier sought social workers willing to surreptitiously license them, now had to figure out ways to avoid other social workers who would come up with excuses to deny them.

To ensure that queer foster parents actually had a chance to foster, activists mobilized the infrastructure they had developed to support queer homeless youth. In 1983, before joining the staff of the Center, Albert Ogle had founded a small organization called the Triangle Project, which aimed to become a street ministry for queer homeless youth.[49] Two months after Hobbs's memo, Ogle and other board members shifted the focus of the organization to placing queer homeless youth in long-term foster homes. Triangle recruited foster parents and educated social workers to overcome their homophobia and allow queer youth to go to queer foster parents.[50] Over the next four years, Triangle recruited and licensed sixty-five queer foster parents.[51]

The Triangle Project's decision to focus on placing queer youth with queer foster parents echoes activists' longstanding vision of foster care as a solution to youth homelessness, but it also may have been strategic. When doing press interviews, Ogle and Triangle Project staff presented queer foster parents as a natural fit for queer foster youth. Queer parents, they argued, were more likely to be "'sensitive' to the needs of these 'high risk' youth." As Triangle Project Executive Director Kathleen Bridgeland explained, the youth were "high risk" because they "don't do well in traditional foster homes. They very often run away—again."[52] By "traditional," Bridgeland meant foster homes run by straight people. By presenting themselves as a "sensitive" alternative for a very particular category of foster youth, Triangle won generally positive press coverage for its mission.[53] The *Los Angeles Times* described queer foster parents as "controversial," but emphasized the "nurturing environment" these parents created. The *Reader*, a free Los Angeles weekly, said that Triangle gave queer foster children "hope."[54] This sympathetic coverage and careful explanation of why queer foster parents were appropriate in very particular cases may have helped make a case about the "best interests of the child" for county social workers contemplating where to place a queer youth.

Although queer foster parenting began as a solution to youth homelessness, it did not end there. The Triangle Project ran out of funding by 1988, but Terry DeCrescenzo absorbed Triangle into GLASS, her organization for gay and lesbian youth.[55] As DeCrescenzo continued finding queer foster parents for queer homeless youth, she soon realized that she had "tapped a motherload." DeCrescenzo says she hadn't realized "how many gay men and lesbian women of a certain era [had] set aside parenting because they assumed you're either going to be gay or lesbian or be a parent." As soon as she approached these queer people about foster parenting, she learned that they "had such a strong, powerful need to parent, and some of them to parent children, the small children."[56] Over the next two decades, DeCrescenzo found openings to help queer people fulfill these needs, persuading the county to allow her to find foster parents for infants and small children as well as teens, and eventually to open the first LGBTQ adoption agency in the United States.[57]

Queer foster parenting in Los Angeles County was a decade in the making, but its effects have lasted well beyond the 1980s. Over the past three decades, activists have fought to make the authorization of queer foster parents mean something in practice. First, they won the right of queer foster parents to care for queer foster children. Over time, they expanded their parenting rights, allowing queer people to foster young children and, eventually, to adopt. For activists who hoped to provide queer homeless youth an alternative to living on the street, foster parenting was a massive victory. For queer people who had thought they would never be able to have children, the creation and expansion of foster parenting made children a possibility. To DeCrescenzo, and to many of these queer people, "it was a remarkable life we made."[58]

Conclusion

Despite an overwhelmingly conservative climate, something remarkable happened in Los Angeles County in 1985. As multiple pressures upon county officials—the emergence of widespread youth homelessness, the growth of an organized network of queer activists, and social workers' quiet decisions to break county policy—converged in the chance encounter between Rosalee Sorenson's foster children and a suspicious police officer in late 1984, their confluence forced the creation of a new policy. The story of queer foster parenting in Los Angeles County is not the story of the 1980s as an era of grand conservative, neoliberal, or liberatory social policies; instead, it reveals the ways in which pragmatic responses to social problems can create lasting effects. When Los Angeles County authorized queer foster parenting in 1985, it set in motion a revolution in queer life. Since 1985, queer access to parenting has expanded dramatically. Simultaneously, queer activists have put family policies—marriage equality and access to adoption among them—at the forefront of the mainstream queer agenda. As part of the first wave of fights to parent, L.A.'s foster policy decision helped shift queer movement priorities across the country.

Studying the place of foster care in the emergence of the fight for queer families restores a missing, early chapter in this fight. In Los Angeles County, queer foster parenting may never have happened without a crisis in which thousands of queer homeless youth appeared seemingly overnight on the streets of Hollywood and West Hollywood. Queer youth homelessness is not a part of the usual story of queer families, but—in the case of Los Angeles—it was a vital catalyst. As an answer to youth homelessness, however, foster families have always been at best a partial, if not flawed, solution. Foster parenting has not ended queer youth homelessness. In 2012, the most recent year for which data is available, 40 percent of homeless youth in the United States identified as LGBTQ.[59] Even when foster parenting succeeded in getting youth off the streets, it is far from clear whether foster parents fully met the needs of the queer youth they took in. Future research needs to expand our knowledge of the aftermath of decisions to authorize queer foster parenting, attending to the experiences of the queer homeless youth who came to live with queer foster parents. The stakes of this research are clear. From its inception, the story of a queer right to parent has been a story about the well-being of children, and how governments support those who are most marginalized. The next question is whether foster parenting has been the source of support it was meant to be.

Notes

1. The author would like to thank Alice O'Connor and Lisa Jacobson for their feedback, and Sarah Crook and Charlie Jeffries for bringing this collection together. Thank you to the staff at the ONE Archives at the University of Southern California for their insight and humor and to the ONE Archives Foundation for the financial support that enabled this research. Most of all, I am indebted to the activists, county employees, and foster parents who spoke to me for this project, including Terry DeCrescenzo, Reverend Canon Albert J. Ogle, and Rob Saltzman.

2. Laura Briggs, *Somebody's Children: The Politics of Transracial and Transnational Adoption* (Durham, NC: Duke University Press, 2012); Daniel Winunwe Rivers, *Radical Relations: Lesbian Mothers, Gay Fathers, and Their Children in the United States since World War II* (Chapel Hill: University of North Carolina Press, 2013).

3. Rob Saltzman, interviewed by Nora Kassner, November 13, 2018.

4. For example, Briggs, *Somebody's Children*; Wendy Brown, *Undoing the Demos: Neoliberalism's Stealth Revolution* (Cambridge: Zone Books, 2015); Melinda Cooper, *Family Values: Between Neoliberalism and the New Social Conservatism* (Cambridge: Zone Books, 2017); Matthew D. Lassiter, "Inventing Family Values," in *Rightward Bound: Making America Conservative in the 1970s*, eds. Bruce J. Schulman and Julian E. Zelizer (Cambridge, MA: Harvard University Press, 2008), 13–28; Rivers, *Radical Relations*; Robert O. Self, *All in the Family: The Realignment of American Democracy Since the 1960s* (New York: Hill & Wang, 2012); Rickie Solinger, *Beggars and Choosers: How the Politics of Choice Shapes Adoption, Abortion, and Welfare in the United States* (New York: Hill and Wang, 2001).

5. George Chauncey, *Why Marriage: The History Shaping Today's Debate over Gay Equality* (New York: Basic Books, 2004); Nancy F. Cott, *Public Vows: A History of Marriage and the Nation* (Cambridge, MA: Harvard University Press, 2000); Michael J. Klarman, *From the Closet to the Altar: Courts, Backlash, and*

the Struggle for Same-Sex Marriage (Oxford: Oxford University Press, 2013); Joyce Murdoch and Deb Price, *Courting Justice: Gay Men and Lesbians v. the Supreme Court* (New York: Basic Books, 2001).

6. For literature on foster care, see Dorothy Roberts, *Shattered Bonds: The Color of Child Welfare* (New York: Basic Civitas Books, 2002), and Catherine E. Rymph, *Raising Government Children: A History of Foster Care and the American Welfare State* (Chapel Hill: University of North Carolina Press, 2017). For changes to the welfare state, see Julilly Kohler-Hausmann, *Getting Tough: Welfare and Imprisonment in the 1970s* (Princeton, NJ: Princeton University Press, 2017); Kim Phillips-Fein, *Fear City: New York's Fiscal Crisis and the Rise of Austerity Politics* (New York: Metropolitan Books, 2017); Alice O'Connor, *Poverty Knowledge: Social Science, Social Policy, and the Poor in Twentieth-Century U.S. History* (Princeton, NJ: Princeton University Press, 2001); Anna Marie Smith, *Welfare Reform and Sexual Regulation* (Cambridge: Cambridge University Press, 2007); and Karen Tani, *States of Dependency: Welfare, Rights, and American Governance, 135–1972* (Cambridge: Cambridge University Press, 2016).

7. "Brown Signs Juvenile Crime Bill into Law," *Oakland Post*, 22 September 1976, 1.

8. Margaret M. Heckler, Secretary of Health and Human Services, "Foreword to the Runaway and Homeless Youth Annual Report to Congress Fiscal Year 1983," *Runaway and Homeless Youth: FY 1983 Annual Report to Congress*, U.S. Department of Human Services, Family and Youth Services Bureau (Washington, DC: Department of Health and Human Services, 1983), i; National Network of Runaway and Youth Services, *To Whom Do They Belong?: A Profile of America's Runaway and Homeless Youth and the Programs That Help Them* (Washington, DC: National Network of Runaway and Youth Services, 1985).

9. Office of Criminal Justice Planning, *Homeless Youth Pilot Projects Annual Report, 1987* (Sacramento: State of California, 1987); Office of Criminal Justice Planning, *Homeless Youth Pilot Projects* (Sacramento: State of California, 1988).

10. Office of Criminal Justice Planning, *Homeless Youth Pilot Projects Annual Report, 1987* (Sacramento: State of California, 1987); Office of Criminal Justice Planning, *Homeless Youth Pilot Projects* (Sacramento: State of California, 1988).

11. Rymph, *Raising Government Children*, 146; The Triangle Project, "Basic Requirements for Becoming a Foster Parent," Circa 1985–1988, Box 2, Folder 8, Donald A. Ferguson Papers, Coll2014.014, ONE National Gay & Lesbian Archives, USC Libraries, University of Southern California; Troy Corley, "To Become a Foster Parent in L.A.," *Los Angeles Times*, 28 August 1986, p. 17.

12. Lois Timnick, "L.A. County Is Facing a Crisis in Foster Care," *Los Angeles Times*, 30 December 1984, OC1, 3; Rich Connell, "Children Lose, Poor Win in Funding for L.A. County Programs," *Los Angeles Times*, 8 July 8 1985, OC_A12.

13. State of California Commission on California State Government Organization and Economy, *The Children's Services Delivery System in California:*

Final Report (Sacramento: State of California, 1987), 66; Gary L. Yates et al., "A Risk Profile Comparison of Runaway and Non-Runaway Youth," *American Journal of Public Health* 78.37 (1988): 820.

14. Reverend Canon Albert J. Ogle, interviewed by Nora Kassner, October 16, 2018.

15. Triangle Project, "Statistics from 7/1/86–6/30/87," Circa June 1987, Box 2, Folder 1, Donald A. Ferguson Papers; Triangle Project Brochure, Circa 1983–1985, Triangle Project Folder, ONE Subject File Collection, Coll2012.001, ONE National Gay & Lesbian Archives, USC Libraries, University of Southern California; Jim Crogan, "A New Angle on the Triangle: Hope for Gay and Lesbian Youth," *Reader* 8.45 (August 1986): 1, Box 2, Folder 4, Donald A. Ferguson Papers.

16. Katie Batza, *Before Aids: Gay Health Politics in the 1970s* (Philadelphia: University of Pennsylvania Press, 2018), 26–32. The Gay Community Services Center was renamed the Gay and Lesbian Community Services Center in 1980. For the sake of clarity, I refer to it as the Gay and Lesbian Community Services Center throughout this chapter.

17. Teresa DeCrescenzo, interviewed by Nora Kassner, October 18, 2018.

18. Ogle, interview; DeCrescenzo, interview.

19. Saltzman, interview.

20. Ogle, interview.

21. Saltzman, interview.

22. Gay Community Services Center, "Displaced Youth Meal Program," circa 1978–1979, Box 1, Folder 3, Teresa DeCrescenzo Papers, Coll2015-006, ONE National Gay & Lesbian Archives, USC Libraries, University of Southern California; Edith Jackson, "Preliminary Application for Funding, County Justice System Subvention Program," circa 1979–1980, Box 1, Folder 14, Teresa DeCrescenzo Papers; Ogle, interview.

23. Ogle, interview.

24. DeCrescenzo, interview.

25. DeCrescenzo, interview.

26. Edmund D. Edelman to Susan McGreivy, Esquire, 7 September 1979, Box 1, Folder 3, Teresa DeCrescenzo Papers.

27. John H. Larson to Supervisor James A. Hayes, 6 January 1978, Box 1, Folder 3, Teresa DeCrescenzo papers.

28. Steven Angelides, "The Emergence of the Paedophile in the Late Twentieth Century," *Australian Historical Studies* 36.126 (2005): 272–295; George Chauncey, "The Post-War Sex Crime Panic," in *True Stories from the American Past*, ed. William Graebner (New York: McGraw Hill, 1993), 160–178; Elise Chenier, "The Natural Order of Disorder: Pedophilia, Stranger Danger, and the Normalising Family," *Sexuality & Culture* 16.2 (2012): 172–186; Rachel Hope Cleves, "From Pederasty to Pedophilia: Sex between Children or Youth and

Adults in U.S. History," *History Compass* 16.1 (2017): 1–9; Simon A. Cole, "From the Sexual Psychopath Statute to 'Megan's Law': Psychiatric Knowledge in the Diagnosis, Treatment, and Adjudication of Sex Criminals in New Jersey, 1949–1999," *Journal of the History of Medicine and Allied Sciences* 55.3 (2000): 292–314; Philip Jenkins, *Moral Panic: Changing Conceptions of the Child Molester in Modern America* (New Haven, CT: Yale University Press, 1998); Stephen Robertson, "'Boys, of Course, Cannot be Raped': Age, Homosexuality, and the Redefinition of Sexual Violence in New York City, 1880–1955," *Gender & History* 18.2 (2006): 357–379. For a popular example of this rhetoric, see "Voter's Pipeline; Election '78-Prop. 5-Smoking Initiative and Prop. 6-Homosexuals in Education," PBS SoCal, 1978, American Archive of Public Broadcasting (WGBH and the Library of Congress), Boston and Washington, DC.

29. Teresa DeCrescenzo and Stephen Schulte, "Concept Paper for Residential Adolescent Treatment Program," Circa 1980–1981, Box 1, Folder 13, Teresa DeCrescenzo Papers.

30. David D. Wexler, letter to Stephen E. Schulte, March 3, 1983, Box 1, Folder 16, Teresa DeCrescenzo Papers.

31. Bill Fenske, Youth Subvention Concept Paper, Preliminary Application for Funding, County Justice System Subvention Program, Box 1, Folder 14, Teresa DeCrescenzo Papers.

32. DeCrescenzo, interview; Ogle, interview.

33. DeCrescenzo, interview.

34. DeCrescenzo, interview.

35. Ogle, interview.

36. Connell, "Children Lose, Poor Win."

37. DeCrescenzo, interview.

38. Saltzman, interview.

39. DeCrescenzo, interview.

40. Saba Hamedy, "New Owner Plans Relaunch of LGBT Magazine," *Los Angeles Times*, February 13, 2014, online edition.

41. Tricia Lootens, "Lesbian Foster Home: 'Pornographic?!,'" *Off Our Backs* 14.10 (November 1984): 7.

42. Rosalee Sorenson to Anthony Day, editor of the *Los Angeles Times*, 5 August 1989, Box 2, Folder 6, Donald A. Ferguson Papers; Crogan, "A New Angle on the Triangle"; Elizabeth J. Mann, "On the Side of Gay Foster Families: Triangle Project's Goal is to Give Teens Nurturing Environment," *Los Angeles Times*, 5 August 1989, online edition.

43. Unruh Civil Rights Act, ch. 1866 § 1, 1959 Cal. Stat. 4424, 4424.

44. In re Cox (1970) 3 Cal. 3d 205; *Gay Law Students Assn. v. Pacific Tel. & Tel. Co.* (1979) 24 Cal. 3d 458; *Marina Point, Ltd. v. Wolfson* (1982) 30 Cal. 3d 721; *Hubert v. Williams* (1982) Civ. A. No. 15101.

45. Rosalee Sorenson to Anthony Day.

46. Rosalee Sorenson to Anthony Day; Los Angeles County Code of Ordinances Section 87017 (a), Title 22 CAC, emphasis added.

47. Teresa DeCrescenzo, quoted in Mann, "On the Side of Gay Foster Families."

48. Hobbs to all Managers, SCWs, CSWs, and Licensing SWs.

49. Albert J. Ogle, "A Proposal to Establish a Ministry Directed to Young People Involved in Prostitution in the West Hollywood Area of Los Angeles," Circa 1983, Triangle Project Folder, ONE Subject File Collection; Ogle, interview.

50. Richard Hitt, "Minutes of the Board of Directors of the Triangle Project," May 7, 1985, Box 2, Folder 1, Donald A. Ferguson Papers.

51. Alicia Gelpi to Licensing Staff of the County of Los Angeles Department of Children's Services, March 13, 1987, Box 2, Folder 1, Donald A. Ferguson Papers; for directories of Triangle foster parents between 1986 and 1989, see Box 2, Folder 8, Donald A. Ferguson Papers.

52. Crogan, "A New Angle on the Triangle."

53. See, for example, Al Ballesteros, "Triangle Project Fostering Gay and Lesbian Parents," *Update* 253 (October 19, 1986), Box 2, Folder 4, Donald A. Ferguson Papers; Mann, "On the Side of Gay Foster Families."

54. Mann, "On the Side of Gay Foster Families"; Crogan, "A New Angle on the Triangle."

55. Triangle Project, "Minutes: Emergency Board Meeting," March 23, 1988, Box 2, Folder 2, Donald A. Ferguson Papers.

56. DeCrescenzo, interview.

57. DeCrescenzo, interview; Japhy Grant, "First LGBT Adoption Agency Declares Bankruptcy," *Queerty*, February 19, 2009, online edition.

58. DeCrescenzo, interview.

59. Laura E. Durso and Gary J. Gates, *Serving Our Youth: Findings from a National Survey of Service Providers Working with Lesbian, Gay, Bisexual, and Transgender Youth who are Homeless or at Risk of Becoming Homeless* (Los Angeles: Williams Institute, 2012).

Works Cited

ARCHIVAL COLLECTIONS

Donald A. Ferguson Papers. Coll2014.014. ONE National Gay & Lesbian Archives. USC
Libraries. University of Southern California.
ONE Subject File Collection. Coll2012.001. ONE National Gay & Lesbian Archives. USC

Libraries. University of Southern California.
Teresa DeCrescenzo Papers. Coll2015-006. ONE National Gay & Lesbian Archives. USC Libraries. University of Southern California.

Published Primary Sources

Durso, Laura E., and Gary J. Gates. *Serving Our Youth: Findings from a National Survey of Service Providers Working with Lesbian, Gay, Bisexual, and Transgender Youth who are Homeless or at Risk of Becoming Homeless.* Los Angeles: Williams Institute, 2012.
Heckler, Margaret M. "Foreword to the Runaway and Homeless Youth Annual Report to Congress Fiscal Year 1983." *Runaway and Homeless Youth: FY 1983 Annual Report to Congress*, US Department of Human Services, Family and Youth Services Bureau. Washington, DC: Department of Health and Human Services, 1983.
National Network of Runaway and Youth Services. *To Whom Do They Belong?: A Profile of America's Runaway and Homeless Youth and the Programs That Help Them.* Washington, DC: National Network of Runaway and Youth Services, 1985.
Office of Criminal Justice Planning. *Homeless Youth Pilot Projects Annual Report, 1987.* Sacramento: State of California, 1987.
Office of Criminal Justice Planning. *Homeless Youth Pilot Projects.* Sacramento: State of California, 1988.
State of California Commission on California State Government Organization and Economy. *The Children's Services Delivery System in California: Final Report.* Sacramento: State of California, 1987.
"Voter's Pipeline: Election '78-Prop. 5-Smoking Initiative and Prop. 6-Homosexuals in Education." PBS SoCal, 1978. American Archive of Public Broadcasting (WGBH and the Library of Congress). Boston and Washington, DC.
Yates, Gary L. et al. "A Risk Profile Comparison of Runaway and Non-Runaway Youth." *American Journal of Public Health* 78.37 (1988): 820–821.

Secondary

Angelides, Steven. "The Emergence of the Paedophile in the Late Twentieth Century." *Australian Historical Studies* 36.126 (2005): 272–295.
Batza, Katie. *Before Aids: Gay Health Politics in the 1970s.* Philadelphia: University of Pennsylvania Press, 2018.
Briggs, Laura. *Somebody's Children: The Politics of Transracial and Transnational Adoption.* Durham, NC: Duke University Press, 2012.

Brown, Wendy. *Undoing the Demos: Neoliberalism's Stealth Revolution*. Cambridge: Zone Books, 2015.

Chauncey, George. "The Post-War Sex Crime Panic," in *True Stories from the American Past*, ed. William Graebner. New York: McGraw Hill, 1993. 160–178.

Chauncey, George. *Why Marriage?: The History Shaping Today's Debate over Gay Equality*. Cambridge: Basic Books, 2004.

Chenier, Elise. "The Natural Order of Disorder: Pedophilia, Stranger Danger, and the Normalising Family." *Sexuality & Culture* 16.2 (2012): 172–186.

Cleves, Rachel Hope. "From Pederasty to Pedophilia: Sex between Children or Youth and Adults in U.S. History." *History Compass* 16.1 (2017): 1–9.

Cole, Simon A. "From the Sexual Psychopath Statute to 'Megan's Law': Psychiatric Knowledge in the Diagnosis, Treatment, and Adjudication of Sex Criminals in New Jersey, 1949–1999." *Journal of the History of Medicine and Allied Sciences* 55.3 (2000): 292–314.

Cooper, Melinda. *Family Values: Between Neoliberalism and the New Social Conservatism*. New York: Zone Books, 2017.

Cott, Nancy F. *Public Vows: A History of Marriage and the Nation*. Cambridge, MA: Harvard University Press, 2000.

Jenkins, Philip. *Moral Panic: Changing Conceptions of the Child Molester in Modern America*. New Haven, CT: Yale University Press, 1998.

Klarman, Michael J. *From the Closet to the Altar: Courts, Backlash, and the Struggle for Same-Sex Marriage*. Oxford: Oxford University Press, 2013.

Kohler-Hausmann, Julilly. *Getting Tough: Welfare and Imprisonment in the 1970s*. Princeton, NJ: Princeton University Press, 2017.

Lassiter, Matthew D. "Inventing Family Values," in *Rightward Bound: Making America Conservative in the 1970s*, eds. Bruce J. Schulman and Julian E. Zelizer. Cambridge, MA: Harvard University Press, 2008. 13–28.

Murdoch, Joyce, and Deb Price. *Courting Justice: Gay Men and Lesbians v. the Supreme Court*. New York: Basic Books, 2001.

O'Connor, Alice. *Poverty Knowledge: Social Science, Social Policy, and the Poor in Twentieth-Century U.S. History*. Princeton, NJ: Princeton University Press, 2001.

Phillips-Fein, Kim. *Fear City: New York's Fiscal Crisis and the Rise of Austerity Politics*. New York: Metropolitan Books, 2017.

Rivers, Daniel Winunwe. *Radical Relations: Lesbian Mothers, Gay Fathers, and Their Children in the United States since World War II*. Chapel Hill: University of North Carolina Press, 2013.

Roberts, Dorothy. *Shattered Bonds: The Color of Child Welfare*. New York: Basic Civitas Books, 2002.

Robertson, Stephen. "'Boys, of Course, Cannot be Raped': Age, Homosexuality, and the Redefinition of Sexual Violence in New York City, 1880–1955." *Gender & History* 18.2 (2006): 357–379.

Rymph, Catherine E. *Raising Government Children: A History of Foster Care and the American Welfare State*. Chapel Hill: University of North Carolina Press, 2017.
Self, Robert. *All in the Family: The Realignment of American Democracy Since the 1960s*. New York: Hill & Wang, 2012.
Smith, Anna Marie. *Welfare Reform and Sexual Regulation*. Cambridge: Cambridge University Press, 2007.
Solinger, Rickie. *Beggars and Choosers: How the Politics of Choice Shapes Adoption, Abortion, and Welfare in the United States*. New York: Hill and Wang, 2001.
Tani, Karen. *States of Dependency: Welfare, Rights, and American Governance, 135–1972*. Cambridge: Cambridge University Press, 2016.

Thatcherism, the Black Women's Movement, and the Politics of Motherhood in Britain

KATE TURNER

Margaret Thatcher's government and the British Black Women's Movement (BWM) emerged in tandem, both experiencing their rise and fall against the backdrop of the long 1980s.[1] Thatcher entered Downing Street within two months of the first national BWM conference, held in Brixton in March 1979.[2] By the turn of the 1990s, both had seen brighter days. Tracing these parallel trajectories reveals two shadow sides of the long 1980s in Britain. While historians are accustomed to viewing the period through the lens of the changes wrought by Thatcherism, and thus packaging it as the exemplary "Me Decade," the less familiar history of the BWM provides a striking counternarrative, a kind of alternative "Us Decade," if we choose to look for it. Along the key axes of gender, race, and the economy, the BWM's rhetoric and political activism challenged the ideological "common sense" that Thatcher and her government sought to establish. This chapter is focused on the intersection of those axes, where we can find two very different, racialized politics of motherhood and the family: a Thatcherite model that we might describe as the implicitly white embodiment of domesticated "Victorian Values," and the BWM's approach to motherhood as an activist identity and mothering as a political act. By comparing these two visions of motherhood, we can better understand the ideological threads that constituted Thatcherite neoliberalism, as well as the diverse social movements that sought to challenge its hegemony throughout the long 1980s. Indeed, this chapter shows that, by dint of both their identities and their radical politics, BWM activists posed important challenges to the period's ascendant ideologies.

Very often, the history of the long 1980s in Britain is reduced to the economic transition from social democracy to Thatcherite neoliberalism, particularly in popular memory of the period.[3] This account sidelines the era's other important transformations, including radical changes to public discourse around gender and the family, and race and national identity. Following Stephen Brooke's call for a historical reassessment of the decade, and a diversification of foci beyond the formal politics of Thatcherism, this chapter employs a different historical lens.[4] Specifically, it demonstrates the value of an intersectional approach to the long 1980s, arguing that we cannot understand the history of capitalism, gender, or race in a vacuum, in this period or in any other. Discourse about motherhood—a topic at once deeply private and personal, and caught up in public debates about morality and the nation's future—provides a key site for analyzing the everyday entanglements of these three ideological axes. The "Victorian Values" rhetoric of motherhood and the family promoted by the Thatcher government, while expressed in the apparently apolitical register of "common sense" or "tradition," articulated a mutually reinforcing set of prescriptions relating to the economy, gender roles, and race relations. Likewise, the BWM's counter-politics of motherhood articulated a larger ideological agenda. This agenda explicitly identified and resisted the very economic, racial, and gendered "common sense" of Thatcherism, and contextualized it within a longer British history of liberal capitalism, imperialism, and patriarchy. This chapter outlines the racial politics of motherhood articulated by both the Thatcher government and the Black Women's Movement in the long 1980s.[5] Like other activists of the period, members of the BWM functioned as both authors and disseminators of powerful counternarratives to the Thatcherite status quo, in this case crafting a different vision of motherhood and family life. The chapter ends by examining the material and rhetorical challenges faced by the movement in its opposition to the Victorian Values agenda, and considers the legacies of their efforts to use to a communalist, matriarchal politics to construct a kind of "Us Decade" in the midst of the long 1980s.

Victorian Values: The Thatcherite Politics of Motherhood

In the first few months of 1983, as Thatcher and her party mounted their re-election campaign, the prime minister launched a mission to revive "Victorian Values." It soon became apparent that family life, and specifically mothering, would play a crucial role in this mission. As the historian Raphael Samuel argued a few years later, the use of Victorian Values as a rallying cry was a deliberately vague catch-all, providing a nostalgic solution to any concerns that potential voters had about the state of modern Britain.[6] This applied whether those pet anxieties were feminism, homosexuality, immigration, or "benefit scroungers"; all roads eventually led back to the degrading effects of modern life on the family, the "bedrock of national life."[7] Samuel contended that Victorian Values rhetoric was particularly effective in the early eighties because it exploited an existing belief that "Britain was becoming ungovernable" because of the moral decline some associated with the welfare state, Commonwealth immigration, and the ascendency of a "permissive" approach to premarital sex, divorce, and the gendered division of labor.[8] Under the auspices of Victorian Values, the government set their sights on solving these "problems" in the private realm of family life and individual conduct.

The "Victorian" ideal of the family, and specifically of motherhood, that the Tory government sought to "return" to throughout the long 1980s embodied the three central rhetorical threads of the Thatcherite agenda: (neo-)liberal individualism; traditional gender roles and family structures; and a narrow, racialized understanding of national identity. The ideological mobilization of Victorian Values rested on more than traditional ideas about morality and was more than a straightforward "backlash" to sixties' permissiveness. It was, rather, a vision of the social order forged out of the longer, intertwined histories of empire, capitalism, and modern forms of patriarchy.

In an April 1983 interview with the *Evening Standard*, titled "The Good Old Days," Thatcher proudly described how she had been "brought up by a Victorian grandmother":

> we were taught to work jolly hard. We were taught to prove yourself; we were taught self-reliance; we were taught to live within our income. You were taught that cleanliness is next to godliness. You were taught self-respect. You were taught always to give a hand to your neighbour. You were taught tremendous pride in your country.[9]

In this account, her grandmother's care instilled in the young Margaret the very tenets of individual responsibility and self-sufficiency that would become associated with her own premiership's neoliberal policies and rhetoric. As she concluded, "all of these things are Victorian values. They are also perennial values."[10] While the "Thatcherite revolution" is often considered a firmly twentieth-century phenomenon, which unleashed "new" impulses from entrepreneurialism to selfishness, it was profoundly influenced by the classical liberal values that Thatcher and others nostalgically associated with the Victorians. In this way, the British narrative of the "selfish turn" in the long 1980s is best described as an embrace of "(neo-)liberal individualism": a liberal capitalist ethos with a late twentieth-century twist.

As Thatcher's own memories attest, while self-reliance and financial independence could be described as "perennial values," in practice they had to be taught, in her case by a "Victorian" grandmother. Two months before the *Evening Standard* interview, the *Guardian* carried a front-page story leaking the details of the Family Policy Group (FPG), a secret group of cabinet members working on proposals to use family policy to teach these values on a national scale.[11] The report highlighted the group's controversial "social engineering" plans to encourage a return to "family values" and "self-sufficiency" among British people.[12] The ideological heart of the Group was Ferdinand Mount, a journalist and strong believer in the importance of traditional family values.[13] Mount authored the FPG's initial briefing paper, "Renewing the Values of Society: Suggestions for the mid-80s," laying out a policy vision echoing Thatcher's own Victorian values. Mount argued that the overall goal of the Group was to "ensure that all the Government's domestic policies help to promote self-respect and a sense of individual responsibility."[14]

The Family Policy Group's grand mission and broad purview reveals the central place of family life, and specifically of parenting, to the Thatcher government's hopes for a social transformation in Britain. The FPG argued that the family home was the most effective place to instill values like self-reliance, in just the way Thatcher's grandmother had. Mount called this the "children first" approach, and argued that competent, attentive parenting was crucial to the creation of "a free, self-governing society," where (neo-)liberal values came naturally.[15] The FPG's proposals also made it clear that mothers would do the bulk of this parenting work; the very first plan leaked by the *Guardian* was a taxation scheme to "encourage married mothers to stay at home."[16] The Group argued that families should be impelled "to reassume responsibilities taken on by the state."[17] The implication was that married mothers should be incentivized to replace paid work with unpaid caring duties that had previously been provided as public services; as a *Guardian* cartoon lambasting the FPG put it, "I believe a woman's place is undermining the welfare state."[18]

The FPG's suggestion that mothers should be induced to stay at home reveals the complex intersection between at least two threads of the Victorian Values agenda: neoliberal individualism and traditional gender roles. While the Thatcher government encouraged financial independence, property ownership, and entrepreneurialism as universal British values, here mothers were implicitly excluded, relegated to teachers of values, not embodiments of them. In her autobiography *The Downing Street Years*, Thatcher described her battle against the "great pressure" to subsidize childcare, a policy she opposed because it "would have swung the emphasis further towards discouraging mothers from staying at home."[19] Though she acknowledged that it was "possible" for other mothers to pursue careers outside the home, just as she had, she implied that this was the exception rather than the rule, dependent on women making "a great effort" to manage their time carefully, and also taking on "extra help." Given this, she prioritized protecting women's "choice" to stay at home and "bring up their families on the one income," opposing "unfair" fiscal policies—such as tax reliefs for childcare—that might support mothers who made the choice to go out to work. She even expressed bafflement that the Women's Movement would support subsidized childcare: "It always seemed odd to me that the feminists," who were "so keenly sensitive to being patronized by men," were "without any such sensitivity to the patronage of the state." Using the discourse of choice and independence from state "patronage" to celebrate full-time motherhood, she smoothed over the rhetorical tension between her party's neoliberal social vision and its belief in the importance of traditional family values.

In *The Downing Street Years*, Thatcher describes her broad commitment to protecting the "traditional family" as she understood it, and her particular investment in stemming the rising number of single-parent families in Britain. She wrote that "one in four children were born to unmarried parents," asserting that "all the evidence" indicated that single-parent households were a key source of many "social ills" from criminality and poverty, to learning difficulties, abuse, and homelessness.[20] Similarly, a 1982 FPG policy paper highlighted single mothers among "the fastest growing groups of those dependent on the state," and suggested the government rethink child support to encourage unmarried mothers, unlike their married counterparts, to go out to work and develop "responsible and self-reliant behavior."²¹ This was an indication of an ongoing political trend that continued throughout the long 1980s. As Pate Thane and Tanya Evans argue, this period saw "the most outspoken and persistent attack on lone mothers by representatives of any government of the century," and much of this "attack" was rooted in gendered assumptions about the proper workings of the self-sufficient family.²² It is clear from the FPG's own framing that the twin Thatcherite crusades of economic and family policy reform were mutually constitutive. In theory, "rolling back the state" would encourage more self-reliance within families as women took on caring responsibilities, and taught their children an independent, entrepreneurial mindset. This vision was, however, reliant upon the nineteenth-century ideal of the bourgeois nuclear family and was often frustrated by the realities of late twentieth-century Britain.

The growing number of single mothers in Britain had a multifaceted significance for the Victorian Values agenda. Due to the growing mythology of the single-mother "benefit scrounger," it could be mobilized to critique the "over-generosity" of the post-war consensus and to argue for a more limited safety net that "encouraged" individual responsibility and restraint.²³ Moreover, as the decade wore on, conservative politicians and journalists began to cast the "problem" of single-parent homes as an implicitly racialized undercurrent, contributing to the sense that single-parent homes were an external threat to "natural" British values. As Thatcher's own celebration of Victorian values as intrinsic to the "British character" demonstrates, a common understanding of British national identity centered on an Anglo-Protestant, middle-class ethos of self-restraint, industriousness, and financial independence. This was a colonial imaginary of the "British character," as embodied in white, male, middle- and upper-class British figures like the "self-made man" of free-market capitalism or the imperialist settler.²⁴ This long history provided a fertile backdrop against which the racialized connotations of terms such as "dependent" might be interpreted. While Thatcher insisted that the polite, disciplined individualism of Victorian values was "natural to the British," the government was not certain that these values came so naturally to migrants and people of color. The FPG suggested that a "special effort" may be necessary to "strengthen the sense of self-respect, confidence and hence individual responsibility of members of ethnic minority communities."²⁵ Within this context, working-class, Black single mothers could be portrayed as the very antithesis of "British" values.

Race and national identity were integral to the Thatcherite social agenda; as Camilla Schofield has shown, immigration was "'always' the most popular subject in the Prime Minister's postbag."²⁶ Since the Empire Windrush docked in 1948, British public discourse had seen a gradual "racialization of national belonging," which excluded people of color from the national community, regardless of legal citizenship.²⁷ In the 1980s, the Thatcher government worked a rhetorical ground already thoroughly exploited by Enoch Powell, which mobilized a particular notion of "essential Britishness," rooted in a liberal-capitalist ethos and the traditional domestic ideal.²⁸ It was this racial and cultural logic that allowed Thatcher to present the 1982 Falklands War as the defense of people living 8,000 miles from London, but who were "British in stock and tradition," soon after promising to protect white Britons from the "swamping of their country" and "culture" from British subjects arriving from the Commonwealth.²⁹ In addition to this deep-rooted subtext, explicitly racialized descriptions of single-parent families became increasingly common in the conservative media toward the end of the 1980s.³⁰ By the early 1990s, British tabloids were carrying front-page stories about the prominence of single-parent households among Black Britons.³¹ In 1991, Adrian Rogers of the Conservative Family Campaign argued that this demographic trend proved that "the permissive society has given way to the lawless society," and that unmarried parents were "feckless beyond belief," implicitly casting Black single mothers as the "feckless" antithesis to the restrained British character of Victorian Values.³²

During the 1983 "Victorian Values" election campaign, the Conservative party distributed an advertisement that encapsulated the conflicted position of Black Britons in its vision of the nation. The ad featured a prominent image of a young Black man neatly dressed in a suit. It announced that "LABOUR SAYS HE'S BLACK. TORIES SAY HE'S BRITISH": "With the Conservatives there are no 'blacks,' no 'whites,' just people, because everyone wants to work hard and be rewarded for it."³³ Four years later, Paul Gilroy highlighted this campaign material as a prime example of the Thatcher government's work to articulate a supposedly inclusive notion of British identity, which actually recentered the nation around whiteness and liberal capitalism. He noted that the poster was rejected by many people of color because it was seen to suggest that "the categories black and British were mutually exclusive."³⁴ As Gilroy argued, it "conveys what is being asked of the black readers as the price of admission to the colour-blind form of citizenship": "to forsake all that marks them as culturally distinct."[35] Instead, the advert reiterated a vision of British cultural values firmly rooted in a capitalist-individualist liberal ethos, expressed in the "common-sense" claim that "everyone wants to work hard and be rewarded for it" and embodied in the professional respectability of the man's suit.[36]

Gilroy also suggested that the decision to present an isolated *male* figure as the face of the Black British electorate had very specific gendered and racialized implications: "It avoids the hidden threat of excessive fertility which is a constant presence in the representation of black women. The lone young man is incapable of swamping 'us.'"[37] In the context of Thatcher's "swamping" narrative, it was possible to portray women of color, and their embodied implication of fertility and futurity, in a threatening light. This threat was heightened in the case of Black single mothers, who sat at the uncomfortable intersection of renewed norms around gender, race, class, and personal conduct encapsulated in the Conservative agenda. As part II explores, the Black Women's Movement developed their own counter-politics of motherhood within this hostile climate, constructing a vision that challenged all three central threads of the Victorian Values agenda.

Communalist Matriarchy: The BWM's Politics of Motherhood

While the white-dominated women's liberation movement has benefited from increasing attention from British historians, the BWM has attracted sustained historical consideration only relatively recently.[38] Natalie Thomlinson's work is one example of this, and argues against an accepted narrative that presents the BWM as a mere offshoot of the mainstream feminist movement, insisting that "there was a *parallel* development of Black women's activism alongside white feminism," and that the BWM constitutes a distinct movement with its own ideology.[39] The prominent Black feminist Gail Lewis has echoed this sentiment, noting that she "refused" the narrative that presented the Black Women's Movement as "subsequent to" and therefore indebted to the WLM: "factually it's not true and certainly ideologically it's not true."[40] She highlighted the BWM's distinct political origins and methodology to demonstrate the fallacy of this narrative, emphasizing its "central" commitment to "work with the community," which, she suggested, the WLM did not share.

Lewis's reference to "commitment to the community" is characteristic of the ways that activists sought to distinguish the BWM from other post-war social movements.[41] Many prominent voices in the BWM positioned women of color as community leaders, via their role as mothers (both biological and otherwise). This communalist, matriarchal ideal suggested that the political change for marginalized people in Britain might be powered by a mothering ethos rooted in service to the "family" writ large: a large, fluidly defined community. The BWM's politics of motherhood was a product of its unique position in the late- and postcolonial order, which often included firsthand understanding of racial, gender, and class politics in both "colony" and "metropole." For many BWM activists, this understanding fostered a critical perspective on the relationship between imperial, patriarchal, and capitalist oppression and the liberal rhetoric of individual rights that, they argued, was often accepted as "common sense" by other post-war social movements, including the WLM. Instead, BWM members developed their own communalist vision of political change led by Black women, and especially Black mothers. From this politics there emerges a counternarrative to the story of the long 1980s as a decade defined by the Victorian Values of individualism, traditional gender and family roles, and racialized national identity.

To some extent, the BWM's dedication to community-level politics predated the movement itself. *The Heart of the Race*—the 1985 text by a collective of BWM activists, which remains an exemplary account of Black women's experience in Britain—underscores the significance of Black mothers' community action in the history of Black people in post-war Britain.[42] The authors argued that women, and specifically mothers, were central to the initially informal efforts—often found in makeshift hair salons and "embryonic churches"—which they describe as "our own spontaneous response to the isolation and alienation we felt when we first arrived."[43] These spaces created opportunities for women of color to gather safely and provide one another's families with "support and sustenance."[44] By the late 1950s, these informal groupings began to produce more official political organizations, focused on systematically fighting racism.[45]

Like these older models of women-led community action, the BWM was rooted in particular scripts surrounding gender and the family, which highlighted Black women's social role as leaders and protectors of their families and broader social networks.[46] They also emphasized the power of mothering—in its most expansive sense—to improve people's lives.

Co-author and BWM leader Stella Dadzie asserted that *The Heart of the Race*'s title was intended to capture the "sense of women being the preservers of history . . . the same hand that rocks the cradle rules the world" and attest to "the fact that we were quite often from very matriarchal families; it was the grandmothers, and the mothers . . . who told the stories and kept stuff around."[47] The book describes the BWM as an opportunity for Black women, and specifically mothers, to express their "anger," often after generations of struggle against racism and misogyny, and specifically the anger that was felt at mistreatment of their "children at the hands of the police, education authorities, employers and the courts."[48] The movement harnessed this emotion and channeled it into "overtly political campaigns," mobilizing motherhood as an activist identity and political resource that could be used in the service of the whole community. Dadzie remembers her own firm belief in the transformative politics of mothering: "I really bought into that view that it's all about the way we nurture," and that "we can change the next generation of men and women through our own mothering."[49]

The BWM's matriarchal communalist approach had significant implications for the movement's political agenda. Its most visible campaigns focused on racism in broad areas including housing, employment, education, and policing, even though these issues were not strictly "women's issues" as the WLM might define them. Still, these issues often prompted Black women to organize on behalf of themselves, their communities, and their children. Similarly, from the very beginning, the movement embraced a broad range of organizing strategies, from discussion groups, to boycotts, to media campaigns. For example, the Brixton Black Women's Group was formed in 1973, and started out as a discussion group for women who had been involved in Black Power and African liberation, but who sought an "autonomous" place to explore issues specifically affecting women of color.[50] This group became a crucial early seed of the nascent BWM, and many later local offshoots of the movement similarly began via the formation of discussion and reading groups. In 1980, Black women in North London led a Census boycott, in response to a Test Census carried out in Haringey that sought to

> sound out the response of Black people to having an "ethnic" question in the 1981 National Census. This was something else we thought we had to take on, because our reaction would be used to justify a national head count of Black people . . . we

felt that this was a dangerous move . . . since these kinds of statistics have never been used to improve things for us.[51]

Throughout the eighties, "SCRAP SUS" was a high-profile campaign specifically targeting the institutionalized use of the 1824 Vagrancy Act as a cover for the police's harassment of Black people, as well as the broader problem of racialized police brutality. Organizers arranged public meetings, led demonstrations, distributed petitions, and worked with the press to raise awareness and build pressure around the issue.[52] BWM members also held public meetings and led community fundraising for people of color wrongfully deported or threatened with deportation. In the case of Shirley Graham, who was detained for five days in 1981, "One of the local schools even put on a play to raise money . . . We went up and down the country, giving talks to other immigration and anti-deportation campaigns [including by Graham herself] . . . We worked intensively for a year with petitions, letters to MPs, the whole works."[53]

Many women who attended meetings and organized protests were responding to the urgent problems facing their own families, while others were aware that their identity as mothers might offer them a platform or resource. Baroness Martha Osamor contends that while it "was mainly our men" who were most severely affected by the biased policing, it was "women who are the mothers . . . of the men" who led much of the campaigning on this issue.[54] A major reason for this, she proposes, was the very fact of Black men's increased risk of police harassment; the fear of arrest and violence meant that some men were "not forthcoming" when it came to activism; she even encouraged men to "stay away" for this reason.[55] Osamor also remembers the effectiveness of mobilizing visible markers of motherhood to gain political support, describing how the sight of a group of mothers "with the pram and the placard" could reassure and encourage others, including Black men, to join a rally.[56]

The BWM's politicization of motherhood was profoundly shaped by the material conditions of its members. *The Heart of the Race* argued that, although many Black women did display great resourcefulness in leading their families, often as single parents, this reality should not be "romanticised," but understood as an example of "making do" with limited options.[57] And yet, in forging a political identity and methodology from what was available to them, Black mothers celebrated their own cultural and family values and highlighted the structural barriers that stood between them and the "achievement" of the British ideal of motherhood.

They also questioned the very desirability of that ideal. By harnessing motherhood as a political identity and a source of community authority, BWM activists challenged traditional gender scripts that suggested that mothering was best done in the nuclear family home. They resisted the narratives that demonized their families, and instead mobilized their motherhood as a source of power and a model for political transformation. As *The Heart of the Race* acknowledged, the activism of Black single mothers demonstrated "a different kind of strength . . . which the pervading oppressive sexual stereotypes have not undermined."[58]

The BWM's matriarchal communalism was also reflected in the movement's explicit critique of the liberal individualism as a longstanding tool of racist, imperial domination.[59] The authors of *The Heart of the Race* argued that contemporary British stereotypes that presented Black people as "only being fit for manual and menial labour, or as idle scroungers who do not wish to work" were products of this colonial history.[60] They contended that associations between people of color and economic dependency were not incidental but the outcome of a racialized ideology that accompanied Britain's imperial-capitalist expansion in the eighteenth and nineteenth centuries:

> The attitudes of social workers and journalists about our "childlike dependence," the fears of politicians and police when we rebel—all have their roots in Britain's racist past, when the possibility of Black equality became the source of the society's most fundamental paranoia.[61]

Before it emerged as a common narrative in academic historical accounts of modern Britain, *The Heart of the Race* argued that the naturalization of independence and self-restraint as "universal" liberal values was the product of an imperialist history, and persisted into the twentieth century, only to be reenergized in the 1980s. It was this history of liberal individualism and its exclusions, they suggested, that ensured that Black people in Britain were scorned for their "childlike dependence," while simultaneously feared as irrational and immoral. Rejecting this narrative, the BWM built on leftist and anticolonial thought to propose a counter-politics rooted in a matriarchal vision of community action and identity, challenging centuries of liberal individualist thought in Britain and its Empire and resisting the Thatcher government's social agenda.[62]

In many ways, the BWM's communalism was marked by radical inclusiveness and its openness to re-definition. For example, Dadzie describes how OWAAD, the movement's national umbrella organization, originally stood for the Organization for Women of Africa and African Descent, but became Women of *Asian* and African Descent "within a few meetings," because "Asian sisters started turning up and saying . . . 'Where are we in all this?' "[63] As the group grew, OWAAD remained dedicated to cross-racial solidarity between women of color, as did prominent Asian-led organizations, including the Southall Black Sisters.[64] The BWM was generally notable for its commitment to women from *all* ethnic and racial minorities, and for embracing the capacious definition of Black identity associated with Political Blackness, which could encompass *all* people of color. As Jade Bentil analyzes in this volume, however, there was a "lack of consensus throughout the BWM as to whether Blackness as a political identity could effectively represent the specific forms of racialized and gendered violence that Black and Asian women were experiencing."[65]

Though the immediate origins of Political Blackness lie in British anti-racist organizations of the 1960s, sociologist Claire Alexander argues that the identity came to fruition in the 1970s and 1980s.[66] Within a polarized racial climate, a commitment to cross-racial "solidarity and resistance" was particularly appealing to young people of color who might view the very notion of specific ethnic identity "with suspicion" and as "part of the colonial 'divide and rule' policy."[67] Alexander suggests that Political Blackness is best understood as a deliberately "constructed unity," consciously designed to counter divisive racial politics. Within the BWM, Political Blackness is often portrayed as an active mobilization of a shared history and experience of colonization and racism. As one unnamed woman quoted in *The Heart of the Race* put it: "When we use the terms 'Black,' we use it as a political term. It doesn't describe skin colour, it defines our situation here in Britain. We're here as a result of British imperialism, and our continued oppression in Britain is the result of British racism."[68]

An understanding of the shared legacies of British imperialism was used by the BWM to anchor relationships between people of color within Britain, and to reach across geographic space to facilitate engagement with women in former and current colonies.[69] Indeed, Gerlin Bean argued that these connections shaped the BWM's core mission, which she described as "an anti-imperialist struggle" fought for all people of color, and not limited by racial categories or national boundaries.[70] Thus, the BWM's matriarchal communalism posed a third challenge to the Victorian Values agenda: a cross-racial, transnational vision of its political community that consciously countered its rhetorical narrowing of racial and national identity.

"That Margaret Thatcher Phase": The BWM, Victorian Values, and Memories of the Long 1980s

In the conclusion to *The Heart of the Race*, the authors reflected on the state of the BWM halfway through the 1980s. Despite the political achievements detailed in the previous pages, they struck a cautionary tone for the future: "it is clear that the task ahead is not going to get any easier for us," and that they faced challenges "both from within and outside our community."[71] The BWM's internal problems were, arguably, rooted in the very matriarchal communalism described in this chapter. While many members initially celebrated the movement's ability to unite a wide diversity of women, over time it became clear that this expansive vision of communalism also brought with it its own significant challenges.[72] In accounts of the BWM's fate in the late 1980s, these challenges were often identified as a major factor in the movement's eventual fragmentation.[73] Likewise, its commitment to campaigning on behalf of the whole Black community, rather than focusing on specific "women's issues," also came into question.[74] Finally, the BWM's mobilization of motherhood as a political identity had the potential to isolate women without children, and particularly lesbians and bisexuals, who already held a conflicted position in the movement.[75]

Despite these internal challenges, it is arguable that the biggest obstacles to the long-term health of the movement came from the "outside." *FOWAAD!*, OWAAD's national newsletter, was launched within two months of Thatcher's entry to 10 Downing Street and, from its inaugural issue, the authors consistently identified her tenure as a threat to the BWM and broader Black community in Britain. Commenting on the cuts made by the Conservative government in their first four months in office, the *FOWAAD!* editorial collective wrote that "more and more" Black women "are being deprived of our right to maintain our families, and are being forced back into the home to do work that is the responsibility of the state."[76] They noted that this would take a toll on the very high rate of Black British women's involvement in the workforce ("90% of black women work, a lot of the time double and treble shifts") seemingly undermining the government's desire to encourage financial independence. After less than a year, *FOWAAD!* declared that Thatcher's government was "responsible for some of the most vicious attacks that the Black community has had to deal with in many years."[77]

Cuts to public services—which did indeed fall particularly hard on women of color, who were disproportionately likely to rely on state support and to work in the public sector—were accompanied by a more hostile immigration climate and a more aggressive approach to policing communities of color. All of this put added pressure on BWM activists, affecting their personal lives and often limiting political activism to a set of reactions to the latest round of service cuts, immigration restrictions, or police hostility. For example, many women identify the impact that cuts to local authority funding had on the long-term viability of the movement.[78] In many memories of the mid- to late 1980s, the impact of these material challenges was accompanied by a set of ideological changes. Many BWM accounts echo the grand narrative of the long 1980s, and associate the decade with the Victorian Values agenda, particularly the rise of individualism, which is linked to a waning interest in political activism within their own communities. Though the BWM reached its own peak during the 1980s, Judith Lockhart remembered the period between 1979 and 1990 as "that Margaret Thatcher phase," which affected the Black British community "very, very seriously."[79] She described how a longstanding commitment to inclusive communalism was replaced by "the Margaret Thatcher model," which meant "everybody looking out for themselves."[80]

While BWM leaders had hoped to empower and inspire their children through their politics of mothering, the movement faced stiff competition in this regard. Lockhart describes how "that Margaret Thatcher phase" produced a whole generation that had been raised "looking at life very differently," and "thinking more in an individual, rather than the collective level."[81] This rising tide of individualism had particularly powerful impacts when this generation reached adulthood in the following decades. Bean focused on the power of these emerging social values to erode political action, contending that it had become "very hard to mobilise people" by the early twenty-first century, and limited the ability to maintain trust and a shared vision within activist circles.[82] She argued that these changing priorities not only had serious practical impacts but represented a broader ethical malaise. Bean described a balance between "love for the self" alongside "love for one another" as the basis of community politics, and lamented that this had been abandoned in recent decades: "Now we've become just . . . greed, that's what individualism breeds . . . [the] self says I just want want want."[83]

Thus, the BWM's heyday in the early 1980s is remembered as a period of unusual community cohesion, when women from an extraordinary range of backgrounds coalesced around a common cause. This is a story of the movement as an anomaly: a short-lived island of true communalism and matriarchy surrounded by a sea of selfishness and paternalism, as embodied by the ascendant Victorian Values agenda. This vision resonates with Gilroy's depiction of a "utopian, democratic populism" specific to the radical openness of the Black British coalition in the late twentieth century.[84] In the end, the story goes, this utopian island would also be overcome by an external threat: a wave of Thatcherite individualism, which came just as the movement was also facing unsustainable pressures wrought by its own internal diversity. There are, however, some counternarratives to this account. Several BWM members remember that there were always problems balancing individual needs with those of the community.[85] Dadzie explained how, even at the height of the movement, "there were a lot of hangers-on who just turned up for the beer, whereas I can remember sitting up night after night."[86]

Still, despite this imbalance Dadzie argued that she and the rest of the "work horses" remained committed to an inclusive, communalist political methodology that was "fluid enough to allow women to come and go" and to include all women, "whatever their level of consciousness." It is revealing that memories of the movement share a near-universal emphasis on the importance of its expansive communitarianism. In fact, while sources from the 1980s share this vision of the BWM, the impression of communalism appears to have been distilled and purified with hindsight in oral history interviews, perhaps thrown into relief against other memories of the long 1980s as a "Me Decade."

Conclusion

This chapter has sought to show that the social transformations of the long 1980s cannot be boiled down to economic changes or an amorphous rise of "individualism" in British society. The "Thatcherite revolution" comprised a complex rhetorical network and, as the "Victorian Values" rhetoric of motherhood demonstrates, the "apolitical" domestic sphere had a central place in its vision. Motherhood also played a central symbolic role in the BWM's radical counter-politics, which—like the FPG's "children-first approach"—conceived of mothering as a powerful ideological tool. However, the matriarchal communalism that shaped, and shapes, the movement's self-image represented a three-pronged challenge to the ascendancy of "Victorian Values": it rejected the primacy of patriarchal gender roles and the notion that mothering should happen in private; it denaturalized Britain's historical investment in (neo)liberal individualism; and, by building a transnational coalition centered on *all* women of color, it opposed a narrowing vision of racial and national identity.

While this "triple threat" reveals the potent radicalism of the BWM in both practical and symbolic terms, it also hints at the gravitational pull of the narrative of the long 1980s as Thatcher's decade. Particularly in memories of the movement, the BWM's priorities are at least partially framed in reaction to Thatcher and the racial, gendered, and economic agenda her government set. This feeling also appears in accounts of the movement's demise, and the individualist apathy it left in its wake— accounts that tend to reinforce the idea that, on balance, the long 1980s really were a "Me Decade." And yet, the long-term impact of the BWM on changing understandings of national identity, racial politics, and family values in Britain should not be underestimated. Speaking in 2018, Dadzie insisted that the movement's legacy lived on, and that this legacy could do its own kind of mothering, inspiring and nurturing "the enthusiasm and the energy of the next generation," because "we ain't done yet!"[87]

Notes

I wish to acknowledge my own identity as a white British scholar writing about the history of Black women in the UK; this should be read with that in mind. My hope is that more scholars of color, particularly women, will soon have a greater platform for their own work. For more on the lack of racial diversity in the history profession in Britain, see "The UK's Only Black Female History Professor," BBC News, November 19, 2018, www.bbc.com/news/uk-46247776. My thanks to the staff at the Black Cultural Archives and the National Archives at Kew for their assistance accessing the materials that underpin this chapter. I'm deeply grateful for the support of the History Department at UW-Madison, which has made this work possible. In particular, thank you to Lou Roberts, Daniel Ussishkin, and Leslie Abadie, who provided their usual rigorous critical insight, tireless cheerleading, and emotional guidance. Finally, thank you to Elena McGrath, my wife, champion, and intellectual partner.

1. This chapter uses "Black" throughout to refer to women of color, in recognition of the shared identity of Political Blackness which many people of color in Britain organized around in the post-war decades, and that was used to describe the cross-racial alliances of many Black women's groups. See Jade Bentil's chapter for discussion of this. However, my chapter focuses on the experiences of women of African and Caribbean origin and descent, who were positioned very specifically in relation to the politics of motherhood in the long 1980s. It also deliberately uses "Black women's movement" as an alternative to "Black feminism" because of the controversy around the latter term, particularly during the long 1980s themselves. As historian Natalie Thomlinson has noted, " 'Feminist' was a deeply loaded term and was often taken to represent only white women. Far from being a positive politics by and for women, declaring oneself a 'feminist' could represent acquiescence with the white oppressor." Natalie Thomlinson, *Race, Ethnicity and the Women's Movement in England, 1968–1993* (Basingstoke: Palgrave Macmillan, 2016), 65.

2. See Jade Bentil's chapter in this volume for a rich exploration of the BWM in the context of Thatcherism.

3. "The 'Me' Decade," *BBC News Magazine*, 14 June 2007. http://news.bbc.co.uk/2/hi/uk_news/magazine/6742385.stm. It has also provided an anchor for much scholarly work on the period. For example, Geoffrey K. Fry argues that a cluster of "Economic Liberal Crusades" lay at the heart of the "Thatcher Revolution." G. Fry, *The Politics of the Thatcher Revolution: An Interpretation of British Politics 1979–1990* (Basingstoke: Palgrave Macmillan UK, 2008), vii–viii, https://doi.org/10.1057/9780230594111. Despite the centrality of "Thatcherism" within most accounts of the long 1980s, some historians now question the viability of portraying Thatcherism as a coherent political project or economic ideology. Ben Jackson and Rob Saunders contend that the label functioned as "a receptacle for a dizzying array of ideas and never achieved a stable meaning, even among Thatcher's closest allies," and that historians should use it only because it was "central" to the contemporary political lexicon, suggesting that it should be considered "a discourse to be interrogated, not . . . an explanatory tool for the actions" of her governments. Ben Jackson and Robert Saunders, eds., *Making Thatcher's Britain* (Cambridge: Cambridge University Press, 2012), 12–13.

4. Stephen Brooke, "Living in 'New Times': Historicizing 1980s Britain," *History Compass* 12.1 (2014): 20–32. https://doi.org/10.1111/hic3.12126

5. Part I, focusing on the Thatcherite Victorian Values agenda, pulls primarily on government documents from the early 1980s relating to the Family Policy Group, alongside media depictions of mothers taken from a range of contemporary national newspapers. Part II, focusing on the BWM's matriarchal communalism, uses interviews from the Black Cultural Archive's "Heart of the Race: Oral Histories from the Black Women's Movement" collection, as well as newsletters and books produced by the BWM.

6. Raphael Samuel, "Mrs. Thatcher's Return to Victorian Values," *Proceedings of the British Academy* 78 (1992), 10. Samuel also argues that Thatcher's own mobilization of the nineteenth century was "more a matter of style than substance," and lay in contrast to her own enthusiasms for certain aspects of late twentieth-century life, such as "Cable TV" and "hi-tech industry."

7. Samuel, 11. The passing of Section 28 in 1988 is an archetypal example of the Thatcherite concern with the morality of the nation. Similarly, feminist scholars have noted that the 1980s represented a period of revival for domesticity and conventional, or even "Victorian" family values. Helen McCarthy, "Gender Equality," in Pat Thane, ed., *Unequal Britain: Equalities in Britain since 1945* (London: Continuum, 2010), 116.

8. Samuel, 15; Raphael Samuel, *Island Stories: Unravelling Britain* (London: Verso, 1999), 221, 334.

9. Margaret Thatcher, "The Good Old Days," *The Evening Standard*, April 15, 1983; Samuel, "Mrs. Thatcher's Return to Victorian Values," 14.

10. Thatcher, "The Good Old Days"; Samuel, "Mrs. Thatcher's Return to Victorian Values," 14.

11. Malcolm Dean, "Ministers Rethink the Welfare State," *The Guardian*, February 17, 1983.

12. Dean, 1. Then Shadow Education Secretary and future Labour leader Neil Kinnock even described the FPG's aspirations to alter the nation's social values as a move toward "back door dictatorship, stocking-footed fascism." "Kinnock Hurls Dictator Charge," *The Guardian*, February 19, 1983.

13. His recent book *The Subversive Family* had argued for the protection and celebration of the nuclear family as a natural social form and a bulwark against state overreach. Ferdinand Mount, *The Subversive Family: An Alternative History of Love and Marriage* (London: Jonathan Cape, 1982), 7.

14. Ferdinand Mount, "Family Policy Group: A Guidance Note for Officials by the No. 10 Policy Unit," November 1, 1982, 1, Family Policy Group/Values Of Society Initiatives, National Archive.

15. Ferdinand Mount, "Renewing the Values of Society: Suggestions for the Mid-80s," n.d., 1–2, Treasury ("Renewing the Values Of Society"/Family Policy Group) 6 July 82–18 April 83, National Archive.

16. Dean, "Ministers Rethink the Welfare State," 1.

17. Central Policy Review Staff, "Family Policy Group: Proposals for a Programme of Work," 11 November 1982, 4, Family Policy Group/Values Of Society Initiatives, The National Archive, Kew.

18. "Letters to the Editor," *The Guardian*, February 21, 1983.

19. Margaret Thatcher, *The Downing Street Years* (London: Harper Collins, 1993), 630.

20. Thatcher, 630.

21. Central Policy Review Staff, "Family Policy Group: Proposals for a Programme of Work," 4.

22. Pat Thane and Tanya Evans, *Sinners? Scroungers? Saints?: Unmarried Motherhood in Twentieth-Century England* (Oxford: OUP Oxford, 2012), 179.

23. Thane and Evans, 71.

24. Catherine Hall, *Civilising Subjects: Metropole and Colony in the English Imagination 1830–1867* (Chicago: University of Chicago Press, 2002); Mary Poovey, *Uneven Developments: The Ideological Work of Gender in Mid-Victorian England* (Chicago: University of Chicago Press, 2009); Sonya O. Rose, *Limited Livelihoods: Gender and Class in Nineteenth Century England* (London: Routledge, 2003).

25. Central Policy Review Staff, "Family Policy Group: Proposals for a Programme of Work," 14.

26. Camilla Schofield, *Enoch Powell and the Making of Postcolonial Britain* (Cambridge: Cambridge University Press, 2013), 339.

27. Chris Waters, "Dark Strangers in Our Midst," 208.

28. Waters, 237; Schofield, 166.

29. Anna Marie Smith, *New Right Discourse on Race and Sexuality* (Cambridge: Cambridge University Press), 5; Kathleen Paul, *Whitewashing Britain: Race and Citizenship in the Postwar Era* (Ithaca, NY: Cornell University Press, 1997), 185. She made good on this promise in her introduction of the 1981 British Nationality Act, which created three new tiers of British nationality: British citizenship, British Territories citizenship, and British Overseas citizenship. These categories sorted British subjects according to "their level of 'real' Britishness" and effectively revoked the right of many British citizens to live in Britain, especially citizens of Asian origin. Paul, *Whitewashing Britain*, 183; John Solomos, *Race and Racism in Britain*, 3rd edition (Basingstoke: Palgrave, 2003), 65.

30. For example, in the wake of several years of "race riots" in diverse areas including Toxteth, Moss Side, and Brixton, the journalist and popular historian Paul Johnson wrote that "the foot-soldiers in every inner-city riot are those who have never known a proper home." Quoted in Polly Toynbee, "Happy Families," *The Guardian*, January 12, 1987.

31. In 1991, the *Daily Mail* reported that, according to the latest census data, this number was "three time the average of other races." Michael Seamark, "4 in 10 Black Mothers Are Single," *Daily Mail*, December 8, 1993, p. 1.

32. Jenny Hope Medical Correspondent, "Anger at 200,000 Babies for Unmarried Mothers Single Mothers," *Daily Mail*, September 18, 1991.

33. Paul Gilroy, *"There Ain't No Black in the Union Jack": The Cultural Politics of Race and Nation* (University of Chicago Press, 1991), 58. Emphasis in original.

34. Gilroy, 57.

35. Gilroy, 59.

36. Gilroy, 58.

37. Gilroy, 59.

38. For a range of recent work on the WLM, see, for example, Sarah Crook, "The Women's Liberation Movement, Activism and Therapy at the Grassroots, 1968–1985," *Women's History Review* 27.7 (November 10, 2018): 1152–1168, https://doi.org/10.1080/09612025.2018.1450611; Lucy Delap, "Feminist Bookshops, Reading Cultures and the Women's Liberation Movement in Great Britain, c. 1974–2000," *History Workshop Journal* 81.1 (April 25, 2016): 171–196, https://doi.org/10.1093/hwj/dbw002; Kristina Schulz, ed., *The Women's Liberation Movement: Impacts and Outcomes* (Oxford: Berghahn Books, 2017).

39. Natalie Thomlinson, "'Sisterhood Is Plain Sailing?' Multiracial Feminist Collectives in 1980s Britain," in Schulz, *The Women's Liberation Movement: Impacts and Outcomes*, 201.

40. Gail Lewis, interviewed by Marie Bernard, May 15, 2009, BWM22A, "The Heart of the Race: Oral Histories of the Black Women's Movement," Black Cultural Archives.

41. Thomlinson echoes this account, arguing that the BWM's emphasis on "community politics" constituted the overwhelmingly "distinctive element of its praxis," especially when compared with the mainstream feminist movement. Thomlinson, *Race, Ethnicity and the Women's Movement in England, 1968–1993*, 64.

42. Beverley Bryan, Stella Dadzie, and Suzanne Scafe, *The Heart of the Race: Black Women's Lives in Britain* (London: Virago, 1985), 124.

43. Bryan, Dadzie, and Scafe, *The Heart of the Race*, 130–131.

44. Bryan, Dadzie, and Scafe, *The Heart of the Race*, 131.

45. For example, the Indian Workers Association (IWA) and the West Indian Standing Conference (WISC) were both formed in 1958. In 1961, the IWA and WISC joined forced to form the influential Coordinating Committee Against Racial Discrimination (CARD).

46. The authors of *The Heart of the Race* acknowledged the conflicted history of this matriarchal narrative: "It is true that Black women played an active and positive role in the family, under both slavery and colonialism. But administering to the needs of our children and kinfolk was the only work which we could perform which was not under the direct control of the slavemasters. It also extended the role we were able to play within our communities . . . The burdensome responsibilities we shouldered under slavery cannot, by any stretch of the imagination, be described as 'matriarchal.' Nevertheless, the image of the Black matriarch survives, and has had a profound influence on our relationship with Black men today." "Self-consciousness: Understanding our Culture and Identity," in Beverley Bryan, Stella Dadzie, and Suzanne Scafe, *The Heart of the Race: Black Women's Lives in Britain*, 2nd edition (London: Verso, 2018).

47. Stella Dadzie, interviewed by Ego Ahiawe, March 10, 2009, BWM07, "The Heart of the Race: Oral Histories of the Black Women's Movement," Black Cultural Archives.

48. Bryan, Dadzie, and Scafe, *The Heart of the Race*, 156.

49. Stella Dadzie, interviewed by Rachel Cohen, June 2, 2011, "Sisterhood and After: The Women's Liberation Oral History Project," The British Library. BWM members also highlighted the significance of their own mothers in inspiring their politics. Local politician Gee Bernard recalled how her mother had been an activist during her childhood in Jamaica, and how this had motivated her to "follow her footsteps" when she encountered sexism and racism as an adult in the UK. "What is in you is planted in you," she argued, and "cannot disappear overnight." Ama Gueye, who co-founded the East London Black Women's Organisation, recalled that, when she experienced racism as a child, her "fall back" was simply to remember "my mum loves me . . . so whoever doesn't love me . . . that's your problem." This memory of maternal nurturance provided "strength," which she continued to draw on when she came to organize with other women as an adult. In a similar vein, some women emphasized the significance of their professional work with children, especially as teachers and social workers, in forming their political consciousness and giving authority to their activist identity. Beverley Bryan, interviewed by Kwame Phillips; Stella Dadzie, interviewed by Ego Ahiawe; Judith Lockhart, interviewed by Sheila Ruiz.

Gee Bernard, interviewed by Hayley Reid, September 3, 2009, BWM09, The Heart of the Race: Oral Histories of the Black Women's Movement, Black Cultural Archives; Ama Gueye, interviewed by Yepoka Yeebo, January 3, 2009, BWM04, The Heart of the Race: Oral Histories of the Black Women's Movement, Black Cultural Archives

50. Bryan, Dadzie, and Scafe, *The Heart of the Race*, 148–151.

51. Bryan, Dadzie, and Scafe, *The Heart of the Race*, 170.

52. Bryan, Dadzie, and Scafe, *The Heart of the Race*, 159–160.

53. Bryan, Dadzie, and Scafe, *The Heart of the Race*, 168–169.

54. Martha Otito Osamor, interviewed by Hayley Reed. Baroness Osamor, who was also a leading figure in the civil rights movement of the 1980s and a Labour councilor, was recognized with a life peerage in 2018.

55. Interview, Martha Otito Osamor.

56. Interview, Martha Otito Osamor.

57. Bryan, Dadzie, and Scafe, *The Heart of the Race*, 220–221.

58. Bryan, Dadzie, and Scafe, *The Heart of the Race*, 220–221.

59. Bryan, Dadzie, and Scafe, *The Heart of the Race*, 9. As early as 1964, Black community leader Claudia Jones wrote an untitled essay in the American civil rights journal *Freedomways*, historicizing the state of racism in post-war Britain along similar lines. Jones wrote, "the citizens of 'Mother Democracy' do not yet recognize that the roots of racialism in Britain were laid in the eighteenth and nineteenth centuries . . . All the resources of official propaganda and education . . . were permeated with projecting the oppressed colonial peoples

as lesser breeds, as 'inferior coloured peoples,' 'savages' and the like—in short, 'the white man's burden.' These rationalizations all served to build a justification for wholesale exploitation, extermination and looting of the islands by British imperialism." Claudia Jones (1964), quoted in Bryan, Dadzie, and Scafe, *The Heart of the Race*, 137.

60. Bryan, Dadzie, and Scafe, *The Heart of the Race*, 9.

61. Bryan, Dadzie, and Scafe, *The Heart of the Race*, 9.

62. A key manifestation of the BWM's anti-individualist political rhetoric was the movement's utilization of the first-person plural. For example, *The Heart of the Race* is primarily written in this mode, using "we," "us," and "ours" even when describing the experiences of Black women in the sixteenth and seventeenth centuries. Reflecting on the text twenty-five years later, Dadzie argued that this emphasis on a communal identity for Black women, across time and space, was one of the book's enduring legacies: "Women still read it now and connect with that first-person plural . . . it may not be my personal experience, but it's our experience." This vision of the shared power and strength of Black women, and overwhelmingly of Black mothers, was, arguably, among the movement's foundational interventions, connecting women who had previously been isolated and dispersed in a white-dominated society, and "turned us into a force to be reckoned with." Dadzie, interviewed by Ego Ahiawe. Bryan, Dadzie, and Scafe, *The Heart of the Race*, 177.

63. Dadzie, interviewed by Ego Ahiawe.

64. Ranu Samantrai, *AlterNatives : Black Feminism in the Postimperial Nation* (Stanford, CA: Stanford University Press, 2002), 106.

65. Jade Bentil, in this volume.

66. Early anti-racist organizations in Britain, such as CARD (the Campaign Against Racial Discrimination, founded in 1964), had recognized the power of cross-racial coalitions between people of color in a predominantly white national context. These groups worked to develop a concept of "Political Blackness," which emphasized a shared history of imperial domination and racism in the UK, to unite all racially marginalized people in a common struggle and subaltern identity. Claire Alexander, "Breaking Black: The Death of Ethnic and Racial Studies in Britain," *Ethnic and Racial Studies* 41.6 (May 3, 2018): 1038. https://doi.org/10.1080/01419870.2018.1409902

67. Alexander, "Breaking Black," 1039.

68. On a side note: the authors of *The Heart of the Race* interviewed many women involved in the BWM but chose to keep their testimonies anonymous, at least in part as an expression of the movement's communalist, anti-individualist ethos. Beverley Bryan echoed this unnamed woman, and described Political Blackness as an identity that united those with a "particular experience of imperialism" and Linda Bellos highlighted its power as a "political term." Bryan, Dadzie, and Scafe, *The Heart of the Race*, 171; Beverley Bryan et

al., "Afterword to Second Edition," in *The Heart of the Race: Black Women's Lives in Britain* (2018 edition); Beverley Bryan, interviewed by Kwame Phillips, January 6, 2010, BWM31, "The Heart of the Race: Oral Histories of the Black Women's Movement," Black Cultural Archives. Linda Bellos, interviewed by Nadja Middleton, February 19, 2009, BWM03A, "The Heart of the Race: Oral Histories of the Black Women's Movement," Black Cultural Archives.

69. Bryan, Dadzie, and Scafe, *The Heart of the Race*, 134–135.

70. Gerlin Bean, interviewed by Kwame Phillips, February 20, 2009, BWM032, "The Heart of the Race: Oral Histories of the Black Women's Movement," Black Cultural Archives.

71. Bryan, Dadzie, and Scafe, *The Heart of the Race*, 181.

72. OWAAD, "Editorial," *FOWAAD: Newsletter of the Organisation of Women of Asian and African Descent*, July 1979, 2.

73. Bryan et al., "Afterword to Second Edition." In 1985, *The Heart of the Race* already described questions of how to effectively function according to the pluralistic ethos of Political Blackness as "one of OWAAD's most controversial discussion points." More recently, however, Suzanne Scafe has questioned the significance of this "controversy" in the movement's demise, arguing that there is a "dominant narrative" that argues "that the weakness of the movement was in African and Asian unity. That narrative is out there and it's being authorised and repeated, but I have a different understanding . . . my sense is that people took . . . coalition politics very seriously . . . the demise of OWAAD, such as it was, was not about those single issues; it wasn't that those single stones brought down the whole house." Bryan, Dadzie, and Scafe, *The Heart of the Race*, 165; Bryan et al., "Afterword to Second Edition."

74. As one unnamed woman interviewed in *The Heart of the Race* recalled, "because we were a woman's group, we had to question exactly how much of our energy should go into organising in broad-based campaigns . . . we ran the risk of becoming like a community group." Conversely, some women in the movement viewed the explicit adoption of the label "feminist" with suspicion, often associating the identity with white, middle-class women and an exclusionary attitude to men. Another unnamed woman in *The Heart of the Race* explicitly stated, "We are not feminists. . . . In our culture the term is associated with an ideology and practice which is anti-men. Our group is not anti-men at all." Bryan, Dadzie, and Scafe, *The Heart of the Race*, 173–175.

75. Thomlinson contends that queer sexualities were a particularly fraught issue for the BWM, in part due to its historic relationship with the evangelical church and radical leftist politics, which, she argues, considered activist efforts on behalf of lesbians and bisexual women to be "ungodly" and "bourgeois diversions," respectively, though this should be contextualized within the broader homophobia associated with the Victorian Values agenda. Gail Lewis

had a unique perspective on this "question of sexuality," as she put it, as an out Black lesbian who maintained connections to both the BWM and the WLM. She argued that the "always contentious" debate surrounding the issue fostered a sense that Black lesbians and bisexual women "must keep quiet." In spite of this "don't ask don't tell . . . approach," she was outspoken about her identity: "Of course we did tell." Thomlinson, *Race, Ethnicity and the Women's Movement in England, 1968–1993*, 94; Lewis, interviewed by Marie Bernard.

76. OWAAD, "Editorial," *FOWAAD!*, September 1979, 3.

77. OWAAD, "Editorial," *FOWAAD!*, February 1980, 1.

78. In the late 1970s and early 1980s, funding from progressive local governments had helped establish dedicated Black women's groups and community centers, but this drastically diminished over the course of the eighties. For more on the impact of local authority funding on political organizing, see Lucy Robinson, *Gay Men and the Left in Post-War Britain: How the Personal Got Political* (Manchester: Manchester University Press, 2013); Daisy Payling, "'Socialist Republic of South Yorkshire': Grassroots Activism and Left-Wing Solidarity in 1980s Sheffield," *Twentieth Century British History* 25.4 (February 14, 2014): 602–627. https://doi.org/10.1093/tcbh/hwu001

79. Judith Lockhart, interviewed by Sheila Ruiz, February 3, 2009, BWM05, "The Heart of the Race: Oral Histories of the Black Women's Movement," Black Cultural Archives.

80. Lockhart also credited the ascendency of this "model" with the nichification of community activism as organizers began focusing on "their own sets of issues." Mason-John echoed this sense of fragmentation, noting, for example, that the days when "Black was broader than just Afro-Caribbean and African" were gone; "it's almost like we've gone into our little pockets." Judith Lockhart; Valerie Mason-John, interviewed by Annette Sylvester, February 20, 2009, BWM02, "The Heart of the Race: Oral Histories of the Black Women's Movement," Black Cultural Archives.

81. Judith Lockhart, interviewed by Sheila Ruiz.

82. Bean, interviewed by Kwame Phillips.

83. Bean. Similarly, reflecting on the BWM's communitarianism in 2018, Dadzie argued that "People these days wouldn't necessarily appreciate the idea of a group of women who were self-effacing and didn't bother putting their names on anything." Bryan et al., "Afterword to Second Edition."

84. Gilroy, *"There Ain't No Black in the Union Jack,"* 236.

85. Beverley Bryan, interviewed by Kwame Phillips; Mavis Best, interviewed by Ego Ahiawe, March 10, 2009, BWM06, "The Heart of the Race: Oral Histories of the Black Women's Movement," Black Cultural Archives.

86. Dadzie, interviewed by Ego Ahiawe.

87. Bryan et al., "Afterword to Second Edition."

Works Cited

Alexander, Claire. "Breaking Black: The Death of Ethnic and Racial Studies in Britain." *Ethnic and Racial Studies* 41.6 (May 3, 2018): 1034–1054. https://doi.org/10.1080/01419870.2018.1409902

Bean, Gerlin. Interviewed by Kwame Phillips, February 20, 2009. BWM032. "The Heart of the Race: Oral Histories of the Black Women's Movement, Black Cultural Archives.

Bellos, Linda. Interviewed by Nadja Middleton, February 19, 2009. BWM03A. "The Heart of the Race: Oral Histories of the Black Women's Movement, Black Cultural Archives.

Beverley Bryan. Interviewed by Kwame Phillips, January 6, 2010. BWM31. "The Heart of the Race: Oral Histories of the Black Women's Movement, Black Cultural Archives.

Brooke, Stephen. "Living in 'New Times': Historicizing 1980s Britain." *History Compass* 12.1 (2014): 20–32. https://doi.org/10.1111/hic3.12126.

Bryan, Beverley, Stella Dadzie, and Suzanne Scafe. *The Heart of the Race: Black Women's Lives in Britain*. London: Virago, 1985.

Bryan, Beverley, Stella Dadzie, and Suzanne Scafe. *The Heart of the Race: Black Women's Lives in Britain*. 2nd edition. London: Verso, 2018.

Bryan, Beverley, Stella Dadzie, Suzanne Scafe, and Heidi Safia Mirza. "Afterword to Second Edition," in *The Heart of the Race: Black Women's Lives in Britain*. London: Verso, 2018.

Crook, Sarah. "The Women's Liberation Movement, Activism and Therapy at the Grassroots, 1968–1985." *Women's History Review* 27.7 (November 10, 2018): 1152–1168. https://doi.org/10.1080/09612025.2018.1450611

Dadzie, Stella. Interviewed by Ego Ahiawe, March 10, 2009. BWM07. "The Heart of the Race: Oral Histories of the Black Women's Movement," Black Cultural Archives.

Dadzie, Stella. Interviewed by Rachel Cohen, June 2, 2011. "Sisterhood and After: The Women's Liberation Oral History Project," The British Library.

Delap, Lucy. "Feminist Bookshops, Reading Cultures and the Women's Liberation Movement in Great Britain, c. 1974–2000." *History Workshop Journal* 81.1 (April 25, 2016): 171–196. https://doi.org/10.1093/hwj/dbw002

Gueye, Ama. Interviewed by Yepoka Yeebo, January 3, 2009. BWM04. "The Heart of the Race: Oral Histories of the Black Women's Movement," Black Cultural Archives.

Ferdinand Mount. *The Subversive Family: An Alternative History of Love and Marriage*. London: Jonathan Cape, 1982.

Fry, G. *The Politics of the Thatcher Revolution: An Interpretation of British Politics 1979–1990*. Basingstoke: Palgrave Macmillan UK, 2008. https://doi.org/10.1057/9780230594111

Gee Bernard. Interviewed by Hayley Reid, September 3, 2009. BWM09. "The Heart of the Race: Oral Histories of the Black Women's Movement," Black Cultural Archives.

Gilroy, Paul. *"There Ain't No Black in the Union Jack": The Cultural Politics of Race and Nation*. Chicago: University of Chicago Press, 1991.

Hope, Jenny, Medical Correspondent. "Anger at 200,000 Babies for Unmarried Mothers Single Mothers." *Daily Mail*. September 18, 1991.

Jackson, Ben, and Robert Saunders, eds. *Making Thatcher's Britain*. Cambridge: Cambridge University Press, 2012.

"Kinnock Hurls Dictator Charge." *The Guardian*, February 19, 1983.

Lewis, Gail. Interviewed by Marie Bernard, May 15, 2009. BWM22A. "The Heart of the Race: Oral Histories of the Black Women's Movement," Black Cultural Archives.

Lockhart, Judith. Interviewed by Sheila Ruiz, February 3, 2009. BWM05. "The Heart of the Race: Oral Histories of the Black Women's Movement," Black Cultural Archives.

Mason-John, Valerie. Interviewed by Annette Sylvester, February 20, 2009. BWM02. "The Heart of the Race: Oral Histories of the Black Women's Movement," Black Cultural Archives.

Mavis Best. Interviewed by Ego Ahiawe, March 10, 2009. BWM06. "The Heart of the Race: Oral Histories of the Black Women's Movement," Black Cultural Archives.

Mount, Ferdinand. "Family Policy Group: A Guidance Note for Officials by the No. 10 Policy Unit," November 1, 1982. Family Policy Group/Values of Society Initiatives. National Archive.

Mount, Ferdinand. "Renewing the Values of Society: Suggestions for the Mid-80s," n.d. Treasury ("Renewing the Values of Society"/Family Policy Group) 6 July 82–18 April 83. National Archive.

OWAAD. "Editorial." *FOWAAD: Newsletter of the Organisation of Women of Asian and African Descent*, July 1979.

OWAAD. "Editorial." *FOWAAD!*, September 1979.

OWAAD. "Editorial." *FOWAAD!*, February 1980.

Payling, Daisy. " 'Socialist Republic of South Yorkshire': Grassroots Activism and Left-Wing Solidarity in 1980s Sheffield." *Twentieth Century British History* 25.4 (February 14, 2014): 602–627. https://doi.org/10.1093/tcbh/hwu001

Robinson, Lucy. *Gay Men and the Left in Post-War Britain: How the Personal Got Political*. Manchester: Manchester University Press, 2013.

Samantrai, Ranu. *AlterNatives : Black Feminism in the Postimperial Nation*. Stanford, CA: Stanford University Press, 2002.

Samuel, Raphael. *Island Stories: Unravelling Britain*. London: Verso, 1999.

Samuel, Raphael. "Mrs. Thatcher's Return to Victorian Values." *Proceedings of the British Academy* 78 (1992): 9–29.

Schulz, Kristina, ed. *The Women's Liberation Movement: Impacts and Outcomes.* Oxford: Berghahn Books, 2017.
Thane, Pat, and Tanya Evans. *Sinners? Scroungers? Saints?: Unmarried Motherhood in Twentieth-Century England.* Oxford: Oxford University Press Oxford, 2012.
Thatcher, Margaret. *The Downing Street Years.* London: Harper Collins, 1993.
Thatcher, Margaret. "The Good Old Days." *The Evening Standard.* April 15, 1983.
Thomlinson, Natalie. *Race, Ethnicity and the Women's Movement in England, 1968–1993.* Basingstoke: Palgrave Macmillan, 2016.
Thomlinson, Natalie. "'Sisterhood Is Plain Sailing?' Multiracial Feminist Collectives in 1980s Britain," in *The Women's Liberation Movement: Impacts and Outcomes,* ed. Kristina Schulz. Oxford: Berghahn Books, 2017. 198–213.
Waters, Chris. "Dark Strangers in Our Midst": Discourses of Race and Nation in Britain, 1947–1963," *Journal of British Studies,* 36, 2 (April 1997): 207–238, http://www.jstor.org/stable/176012.

A Framework for Choice

The Lasting Influence of 1980s Advocacy on Reproductive Rights in the United States

TAMAR HOLOSHITZ

The role of the 1980s in American abortion law is not only misunderstood but nearly forgotten; the standard law textbooks, for instance, go directly from *Roe v. Wade*, 410 U.S. 113 (1973), which established the legal right to abortion in 1973, to *Planned Parenthood v. Casey*, 505 U.S. 833 (1992), which significantly reframed that right, nearly two decades later.[1] When the 1980s are given scholarly treatment, it is typically through association with the rise of the religious right, the Reagan administration, and regression of reproductive liberties.[2] This traditional view of the 1980s argues that the United States saw a consolidation of pro-life and conservative forces, accompanied by a rightward shift on the Supreme Court.[3] Scholars believed that, over that decade, "the political climate has reflected a move to the religious right's views, with the result being the infliction on the rest of the population the religious right's views as to abortion and the beginning of human life."[4] More recently, some scholars have argued that this decade not only led to more restrictive abortion law, but also that the abortion decisions of the 1980s led to the rise of conservative legal thinking on other issues.[5]

The truth is that much of the 1980s was actually advantageous for the right to abortion, until the early 1990s when the framework for abortion in the United States was fundamentally altered through *Planned Parenthood v. Casey*.[6] Two cases stand out: *City of Akron v. Akron Center* for *Reproductive Health*,[7] and *Thornburgh v. American College of Obstetricians and Gynecologists*,[8] both instances where the Supreme Court struck down burdensome state legislation threatening women's right of access to abortion. This chapter describes the advocacy strategy that led to those victories. Part I first presents the traditional narrative of the right to abortion through *Roe v. Wade*[9] and *Planned Parenthood v. Casey*.[10] Part II then challenges this narrative, by analyzing the legal activism around abortion in the 1980s. It suggests that activists used three specific techniques to frame the right to abortion: (1) factual accounting of the burdens women faced from state abortion regulation; (2) demonstrating the special burdens faced by poor, minority, and rural women; and (3) arguing that these regulations were passed with the intent to erect barriers to abortion. Part III concludes that the strategies used by 1980s advocates are particularly salient today, given the current state of abortion law and the composition of the United States Supreme Court.

The Traditional Narrative: Creation of the Right to Abortion

The typical account of the right to abortion in the United States focuses on *Roe* in 1973 and *Casey* in 1992. This section briefly reviews the importance of these two cases, before using the lesser-known case-law of the 1980s to challenge this traditional narrative.

The right to abortion in the United States is classically understood to have emerged through the interaction of two forces: on the one hand, nation-wide activism against state criminal abortion statutes, and on the other hand, a series of seemingly unrelated constitutional law decisions that developed the concept of privacy as a constitutional right.[11] On the activism front, feminists called for repeal of state laws making it a criminal offense for a woman to seek, and for a doctor to perform, an abortion. Women's rights groups adopted the issue of abortion law repeal in 1967, and were an especially strong presence in New York, California, Illinois, Pennsylvania, and Massachusetts.[12]

On the constitutional law front, a series of separate decisions led the Court to consider the right to abortion. The Supreme Court began in 1925 by striking down an Oregon state law that had required all children to attend public school.[13] In doing so, the Court asserted the family domain as a protected sphere and expressed the right of parents to decide how their children are educated. The notion of privacy extended through the familial realm: in 1965, the Supreme Court held that a married couple had the right to choose whether to use contraception,[14] and in 1972 extended that right to unmarried couples.[15] These decisions paved the way for a case dealing directly with the right to abortion.

In 1973, Texas was one of several states that criminalized seeking or providing an abortion. A pregnant, single woman who attempted to obtain an abortion but was unable to sought the help of lawyers, who filed the lawsuit on her behalf, using the alias Jane Roe.

The decision in *Roe* is commonly understood as containing two parts. First, the court determined that the Texas state criminal abortion law violated the Due Process clause of the Fourteenth Amendment to the Constitution, which protects the right of privacy against state action. That clause reads that no state shall "deprive any person of life, liberty, or property without due process of law[.]"[16] In *Roe*, the court determined that criminal abortion laws violate a woman's liberty right to the private decision of whether to terminate or continue her pregnancy.

Second, the Court evaluated how this right to privacy is balanced against other interests. The Court explained that, although the State cannot override a woman's privacy right to an abortion, it has legitimate interests in protecting both the health of the woman and in protecting potential life. As such, the Court supplied a trimester framework to attempt to balance those interests. In the first trimester, the woman had an unfettered right to an abortion. The state could not interfere with her right to choose. In the second trimester, the state could regulate abortions in order to advance its policy goal of ensuring maternal health. In the third trimester, the state's interest in protecting fetal life outweighed the woman's right to choose, to the extent that states could prohibit abortions altogether, unless the mother's life was in danger.[17] Crucially, if the state wanted to regulate, the onus was *on the state* to demonstrate that it was doing so to advance a compelling state interest—such as maternal health or potential life.[18]

Today, though it is a target of near-constant attack, the first holding of *Roe* remains undisturbed. What *has* been clearly overturned, however, is the trimester framework, in a case called *Planned Parenthood of Southeastern Pennsylvania v. Casey*, decided in 1992.

Casey involved a Pennsylvania abortion law, which required informed consent and a twenty-four-hour waiting period prior to the procedure.[19] Minors required the consent of one parent prior to the procedure, although the law permitted for a judicial bypass option.[20] A married woman seeking an abortion had to notify her husband.[21] Planned Parenthood of Southeastern Pennsylvania challenged these provisions as being unconstitutional under *Roe*.

At the time of *Casey*, pro-choice activists expected the Court to go so far as to overturn *Roe*.[22] However, in a 5-4, intensely divided opinion, the Court actually reaffirmed *Roe*'s central holding, that women have a privacy right to choose an abortion. Writing for the majority, Justice Sandra Day O'Connor, the first woman appointed to the Supreme Court and a conservative voice on the issue of abortion, wrote, "the essential holding of *Roe v. Wade* should be retained and once again affirmed."[23]

While affirming *Roe*, however, O'Connor introduced a new, more lenient standard for determining whether abortion laws were valid: the undue burden test. An undue burden is any regulation that has "the purpose or effect of placing a substantial obstacle in the path of a woman seeking an abortion."[24] The Court explained that a "a statute which, while furthering [a] valid state interest, has the effect of placing a substantial obstacle in the path of a woman's choice cannot be considered a permissible means of serving its legitimate ends" and that "unnecessary health regulations that have the purpose or effect of presenting a substantial obstacle to a woman seeking an abortion impose an undue burden on the right."[25]

Under *Casey*, courts no longer look at the specific trimester, but rather determine whether a regulation is "unduly burdensome" throughout *all* stages of a pregnancy by using a factual balancing test: the court weighs the state's interest in regulating for the sake of maternal health against the burden imposed by the regulation.[26] Under this test, the onus is no longer on the state, but rather on the woman, who must show that a regulation unduly burdens her right to choose abortion.[27]

The shift from *Roe*'s method of scrutiny to an undue burden framework was viewed as an unfavorable change for those who support a woman's right to choose. In the traditional account of the right to abortion, scholars argued that this shift was caused by the anti-abortion movement's calls, during the 1980s, for the Court to use a more deferential standard of review.[28] However, as I will argue in the next section, during this same decade the pro-choice movement secured several momentous wins in the Supreme Court. The legal history shows that parties—for and against the right to choose—were crafting their arguments in terms of undue burden throughout the decade. This framework predates *Casey*, hearkens back to at least 1979,[29] and gained traction over the course of the 1980s. In the next part, I examine how pro-choice advocates in the 1980s used the advancing undue burden framework to their benefit, engaging in a close, compelling analysis of the burden posed to women.

Demonstrating Burden: *Akron* and *Thornburgh*

In the years after *Roe* was decided, the Reproductive Freedom Project ("RFP") of the American Civil Liberties Union ("ACLU") undertook an enormous nationwide litigation campaign, led by RFP director Janet Benshoof. "Our litigation strategy has been to challenge every statute or policy restricting reproductive freedom, using either [RFP] lawyers or other ACLU lawyers, or cooperating private lawyers where necessary. This is a formidable task since anti-abortion bills have passed the majority of state legislatures every session since 1973."[30] The RFP "function[ed] as the only national clearinghouse on reproductive freedom cases in the country."[31]

During this time, RFP placed a growing focus on defeating omnibus anti-abortion bills.[32] These bills, often drafted based on national models supplied by pro-life groups, were passed in many states and municipalities, and, through their numerous provisions, attempted to restrict women's access to abortion. For example, these statutes often required misleading and inaccurate information to be recited to the woman under the guise of "informed consent," mandated parental consent for minors' abortions, created twenty-four-hour waiting periods, and prohibited second-trimester abortions from taking place in clinics that were not part of a hospital. In 1980 and 1981, RFP was involved in over fourteen omnibus-type cases, "either directly litigating, or acting as a central back-up and clearing-house to ACLU affiliates and private attorneys."[33]

Akron and *Thornburgh* were both challenges to such omnibus abortion statutes. In both cases, RFP used the growing undue burden framework to their benefit, engaging in a close analysis of the burden posed to women. In addition to balancing facts, pro-choice advocates gave special focus to the burdens experienced by minority, rural, and poor women and argued that any intended "medical benefit"[34] of the challenged regulation was actually a pretext for limiting abortion.

Akron

Following the legalization of abortion in 1973, Akron, Ohio, was one of many cities across the country that enacted a restrictive abortion ordinance. The Akron law, passed in February 1978, had seventeen provisions, including requirements that all abortions performed after the first trimester be done in hospitals, parental consent for unmarried minors, counseling by a doctor, a twenty-four-hour waiting period, and that fetal remains be disposed of in a "humane and sanitary manner." The provisions were "specifically intended by its drafters as a 'national model.'"[35] The ordinance was adopted "despite statements by the Akron Director of Health, Akron Mayor and Summit County Medical Society that there was no medical or health-related need for such legislation"[36] and despite testimony by Rutgers Law Professor Nadine Taub, calling the ordinance "blatantly unconstitutional."[37] Once the ordinance was passed, the RFP filed a civil rights class action challenging it.[38] The Court took this case to determine whether these abortion provisions violated a woman's right to an abortion under *Roe*.

At the time, *Akron* was viewed as "the most critical abortion case to reach the Court since *Roe v. Wade*."[39] In June 1983, the Supreme Court struck down all of the challenged provisions, holding that a State's regulation "may be upheld only if it is reasonably designed to further that state interest."[40] Justice O'Connor's dissent in this opinion is important, and, as others have noted,[41] provides a glimpse of the "undue burden" framework that would later emerge in *Casey*. She writes, "In my view, this 'unduly burdensome' standard should be applied to the challenged regulations throughout the entire pregnancy without reference to the particular 'stage' of pregnancy involved."[42] She argues that "the trimester or 'three-stage' approach adopted by the court in *Roe*, and, in a modified form, employed by the Court to analyze the state regulations in these cases, cannot be supported as a legitimate or useful framework for accommodating the woman's right and the State's interests," that it is "completely unworkable," and that "the *Roe* framework . . . is clearly on a collision course with itself."[43] Commenting on O'Connor's dissent in a 1983 position paper, Benshoof wrote that this undue burden standard of review "would effectively undercut the right to choose abortion."[44]

Though Justice O'Connor explicitly foreshadows the undue burden framework in her dissent, the true genesis of this standard lies elsewhere. The concept of an "undue burden" pervades the briefing in *Akron*, as both sides—months before O'Connor penned her dissent, and nearly a decade before she wrote for the majority in *Casey*—framed their arguments in terms of whether or not the Akron ordinance presented a "burden" for women seeking abortion.

Both sides styled their arguments using the framework of undue burden. The City of Akron's request for Supreme Court review posed the question, "Whether the state's interest in maternal health and wellbeing is such that it may regulate abortion in a reasonable manner which is not *unduly burdensome*, even during the first trimester of pregnancy."[45] On the other side, Akron Center for Reproductive Health, represented by the American Civil Liberties Union—including, specifically, Benshoof of the RFP and Stephen Landsman of the Ohio affiliate—organized their brief by arguing that certain provisions "unconstitutionally burden the abortion decision" or "unnecessarily burden[] women."[46]

In preparation for this case, the ACLU viewed it as particularly important and was concerned that the outcome would be unfavorable.[47] In the months leading up to *Akron*, the legal team began building a case, working within the conceptual framework of "undue burden," for striking down the ordinance on three grounds: (1) the facts showed that women faced steep burdens in accessing abortions under the regulations; (2) these burdens fell especially on poor, minority, and rural women; and (3) the ordinance was passed not to promote women's health but to erect barriers to abortion.

The informed consent provision, termed by RFP the "heart of the ordinance,"[48] required an explicit recitation of material that, pro-choice advocates argued, was unduly burdensome. The physician would be required to recite that "the unborn child is a human life from the moment of conception" along with describing in detail "the anatomical and physiological characteristics of the particular unborn child."[49] These anatomical details included "appearance, mobility, tactile sensitivity, including pain, perception or response, brain and heart function, the presence of internal organs and the presence of external members."[50] The physician would further be required to state that "abortion is a major surgical procedure which can result in serious complications, including hemorrhage, perforated uterus, infection, menstrual disturbances, sterility and miscarriage."[51] Moreover, the physician would be required to state that "numerous public and private agencies and services are available to assist [the pregnant woman] during pregnancy and after the birth of her child, if she chooses not to have the abortion, whether she wishes to keep her child or place him or her for adoption" and would be required to provide the woman with a list of such agencies upon request.[52]

In their opposition brief, pro-choice activists argued that the informed consent provision "unconstitutionally burden[s] the abortion decision."[53] The RFP framed these informed consent provisions as mandating the physician to provide a "prepared script" and "foreclose[ing] the exercise of any professional judgment."[54] They argued that the required information was "false, misleading, and emotionally abusive[.]"[55] RFP concluded that this provision "puts a doctor in a 'straightjacket' and *burdens a woman's decision making process.*"[56]

As to the Akron ordinance's second trimester hospitalization requirement, the RFP argued, forcefully, that this provision introduced significant hurdles and challenges for women seeking abortion. First, their brief provides a historical overview of abortion safety and access. "Because abortions are rarely available in hospitals, ambulatory facilities have developed to meet this special need."[57] They argued that, taking the evidence at face value, this requirement served "no health interests because early second trimester abortions performed in clinics are as safe as, or safer than, those performed in hospital facilities."[58] They further argued "that Akron hospitals are not available to meet the need for second trimester abortions, and that the hospital requirement imposes severe burdens on women by making second trimester abortions more expensive, more time-consuming, and less geographically accessible."[59] Their brief notes that "the ban on the performance of second trimester abortions in Akron clinics imposes a substantial burden on women needing second trimester abortions."[60] Other advocates stressed that no second trimester abortion services were available in Akron hospitals, that hospitalization dramatically increases the cost of abortion, and that as a result this provision poses both an economic burden and a health risk to women, who might choose to delay or forego an abortion.[61]

Here, the RFP understood the showing of "burden" to include accounting of factors such as increased cost and decreased clinic access. One manner in which to demonstrate burden was demonstrating that "regulations [] have the effect of raising the cost of abortions" or that "significantly limit the number of places performing abortions . . . [and] forc[e] women to travel."[62] At the time of the decision, at least twenty states had second-trimester hospitalization requirement laws on the books.[63]

Beyond merely accounting for the burdens posed by the Akron ordinance, pro-choice advocates also argued that the burdens of the second-trimester provision would "fall disproportionately on teenage, poor, and minority women who are most likely to need second trimester abortions, and are least able to pay for hospitalization or travel."[64] The RFP coordinated an ambitious amicus[65] effort involving numerous medical, religious, and advocacy organizations.[66] In particular, two amicus briefs characterized the burden posed by the Akron ordinance explicitly in terms of their impact on rural and minority women. First, the National Organization of Women submitted a brief arguing that "although benign sounding on its face, the requirement that a second trimester abortion be performed in a hospital effectively eliminates, for many women, the ability to exercise their fundamental right to reproductive choice" because in many areas of the country "there are few, if any, hospitals that perform second trimester abortion."[67] For instance, testimony in the Akron case demonstrated that there were only two hospitals in Akron performing second trimester abortions, and during 1977, only nine second trimester abortions were performed in these two hospitals.[68] Many Akron women seeking second trimester abortions were referred to clinics in Cleveland, Ohio, and in the state of Michigan.[69] "Where hospitals are unavailable to perform a second trimester abortion," NOW explained, "a government imposed hospitalization requirement essentially acts as a governmental veto of a woman's decision to seek an abortion."[70]

The second important amicus brief was authored by the National Association for the Advancement of Colored People (NAACP)—Jack Greenberg, James M. Nabbit, III, Judith Reed, and Penda D. Hair. Concerned by the Akron ordinance that "erect[s] unduly burdensome and expensive obstacles in the paths of women seeking to exercise the constitutional right to terminate their pregnancies," the NAACP chose to participate in this amicus effort, one of its first such collaborations in an abortion case.[71] In stating the interest of the Amici, these lawyers wrote, "although the Legal Defense Fund's litigation program does not include cases involving abortion rights, the Fund is interested in any litigation which might result in formulating rules of law affecting rights of particular concern to Black people."[72] The brief noted that "in view of economic realities an outcome of this case adverse to [the abortion clinic] could severely affect the poor, among whom Black women are represented disproportionately," and citing to the statistic that "the percentage of all Black women who live below the poverty level is approximately three times the percentage of White women living below the poverty level."[73]

Finally, to further demonstrate the burdens posed by the Akron ordinance, advocates discussed the law as pretextual. Writing about Akron in its 1982 annual report, the RFP explained, "This law was passed, not for health reasons, but to effectively foreclose the abortion option for many women. No hospital in Akron performs first or second trimester abortions, and the women who most need second-trimester abortions—the poor, teenagers, and minority women—can least afford the travel or increased cost of hospital abortions."[74]

The strategies employed by RFP were significant. Not only did they anticipate the legal framework that was developing for the right to abortion—the undue burden test—but they used its parameters to make a compelling factual case about the necessity of abortion in women's lives. They did so through accounting for the costs and burdens experienced by low-income and rural women and through partnership with groups representing the rights of women of color.

On June 15, 1983, the Supreme Court struck down the Akron provisions as unconstitutional in a 6-3 opinion.[75] In announcing their victory, RFP called the decision a "resounding defeat" of the Reagan administration's efforts to preference local legislatures' interpretations of the U.S. constitution, and a "vindication for the thousands of women who have worked to make abortion a safe, legal, and accessible choice for all women."[76] The themes used in *Akron* to advocate for the right to abortion would continue to be developed throughout the decade.

THORNBURGH

Less than three years later, the pro-choice movement gained another victory in the case *Thornburgh v. American College of Obstetricians and Gynecologists*. A five-justice majority reaffirmed the principles laid down in *Roe* and in *Akron*:

> In the years since this Court's decision in *Roe*, States and municipalities have adopted a number of measures seemingly designed to prevent a woman, with the advice of her physician, from exercising her freedom of choice. *Akron* is but one example. But *the constitutional principles that led this Court to its decisions in 1973 still provide the compelling reason* for recognizing the constitutional dimensions of a woman's right to decide whether to end her pregnancy.[77]

Thornburgh was another important win for the pro-choice movement. Through sensitive accounting for the human burdens posed by abortion restrictions as well as through thoughtful coalition building, the pro-choice movement expanded on *Akron*'s strategies and crafted a compelling legal argument.

Thornburgh concerned the Pennsylvania Abortion Control Act, a state law modifying model legislation provided by Americans United for Life.[78] Numerous provisions of this Act were challenged. One Section of the Act involved informed consent and required a detailed method through which "seven explicit kinds of information must be delivered to the woman at least 24 hours before her consent is given, and five of these must be presented by the woman's physician."[79] The five were: (1) the name of the physician who will perform the abortion, (2) the "fact that there may be detrimental physical and psychological effects which are not accurately foreseeable," (3) the "particular medical risks associated with the particular abortion procedure to be employed," (4) the probable gestational age, and (5) the "medical risks associated with carrying her child to term."[80] The remaining two categories of information, which could be provided by a non-physician, were (6) the "fact that medical assistance benefits may be available for prenatal care, childbirth and neonatal care," and (7) the "fact that the father is liable to assist" in the child's support, "even in instances where the father has offered to pay for the abortion."[81]

RFP's involvement in *Thornburgh* actually preceded the enactment of the statute. RFP "provided testimony against the legislation and legal memoranda on earlier, more restrictive versions of it; and [was] part of a litigation team formed to plan strategy for a court challenge to it."[82] Beginning at least by 1981, Benshoof began to work with a Philadelphia team that included Kathryn Kolbert of the Women's Law Project in Philadelphia on this earlier version of the Act.[83] A showing of "irreparable harm" was required in order to stop the Act from going into effect. The team's early legal strategy memos stress the type of factual evidence that would sustain such a finding, such as briefs, reports, and expert affidavits. Much of the evidence collected was framed so as to demonstrate an "undue burden" on women.

Benshoof's team conceptualized "undue burden" in terms of the regulation's potential impact on rural women. A strategy memo explains that "the main task" for arguing against a provision requiring a private medical consultation with a physician would be to "analyze the burden and somehow develop a factual record which would substantiate the burden."[84] Those facts included, for instance, focusing on "certain rural parts of the state" where volunteer physicians "may only work one or two nights giving their time, making the same physician rule particularly onerous."[85] In considering arguments to develop against the twenty-four-hour waiting period provision, Benshoof argued that "rural areas of the state should be looked at and specific affidavits developed showing travel costs, distances women have to travel, limited times clinics are open for abortions, and the psychological and emotional burden put on women by requiring such waiting periods."[86]

On December 23, 1981, Governor Dick Thornburgh vetoed Senate Bill 742 in a seven-paged typed statement analyzing various provisions of the bill, and, in so doing, adopted the basic "pro-choice" position that the bill might "unduly involve government in the private lives of its citizens."[87] His press release, while reiterating his "personal opposition to abortion on demand" and his concern that "too many abortions are too casually undertaken," explained that provisions of the Act could "have the effect of imposing an undue and in some cases unconstitutional burden upon even informed, mature adults intent upon obtaining an abortion under circumstances in which the U.S. Supreme Court has determined they are entitled to do so."[88] He indicated that the bill "threatens to create additional regulation and bureaucracy and to unduly involve government in the private lives of its citizens."[89]

After a later version of this Act was passed, a suit was filed by the Women's Law Project of Pennsylvania with ACLU co-counsel.[90] The case made its way to the Supreme Court and was decided in 1986.

In arguing their case before the Supreme Court, pro-choice lawyers claimed that the regulation was pretextual. "These requirements are plainly designed not to inform the woman's consent but rather to discourage her from having an abortion."[91] Elsewhere in their brief they described the informed consent provisions as a "bald attempt" to force the Commonwealth's message into the private sphere of the doctor-patient relationship.[92] Weighing the medical "benefits" of the regulation, these advocates wrote that information related to fetal gestational age "is not medical information that is always relevant to the woman's decision."[93] The confusion likely to result from these provisions "is a burden that Pennsylvania cannot impose under the guise of informed consent."[94] Furthermore, they argued that these requirements were "contrary to accepted medical practice and inconsistent with the law of informed consent."[95]

The court, too, looked behind the stated purpose of the statute and expressed its view that the legislation was a sham and motivated by anti-abortion animus. "That the Commonwealth does not, and surely would not, compel similar disclosure of every possible peril of necessary surgery or of simple vaccination, reveals the anti-abortion character of the statute and its real purpose."[96] The court stated, powerfully, "The States are not free, under the guise of protecting maternal health or potential life, to intimidate women into continuing pregnancies."[97] It struck down the Pennsylvania statute in a 5-4 opinion on June 11, 1986.

With these victories, pro-choice activists of the 1980s secured abortion access for women against encroaching state regulation attempted to restrict women's access to medical services. In so doing, activists utilized an approach that stressed the real obstacles and burdens posed to women, focused on the special burdens faced by poor, rural women and women of color, and argued that states' intended "health benefit" was merely a pretext for restricting abortion access.

Path to Today

The *Akron* and *Thornburgh* decisions remain significant because they laid the groundwork for pro-choice advocacy today, despite having been over-turned. The activist strategies employed in the most recent abortion cases to reach the Supreme Court—*Whole Woman's Health v. Hellerstedt*,[98] decided in 2016, and *June Medical Services L.L.C. v. Russo*,[99] decided in 2020—directly correspond to the tactics used by 1980s activists nearly forty years beforehand.

Whole Woman's Health involved a Texas state bill, which contained two challenged provisions. The "admitting privileges" provision required that a "physician performing or inducing an abortion . . . must, on the date [of service], have active admitting privileges at a hospital . . . located not further than 30 miles from the" abortion facility.[100] The "surgical-center" provision required an abortion facility to meet the "minimum standards . . . for ambulatory surgical centers" under Texas law.[101]

Following a four-day bench trial, the District Court made extensive factual findings, including: (1) as the admitting-privileges requirement began to be enforced, the number of facilities providing abortions dropped in half, from about forty to about twenty; (2) the number of facilities would drop to seven or eight if the surgical-center requirement took effect; and (3) facilities would remain only in five metropolitan areas.[102]

As with the second trimester hospitalization and informed consent requirements at issue in the 1980s, the "seemingly benign" provisions of the Texas bill would effectively restrict abortion access and increase the hurdles faced by women seeking abortions. In advocating against the Texas bill, pro-choice lawyers drew from a familiar set of strategies.

The advocates in *Whole Women's Health* immediately adopted "undue burden" as the relevant standard.[103] They explained that a regulation in the name of women's health is undue if the health benefit is outweighed by the burden.[104] In their opening brief, they argued that "the Texas requirements will not enhance abortion safety" but rather the requirements "will instead make it harder for women to end a pregnancy safely by reducing their access to legal abortions."[105] Marshalling the factual findings from trial, advocates argued that neither provision provides any health benefit, that together the requirements would force more than 75 percent of Texas abortion facilities to close, and that this drastic reduction in access to legal abortion services harms women's health.[106]

Advocates opposing the Texas law also focused on the special burdens posed to rural women and women of color. For example, they argued that the law unduly burdened Texas women by increasing the distance women had to travel to reach a provider, reducing available appointments, delaying abortion care, and making abortion more expensive and complicated.[107] An amicus brief by the National Network of Abortion Funds described in great detail the number of abortion providers, which providers had closed, and clinic workload. It included vignettes of harmed women and argued that the burdens were not outweighed by purported health benefits.[108]

Advocates also explicitly argued that the law had no valid purpose but rather was a pretext for preventing women from seeking abortion. Because the trial evidence and factual findings had established "in no uncertain terms" that the Texas law "would harm women under the guise of protecting them," the advocates argued that the Texas law "would undermine, not advance, the State's asserted interest in women's health."[109]

In opposition, Texas argued for a less stringent standard. They proposed that the undue burden test did not require factual balancing, but merely asked whether the abortion regulation "has a rational basis and does not impose a significant obstacle to abortion access."[110] They argued that courts were required to defer to legislative findings about medical benefits.[111]

In its decision, the Supreme Court "beg[an] with the standard, as described in *Casey*,"[112] which required courts to "consider the burdens a law imposes on abortion access together with the benefits those laws confer."[113] As pro-choice advocates had argued, the Supreme Court stated that it was correct to "consider[] the evidence in the record—including expert evidence, presented in stipulations, depositions, and testimony" and "weigh the asserted benefits against the burdens."[114]

Four years later, in 2020, in *June Medical Services*, the Supreme Court considered a challenge to a Louisiana state admitting privileges law that was "almost word-for-word identical" to the law struck down in *Whole Women's Health*.[115] Once again, the Court applied the undue burden framework and engaged in careful consideration of the district court's factual findings, including special focus on the law's impact on abortion access. As part of this analysis, the Court considered "the geographic distribution of the doctors and their clinics"[116] and observed that the burdens of cost, travel, and wait time "would fall disproportionately on poor women, who are least able to absorb them."[117] The opinion striking down the Louisiana law was written by Justice Breyer, on behalf of the Court's four liberal justices. Chief Justice Roberts, who had dissented in *Whole Women's Health*, concurred in the judgment in light of the *stare decisis* effect of *Whole Women's Health*. In other words, although he "continue[d] to believe [*Whole Women's Health*] was wrongly decided," the doctrine of *stare decisis* required him to "treat like cases alike" and apply the precedent of *Whole Women's Health* to the facts of this case and to conclude that the law should be struck down.

These recent cases have been largely viewed as victories for the pro-choice movement.[118] But today's political climate also casts great doubt. With the appointment of Brett Kavanaugh to the Supreme Court, the passing of Justice Ruth Bader Ginsburg, and the appointment of Amy Coney Barrett, there is now a solid conservative block on the court. The undue burden framework is decidedly the prevailing standard for assessing abortion regulations. However, pro-choice advocates must anticipate whether this test could be used to further restrict the right to abortion and how best to counter those forces today.

Pro-life activists certainly aim to adjust their strategy in light of *Whole Woman's Health* and *June Medical Services*. One possible trend may be a move away from regulations made in the name of "women's health" and toward more overtly fetal-protective legislation. Pro-life advocates have called for an application of the undue burden framework more explicitly to fetal life: "discussions previous to *Whole Women's Health* were limited to judgments about whether a particular law constituted a 'substantial obstacle' to a woman's access to abortion, almost completely bypassing the moral and legal status of the fetus. But an honest and authentic attempt to perform an interest-balancing test forces a court to directly address both matters being weighed."[119]

Indeed, the model legislation published by Americans United for Life in 2018 shows this gradual shift. Since 2013, Americans United for Life has introduced model legislation restricting abortion access under the guise of "women's health" as part of their "Women's Protection Project."[120] More recently, in 2015, the organization has introduced another set of legislation under the guise of the "Infant Protection Project."[121] This legislation includes the "Born Alive Infant Protection Act," which requires that if, during an attempted abortion, an infant is "born alive," a physician "shall provide immediate medical care to the infant" and request transfer to another physician who can provide "medically appropriate and reasonable care and treatment to the infant."[122] The model legislation provides criminal penalties for physicians who fail to provide "medically appropriate and reasonable care and treatment" to infants born alive.[123] Given these trends, pro-choice advocates must be prepared to use the undue burden test to attack restrictions made in the name of fetal life, not only women's health.[124]

Equally important to constitutional advocacy are strategic efforts to build the factual case that abortion regulations are heavily burdensome. Because the undue burden test involves factual balancing, cases will be decided on the evidence—for example, clinic wait time, distance, availability, or number of physicians. In light of *Whole Woman's Health*, the pro-life movement has renewed calls for building a "factual" case against abortion. Specifically, they have urged new scientific and medical data that would show (1) that existing data collection on abortion in the United States is "inaccurate" and "incomplete"; (2) that abortion is not safer than childbirth; (3) that there are short-term risks to abortion; and (4) that there are long-term risks to abortion.[125] The pro-choice movement must ensure that the factual narrative remains accurate.

Ultimately, advocates today face a very similar reality to those of the 1980s: a conservative Supreme Court and growing calls to eviscerate reproductive rights. There is much to learn about successful activism under such constraints by looking back at the 1980s and the important victories of that decade. Today, as new litigation and restrictive ordinances emerge, we can expect to see advocates drawing from a similar tactical toolbox as those who worked in the 1980s: factual accounting of the human hardship caused by abortion regulations, particularly as it impacts low-income, rural women and women of color. The legacy of 1980s legal activism, its strategies, and lessons learned will be expected to play a fundamental role in protecting reproductive rights in the decade to come.

Notes

1. See, for example, Geoffrey R. Stone, Louis Michael Seidman, Cass R. Sunstein, Mark V. Tushnet, and Pamela S. Karlan, *Constitutional Law* (New York: Walters Kluwer, 2018); Kathleen M. Sullivan and Noah Feldman, *Constitutional Law* (New York: Foundation Press, 2016).

2. The rise of the religious right as a supposed "backlash" to the constitutionalizing of abortion in *Roe v. Wade* has been observed widely. See, for example, William N. Eskridge, Jr., "Channeling: Identity-Based Social Movements and Public Law," *University of Pennsylvania Law Review* 150 (2001): 520; Jeffrey Rosen, *The Most Democratic Branch: How the Courts Serve America* (Oxford: Oxford University Press, 2006), 96. For a comprehensive history of reproductive rights and the role of the 1980s, see, for example, Linda Gordon, "Who is Frightened of Reproductive Rights for Women and Why? Some Historical Answers," *Frontiers: A Journal of Women's Studies* 9.1 (1986): 22 (placing reproductive rights developments of the 1980s in the context of over 150 years of historical political development of the issue, including, for example, criminalization efforts led by physicians and eugenics-motivated arguments for contraceptive rights). For context on the role of culture wars throughout the 1980s and since, see, for example, Andrew Hartman, "The Culture Wars are Dead," *The Baffler*, 39 (May–June 2018): 48 (arguing that a narrative of decline has defined conservative cultural attitudes since the 1960s, and that Donald Trump's rise to power represents just the latest phase of the culture wars). For a more detailed history of the rise of the conservative movement over the later portion of the twentieth Century, see, for example, Donald Critchlow, *The Conservative Ascendancy: How the GOP Made Political History* (Cambridge, MA: Harvard University Press, 2007) (focusing on the expanding conservative base during the 1980s, including the role of anti-abortion activist Phyllis Schlafly).

3. Mark Tushnet, "Understanding the Rehnquist Court," *Ohio Northern University Law Review* 31 (2005): 197 (observing that beginning in the mid-

1980s, social conservatives began to have a larger presence on the U.S. Supreme Court). But, see also, Sara Diamond, *Roads to Dominion* (New York: Guilford Press, 1995), 228–229 (noting that, by the late 1980s, the Christian Right had yet to achieve a major policy win on the issue of abortion and arguing that, although the consolidation of grassroots conservative movements in the 1980s represented a highly influential movement, the Reagan administration's focus on economic and military policies left the movement without a champion for moral traditionalism in the White House).

4. Karen F.B. Gray, "An Establishment Clause Analysis of *Webster v. Reproductive Health Services*," *Georgia Law Review* 24 (1990): 399–400; George J. Wooditch Jr., "A Woman's Right to an Abortion as Affected by the Conservative Era of the 1980s," *Howard Law Review* 34 (1991): 427.

5. Mary Ziegler, "Grassroots Originalism: Judicial Activism Arguments, the Abortion Debate, and the Politics of Judicial Philosophy" *University of Louisville Law Review* 51 (2013): 201; Connor Gearty, "The Politics of Abortion," *Journal of Law and Society* 19 (1992): 451. For an additional, important legal history of the 1980s, see Michael S. Hevel and Charles J. Thompson's history of *Gay Student Services v. Texas A&M University*, in this volume.

6. This positive trend may have mirrored public perception during the decade, as well. Over the 1980s, public support for abortion increased. In 1981, 21 percent of national survey respondents said they thought abortion should be illegal in all circumstances, 52 percent said they thought abortion should be legal in some circumstances, and 23 percent said it should be legal in all circumstances. By contrast, in 1990, only 12 percent of survey respondents said that they thought abortion should be illegal in all circumstances. The number who thought abortion should be legal in some circumstances stayed roughly the same, at 53 percent, while 31 percent said they believed abortion should be legal in all circumstances. "Abortion," Gallup. https://news.gallup.com/poll/1576/abortion.aspx

7. 462 U.S. 416 (1983), hereinafter "*Akron*."
8. 476 U.S. 747 (1986), hereinafter "*Thornburgh*."
9. 410 U.S. 113 (1973), hereinafter "*Roe*."
10. 505 U.S. 833 (1992), hereinafter "*Casey*."
11. The seminal account of the rise of the right to abortion and of the legal activism that led to *Roe* is found in scholar Reva Siegel's work. See, for example, Reva B. Siegel, "Reasoning from the Body: A Historical Perspective on Abortion Regulation and Questions of Equal Protection," *Stanford Law Review* 44 (1992): 267–280; Reva B. Siegel, "Roe's Roots: The Women's Rights Claims that Engendered Roe," *Boston University Law Review* 90 (2010): 1879–1886.

12. Abortion: History of a Victory, in *Civil Liberties* [Part 1 of 4]. 1972–1973. MS Southern Regional Office Files: Southern Regional Office Files,

1945–1990 c03145. Mudd Library, Princeton University, Princeton, New Jersey. American Civil Liberties Union Papers, 1912–1990. http://tinyurl.galegroup.com/tinyurl/8dfki8

13. *Pierce v. Society of Sisters*, 268 U.S. 510 (1925).
14. *Griswold v. Connecticut*, 381 U.S. 479 (1965).
15. *Eisenstadt v. Baird*, 405 U.S. 438 (1972).
16. U.S. Const. Amend. XIV § 1.
17. *Roe*, 410 U.S., 162–164.
18. *Roe*, 410 U.S., 163, 166.
19. *Casey*, 505 U.S., 844.
20. *Casey*, 505 U.S., 844.
21. *Casey*, 505 U.S., 844.
22. A 1992 ACLU newsletter discussing *Casey* stated that "the Justices are likely to use this case to overturn *Roe v. Wade*." Reproductive Freedom Project, Reproductive Rights Update (May 1, 1992) in *[Planned Parenthood v. Casey]* NAACP *(National Association for the Advancement of Colored People) Legal Defense and Education Fund*; American Civil Liberties Union Records: Subgroup 4, MC001.04, Box: 5184, Folder: "ACLU Memos: Sup. Ct.," Public Policy Papers, Department of Rare Books and Special Collections, Princeton University Library, Princeton, New Jersey.
23. *Casey*, 505 U.S., 846.
24. *Casey*, 505 U.S., 877.
25. *Casey*, 505 U.S., 877–878.
26. *Casey*, 505 U.S., 876.
27. *Casey*, 505 U.S., 878.
28. Mary Ziegler, "Facing Facts: The New Era of Abortion Conflict After Whole Woman's Health," *Wake Forest Law Review* 52 (2017): 1239–1261 (arguing that the undue burden framework emerged over the 1980s as a pro-life tactic along with arguments that abortion harms women).
29. Pro-choice advocates frequently framed abortion regulations in terms of the undue burden they posed on women. One of the earliest examples of this framing is in the oral argument for *Bellotti v. Baird*, 443 U.S. 622 (1979) in which attorney Joseph J. Balliro addressed the "undue burdens" posed by a Massachusetts statute requiring parental consent for minors seeking abortion.
30. RFP Annual Report 1980 in *Reproductive Freedom Project Annual Report*; American Civil Liberties Union Records: Subgroup 4, MC001.04, Box: 5418, Folder: "RFP Annual Report 1980," Public Policy Papers, Department of Rare Books and Special Collections, Princeton University Library, Princeton, New Jersey.
31. RFP Annual Report 1980 in *Reproductive Freedom Project Annual Report*; American Civil Liberties Union Records: Subgroup 4, MC001.04, Box:

5418, Folder: "RFP Annual Report 1980," Public Policy Papers, Department of Rare Books and Special Collections, Princeton University Library, Princeton, New Jersey.

32. Derived from the Latin word "for everything," an omnibus bill combines numerous measures into a single document subject to one vote by a legislature. RFP Annual Report 1982 at 4 in *Reproductive Freedom Project Annual Report*; American Civil Liberties Union Records: Subgroup 4, MC001.04, Box: 5418, Folder: "RFP Annual Report 1982," Public Policy Papers, Department of Rare Books and Special Collections, Princeton University Library, Princeton, New Jersey.

33. RFP Annual Report 1981 in *Reproductive Freedom Project Annual Report*, 9; American Civil Liberties Union Records: Subgroup 4, MC001.04, Box: 5418, Folder: "RFP Annual Report 1981," Public Policy Papers, Department of Rare Books and Special Collections, Princeton University Library, Princeton, New Jersey.

34. Much important work has been done on the pro-life movement's use of "women's health" to promote burdensome abortion regulations. For scholarship on this "woman-protective" argument, see, for example, Reva B. Siegel, "The Right's Reasons: Constitutional Conflict and the Spread of Woman-Protective Antiabortion Argument," *Duke Law Journal* 57 (2008).

35. RFP Annual Report 1980 at 5 in *Reproductive Freedom Project Annual Report*; American Civil Liberties Union Records: Subgroup 4, MC001.04, Box: 5418, Folder: "RFP Annual Report 1980," Public Policy Papers, Department of Rare Books and Special Collections, Princeton University Library, Princeton, New Jersey.

36. RFP Annual Report 1980 at 5 in *Reproductive Freedom Project Annual Report*; American Civil Liberties Union Records: Subgroup 4, MC001.04, Box: 5418, Folder: "RFP Annual Report 1980," Public Policy Papers, Department of Rare Books and Special Collections, Princeton University Library, Princeton, New Jersey.

37. Testimony before Akron City Council's Health and Social Service Committee Concerning Proposed Ordinance Amending Chapter 1870 of the Codified Ordinance of the City of Akron, Ohio (January 14, 1978), 1 in *Reproductive Freedom Project Constitutional Convention files*; American Civil Liberties Union Records: Subgroup 4, MC001.04, Box: 4657, Folder: "Con Con Ohio," Public Policy Papers, Department of Rare Books and Special Collections, Princeton University Library, Princeton, New Jersey.

38. RFP Annual Report 1980, *Reproductive Freedom Project Annual Report*, 5; American Civil Liberties Union Records: Subgroup 4, MC001.04, Box: 5418, Folder: "RFP Annual Report 1980," Public Policy Papers, Department of Rare Books and Special Collections, Princeton University Library, Princeton, New Jersey.

39. RFP Annual Report 1982 at 4 in *Reproductive Freedom Project Annual Report*; American Civil Liberties Union Records: Subgroup 4, MC001.04, Box: 5418, Folder: "RFP Annual Report 1982," Public Policy Papers, Department of Rare Books and Special Collections, Princeton University Library, Princeton, New Jersey.

40. *Akron*, 462 U.S., 434.

41. See, for example, Ziegler, "Facing Facts," 1249–1250.

42. *Casey*, 505 U.S., 453

43. *Casey*, 505 U.S., 453–454.

44. Ten Years of Struggle for Equal Rights; The New Supreme Court Abortion Decisions, 1982–1983, 5. TS Years of Expansion, 1950–1990: Series 3: Subject Files: Equality Before the Law, 1941–1987 Box 1147, Folder 21, Item 429. Mudd Library, Princeton University. American Civil Liberties Union Papers, 1912–1990. http://tinyurl.galegroup.com/tinyurl/8dfEi5

45. Petition for a Writ of Certiorari, *Akron v. Akron Center for Reproductive Health*, 81-746 (October 16, 1981), I (emphasis added).

46. Brief of Respondent Akron Center for Reproductive Health, *Akron v. Akron Center for Reproductive Health*, 81-746 (August 27, 1982), 32, 40.

47. Letter from Burt Neuborne to Janet Benshoof and Steve Landsman, Oct. 26, 1982, Designation of Oralist for City of Akron, in *Akron v. Akron Center for Reproductive Health*; American Civil Liberties Union Records: Subgroup 3, Legal Case Files Series, MC001.03.04, Box: 3558, Folder: "*Akron v. Akron Ctr. For Reproductive Health*," Public Policy Papers, Department of Rare Books and Special Collections, Princeton University Library, Princeton, New Jersey.

48. RFP annual report 1982 at 4 in *Reproductive Freedom Project Annual Report*; American Civil Liberties Union Records: Subgroup 4, MC001.04, Box: 5418, Folder: "RFP Annual Report 1982," Public Policy Papers, Department of Rare Books and Special Collections, Princeton University Library, Princeton, New Jersey.

49. *Akron*, 462 U.S. at 444, quoting Akron Codified Ordinances § 1879.06(B).

50. *Akron*, 462 U.S. at 423 n.5, quoting Akron Codified Ordinances § 1879.06(B).

51. *Akron*, 462 U.S. at 423 n.5.

52. *Akron*, 462 U.S. at 423 n.5.

53. Respondents and Cross-Petitioners' Brief, *Akron v. Akron Center for Reproductive Health*, 81-746 (August 27, 1982), 32.

54. Respondents and Cross-Petitioners' Brief, *Akron v. Akron Center for Reproductive Health*, 81-746 (August 27, 1982), 15

55. Respondents and Cross-Petitioners' Brief, *Akron v. Akron Center for Reproductive Health*, 81-746 (August 27, 1982), 32

56. Respondents and Cross-Petitioners' Brief, *Akron v. Akron Center for Reproductive Health*, 81-746 (August 27, 1982), 23 (emphasis added).

57. Respondents and Cross-Petitioners' Brief, *Akron v. Akron Center for Reproductive Health*, 81-746 (August 27, 1982), 8

58. Respondents and Cross-Petitioners' Brief, *Akron v. Akron Center for Reproductive Health*, 81-746 (August 27, 1982), 9

59. Respondents and Cross-Petitioners' Brief, *Akron v. Akron Center for Reproductive Health*, 81-746 (August 27, 1982), 9.

60. Respondents and Cross-Petitioners' Brief, *Akron v. Akron Center for Reproductive Health*, 81-746 (August 27, 1982), 12

61. Amici Curiae Brief on behalf of National Organization for Women et al., Akron v. Akron Center for Reproductive Health, 81-746 (August 4, 1982) at 31–33.

62. Ten Years of Struggle for Equal Rights; The New Supreme Court Abortion Decisions, 15. 1982–1983. TS Years of Expansion, 1950–1990: Series 3: Subject Files: Equality Before the Law, 1941–1987 Box 1147, Folder 21, Item 429. Mudd Library, Princeton University, Princeton, New Jersey. American Civil Liberties Union Papers, 1912–1990. http://tinyurl.galegroup.com/tinyurl/8dfEi5

63. Ten Years of Struggle for Equal Rights; The New Supreme Court Abortion Decisions, 19–25. See also States with Laws or Regulations Requiring that Second Trimester Abortions be Performed in Hospitals in *Planned Parenthood Legal Cases*; American Civil Liberties Union Records: Subgroup 4, MC001.04, Box: 5124, Folder: 7, Public Policy Papers, Department of Rare Books and Special Collections, Princeton University Library, Princeton, New Jersey (listing California, Connecticut, Georgia, Hawaii, Idaho, Illinois, Indiana, Kentucky, Massachusetts, Louisiana, Missouri, Montana, New York, North Dakota, Oklahoma, Tennessee, Nevada, Utah, Virginia, and Wisconsin).

64. Respondents and Cross-Petitioners' Brief, *Akron v. Akron Center for Reproductive Health*, 81-746 (August 27, 1982), 12.

65. In Supreme Court cases, amicus, or "friend of the court" briefs are filed by individuals and groups that are not a party to the lawsuit but have a vested interest in the outcome of the case.

66. RFP Annual report 1982 at 6, in *Reproductive Freedom Project Annual Report*; American Civil Liberties Union Records: Subgroup 4, MC001.04, Box: 5418, Folder: "RFP Annual Report 1982," Public Policy Papers, Department of Rare Books and Special Collections, Princeton University Library, Princeton, New Jersey.

67. Amici Curiae Brief on behalf of National Organization for Women et al., *Akron v. Akron Center for Reproductive Health*, 81-746 (August 4, 1982) at 11.

68. Respondents and Cross-Petitioners' Brief, *Akron v. Akron Center for Reproductive Health*, 81-746 (August 27, 1982), 12.

69. Amici Curiae Brief on behalf of National Organization for Women et al., *Akron v. Akron Center for Reproductive Health*, 81-746 (August 4, 1982), 12.

70. Amici Curiae Brief on behalf of National Organization for Women et al., *Akron v. Akron Center for Reproductive Health*, 81-746, 14–15.

71. See Brief of Amici Curiae NAACP Legal Defense and Educational Fund, Inc., *Akron v. Akron Center for Reproductive Health*, 81-746 (August 30, 1982), 2 (citing a prior sex discrimination case in which the NAACP had served as amici but listing no prior reproductive rights cases.) The ACLU would continue to work with minority groups in its legal strategy throughout the 1980s. For instance, in *Ohio v. Akron*, 497 U.S. 502 (1990), the ACLU solicited an amicus brief written on behalf of the American Indian Health Care Association, Asian American Legal Defense and Education Fund, Choices Women's Medical Center, Committee of Interns and Residents, DC Rape Crisis Center, Hispanic Health Council, National Center for Lesbian Rights, National Rainbow Coalition, and Women's Commission, among others. The brief argued that mandating parental notice would "unduly burden" the right to abortion. The brief stated that "over twenty-five civil rights, women's, labor organizations" joined in the writing of the brief because they "represent various segments of American society with diverse interests" and are all "concerned that adolescent women's right to choose not be destroyed or infringed." In Case Files; American Civil Liberties Union Records: Subgroup 3, Project Files Series, MC001.03.02, Box: 2943, Folder: "*Ohio v. Akron*—Amici Curiae Brief, American Indian Health Care Assoc. et al.," Public Policy Papers, Department of Rare Books and Special Collections, Princeton University Library, Princeton, New Jersey.

72. Brief of Amici Curiae NAACP Legal Defense and Educational Fund, Inc., *Akron v. Akron Center for Reproductive Health*, 81-746 (August 30, 1982), 2.

73. Brief of Amici Curiae NAACP Legal Defense and Educational Fund, Inc., *Akron v. Akron Center for Reproductive Health*, 81-746, 3, n.1.

74. RFP Annual Report 1982 at 6 in *Reproductive Freedom Project Annual Report*; American Civil Liberties Union Records: Subgroup 4, MC001.04, Box: 5418, Folder: "RFP Annual Report 1982," Public Policy Papers, Department of Rare Books and Special Collections, Princeton University Library, Princeton, New Jersey.

75. *Akron*, 462 U.S. 416 (1983).

76. ACLU Press Statement, June 16, 1983, in *Press Statement—Akron Center for Reproductive Health v. Akron*; American Civil Liberties Union Records: Subgroup 3, Regional Offices Files Series, MC001.03.05, Box: 4370, Folder: "Press Statement 6/16/83 Akron Ctr. For Rep. Health v. Akron," Public Policy Papers, Department of Rare Books and Special Collections, Princeton University Library, Princeton, New Jersey.

77. 476 U.S. at 758 (emphasis added).

78. Incorporated in 1971, Americans United for Life "protects and defends human life from conception to natural death through vigorous legislative,

judicial, and educational efforts" and is the first national pro-life organization in America. https://aul.org/about

79. *Thornburgh*, 476 U.S. 747, 760–761 (1986).

80. *Thornburgh*, 476 U.S. 747, 760–761 (1986). Quoting Pennsylvania Consolidated Statutes §§ 3205(a)(1) and (2).

81. *Thornburgh*, 476 U.S. 747, 760–761 (1986). Quoting Pennsylvania Consolidated Statutes §§ 3205(a)(1) and (2).

82. RFP Annual Report 1982 at 10 in *Reproductive Freedom Project Annual Report*; American Civil Liberties Union Records: Subgroup 4, MC001.04, Box: 5418, Folder: "RFP Annual Report 1982," Public Policy Papers, Department of Rare Books and Special Collections, Princeton University Library, Princeton, New Jersey.

83. Letter from Lloyd R. Ziff to Kathryn Kolbert, copying Janet Benshoof (Dec. 29, 1981); memoranda from Julia A. Conover to the Pennsylvania Litigation Team regarding the Pennsylvania Abortion Control Act, Dec. 22, 1981, at 1 (discussing meetings held in December attended by Kitty Kolbert); and letter from Kathryn Kolbert to Janet Benshoof, dated January 7, 1982, in *Planned Parenthood Legal Cases*; American Civil Liberties Union Records: Subgroup 4, MC001.04, Box: 5124, Folder: 7, Public Policy Papers, Department of Rare Books and Special Collections, Princeton University Library, Princeton, New Jersey.

84. Memoranda from Julia A. Conover to The Pennsylvania Litigation Team regarding The Pennsylvania Abortion Control Act, Dec. 22, 1981 at 8 in *Planned Parenthood Legal Cases*; American Civil Liberties Union Records: Subgroup 4, MC001.04, Box: 5124, Folder: 7, Public Policy Papers, Department of Rare Books and Special Collections, Princeton University Library, Princeton, New Jersey.

85. Memorandum from Janet Benshoof to Litigation Team & Persons Concerned with the Recently-Passed Senate Bill 742 in the State of Pennsylvania, Dec. 17, 1981, at 2 in *Planned Parenthood Legal Cases*; American Civil Liberties Union Records: Subgroup 4, MC001.04, Box: 5124, Folder: 7, Public Policy Papers, Department of Rare Books and Special Collections, Princeton University Library, Princeton, New Jersey.

86. Memorandum from Janet Benshoof to Litigation Team & Persons Concerned with the Recently Passed Senate Bill 742 in the State of Pennsylvania, Dec. 17, 1981, at 2. The memo suggested, as one discrete advocacy assignment, "for someone to chart all the abortion clinics and other abortion facilities throughout the state, when they are open, and the amount of travel time to any of these facilities, in order to demonstrate the incredible burden upon women who want abortions, particularly those living in outlying rural areas."

87. The Pennsylvania abortion act attracted record public attention. In fact, more than 25,000 people sent messages to the governor both in favor and

against the bill. Frederick Cusick, "Why Foes of Abortion in Pa. Lost on the Veto," *Inquirer* (Dec. 27, 1981) in *Planned Parenthood Legal Cases*; American Civil Liberties Union Records: Subgroup 4, MC001.04, Box: 5124, Folder: 7, Public Policy Papers, Department of Rare Books and Special Collections, Princeton University Library.

88. Press Release, Dec. 23, 1981, in *Planned Parenthood Legal Cases*; American Civil Liberties Union Records: Subgroup 4, MC001.04, Box: 5124, Folder: 7, Public Policy Papers, Department of Rare Books and Special Collections, Princeton University Library.

89. Press Release, Dec. 23, 1981, in *Planned Parenthood Legal Cases*; American Civil Liberties Union Records: Subgroup 4, MC001.04, Box: 5124, Folder: 7, Public Policy Papers, Department of Rare Books and Special Collections, Princeton University Library.

90. RFP Annual Report 1982 at 10–11 in *Reproductive Freedom Project Annual Report*; American Civil Liberties Union Records: Subgroup 4, MC001.04, Box: 5418, Folder: "RFP Annual Report 1982," Public Policy Papers, Department of Rare Books and Special Collections, Princeton University Library, Princeton, New Jersey.

91. Brief for *Appellees, Thornburgh v. American College of Obstetricians and Gynecologists*, 84–495 (1985) 1985 WL 669697 at *4.

92. Brief for *Appellees, Thornburgh v. American College of Obstetricians and Gynecologists*, *18.

93. Brief for *Appellees, Thornburgh v. American College of Obstetricians and Gynecologists*, *19.

94. Brief for *Appellees, Thornburgh v. American College of Obstetricians and Gynecologists*, *20.

95. Brief for *Appellees, Thornburgh v. American College of Obstetricians and Gynecologists*, *22.

96. *Thornburgh*, 476 U.S., 764.

97. *Thornburgh*, 476 U.S., 759.

98. 136 S. Ct. 2292 (2016) (hereinafter "*Whole Woman's Health*").

99. 591 U.S. ____ (2020) (hereinafter "*June Medical Services*").

100. Ibid. at 2300, quoting Texas Health and Safety Code Annotated § 171.0031(a).

101. Ibid. at 2300, quoting Texas Health and Safety Code Annotated § 245.010(a).

102. Ibid. at 2301–2303.

103. Brief for Petitioners Whole Woman's Health et al., *Whole Woman's Health v. Hellerstedt*, 15–274 (Dec. 28, 2015) (hereinafter "Petitioners' Brief"), i.

104. Petitioners' Brief, 44–54.

105. Petitioners' Brief, 3.

106. Petitioners' Brief, 3.

107. Petitioners' Brief, 20.

108. Brief of Amici Curiae National Network of Abortion Funds and 41 Member Abortion Funds in Support of Petitioners, *Whole Woman's Health v. Hellerstedt*, 15–274 (Jan. 4, 2016), 12–23.

109. Petitioners' Brief, 2, 35–44.

110. Brief for Respondents John Hellerstedt et al., *Whole Woman's Health v. Hellerstedt*, 15–274 (Jan. 27, 2016), I.

111. Brief for Respondents John Hellerstedt et al., *Whole Woman's Health v. Hellerstedt*, 20–29.

112. 136 S. Ct. 2292 at 2309.

113. 136 S. Ct. 2292 at 2309.

114. 136 S. Ct. 2292 at 2310.

115. Slip Op. at 2.

116. Slip Op. at 31.

117. Slip Op. at 34.

118. See, for example, Hannah Haksgaard, "Rural Women and Developments in the Undue Burden Analysis: The Effect of *Whole Woman's Health v. Hellerstedt*," *Drake Law Review* 65 (2017); Pamela C. Corley, "Undue Burden on Women's Right to Seek Abortion: *Whole Woman's Health v. Hellerstedt*," *Justice System Journal* 37 (2016) 386 (concluding that "*Whole Woman's Health* strongly reaffirms a woman's constitutional right to obtain an abortion").

119. Charles C. Camosy, "Casey's Undue Burden and Whole Woman's Health's Interest-Balancing Tests are Pro-Life Opportunities," *Quinnipiac Law Review* 35 (2017): 647.

120. Americans United for Life, "Defending Life." See https://aul.org/defendinglife

121. Americans United for Life, "Defending Life."

122. Americans United for Life, "Defending Life."

123. Americans United for Life, "Defending Life."

124. At the time of writing, two lawsuits appeared set for potential Supreme Court consideration; both are abortion prohibitions sought in the interest of fetal life and "women's health":

> First, in March 2018, Mississippi passed a fifteen-week abortion ban. The District Court struck down this law, strongly criticizing the state in its decision. The Court wrote that "the State chose to pass a law it knew was unconstitutional to endorse a decades long campaign, fueled by national interest groups, to ask the Supreme Court to overturn *Roe v. Wade*. This Court follows the commands of the Supreme Court and the dictates of the United States Consti-

tution, rather than the disingenuous calculations of the Mississippi Legislature." The Court stated that "the Mississippi Legislature's professed interest in 'women's health' is pure gaslighting."

Second, in 2017 the Texas legislature passed a law banning the most common and safe method of ending a pregnancy after fifteen weeks. The District Court struck down the ban as unconstitutional, the case was appealed to the Fifth Circuit, and may be appealed to the Supreme Court.

125. Americans United for Life, "Defending Life."

Works Cited

Akron v. Akron Center for Reproductive Health; American Civil Liberties Union Records: Subgroup 3, Legal Case Files Series, MC001.03.04, Box: 3558, Folder: "*Akron v. Akron Ctr. For Reproductive Health*," Public Policy Papers, Department of Rare Books and Special Collections, Princeton University Library, Princeton, New Jersey.

Americans United for Life. https://aul.org/about

Americans United for Life. "Defending Life" (2018). https://aul.org/defendinglife

Case Files; American Civil Liberties Union Records: Subgroup 3, Project Files Series, MC001.03.02, Public Policy Papers, Department of Rare Books and Special Collections, Princeton University Library, Princeton, New Jersey.

Civil Liberties [Part 1 of 4]. 1972–1973. MS Southern Regional Office Files: Southern Regional Office Files, 1945–1990 c03145. Mudd Library, Princeton University, Princeton, New Jersey. American Civil Liberties Union Papers, 1912–1990. http://tinyurl.galegroup.com/tinyurl/8dfki8

Corley, Patricia C. "Undue Burden on Women's Right to Seek Abortion: *Whole Woman's Health v. Hellerstedt*." *Justice System Journal* 37 (2016): 386

Critchlow, Donald. *The Conservative Ascendancy: How the GOP Made Political History*. Cambridge, MA: Harvard University Press, 2007.

Diamond, Sara. *Roads to Dominion*. New York: Guilford Press, 1995.

Eskridge, William N. Jr., "Channeling: Identity-Based Social Movements and Public Law." *University of Pennsylvania Law Review* 150 (2001).

Gallup. "Abortion." https://news.gallup.com/poll/1576/abortion.aspx

Gearty, Connor. "The Politics of Abortion." *Journal of Law and Society* 19 (1992).

Gordon, Linda. "Who is Frightened of Reproductive Rights for Women and Why? Some Historical Answers." *Frontiers: A Journal of Women's Studies* 9.1 (1986).

Gray, Karen F. B. "An Establishment Clause Analysis of *Webster v. Reproductive Health Services.*" *Georgia Law Review* 24 (1990).
Haksgaard, Hannah. "Rural Women and Developments in the Undue Burden Analysis: The Effect of *Whole Woman's Health v. Hellerstedt.*" *Drake Law Review* 65 (2017).
Hartman, Andrew. "The Culture Wars are Dead." *The Baffler*, 39 (May–June 2018).
The New Supreme Court Abortion Decisions, 5. 1982–1983. TS Years of Expansion, 1950–1990: Series 3: Subject Files: Equality Before the Law, 1941–1987 Box 1147, Folder 21, Item 429. Mudd Library, Princeton University, Princeton, New Jersey. American Civil Liberties Union Papers, 1912–1990. http://tinyurl.galegroup.com/tinyurl/8dfEi5
Planned Parenthood Legal Cases; American Civil Liberties Union Records: Subgroup 4, MC001.04, Box: 5124, Folder: 7, Public Policy Papers, Department of Rare Books and Special Collections, Princeton University Library, Princeton, New Jersey.
Planned Parenthood v. Casey NAACP (National Association for the Advancement of Colored People) Legal Defense and Education Fund; American Civil Liberties Union Records: Subgroup 4, MC001.04, Public Policy Papers, Department of Rare Books and Special Collections, Princeton University Library, Princeton, New Jersey.
Press Statement—Akron Center for Reproductive Health v. Akron; American Civil Liberties Union Records: Subgroup 3, Regional Offices Files Series, MC001.03.05, Public Policy Papers, Department of Rare Books and Special Collections, Princeton University Library, Princeton, New Jersey.
Reproductive Freedom Project Annual Report; American Civil Liberties Union Records: Subgroup 4, MC001.04, Public Policy Papers, Department of Rare Books and Special Collections, Princeton University Library, Princeton, New Jersey.
Reproductive Freedom Project Constitutional Convention files; American Civil Liberties Union Records: Subgroup 4, MC001.04, Public Policy Papers, Department of Rare Books and Special Collections, Princeton University Library, Princeton, New Jersey.
Rosen, Jeffrey. *The Most Democratic Branch: How the Courts Serve America*. Oxford: Oxford University Press, 2006.
Siegel, Reva B. "Reasoning from the Body: A Historical Perspective on Abortion Regulation and Questions of Equal Protection." *Stanford Law Review* 44 (1992).
Siegel, Reva B. "The Right's Reasons: Constitutional Conflict and the Spread of Woman-Protective Antiabortion Argument." *Duke Law Journal* 57 (2008).
Siegel, Reva B. "Roe's Roots: The Women's Rights Claims that Engendered Roe." *Boston University Law Review* 90 (2010).

Stone, Geoffrey R., Louis Michael Seidman, Cass R. Sunstein, Mark V. Tushnet, and Pamela S. Karlan. *Constitutional Law*. New York: Walters Kluwer, 2018.

Sullivan, Kathleen M., and Noah Feldman. *Constitutional Law*. New York: Foundation Press, 2016.

Tushnet, Mark. "Understanding the Rehnquist Court." *Ohio Northern University Law Review* 31 (2005).

Wooditch Jr., George J. "A Woman's Right to an Abortion as Affected by the Conservative Era of the 1980s." *Howard Law Review* 34 (1991).

Ziegler, Mary. "Facing Facts: The New Era of Abortion Conflict after Whole Woman's Health." *Wake Forest Law Review* 52 (2017).

Ziegler, Mary. "Grassroots Originalism: Judicial Activism Arguments, the Abortion Debate, and the Politics of Judicial Philosophy." *University of Louisville Law Review* 51 (2013).

Opening DOORWAYS and Closing Others

Tactical Deployments of Respectability, Religion, and Race in the St. Louis Early-AIDS Response

KATIE BATZA

The AIDS crisis is a defining component of the 1980s, especially with regard to feminist and queer history, and yet our historical understanding of the epidemic is distorted by a bifurcated approach that foregrounds either large urban centers or broad national histories.[1] These perspectives illuminate robust political responses buoyed by the preexistence and creation of extensive gay social services as well as by large gay and lesbian communities on one side and a sharp neoliberal and conservative political turn at the national level that trickled down to socially construct the epidemic at the local level on the other. Both approaches either exclude or marginalize the AIDS crisis and response in smaller cities, towns, and rural places, particularly in the United States Heartland.[2] However, a closer examination of the Heartland's response to AIDS reveals a number of the political tactics and framings that came to define the lesbian, gay, and bisexual, if not transgender or queer, political agenda for a full generation after the emergence of the epidemic in 1981.

The history of AIDS in the Heartland region challenges many of the paradigms about the epidemic put forth by the dominant historical narrative that focuses on the coastal cities like New York and San Francisco. For one, the disease itself presented very differently in this region than on the coasts—though St. Louis is home to the first documented case of HIV within the United States with the death of Robert Rayford in 1969, the epidemic of the 1980s hit the Heartland later, thus with more warning, and on a much smaller scale than in New York City or San Francisco.[3] Additionally, the political landscape of the epidemic in the Heartland proved vastly different and in ways more representative of the nation at large than the major metropoles on the coasts. The lack of a healthy and multifaceted political and social service infrastructure within the region's gay communities, in part a result of a relatively small out gay population, demanded a politically collaborative response to the epidemic relying on groups not often thought of as allies to gay communities. Thus, the need for buy-in from religious institutions and traditionally more conservative community stakeholders shaped the early AIDS response in the Heartland. The creation and evolution of DOORWAYS, a housing organization for people with HIV/AIDS in St. Louis, provides a window into the mechanics of the epidemic's political framing in order to address the crisis in the political landscape of the region—a framework that resonated throughout the region and reverberated back into the national lesbian, gay, and bisexual political agenda of the 1980s, 1990s, and 2000s. Upon the Heartland landscape, organizations such as DOORWAYS emerged as some of the most transformational sites of activism as they provided desperately needed services while simultaneously challenging people largely unaffected by the HIV/AIDS epidemic to engage and invest in the epidemic morally, spiritually, and financially. Though less bombastic and confrontational than some of the important activism on the coasts, broadening the scope of activism to include DOORWAYS and similar organizations allows for a deeper understanding of AIDS activism beyond major urban landscapes.

This brief story provides both an introduction to DOORWAYS and an analytical jumping-off place: Michael Edland, a well-regarded interior designer in St. Louis, cajoled many of his designer friends and high-end clients to donate antiques and valuable furniture pieces to sell in a garage sale, a three-day high-end fundraiser wherein Edland designed the parking garage of St. Louis' luxurious Plaza Frontenac, a mall anchored by Saks Fifth Avenue, like a showroom. The event raised $40,000 for DOORWAYS, a nonprofit tasked with providing housing for people with AIDS. The funds, along with significant financial contributions from Catholic Charities, the Jewish Foundation, and the major service and funding arms of a handful of Protestant denominations, went to refurbishing a gifted but dilapidated building on the city's racial dividing line, Delmar Boulevard, on St. Louis' North side.[4] Congregations from across the city and religious spectrum adopted individual apartments to rehab using volunteer labor and donated second-hand fixtures, furniture, and even cleaning supplies.[5] Many of those interviewed reminisced the five-story building had bathroom vanities, toilets, and showers of nearly every hue because they were all donated. Envisioned as a mixture of a "country club and fraternity house" for gay men dying of AIDS with nowhere else to go, Edland's volunteer designer team used a donated piano, bookshelves, and thick cushioned armchairs to create warm and comfortable communal spaces for young men suddenly faced with the physical capacities of much older and infirm men.[6] According to many recollections, just as they "finished fluffing the last decorative pillow and opened the space" for the AIDS "fraternity house," a low-income Black woman and her two children walked in as their first residents.[7] They had just arrived in St. Louis, courtesy of one-way bus tickets bought with pooled funds from her fearful neighbors in a small rural town in southeast Missouri, with one suitcase for each of them. "That was it, that was all they had," recalled one DOORWAYS founding board member.[8] "Pat," not her real name, recalled in a 1988 interview, "I can't tell you what my life would be like without DOORWAYS because I can't even bring myself to think about it."[9] She and her children turned the vision Edland had had for potential residents on its head, but they also represented an important new doorway of opportunity for the political framing of AIDS in the region.

There are many noteworthy aspects of the Heartland AIDS crisis introduced by this brief story. First and most obviously, the creative fundraising approaches and community partnerships in the absence of sufficient state services and support. Second, the need for DOORWAYS reflects that changing prognosis of HIV/AIDS at this particular moment in the late 1980s when AZT (1987), Trimetrexate (1988), and interferon Alpha injections (1988) extended the lifespan for some.[10] Relatedly, "Pat's" arrival signifies the infections among Black women (and people of color generally) that hit *simultaneously* with the emergence of AIDS among gay men in the region, challenging the often white-washed origins of AIDS that focus entirely on white gay communities. Pat's experience also illuminates one of the many forms of migration inspired/forced by AIDS. Regional migration from rural areas into urban centers both for care and at the insistence of AIDS-phobic communities became a hallmark of the Heartland AIDS experience, as one interview revealed "they either moved here for services or were brought here and dumped."[11] The in-migration extended beyond the rural surroundings as gay men returning to the Midwest in their final months of life and often in dire financial and medical situations as their coastal gay enclaves could no longer support them played an important role in the Heartland epidemic and response.[12] Finally, a number of interviewees for this project either moved to St. Louis in the hopes of fleeing the trauma of AIDS they had experienced on the coasts, or, less frequently, moved away from St. Louis to coastal cities in the hopes of helping a larger HIV+ population.[13] Indeed, the notion of "home" both in this region and in DOORWAYS itself is ripe for greater analysis and exploration that I will take up in future work.

Though difficult to disentangle and set aside the above articulated themes, this chapter explores the importance of religion, religious communities, and interdenominational alliances in the St. Louis HIV/AIDS response. My research suggests that religion is one of the strongest forces in the regional response and also stands in stark contrast, both in terms of positive leadership and negative obstacles, to the role of religion in existing histories of the epidemic. One person who served on numerous St. Louis boards stated that without religious organizations, "there would not have been any response" to AIDS in St. Louis.[14] Though nonreligious responses did exist, they were certainly meager by comparison and regularly interwoven into religious outreach or services. Within the religious responses there is certainly a great deal to pick apart, analyze, and understand. Further, the ripple effects of the close relationship between organized religion and the St. Louis AIDS response echoed and perhaps informed the national lesbian, gay, and bisexual political agenda in the final decades of the twentieth century.

Religion and the St. Louis Response

Before expanding further on the role of religion in St. Louis, I want to quickly revisit how religion intersects with current historical depictions of HIV/AIDS and related politics. Religious institutions, particularly the Catholic Church, fueled much of the most memorable and documented AIDS activism of the pre-HAART period, meaning before 1996. Consider the numerous ACT-UP protests and vivid artworks and posters aimed at the outspoken homophobia and firm anti-condom stance of the Catholic Church, and specifically New York's archbishop Cardinal John O'Connor.[15] Beyond street protests, the rise of the Religious Right that coincided with the first decade of the AIDS epidemic is frequently, and rightfully, implicated in the social and political construction of the epidemic. With closer examination, we see that individual religiously affiliated hospitals and liberal congregations in many large coastal cities served as important frontline responders to the disease. However, the official stances held by many denominations on homosexuality and safe sex, not to mention the fuel for AIDS-discrimination, phobia, and violence offered by "hate the sin, not the sinner" rhetoric has rendered organized religion an overwhelmingly negative force in the AIDS epidemic.[16]

St. Louis' relationship to religion is more nuanced and complex. In ways not reflected in the existing AIDS histories of New York or San Francisco, religion steeped the social and political landscape of the entire Heartland region and also made up, and even instigated, much of the AIDS response. We can see this at the personal, organizational, and cultural level in this St. Louis case study. With a small number of exceptions, the nearly thirty people I have interviewed thus far have had strong religious roots and many continued to be active in their religious communities that spanned from Catholic to Protestant to Judaism after their coming out or involvement with AIDS activism. In short, St. Louis is a religious town. In the words of one man who moved to St. Louis from Washington, DC, mid-crisis, "For gays . . . there was this still real desire to remain in the church verses people we knew in DC who would be like ex-Catholics."[17] Religious congregations proved important cultural, political, and social institutions regardless of faith or agnosticism so that activists and congregants knew the names of liberal congregations across the religious spectrum and were fluent enough in doctrines and ethos to know how best to harness each group for an effective AIDS response. Religious groups were tied to social services here as they either administered them, legitimated them through endorsement, or funded them through congregational fundraising or charity granting organizations, and often all three. Catholicism dominated this landscape, not because its subscribers far outnumber those of other religious denominations, but because of the city's strong and historic Catholic roots shaped the politics and culture of the city since its founding.

Archbishop of St. Louis John L. May is nearly universally credited with mainstreaming the city's AIDS response, as he declared in early 1987 that AIDS required compassion, voicing the official stance taken at the National Conference of Catholic Bishops in the spring of 1988.[18] Similar proclamations from Catholic leaders in major coastal cities following the Conference drew derision as activists fixated on the underlying homophobia and anti-condom stance of the church. However, St. Louisans responded to the call for compassion differently. In fact, Catholic Archbishop of St. Louis John May is frequently referred to as "the Spiritual parent of DOORWAYS."[19] He instigated an interdenominational working group including religious leaders from the biggest religious congregations in the city (such as Rabbi Ruben from Temple Israel and Reverend Michael Allen from Christ Church Cathedral), community activists, and representatives from the city's main AIDS Service Organization. Within these meetings housing emerged as the most obvious and basic roadblock for health services, a concept that fueled the interdenominational funding and volunteering commitment. All the religious leaders both present and represented in those meetings echoed this notion of housing as essential to health to their congregants and to other liberal religious leaders in the city. Michael Allen, a liberal Episcopal priest with Christ Church Cathedral (the main Cathedral for St. Louis) "was masterful . . . at tapping his wealthy and connected parishioners, particularly in the business community [to fundraise for DOORWAYS]. He said in his pulpit that St Louis has AIDS and we have AIDS, Christ Church has AIDS."[20] It became a *cause célèbre* among liberal churches and temples, evidenced by funds raised and volunteers regularly recruited over the next several years.

Digging just behind this carefully polished savior narrative in which AIDS housing facilities and DOORWAYS service awards are unironically named after a Catholic Archbishop reveals that St. Louis' largest AIDS Service Organization, St. Louis Effort for AIDS (EFA), had actually curated, pruned, and presented the idea of housing to the Archbishop and the interdenominational working group of the city's religious leaders. EFA first began its work of connecting people with AIDS with additional services in June of 1985 but didn't formally become a 501-c3 until the end of that year.[21] By then it provided a buffet of services. EFA's buddy program paired those living with the disease with volunteers who would check in daily, provide friendship, aid in navigating/informing families, and provide social and emotional support to health crises and end of life.[22] Initially, buddies often lived for only a matter of weeks before succumbing to the disease, but as treatments became available these relationships lasted longer and those relationships and services evolved accordingly to provide long-term support, sometimes spread across several EFA volunteers. Additionally, EFA had a help-line, support groups for family members and partners, and connected people with AIDS with the small number of AIDS-knowledgeable doctors (three or four for the city and surrounding region) and other medical services (often based out of Washington University's or St. Louis University medical schools). EFA dominated the AIDS service organization landscape throughout the early epidemic, though eventually became buttressed by a food outreach organization, a political organization, a specific organization for AIDS in the Black community, and DOORWAYS, many of which were started by EFA board members and volunteers.[23] As one volunteer explained, "though it had to navigate a very political terrain, it was not political."[24] However, it did not shy away from making people uncomfortable. EFA founder and well-known local drag performer Daniel Flier remembered performing in drag shows and incorporating safe sex education: "I would unravel condoms out of packages and I'd say 'this is a condom and this is made of latex and this can save your life.' I would do this in drag and get right in people's faces and say 'this goes on your junk before you do anything sexually because if you don't, you die.' "[25]

Publicly embracing the gay community and speaking bluntly and openly about sex epitomized the EFA mission and made outspoken support or financial backing from religious organizations difficult. Yet, even EFA's origin includes a religious intervention of sorts, speaking to the ubiquity of religion in the larger city landscape and in the AIDS response as a whole. Flier recalled that the very first meeting of what would become EFA was held in the drag queen dressing room upstairs of a local gay bar with twelve people attending, including "some little lady in nun garb named Sister Regina." Sister Regina, who no one recognized or even knew of, proceeded to instruct the others on the importance of and steps to getting tax-exempt status, and then, somewhat prophetically, according to Flier, she said, "What's going to happen is going to blow you all away and you are not going to believe what is to come. So fasten your seatbelts, because it is going to be very rough and God give you power and strength to get through it."[26] The mysterious Sister Regina did not appear again, but her story factors centrally in the recollections of EFA's origin. However, she constitutes all formal religious involvement in EFA. An early DOORWAYS board member and EFA volunteer recalled, "They [religious groups] wouldn't support EFA but they would support DOORWAYS."[27] Instead, Effort for AIDS relied heavily on small grants, volunteer labor, and private fundraising (until looking to corporations in 1988 and then to the 1990 passage of the Ryan White ACT), at times drawing their entire budget from benefit drag performances.[28] With the approval of AZT and other early drugs that granted longer life to some, those at EFA saw the need for housing grow and also saw a potential partner in the city's religious groups, if they were careful in simplifying and sanitizing the mission. Thus, when Archbishop May declared compassion for people with AIDS and created an interdenominational working group to which an EFA board member was invited, EFA had already identified the need for housing, articulated an argument that "housing equaled health," and imagined a solution that it simply could not execute without significant resources beyond its own abilities.[29] It was a match made either out of strategic necessity or in heaven, depending on perspective.

From its inception, DOORWAYS was designed for maximum palatability and highest impact. To accomplish this and foster necessary partnerships with conservative stakeholders, DOORWAYS divorced itself from any services beyond housing. Its housing services were very robust and included, from the start, rent subsidies to allow people to remain in the homes they already had, agreements with local landlords to facilitate discounted and subsidized rents, and also building construction, ownership, and management for those without housing. Today, the organization serves just under three thousand people in housing that spans from fully independent apartments to end-of-life care facilities.[30] DOORWAYS was not allowed to offer any additional services for fear of encouraging residents to practice safe sex or "encouraging" homosexuality. Thus, in the interdenominational meetings, EFA and religious leaders envisioned DOORWAYS as devoid of all counseling or support services beyond housing, with the understanding that EFA could and likely would provide those services separately.[31] Thus, DOORWAYS remained, in the words of one early board member, "vanilla."[32]

With housing the sick and needy foregrounding homosexuality and condoms, liberal religious congregations and individuals across the faith spectrum threw their full support behind DOORWAYS in multiple ways. Fundraising ranged from passing the basket during weekly services to business leaders with religious ties providing event sponsorships and from generous start-up funding (e.g., $75,000 from the Jewish Foundation) to quarterly obligations taken on by religious foundations.[33] In the early years, Catholic Charities was donating "something like $50,000" quarterly.[34] There was also evidence of "God on the Ground" with congregants volunteering but also with individuals with strong religious ties literally running DOORWAYS. The first executive director of DOORWAYS was an ex-nun named Lynn Cooper who "could talk anybody into anything" and who partnered with an active nun, Sister Betty, an administrator at a local Catholic Hospital, to bring DOORWAYS to life.[35] Both women were "tough" and people "you didn't say no to" but also "incredibly kind."[36] Sister Betty used her power as a hospital administrator to secure the city's first designated hospital beds for AIDS patients, and when nurses and doctors balked at her decision, she fired them. She also helped Lynn identify a convent in the city that had unused living quarters and instigated negotiations for their use as DOORWAYS' first living spaces for people with AIDS.[37] The hospital beds, convent quarters, and rent subsidy program provided the starting foundation upon which DOORWAYS could build. As word spread about the DOORWAYS mission through congregations and announcements in weekly religious bulletins, property owners began to donate properties or sought rental partnerships with DOORWAYS.[38] The organization offered more than altruistic incentives for business-minded property owners as DOORWAYS "always paid on time" with its religiously funded bank accounts and initially (before becoming more discerning) offered unscrupulous property owners opportunities to offload dilapidated buildings for a tax break.[39] Seemingly, in St. Louis, and in other cities that copied the DOORWAYS model, religious association opened many doors that otherwise would have been closed.

Though the success and exponential growth of DOORWAYS speaks to an acceptance of people with AIDS and the religious-infused mission to help them, simply associating religion and the act of housing people with AIDS did not defuse the fear and bigotry associated with the illness. There is an equal number of examples of AIDS-phobia and homophobia that housing people with AIDS inspired. Initially, a number of area residents around potential DOORWAYS buildings or rentals had a "not in my backyard" response. Even as recently as 2018, the organization encountered a repairman who refused to do work on a building when he learned that it housed AIDS patients.[40] When an order of nuns wanted to rent a portion of their convent at a discounted rate to DOORWAYS in 1988, an adjacent hospital brought the deal to a halt because "it did not want people [with AIDS] coming into their emergency room without insurance."[41] Equally important, if perhaps obviously, religious responses to AIDS in St. Louis and the Heartland more generally were far from monolithic and certainly not universally positive. While religiously sponsored and endorsed services and agencies made up a significant portion of the region's AIDS response, other denominations faced the epidemic with an intense bigotry that became central to their religious missions. The most well-known and aggressive example of this is the Westboro Baptist Church based in Topeka, Kansas, led by Fred Phelps, who made picketing the funerals of people who died from AIDS and of United States soldiers central to his ministry.[42] Despite the strong grip of AIDS-phobia and homophobia exemplified here, the affiliation of the Catholic Diocese and a number of other major religious institutions in St. Louis made DOORWAYS more palatable to the broader St. Louis public, in part by distancing the disease from the gay community in the eyes of their congregants.

Bridging Some Divides and Expanding Others

Like "Pat" from the opening vignette, women, and specifically women of color, made up the majority of new HIV/AIDS infections in the city, allowing DOORWAYS to further disassociate itself from homosexuality. By centering women rather than gay men in the DOORWAYS mission and the AIDS crisis more generally, DOORWAYS increased the palatability of its work to its religious stakeholders, particularly among Black pastors. Though Archbishop May's interdenominational working group, and many of the nonprofits that also made up to St. Louis AIDS response, repeatedly extended invitations to numerous Black pastors, they proved unwilling to openly engage, at least initially.[43] This reluctance appears to have been a response not only to AIDS and its association with homosexuality but also a response required by the Black respectability politics at work within the highly segregated city of St. Louis. Too often do scholars associate Black churches with homophobia without digging deeper beyond an assumed bigotry to reveal the political enactment of respectability and rebuttal of negative sexual stereotypes that all but necessitates the shunning of the sexual practices or drug use behind the AIDS epidemic. The work of Cathy Cohen and Daniel Royles, Darius Bost, and others tease out and provide nuanced insight into this political conundrum.[44] However, as the impact of AIDS among communities of Black women became more pronounced and stood outside the bounds of gay and/or intravenous drug using populations, Black churches became more engaged in the St. Louis AIDS response, often through the carefully sanitized work of DOORWAYS. All religious stakeholders in DOORWAYS, including Black churches, mobilized the innocent (and respectable) victim narratives offered by mothers and women infected with the disease to raise funds, awareness, and sympathy among their congregants.[45] DOORWAYS shifted its vision from "country club/fraternity house(s)" for gay men with AIDS to family-friendly housing and housing for all low-income people with AIDS.

In this way, DOORWAYS, more than any other AIDS service organizations in St. Louis, successfully bridged the highly segregated St. Louis landscape with buildings and apartments located all over the city, integrated living spaces in predominantly white or Black neighborhoods, and with invested stakeholders spanning much of both the religious and racial spectrums. Against the backdrop of infected women, Black pastors and neighborhood leaders welcomed DOORWAYS with open arms, inviting the organization to build and rent numerous housing developments, including the Mama Nyumba and Kaya Malaika buildings designed specifically for mothers and children, two of just a few in the nation of their kind.[46] Meanwhile, the organization continued to provide outreach and services for gay men and those infected through intravenous drug use as well. This somewhat clandestine and collaborative relationship between the straight Black community and gay communities played out beyond the AIDS crisis in the city.[47] When City Alderman Mary Ross, former chairwoman of the Black caucus, introduced and pushed through a Civil Rights Ordinance in 1992 that included some of the strongest protections for gays and lesbians in the country, she did so by highlighting the creation of a civil rights commission with investigative and disciplinary power and downplaying the inclusion of gay rights.[48] In an interview with the *New York Times* several weeks after the passage, Ross explained, "I think we covered, hopefully, everybody in this legislation who could possibly be discriminated against in one manner or another, and that is the intent. It is not a gay-rights thing."[49] As a result, St. Louis' protections for gays and lesbians passed unanimously and without incident while, by contrast, the Kansas City "gay" ordinance spear-headed by local gay and lesbian activists took years of protracted debate and protests.[50]

While the religiously inspired sanitizing politics deployed by DOORWAYS opened many, well, doorways, it darkened others. For DOORWAYS, fundraising in the larger community, away from the official churches, was conscientiously tailored to be appropriate for the nuns and ex-nuns associated with the organization.⁵¹ This is just one example of how such firm ties with religion had a comparatively conservatizing effect on the gay community's response to AIDS. Looking beyond DOORWAYS, we can see the religious influence in the broader St. Louis AIDS response in other ways—specifically the power of the closet. Though St. Louis has a rich LGBTQ history, nearly all of my interviewees point to the closet as the greatest impediment to a more robust AIDS response.⁵² "The gays that were here at that time in St. Louis at that time were much more closeted . . . some of it had to do with religion, some of it had to do with, um, they were from here and their families were still here."⁵³ Certainly, stories of the closet appear in coastal histories of AIDS as well, but St. Louis, though one of the twenty most populous cities in the country in the early 1980s and the largest in the state at the time, operated very much as a small town. Numerous interview subjects commented on the city's insular nature by explaining that people commonly included their high school in their initial introductions and that often relationships with or knowledge of extended family preceded them.

Generally, this close-knit nature inspired three reactions that hint at the role of religion and social policing in St. Louis: easy gay chain-migration patterns from surrounding rural towns; a vibrant, well-defined, and decidedly not politically focused gay neighborhood within which gay men were out and beyond which they were assumed closeted; and an exodus of gay men wanting greater anonymity and the ability to live without consequence for or from their families from St. Louis to larger cities. Gay chain migration in St. Louis, in which numerous gay men built on friendships forged in small rural and often evangelical congregations to gain entry into gay networks and spaces in St. Louis as an older youth or youth minister moved to St. Louis, came out, and others followed, appears as a shared experience among many who migrated to the city. These homegrown friendships served as both a gateway and a checkpoint, meaning new arrivals had a built-in community that connected them to gay spaces and people, but also that reported, or could potentially report, back home.⁵⁴ St. Louis' Central West End neighborhood has been associated with the gay community for many decades. However, unlike other gay enclaves, the Central West End's gay spaces consisted almost entirely of bars and religious sites, including churches and a synagogue, with no long-sustained social service organization existing outside a religious institution and very little politically specific activism.⁵⁵ These religious congregations were an important part of the gay communities in the city while they simultaneously intertwined gay congregants with their straight counterparts and the larger religious institutions. Meanwhile, this intermingling of gay and straight communities combined with the small-town feel of St. Louis sparked concern among many gay men that their families would inadvertently learn they were gay or that their sexuality would somehow disparage the family reputation to such an extent that they simply left town. There were also a number of gay men who found the apolitical nature of gay communities and the conservatism and religiosity of the city grating enough to go elsewhere.[56] Thus the closet door wasn't shut in the city, but swung in both directions and operated best when greased with discretion, religious fluency, and awareness of potential familial oversight.

With regard to the AIDS epidemic, this ethos played out in countless ways, regardless of how out an individual was: families learned of their sons' sexuality and infection in the same breath in hospital waiting rooms; gay men limited their involvement with gay politics to avoid word getting back to the families; and safe-sex workshops modeled after those in coastal cities toned it down for the St. Louis crowd.[57] Commenting on how St. Louis was more conservative about sex than other big cities he had lived in and visited, one DOORWAYS and EFA board member recalled, "In San Francisco when they did [a safe-sex workshop called] Hot, Healthy, and Horny they did the education training and then would have a safe-sex party. Well the safe-sex party would never work in St. Louis. The board members of Effort for AIDS did not want it to be said . . . [in] St. Louis you could talk about it, but you can't get together and do it." The religiosity of the city translated into a "prudish"-ness in public, even within gay spaces and culture. The religious attempts to erase sexuality from AIDS discussions in ways that inherently placed blame and shame on certain sexualities and acts reinforced the St. Louis gay community's assumption that "you weren't gonna get AIDS if you weren't out there every night having sex with ten people . . . and only people that did that would ever get AIDS." This, in turn, fueled AIDS discrimination from within the gay communities of St. Louis and associated it with the judgment-laden notion of promiscuity that operated within both gay communities and in conservative political rhetoric.[58] This conservatism was informed by the larger political landscape of the city and region. Not acting with discretion could and did have real consequences, particularly around AIDS. When word got out to the larger St. Louis community that a local AIDS service organization specifically for the Black community had invited a famous gay stripper and porn actor to an event, the resulting negative press and funding recoil shuttered the organization within months.[59]

The St. Louis AIDS response deployed respectability out of necessity and relied on collaborations with religious groups because without those partnerships the response would have been meager and anemic, if not entirely impossible. Though gay culture in the city was vibrant and multifaceted, it simply did not have the capacity or the preexisting foundations for the creation of multiple social service agencies and fundraising that the epidemic required and that materialized in places like New York, Los Angeles, and San Francisco. In short, partnering with religious organizations and using the city's religious infrastructure to mobilize an AIDS response grew from practicality. Two activists from EFA and DOORWAYS explained that "St. Louis was a hard nut to crack . . . making them say the word AIDS, making them admit they had a gay son . . . it's pretty conservative."[60] Though an ACT-UP St. Louis chapter existed briefly, its actions were poorly attended and its founders felt ostracized by other AIDS service organizations to the extent that both quickly moved to larger cities within a year of its founding, at which point it dissolved.[61] In many ways, the positive potential of typical ACT-UP tactics, beyond making all other AIDS service organizations and their traditional tactics appear more conservative and thus palatable by contrast, was simply lost amidst the St. Louis cultural landscape because it seemed too radical and impractical. One founding board member of DOORWAYS remarked that "people were more politically conservative here . . . St. Louis is known for being more conservative in their money, their banks, their investing—the medicine here is more conservative. The joke is that St. Louis was founded by the people who were not risk takers and not willing to go the rest of the way out west, so they stayed here."[62] Religion is a central part of this conservative landscape, even the more liberal pockets of it.

However starkly different the St. Louis response was from those of New York or San Francisco, its reliance on religious partnerships, respectability politics, tactically created palatability, and disdain for the aggressive tactics deployed by ACT-UP seemingly mirrored the AIDS response in many mid- and small-sized cities removed from the country's coasts.[63] These cities similarly enjoyed a slightly delayed and smaller-scale epidemic but also met the disease with vastly different tools and actors that often involved religious organizations and their congregations.

Necessity and reality dictated that the battle against AIDS began from a different stance in these places, rather than the progressive or even revolutionary positions on the coast. Thus, when considering the long 1980s and its conservative progression, we must consider and recalibrate the starting points from which we measure this conservative rise. The St. Louis response arguably illuminates this rise of the Right in some ways, whether through Pat's forced migration to St. Louis or Fred Phelps's funeral protests.

However, there is also the reality of religion serving as a catalyst for congregations and business elites to provide housing to people with AIDS and congregants becoming central figures in the city's AIDS organizations. One observant Jewish woman, along with her husband, became a strident AIDS activist and critical volunteer at both EFA and DOORWAYS after her son's death from AIDS in 1987. She remembered a moment working the EFA hotline with another frequent volunteer when "we got the giggles because here I was, a nice Jewish matron from the West county and here she was this nice Catholic lady [Sister Margaret] from St. Louis City and we're telling all these young people how to have safe sex! Can you imagine!?"[64] From this vantage point, the political and cultural narrative of the long 1980s seems far more complex than one of a simple conservative rise and radical fall or queer politics giving way to respectability.

Notes

    1. Tamar Carroll, *Mobilizing New York: AIDS, Antipoverty, and Feminist Activism* (Chapel Hill: University of North Carolina Press, 2015); Jennifer Brier, *Infectious Ideas: U.S. Political Responses to the AIDS Crisis* (Chapel Hill: University of North Carolina Press, 2009; Deborah Gould, *Moving Politics: Emotion and ACT-UP's Fight Against AIDS* (Chicago: University of Chicago Press, 2009); Cathy Cohen, *The Boundaries of Blackness: AIDS and the Breakdown of Black Politics* (Chicago: University of Chicago Press, 1999).

    2. The concept of the Heartland as a geographical region is both amorphous and disputed, though less so than the "Midwest." The research presented here focuses almost entirely on Missouri, southern Illinois, and Kansas though my larger project expands this region to include Iowa and Nebraska as well as some partnerships spilling into Oklahoma. This region shares a similar topography, demography, history of migration and immigration, similar relationship to religion (though the most influential religion changes depending on specific

locale), political landscape, and small and relatively conservative populations of both racial and sexual minorities.

3. For more on Robert Rayford see, The Albion Centre, "A HIV/AIDS Timeline," (New South Wales: The Albion Centre, 2012), 3; W. Pate McMichael, "The Pre-Pandemic Puzzle," *St. Louis Magazine*, August 31, 2007.

4. Evelyn Cohen, interview by telephone, Katie Batza, November 1, 2018; Chuck Gulas, interview by telephone, December 14, 2018; Keith Price, interview by telephone, October 29, 2018.

5. "DOORWAYS Needs Help Furnishing Residences," *Frontline: The Monthly Newsletter of St. Louis Effort for AIDS*, August 1988, Box 1, Folder Newsletters 1988, St. Louis Effort for AIDS Collection, Missouri History Museum.

6. Gulas, interview.

7. Cohen, interview; Gulas, interview; Opal Jones, interview by telephone, November 30, 2018.

8. Gulas, interview. Michael Allan to John May, "The doors are open Letter," 14 September 1988, Box "Executive," Folder "Archbishop and Bishop— Correspondence—1988–1997," St. Louis Archdiocese Library and Archive, St. Louis Archdiocese. "Just Months Old, Doorways Becomes a Community and a Place PWAs Call " 'Home,' " *Frontline: The Monthly Newsletter of St. Louis Effort for AIDS*, November 1988, Box 1, Folder Newsletters 1988, St. Louis Effort For AIDS Collection, Missouri History Museum.

9. "Just Months Old, Doorways Becomes a Community and a Place PWAs Call " 'Home.' "

10. Food and Drug Administration, "HIV/AIDS Historical Time Line 1981–1990," fda.gov, www.fda.gov/ForPatients/Illness/HIVAIDS/History/ucm151074.htm

11. Gulas, interview.

12. Mayer and Pat Levy, interview by telephone, Katie Batza, December 4, 2018; Gulas, interview. Brenda Armour, interview by telephone, Katie Batza, December 11, 2018; Gary Hirshberg, interview by telephone, Katie Batza, September 26 and 27, 2018.

13. Gulas, interview; Bill LaRock, interview by telephone, Katie Batza, July 10, 2018; Cathy Johnson, interview by telephone, Katie Batza, July 9, 2018.

14. Price, interview.

15. Douglas Crimp and Adam Rolston, *AIDS demo graphics* (Seattle: Bay Press, 1990).

16. Heather Murray, *Not in this Family: Gay and the Meaning of Kinship in Postwar North America* (Philadelphia: University of Pennsylvania Press, 2011); Anthony Petro, *After the Wrath of God: AIDS, Sexuality, and American Religion* (London: Oxford University Press, 2015); Thomas Rzeznik, "The Church and the AIDS Crisis in New York City," *U.S. Catholic Historian* 34.1 (Winter 2016); Whitney Cox, "Christian, Philadelphian, and gay-affirming responses to AIDS

1982–1992" PhD diss. Temple University, 2016, Proquest Publishing (10144379); Jonathan Bell, "Between Private and Public: AIDS, Health Care Capitalism, and the Politics of Respectability in 1980s America," *Journal of American Studies* (2018): 1–25; Mark Kowalewski, *All Things to All People: The Catholic Church Confronts the AIDS Crisis* (Albany, NY: SUNY Press, 1994).

17. Gulas, interview.

18. Minutes of the Ad Hoc Task Force on AIDS, 6 March 1987, Box "Administrative," Folder "Files-RG03C13," St. Louis Archdiocese Library and Archive, St. Louis Archdiocese; "Task Force on AIDS to Start Work Here," *St. Louis Review*, 3 April 1987, 1, 7. National Conference of Catholic Bishops and United States Catholic Conference, "Called to Compassion and Responsibility," www.usccb.org, www.usccb.org/issues-and-action/human-life-and-dignity/global-issues/called-to-compassion-and-responsibility.cfm

19. The Vital Voice, "Doorways Announces New President and CEO," www.thevitalvoice.com, http://thevitalvoice.com/tag/aids/page/3

20. Gulas, interview.

21. "St. Louis Effort for AIDS Fact Sheet," c. 1986, Box 1, Folder Newsletters, Timothy Cusick Collection, Missouri History Museum.

22. Levy, interview; Gulas, interview; Anonymous, interview by telephone, Katie Batza, December 28, 2018.

23. Daniel Flier, interview by telephone, Katie Batza, January 10, 2019.

24. Anonymous, interview.

25. Flier, interview.

26. Flier, interview.

27. Gulas, interview; Flier, interview. Though this is largely true, there are a few notable exceptions where EFA received grants from religious groups, such as the 1988 grant from the St. Luke's Episcopal-Presbyterian Charitable Fund that allowed EFA to hire its first paid staff. "EFA Received $71,500 Grant for Hiring Paid Staff," *Frontline: The Monthly Newsletter of St. Louis Effort for AIDS*, August 1988, Box 1, Folder Newsletters 1988, St. Louis Effort For AIDS Collection, Missouri History Museum.

28. Flier, interview. "Corporate Funding Has $100,000 Goal" *Frontline: The Monthly Newsletter of St. Louis Effort for AIDS*, February 1988, Box 1, Folder Newsletters 1988, St. Louis Effort For AIDS Collection, Missouri History Museum.

29. Gulas, interview. Minutes of the Core Committee of the Catholic Task Force on AIDS, 25 April 1988, Box "Executive," Folder "Archbishop and Bishop—Correspondence—1988," St. Louis Archdiocese Library and Archive, St. Louis Archdiocese.

30. DOORWAYS, "Impact Report 2018." www.doorways.org, www.doorwayshousing.org/wp-content/uploads/2018/12/FY18-impact-report-final_print_web.pdf

31. Minutes of the Core Committee of the Catholic Task Force on AIDS, 27 June 1988, Box "Executive," Folder "Archbishop and Bishop—Correspondence—1988," St. Louis Archdiocese Library and Archive, St. Louis Archdiocese.

32. Gulas, interview.

33. Cohen, interview. Both the Episcopalian communities and the Lutherans also gave regularly, though the number often fluctuated. Minutes of the Core Committee of the Catholic Task Force on AIDS, 25 April 1988, Box "Executive," Folder "Archbishop and Bishop—Correspondence—1988," St. Louis Archdiocese Library and Archive, St. Louis Archdiocese. Also, the United Way provided some significant start-up funds. "AIDS Housing Program Gets Strong Start-Up Support," *Frontline: The Monthly Newsletter of St. Louis Effort for AIDS*, February 1988, Box 1, Folder Newsletters 1988, St. Louis Effort For AIDS Collection, Missouri History Museum.

34. Gulas, interview; Cohen, interview. Minutes of the Core Committee of the Catholic Task Force on AIDS, 26 September 1988, Box "Executive," Folder "Archbishop and Bishop—Correspondence—1988," St. Louis Archdiocese Library and Archive, St. Louis Archdiocese. Minutes of the Core Committee of the Catholic Task Force on AIDS, 27 June 1988, Box "Executive," Folder "Archbishop and Bishop—Correspondence—1988," St. Louis Archdiocese Library and Archive, St. Louis Archdiocese. Minutes of the Core Committee of the Catholic Task Force on AIDS, 25 April 1988, Box "Executive," Folder "Archbishop and Bishop—Correspondence—1988," St. Louis Archdiocese Library and Archive, St. Louis Archdiocese.

35. Cohen, interview

36. Price, interview; Cohen, interview; Jones, interview; Jim Timmerberg, interview by telephone, Katie Batza, December 6, 2018; "St. Francis Residence Opens Its Doors in Clayton," *Frontline: The Monthly Newsletter of St. Louis Effort for AIDS*, March 1988, Box 1, Folder Newsletters 1988, St. Louis Effort For AIDS Collection, Missouri History Museum.

37. Cohen, interview; Gulas, interview; Price, interview; Flier, interview. Minutes of the Core Committee of the Catholic Task Force on AIDS, 25 April 1988, Box "Executive," Folder "Archbishop and Bishop—Correspondence—1988," St. Louis Archdiocese Library and Archive, St. Louis Archdiocese.

38. Michael Allan to John May, "The doors are open Letter," 14 September 1988, Box "Executive," Folder "Archbishop and Bishop—Correspondence—1988–1997," St. Louis Archdiocese Library and Archive, St. Louis Archdiocese. "Just Months Old, Doorways Becomes a Community and a Place PWAs Call "'Home.'"

39. Gulas, interview. "Just Months Old, Doorways Becomes a Community and a Place PWAs Call "'Home.'"

40. Cohen, interview; Jones, interview; Armour, interview.

41. Gulas, interview.

42. Rebecca Barrett-Fox, *God Hate: Westboro Baptist Church, American Nationalism, and the Religious Right* (Lawrence: University of Kansas, 2016).

43. Michelle O'Brien, "Catholic Health Outreach Program Survey on AIDS Response," February 1987, Box "Executive," Folder "Archbishop and Bishop—Correspondence—1987," St. Louis Archdiocese Library and Archive, St. Louis Archdiocese.

44. Cathy Cohen, *Boundaries of Blackness: AIDS and the Breakdown of Black Politics* (Chicago: University of Chicago Press, 1999); Daniel Royles (2014) "Don't We Die, Too?": The Political Culture of African American AIDS Activism" PhD diss., Temple University, Proquest Dissertations, 2014, 3611169; Darius Bost, "At the Club: Locating Early Black Gay AIDS Activism in Washington, DC," 2015; Jacob Levenson, *The Secret Epidemic: The Story of AIDS and Black America* (New York: Anchor Books, 2005).

45. Michael Allan to John May, "The doors are open Letter," 14 September 1988, Box "Executive," Folder "Archbishop and Bishop—Correspondence—1988-1997," St. Louis Archdiocese Library and Archive, St. Louis Archdiocese.

46. Jones, interview; Gulas, interview.

47. This type of collaborative politics is examined in depth in Tim Stewart-Winter, *Queer Clout: Chicago and the Rise of Gay Politics* (Philadelphia: University of Pennsylvania Press, 2015).

48. "Readers' Advocate explains why gay rights bill was not covered in Post-Dispatch," *St. Louis Post-Dispatch* (St. Louis, Missouri), December 13, 1992, p. 40; Tim O'Neil, "Revised Gay Rights Code Beyond 'Routine,'" *St. Louis Post-Dispatch* (St. Louis, Missouri), December 13, 1992, pp. 40, 44.

49. Associated Press, "Virtually Unnoted, St. Louis Approves Gay Rights Measure," *New York Times*, December 28, 1992. www.nytimes.com/1992/12/28/us/virtually-unnoted-st-louis-approves-gay-rights-measure.html?fbclid=IwAR2YidDv8oB_RPLcxow_p99Xwi_rEKHG6SAWNdfqSxFFAQWUSGgBNk7g_R4

50. Austin Williams, *The Ordinance Project*, Documentary Film, 2018, Gay and Lesbian Archive of Mid-America.

51. Gulas, interview; Cohen, interview.

52. Steven Louis Brawley and the St. Louis LGBT History Project, *Images of Gay and Lesbian St. Louis* (Charleston: Arcadia Publishing, 2016).

53. Gulas, interview.

54. Rodeny Wilson, interview by telephone, Katie Batza, July 17, 2018; Michael Slawin, interview by telephone, Katie Batza, June 12, 2018; Jim Thomas, interview by telephone, Katie Batza, August 27, 2018.

55. Andrea Friedman and Miranda Rectenwald, "Mapping LGBTQ St. Louis," www.wustl.edu, http://wustl.maps.arcgis.com/apps/Cascade/index.html?appid=d650dce414924b07b35a591d1202a6b5 (October 11, 2018; Katie Batza and Michelle Diedriech, Trinity Episcopal Church Nomination for the National

Register of Historic Places, January 5, 2018; Rodney Wilson, interview by telephone, Katie Batza, July 17, 2018; Philip Deitch, Interview by telephone, Katie Batza, September 12, 2018; Jym Andris, interview by telephone, Katie Batza, August 21, 2018; Thomas, interview.

    56. LaRock, interview; Johnson, interview.
    57. Levy, interview; Gulas, interview; Cohen, interview.
    58. Gulas, interview.
    59. Erise Williams, interview in person, Katie Batza, May 31, 2018; Gulas, interview.
    60. Levy, interview.
    61. LaRock, interview; Johnson, interview.
    62. Gulas, interview.
    63. One such town is Minneapolis, which had direct contact with St. Louis organizations, including DOORWAYS, and modeled a number of their political strategies and AIDS service organizations after those in St. Louis, which capitalized on strong religious foundation in the city. Gulas, interview.
    64. Levy, interview.

Works Cited

Archives

Kansas City, Missouri
    Gay and Lesbian Archive of Mid-America
    The Ordinance Project, 2018
St. Louis, Missouri
St. Louis Archdiocese Library and Archive
    Record from the Ad Hoc Task Force on AIDS Collection
Records from the Core Committee of the Catholic Task Force on AIDS Collection
Missouri History Museum
Records from St. Louis Effort for AIDS Collection
Record from the Timothy Cusick Collection

Books and Book Chapters

Barrett-Fox, Rebecca. *God Hate: Westboro Baptist Church, American Nationalism, and the Religious Right*. Lawrence: University of Kansas, 2016.
Bost, Darius. "At the Club: Locating Early Black Gay AIDS Activism in Washington, DC." *Special Issue on Race, Place and Scale, Occasion* 8, 2015.
Brawley, Steven Louis. *Gay and Lesbian St. Louis*. Charleston, SC: Arcadia Publishing, 2016.

Brier, Jennifer. *Infectious Ideas: U.S. Political Responses to the AIDS Crisis.* Chapel Hill: University of North Carolina Press, 2009.
Carroll, Tamar W. *Mobilizing New York: AIDS, Antipoverty, and Feminist Activism.* Chapel Hill: University of North Carolina Press, 2015.
Cohen, Cathy J. *The Boundaries of Blackness: AIDS and the Breakdown of Black Politics.* Chicago: University of Chicago Press, 2006.
Crimp, Douglas, and Adam Rolston. *AIDS Demo Graphics.* Seattle: Bay Press, 1990.
Gould, Deborah B. *Moving Politics: Emotion and ACT UPs Fight against AIDS.* Chicago: University of Chicago Press, 2009.
Kowalewski, Mark R. *All Things to All People: The Catholic Church Confronts the AIDS Crisis.* Albany, NY: SUNY Press, 1994.
Murray, Heather A.A. *Not in This Family: Gays and the Meaning of Kinship in Postwar North America.* Philadelphia: University of Pennsylvania Press, 2011.
Petro, Anthony Michael. *After the Wrath of God: AIDS, Sexuality, and American Religion.* Oxford: Oxford University Press, 2015.
Stewart-Winter, Timothy. *Queer Clout: Chicago and the Rise of Gay Politics.* Philadelphia: University of Pennsylvania Press, 2015.

DISSERTATIONS

Cox, Whitney. "Christian, Philadelphian, and Gay-Affirming Responses to AIDS, 1982–1992." Dissertation, Proquest Publishing, 2016.
Royles, Daniel. "'Don't We Die, Too?': The Political Culture of African American AIDS Activism." Dissertation, Proquest Dissertations, 2014.

INTERVIEWS

Andris, Jym. Telephone interview by Katie Batza, August 21, 2018.
Anonymous. Telephone interview by Katie Batza, December 28, 2018.
Armour, Brenda. Telephone interview by Katie Batza, December 11, 2018.
Cohen, Evelyn. Telephone interview by Katie Batza, November 1, 2018.
Deitch, Philip. Telephone interview by Katie Batza, September 12, 2018.
Flier, Daniel. Telephone interview by Katie Batza, January 10, 2019.
Gulas, Chuck. Telephone interview by Katie Batza, December 14, 2018.
Hirshberg, Gary. Telephone interview by Katie Batza, September 26 and 27, 2018.
Johnson, Cathy. Telephone interview by Katie Batza, July 9, 2018.
Jones, Opal. Telephone interview by Katie Batza, November 30, 2018.
LaRock, Bill. Telephone interview by Katie Batza, July 10, 2018.
Levy, Mayer, and Pat Levy. Telephone interview by Katie Batza, December 4, 2018.
Price, Keith. Telephone interview by Katie Batza, October 29, 2018.
Slawin, Michael. Telephone interview by Katie Batza, June 12, 2018.
Thomas, Jim. Telephone interview by Katie Batza, August 27, 2018.

Timmerberg, Jim. Telephone interview by Katie Batza, December 6, 2018.
Williams, Erise. In-person interview by Katie Batza, May 31, 2018.
Wilson, Rodney. Telephone interview by Katie Batza, July 17, 2018.

Journal Articles

Bell, Jonathan. "Between Private and Public: AIDS, Health Care Capitalism, and the Politics of Respectability in 1980s America." *Journal of American Studies* 54, no 1 (2020): 159–183.

Rzeznik, Thomas. "The Church and the AIDS Crisis in New York City." *U.S. Catholic Historian* 34.1 (2016).

Magazine and Newspaper Articles

Associated Press. "Virtually Unnoted, St. Louis Approves Gay Rights Measure." *New York Times*, December 28, 1992. www.nytimes.com/1992/12/28/us/virtually-unnoted-st-louis-approves-gay-rights-measure.html?fbclid=IwAR2YidDv8oB_RPLcxow_p99Xwi_rEKHG6SAWNdfqSxFFAQWUSGgBNk7g_R4

McMichael, W. Pate. "The Pre-Pandemic Puzzle." *St. Louis Magazine*, August 31, 2007.

O'Neil, Tim. "Revised Gay Rights Code Beyond 'Routine." *St. Louis Post-Dispatch*, December 13, 1992.

"Readers' Advocate Explains Why Gay Rights Bill Was Not Covered in Post-Dispatch." *St. Louis Post-Dispatch*, December 13, 1992.

"Task Force on AIDS to Start Work Here." *St. Louis Review*, April 3, 1987.

Websites

"Called to Compassion and Responsibility." National Conference of Catholic Bishops and United States Catholic Conference. United States Catholic Conference, Inc., January 1990. www.usccb.org/issues-and-action/human-life-and-dignity/global-issues/called-to-compassion-and-responsibility.cfm

"Doorways Announces New President and CEO." The Vital Voice. http://thevitalvoice.com/tag/aids/page/3

Friedman, Andrea, and Miranda Rectenwald. "Mapping LGBTQ St. Louis." Washington University in St. Louis. http://wustl.maps.arcgis.com/apps/Cascade/index.html?appid=d650dce414924b07b35a591d1202a6b5

HIV/AIDS Historical Time Line 1981–1990, HIV/AIDS Historical Time Line 1981–1990 §. www.fda.gov/ForPatients/Illness/HIVAIDS/History/ucm151074.htm

"Impact Report 2018." Doorways, 2018. www.doorwayshousing.org/wp-content/uploads/2018/12/FY18-impact-report-final_print_web.pdf

IV
Grassroots Images, Speech, and Power

Polareyes

A Magazine by and for Black British Women Photographers as a Site of Resistance in London, 1987

Taous R. Dahmani

Tired
of struggling
for my right
to create
Tired
of struggling
with the politics and
ethics
surrounding my right
to photograph
I retreat
to create

—Mumtaz Karimjee, *Polareyes*, 1987

Introduction

Leafing through the Stuart Hall Library's collection of periodicals, I noticed a bright pink- and yellow-covered journal entitled *Polareyes*.[1] As I came to realize, the photography and text magazine had been largely overlooked in broader discourses on visual arts and its printed matter:

the uncovering of this publication marked the beginning of a long quest to understand its creation and production.[2] As such, this chapter is an analysis of the magazine but is also made out of conversations with its key creators and contributors, Molly Shinhat, Anita McKenzie, Mumtaz Karimjee, Amina Patel, Joy Gregory, Sharron Wallace, and Ingrid Pollard. Against all conventional definitions, *Polareyes* was a "one shot magazine,"[3] meaning that its first issue was also its last. Published in 1987, *Polareyes* needs to be included and examined within the larger scope of its contemporaries—British photography periodicals—including *Camerawork* and *Ten.8*. But *Polareyes* was more than just a photography magazine. As stated in its subtitle, "A journal by and about Black Women working in photography," *Polareyes* emphasized its race and gender focus, making it a unique publication at that time in Britain. Thus, in order to understand the challenges of designing such a project, it is necessary to see it within the context of 1980s British visual arts, but also in the context of the editorial offerings on Black Feminism that emerged at the same time. Its distinctiveness is reinforced when we know how much photography, as an art practice, struggled to gain recognition and institutionalization in Britain.[4] As art historian and art critic Abigail Solomon-Godeau wrote, photography was a "discrete artistic medium."[5]

Polareyes' existence is even more remarkable when we consider the racial, social, and gendered prejudices in 1980s British society.[6] As Graham Stewart stated in *Bang! A History of Britain in the 1980s*, "It was a time of primary colours, clashing ideologies and divisive personalities."[7] Framed by Margaret Thatcher's terms in office (1979–1990), the 1980s saw unemployment, IRA hunger strikes, the Anti-Nuclear Movement, the Falklands War, the Miners' strike, deregulation and privatization, the AIDs epidemic, and the Anti-Apartheid Movement.[8] Even if Thatcher is not solely responsible for the climate of 1980s Britain, her policies led to widespread unrest for those fighting along the axes of race, gender, sexuality, and class.[9] During her 1979 electoral campaign, Thatcher adopted a strong anti-immigration stance. Later, her government would continue to be driven by racism. It is within this cultural and political context that *Polareyes* should be seen as a platform for marginalized voices. In that respect, through a detailed account of its content and a study of its backdrop, I will consider *Polareyes* as a site of resistance for Black British women photographers active in the 1980s in London. In this chapter, I highlight how the editors of *Polareyes* were able to bring to the fore their artistic and political agency. I also highlight their struggle against a monolithic gaze on "Otherness" and their kaleidoscopic vision on photography and creative text making. *Polareyes* was a site of resistance for Black women photographers in 1980s England.

Polareyes' Inception

The group that came together to work on the magazine was a result of a double exclusion. On the one hand, collectives and associations of Black photographers were dominated by men, while white women photographers struggled to be inclusive in their thinking.[10] In London in 1986, after the heated conference "Women and Photography,"[11] a group of fifteen Black female photographers—who already knew each other from using collective darkrooms in London—decided to separate from their white counterparts.[12] In some artistic and activist circles in 1980s Britain, populations of African Caribbean, African, and South Asian descent identified as "Black": the term was employed as a unifying notion, imbedded in a pan-Africanist vision, to rally those involved in anti-racist and decolonizing struggles around the same demands for rights and an end to discrimination.[13] "Black"—with a capital letter—referred to a conscious political embodiment by all people of color. It was thus a heterogeneous, composite, and hybrid Blackness built against the British racist and sociopolitical system.[14] By stating, "All of us come from African, Asian and Afro-Caribbean backgrounds,"[15] *Polareyes'* editorial team rooted itself in this multiracial political category and adopted the term "Black" as a collective voice, for its inclusive force, but it did not mean they affirmed any uniformity or homogeneity.[16] As Jade Bentil has outlined in her chapter in this collection, there was a "lack of consensus throughout the BWM as to whether Blackness as a political identity could effectively represent the specific forms of racialized and gendered violence that Black and Asian women were experiencing."[17] Because the women involved in *Polareyes* organized under this term, I deploy it throughout this chapter.

These photographers first gathered as an informal thinking group at each other's homes. Later, led by McKenzie and Walker, nine of them established themselves as an editorial board in order to publish a journal dedicated to their photographic practices and those of their network. The magazine form became an accessible choice for the group of editors-to-be looking for an outlet. The 1980s were the height of small-scale independently owned printed magazine such as "zines" or "fanzines."[18] Popular in underground scenes and countercultures, used to assert subjectivities, the flexibility of magazines seemed ideal to accommodate *Polareyes'* variety of texts and photographs. The creators of *Polareyes*, and the writers, artists, and photographers featured in its pages, together created a one-of-a-kind printed object. Its glossy and colorful cover paired with its bold and unrestrained black-and-white inside design[19] were similar in aesthetic to "the new women's magazine" *Spare Rib* (1972–1993).[20] Moreover, *Polareyes'* origin story is reminiscent of *Spare Rib*'s: "Liberation, the lady said. Rubbish we thought. Then we thought some more. Then we talked some more. Then we came together. That was it. *Spare Rib* is the result."[21] Like *Spare Rib*'s early purpose to try and explain Women's Liberation, *Polareyes'* political goal can be understood in its materiality, look, inspirations, and writing.[22] As such, the politics of zines and other independent publishing ventures such as pamphlets inspired *Polareyes'* editors for their manifesto-like editorial. *Polareyes'* opening text was in line with the politics and writings of other women in the Black British art movement, such as that of Chila Kumari Burman's (1986) *There Have Always Been Great Blackwomen Artists*[23] or, subsequently, Lubaina Himid's (1990) *Mapping: A Decade of Black Women Artists 1980–1990*.[24] *Polareyes'* opening essay consists of a list of statements that highlight the forms of resistance taken by the magazine.

The magazine opens with a self-definition, an explanation of their name by giving its technical explanation: "Polar'eyes, v. (ref photography)—use of an optical filter that cuts extraneous reflected images from transparent surface (e.g., glass) to give a clearer view."[25] Through the use of technical photographic vocabulary, the members of the publication stress their belonging to a milieu that had endlessly rejected them. The rest of the editorial is an assertion of their existence within photography's very white ecosystem: "*Polareyes* attempts to include the many voices of Blackwomen who have been silenced by their absence from mainstream and alternative photography magazines be they white-male or white-female dominated."[26] The editorial is blunt and straightforward; pointing to the problems and their culprits (mostly the white press and white journalists), criticizing mainstream photographic discourse and its blinkered vision.[27] Not wanting to be a "token Black issue"[28]—or a "last special issue," as exposed by Kobena Mercer and Isaac Julien a year later in *Screen*[29]—*Polareyes* denounced the limitations of a single issue magazine as a means of addressing the multiplicity of subjects that

Black women photographers tackled and deplored the fact that they had received enough funding for only one issue.[30] Created a year after the abolition of Ken Livingstone's Greater London Council,[31] *Polareyes* did not benefit from the GLC's ambitious support programs for people of color initiatives.[32] However, the publication benefited from funding from the Greater London Authority (GLA) and the Arts Council. Yet, as stated in *Polareyes*' editorial: "Giving some Blackwomen photographers a couple of thousand pounds and expecting that to fund projects focusing on the plethora of issues Blackwomen photographers would like to deal with is a joke."[33] Touching on the cynicism of such funding, *Polareyes* was largely made possible thanks to the editors and contributors' free labor and voluntary dedicated work, as explained by Maxine Walker:

> "Jenny McKenzie and myself [Maxine Walker] had presented the idea of a magazine initially to a wide group of black women in an early meeting. The groundwork of application, form-filling and keeping the enthusiasm going was instigated by Mumtaz Karimjee and Samena Rana; Amina Patel succeeded in securing the group a space at the Cockpit; Brenda Agard provided a great deal of support in meeting deadlines and liaising with grant bodies; Leslie Mitchell provided support through her work at Brixton Recreation Centre, which helped with organizing the launch. Molly Shinhat, Geraldine Walsh and Similola Coker were particularly crucial in keeping momentum going during the last stages of production. And, of course, without all the work from the contributors, there could be no magazine."[34]

Even if they knew they did not have enough money to make subsequent issues, the editors still decided to append "Issue No. 1 1987" on the cover, probably hoping for a brighter future for Black women's photography and editorial endeavors. Nevertheless, the state of affairs was not as bleak as one might think. For example, support from their colleagues from other publications—such as *Camerawork, Bazaar, Art Express*, and *The Voice*[35]—can be found inside the journal through advertisements. The other advertisements were from small institutions that had a link with the editors, such as the Women Artists Slide Library, the Cockpit Gallery[36] and the Commission for Racial Equality. *Polareyes* also had pages dedicated to reviews, a reading list, and a directory of resources available for women, including addresses and contacts for darkrooms and other photo groups. *Polareyes'* review page,[37] dedicated to references to publications, reveals a relative dearth of available books but emphasizes the strong link with the United States by presenting *Viewfinders—Black Women Photographers* published in 1986 by photographer and historian of North American photography, Jeanne Moutoussamy-Ashe.[38] As presented, *Viewfinders* also became an object of legitimization that allowed a journal like *Polareyes* to fit into a historical and transatlantic tradition.[39]

However, *Polareyes* was primarily dedicated to photographic portfolios and to critical texts about photographic practices using an array of textual forms. The issue included essays such as Brenda Agard's "Photography: An Extension Of" and Similola Coker's "Thoughts on Creating / Re-Creating ourselves in Films"; peer-to-peer interviews such as Maxine Walker's conversation with Joy Gregory and Molly Shinhat's conversation with Ingrid Pollard; and poems such as the one next to Mumtaz Karimjee's photographs[40] as well as "Today I'm feeling colourful" by Laeticea Phoenix and Geraldine Walsh.[41] The printed volume comprised nineteen widely varying black-and-white portfolios, including documentary, staged photography, experimental images, and montages. A quick overview of the textual and photographic proposals one can find in *Polareyes* shows the diversity of the subjects tackled, but nevertheless highlights their common interests for reflexivity on the photographic medium, the politics of being a woman, the state of racism in Britain, and the difficulty of having a photographic practice—and career—when one's financial situation is challenging.

The 1980s was a decisive decade for Black art in Britain.[42] The Black art scene was pushed by Naseem Khan's 1976 report *The Arts Britain Ignores: The Arts of Ethnic Minorities in Britain*,[43] and then aided by the GLC initiatives and crafted thanks to their Do-It-Yourself philosophy. As outlined by Stuart Hall, "Somewhere during the 1980s, the world, our world, changed dramatically and decisively. . . . The very intensity of the deluge produced an extraordinary creativity from the most marginal spaces."[44] Just after the 1981 uprisings and its Scarman Report,[45] in 1982, Black British visual art students from the Midlands organized the first National Black Art Convention at Wolverhampton Polytechnic—a starting point and the first visible sign of an emerging Black British art scene[46]—linking the decade's artistic production with the political climate.[47] Debates, alliances, and dissent animated the 1980s, giving rise to the creation of a multitude of networks and subgroups chiefly reflecting queer and feminist struggles. As explained by Juliette Jarette, "the artist has, historically, been constructed as male, independent, anti-social and having a creative prerogative"[48]; as such, groups of Black British women artists were easily considered alien to the dominant definition. These networks were a revolution within a revolution, leading to Black women artists organizing and exhibiting separately from men. *Polareyes* can be considered one of the many results of such insurgencies.[49]

Wedged between male-dominated Black Art groups and white-dominated photography networks, *Polareyes* attempted to find a place in the ecosystem of magazines. It tried to refresh the discourse found in mainstream publications and challenged peers in journals such as *Ten.8* and *Camerawork*, even if most of them had already started examining themselves and had published inclusive content.[50] When *Polareyes* was launched, they showed their support: *Camerawork* published an advertisement and *Ten.8* gave a platform to *Polareyes* in its twenty-seventh issue by letting Maxine Walker present the publication.[51]

As I have suggested, *Polareyes*' team suffered from considerable invisibilization from key players in different spheres.[52] There was a marked lack of recognition of photographers of color when the photographic medium was celebrated, as exemplified by the Museum of Modern Art's all-male and all-white exhibition, *British Photography from the Thatcher Years* (1991).[53] If one would expect mainstream photography narratives to overlook endeavors such as *Polareyes*, Black women artists and photographers were, more often than not, overlooked by some of the key commentators of the larger Black Art "movement."[54] Critics and observers' primary interest was in trying to define the existence of a possible "movement" and discuss its aesthetic ramifications as exemplified in Eddie Chambers and Rasheed Araeen, "Black Art: A Discussion," Aubrey Williams's "Seeking a Black Aesthetic," and Araeen's "Preliminary Notes for a Black Manifesto."[55] The debates on the use of the term was then summarized by Stuart Hall: "Two visions or pathways for the black arts seem to be in contention here. They are not diametrically opposed. Both are informed by a political critique; both want an art practice that is engaged with these larger political questions. But they register deep differences of experience and political perspective, which plays through into the aesthetics."[56]

In line with the questions raised by political Blackness, the issue of racism was at the heart of *Polareyes* and the fight against racism was omnipresent. The most radical proposal seems to be that of Molly

Shinhat, entitled "I'm the Problem, I'm not White."⁵⁷ This series was comprised of superimposed photographs and a text that took the form of a militant anti-racism essay and a manifesto in the defense of photography, in which she wrote "I'm the Problem, I'm not White" as an attempt to explore modes through which Black people can be empowered through photography, a medium that in both historical and contemporary contexts has usually been yet another aspect of how Black people have been oppressed.⁵⁸ Created in 1987, *Polareyes* was published following the 1981 and 1985 uprisings that took place in major inner cities.⁵⁹ In 1985, the British jazz band Working Week picked up Marvin Gaye's "Inner City Blues" (1971) and offered a soundtrack to the uprisings, singing about crime and policing. This musical environment, among other cultural factors, significantly influenced *Polareyes'* editors and contributors, as shown by the two-page spread entitled "Young gifted and black" by photographer Rhona Hariette in which she made a reference to Nina Simone's civil rights anthem and wondered, in her article, how familiar or acquainted people were with young Black British vocalists and artists, addressing the issue through the prism of music and paying homage to singers like Juliet Roberts from Working Week.⁶⁰

Polareyes: A Site of Resistance

By creating *Polareyes*, the editors—Maxine Walker, Molly Shinhat, Mumtaz Karimjee, Jenny McKenzie, Amina Patel, Samena Rana, Similola Coker, Brenda Agard, and Leslie Mitchell—created a site of resistance against racism and sexism in British society and the photography world. Underground magazines like *Polareyes* function as important cultural artefacts of the political movement they were born out of. In *Magazine Movements*, Laurel Forster stated that "magazines are perhaps the ultimate zeitgeist media form."⁶¹ Magazines can reveal intellectual disputes and reflect the cultural climate. While mainstream magazines work from the top down, small publications such as *Polareyes* are rooted in communities. They are often an expression of dissident thinking and offer a way into subgroups and "subaltern counterpublics," as Nancy Fraser phrased it.⁶² As such, magazines remain a popular vehicle of political expression. As Adelaide Bannerman put it, *Polareyes'* editors "creat[ed] centrality for themselves."⁶³ By making it a text-heavy publication, the editors incorporated popular ways of thinking emanating from Birmingham's Centre for Contemporary Cultural Studies[64] and put forward ideas inspired by Black Feminist literature.[65] As photographers, they were also aware of the implications of representation and appreciative of photographs as "both images and physical objects that exist in time and space and thus in social and cultural experience."[66] At a time in the history of the country, where minority populations and minoritized individuals were referred to as a shapeless body or an opaque horde, highlighting the multiplicity of individual perspectives as shaped by social and political experiences could deconstruct mainstream conceptions and challenge the social, political, and economic status quo. By using photography, *Polareyes* weaved its images into the fabric of society, while at the same time revealing its vantage point on that world and on its world.

It is worth underlining *Polareyes'* innovative elements compared to its predecessors. In the 1950s and 1960s, photography journals were mainly dedicated to amateurs and focused on a technical dimension, as found in *Practical Photography* (1959), *Professional Photographer* (1961), and *Camera Owner* (1964). In 1967, Bill Jay took over *Creative Owner* and transformed it in 1968 into *Creative Camera*, making it one of the first British photography magazines to look at photography as an art form.[67] A decade later, in 1976, the members of the Half Moon Photography Workshop created *Camerawork*, introducing critical thinking in its analysis of the medium and addressing its politics.[68] In 1979, in order to create a platform for local photographers Derek Bishton, Roy Peters, Nick Hedges, John Taylor, Brian Homer, and John Reardon launched *Ten.8*. In this context, *Polareyes* can be considered part of the legacy of *Ten.8*'s political commitment—especially to class- and gender-related issues—and inherited *Camerawork*'s collective way of proceeding; however, its being anchored in women-of-color activism is unique. A link could also be found with Rasheed Araeen's 1978, *Black Phoenix* magazine—which, similarly to *Polareyes*, reads as a manifesto.[69]

Polareyes also needs to be framed within British feminist periodicals and print culture and needs to be included in such literature, the likes of which have been explored by Laurel Forster,[70] Maria DiCenzo, Lucy Delap, and Leila Ryan for *Feminist Media History*, but also Barbara Green, Simone Murray, and Catherine Clay.[71] Moreover, the scholarship on Black British women's organizing and publishing in post-war Britain seems imperative to understanding *Polareyes'* genesis and outcome. Natalie Thomlinson has argued that publications such as *FOWAAD*, *Speak Out*, *We Are Here*, and *Mukti* should be seen as "sites of contestation."[72] Indeed, periodicals made by and for Black women in Britain in the 1980s should be considered as forms of print activism[73] wherein the printed matter is made to be the voice of a struggle.[74]

In the 1984 *Feminist Review* issue "Many Voices, One Chant—Black Feminist Perspectives," edited by Valerie Amos, Gail Lewis, Amina Mama, and Pratibha Parmar, the publishers called on Black women to create their own forms and their own content; they also specifically called upon photographers: "The photographs of and by Black women are symbolic of the process of creating and projecting new images of ourselves."[75] This call resonated with *Polareyes*' editors. Published three years later, the journal became the expression of the ability of its founders to act. The agency expressed in the making of *Polareyes* turned a space of deprivation—that is, the art world and publishing—into sites of resistance.[76] In 1990, bell hooks used this concept twice, in her essay "Homeplace (a site of resistance)" and in "Marginality as Site of Resistance."[77] It applies in the case of *Polareyes*, as it was a site of resistance to the silencing of Black women artists in mainstream spaces.[78] Driven by the recognition that individual oppression is experienced at the collective level, *Polareyes* challenged power relations and addressed the politicization of personal experiences in order to fight discrimination. The cover of *Polareyes*, a self-portrait by Molly Shinhat, is a color photograph that represents, symbolizes, and embodies the majority of the issues addressed in the journal. Shinhat's raised fist, symbol of struggle, doubled by the superposition of the shots, represents the convergence of the struggles of the editors and the photographers of *Polareyes*.

For the editors, *Polareyes* was the embodiment of their desire to see a new critical space appear in the photographic field.[79] The journal was a unique place for speaking up and out, allowing the editors to blur the lines of the status quo and to open up practices and photographic discourses to minority people and minoritized individuals. The journal was a space of freedom and experimentation, a critical space of social, sexual, and racial representations but also a space of free self-representation. The magazine format was perfect as they believed that "the act of publishing is . . . an inherently political act," as stated by Simon Murray.[80] Alienated in many ways, the photographers developed *Polareyes* as an act of solidarity, as an object of "consciousness raising," and as the expression of the political role of photography. They were fully aware of this and wrote: "To be a Blackwoman and to be a photographer constitutes a strong political statement" and "*Polareyes* wants to ENGAGE in the discourse around Blackwomen photographers' struggles."[81]

If *Polareyes* was the material result of a joint effort, and as such constituted a community of resistance, it was achieved because of the contributors' determination to carry out their double objective: (1) the affirmation of their existence and (2) the expression of the diversity of their subjectivities. *Polareyes* as a site of resistance was not homogeneous and valued its plurality. In her article "We Do Not Wish to Do It Quietly," Maxine Walker emphasized this intention of collaboration but also the importance of highlighting individualities, summarizing the project this way: "Our Blackness brings us together. Our work as photographers brings us together. These two elements alone have not cemented the individuals into a group. . . . Vast differences can be found within the community of black women photographers."[82] The forty-seven pages that compose it deliver a plurality of photographic and textual projects, through which a variety of practices and multiple subjectivities unfold. It is essential to understand this object as a literal appropriation of Standpoint theory as conceptualized by Sandra Harding: a relevant notion for analyzing intersubjective discourses.[83]

Another way that *Polareyes* was a site of resistance is in the way it blended the personal and political. By using photography, *Polareyes* weaved its images into the fabric of society, while at the same time revealing its vantage point on that world. In the magazine, the intimate, the personal, the familiar, the private, and the confidential were exposed to the public eye. Self-taught photographer Jenny McKenzie[84] displayed pictures taken by her daughter, allowing, from the first couple of pages, the issue of motherhood to be addressed.[85] McKenzie's daughter, Nasiché, took black-and-white photographs, surrounded by a black edge, showing scenes of everyday life. Taken from a child's perspective, the images are often blurry and framed so that the subject is fragmented or cut off as a result. In the text that supported the images, McKenzie reversed the idea of motherhood as a burden to women's creativity.[86] In *Polareyes*, photographers disrupted mainstream feminist assumptions, especially around issues related to the domestic.[87] Rejecting any dichotomous vision of "the house"—between an ultra-positive or ultra-negative conception—Black feminists like Angela Davis,[88] Hazel V. Carby, and bell hooks[89] were determined to review conceptually the issues related to the home.[90] This was also addressed by Maxine Walker in the last pages of *Polareyes*. "Boxed Gems" consists of a short text and a photograph from a then ongoing series and broader project by Birmingham-based photographer Maxine Walker when she turned her camera on the "front rooms" of houses owned by people from the Afro-Caribbean diaspora.[91] Entitled *Auntie Linda's front room*, the image is therefore a close-up of an overcharged living room with wallpaper, knick-knacks, and flowers that Walker explained as the result of a need to "continue to be certain that we produce images of ourselves" adding that she loved "the crochet, the silk flowers, the plastic fruit, the colour, the grandeur."[92] Elizabeth Robles wrote that Walker "makes room for the possibilities of the homeplace as a paradigm for a radical domesticity rooted in black womanhood."[93] By reexamining feminist struggles such as motherhood, family and domesticity, Black women photographers argued for more complex stances on such subjects. The expression of their situated subjectivities became central when addressing such areas.[94] About Walker's photograph, art critic Gilane Tawadros wrote that she "frames individual identity and experience in terms of material objectivity."[95] Tawadros stressed the—contested—power of photography to bring to the surface images of the unthought-of society and history. If Walker's aunt, Auntie Linda, was fundamental in her work on British-Caribbean interiors, it would be the figure of the grandmother who would preoccupy photographer Gloria Walsh. For Walsh, taking a picture of her grandmother was proof of her passage on earth; she wrote, "This slide was taken to prove that she was here and whenever she dies, I will have visual memories of her to pass-on to my children etc."[96] Photography becomes a memory aid and embodies the photographic essence, the photographic "it has been," according to Roland Barthes, oscillating between life and death.[97] This idea is also defended by Similola Coker, who alongside her portrait photography, wrote, "One of the functions of photography is as a record that we exist. Long after memories fade, they are renewed by the image of our physical selves and (sometimes) our personality on a sheet of paper."[98]

Polareyes was not important only in its representation of feminist issues. It was also significant in the platform it gave to a disabled photographer. Samena Rana wrote a striking testimony about the difficulties of being a disabled female photographer. Rana questioned norms, conceptions of and relationship to the body, and the relationship we have with it as a society, writing, "disability is not a game of words but a way of life, which is full of physical limitations, and mental and emotional barriers which create the loss of opportunities to participate in the community on an equal level."[99] Because of her inability to move freely, Rana testified to her difficulties in accessing darkrooms with her wheelchair, but also told the story of how she managed to get some laboratories to improve their accessibility.[100] From 1989, she completely dedicated herself to photography, using an adjusted camera with a trigger mechanism that could be placed in her mouth.[101] Thus, Rana's lived experience provides a fundamental context for understanding her images. The same goes for Zarina Bhimji, who in "And then I woke up" wove questions about identity, displacement, exile, childhood, and family space through a poetic and photographic proposal.[102] Her reflexive poem is accompanied by documentary-style images showing childhood toys such as a doll's head in rather chaotic surroundings. Lived experiences are then translated by photography, underlining the rhetorical and political potency of the feminist axiom "the personal as political."

Polareyes also formed a site of resistance through demonstrating an intersectional lens before the popular writing on the subject. As such, the magazine should be considered a forerunner to intersectionality, in the way that it simultaneously addressed oppressions related to gender, race, sexual orientation, and abilities. When, in 1989, Kimberlé Williams Crenshaw coined the term "intersectionality," she did so based on her personal experience and that of the women around her: "I consider how the experiences of women of color and frequently the product of intersecting patterns of racism and sexism, and how these experiences tend not to be represented within the discourses of either feminism or antiracism."[103] Two years before, Maxine Walker recounted, "One of the most interesting and important aspects of *Polareyes* is that it touched on many different parts of black women's lives through photography."[104] Subtitled "A journal by and about Black Women working in photography," *Polareyes* was a space for thinking about the intersection of their condition as women, as female photographers, and as Black women photographers active in England in the 1980s.[105] *Polareyes*, like other Black women's periodicals in Britain, as Thomlinson explained, "insisted on the interconnected nature of gendered, race and class oppression in a manner that foreshadowed many contemporary theoretical developments around the politics of intersectionality."[106] Hence, *Polareyes*, appears as a precursor to Crenshaw's theory of intersectionality.[107]

In 1991, in her article "Mapping the Margins" Crenshaw developed the idea that "the devaluation of women of color . . . is linked to how women of color are represented in cultural imagery."[108] It is precisely by considering these undesirable reflections or negative representations that Crenshaw developed the idea of "representational intersectionality." By developing a visual ramification to intersectionality, Crenshaw points out the political stakes of the visual. In the context of photography, who is in front and who is behind the camera is indicative of relationships of domination and discrimination. The relationships of power intrinsic to the history of photography, particularly through colonial or anthropological photography, are questions that concerned most members of *Polareyes*. Walker, for example, wrote in her short essay, "I have found the majority of anthropological works offensive."[109] Bouncing back on such a—widely shared—feeling, Joy Kahumbu wondered if she could take a photo of an African woman and if it would look different to one taken by a white photographer.[110] The questions are: Who represents whom? Which voices are heard? The women photographers who collaborated in the setting up and publication of *Polareyes* are fully aware of the conflicting history between the camera and the representation of the Black body. Because of this, it is essential to understand the empowerment to be found in a publication such as *Polareyes* that presented itself as a journal *by* and *about* Black women photographers.

It was in the 1980s, thanks in particular to transatlantic dialogue, that the discussion on the multiplicity of feminisms, especially in periodicals, developed. As Thomlinson has explained, "Black feminist periodicals in the UK became focal points for the development of black feminist theory."[111] Black feminists were witnesses to, and sometimes participants in, the multiplication of "consciousness raising" (CR) groups developing among the population of Black women living in large British cities, as exemplified by activist groups such as the Organisation of Women of Asian and African Descent (aka OWAAD).[112] Indeed, OWAAD[113] was a "concrete expression of black feminists' critical distance from 'white' feminism."[114] The organization also published booklets and pamphlets, as a means of disseminating their ideas and debates within communities.[115] FOWAAD (OWAAD's newsletter), *Speak Out*, and *We Are Here* were the first periodicals born out of Black feminism in England.[116] However, in the mid-1980s these publications disappeared, leaving a void that would be a necessary vector for the creation of *Polareyes* in 1987.

Beyond their philosophy, they also left to *Polareyes*' editors a *modus operandi* of sorts. Collaboration, groups, gatherings, even temporary ones, were crucial to the creation of this critical mass. Reflecting back on this decisive decade, Heidi Safia Mirza explained, "In Britain in the 1980s, this shared sense of objectification was articulated when the radicalized, disempowered and fragmented sought empowerment in a gesture of politicized collective action."[117] The question of group work and the constitution of collectives made meetings and gatherings fundamental for exchanges and encounters. In the pages of the journal, Barbara Jones recounted the role and place of the "workshops" in 1980s London.[118] The Lenthall Road Workshop in Hackney (North East London) was an additional space for gatherings and mutual help. It was a place where minority women photographers could talk freely.

Polareyes was also a way of breaking out of isolation. Walker explained the importance of interaction among peers: "I had been working in virtual isolation from other black women photographers, and the conference brought home to me just how acute that isolation was."[119] This testimony raises the significance of meetings in order to think together about ways of action. Walker adds: "Talking to other black women photographers who were all experiencing similar forms of racism convinced me that I wanted and needed to be involved in something where black women were taking charge of things for themselves."[120] The issue of collective action by women artists also preoccupied North American feminist art historian Linda Nochlin. Indeed, in her famous 1988 essay "Why Have There Been No Great Women Artists?," Nochlin addressed the strength of the collective form: "The art produced by a group of consciously united and purposefully articulate women intent on bodying forth a group consciousness of feminine experience might indeed be stylistically identifiable as feminist, if not feminine, art."[121] At the heart of these groupings was the sharing of similar experiences and the will to take action, and to find a form of political expression. Summing up the intention behind the creation of the journal, Walker explained that *Polareyes* was initially constituted as "a forum for, and network of, black women photographers."[122]

Conclusion

In 1984, a few years before the publication of *Polareyes*, filmmaker Pratibha Parmar wrote:

> Many photographers who consider themselves to be "on the side of" (for instance) Black people, continue to use their skills

and power to represent "multi-ethnic" Britain in the belief that they are doing so in the interests of Black people. But their photographs are constructed through a series of choices based on their race, class and gender positions and often complement the hegemonic system which uses photographs as a way of representing, classifying and evaluating Black people in particular ideological ways.[123]

Pratibha Parmar's powerful and apt statement prefigures Maxine Walker's testimony written three years later in *Polareyes*: "Without putting definitions on myself I find them put on to me. The photography circuit is no exception."[124] In that respect, *Polareyes* should be understood as an effort toward self-determination. Spreading the word about their artistic existence—through the medium of a publication—allowed access to a freedom in telling their stories. Their autonomy in crafting *Polareyes* meant they could determine the content and conditions, words, and images: something that had been denied to them until *Polareyes* came into being. Through an oppositional photographic practice and alternative approach to publishing, the Black women photographers that constituted *Polareyes*' editorial board made a transgressive object that had the form of a magazine but the content of a zine. As a hybrid object it was made in the image of its creators: a defiant object produced by imagemakers, disenfranchised by dominant economic and cultural systems. The production of the magazine resulted in an avant-garde visual and textual vernacular language the editors-photographers created for themselves: a new kind of grassroots publication. In the United States, a few years later, Black feminist writer and activist Barbara Smith wrote about setting up Kitchen Table Press: "Starting a press for women of color in 1980 may have defied logic, but it was one of those acts of courage that characterize Third World women's lives,"[125] a statement backed by founding member Anita McKenzie, who reported that "Black women organize to get their voices heard, that's what we do."[126] *Polareyes* is the result of a mixture of personal narratives and politics, and had the ability to convey urgent ideas, foster creativity, and connect likeminded photographers. With this magazine, editors and contributors asserted a way of working, creating a support system for themselves and their practices, focusing on their politics, and forming a hub for their peers. However, *Polareyes* did not experience commercial success. More than thirty years after its launch, Anita McKenzie told me that she "had boxes of it, but nobody was interested, so [I] threw them all away." The question of its legacy comes into question, as many doors remained closed for the *Polareyes* team as a collective and as individuals. It is in this context that this chapter was written and published.

Perhaps by considering this modestly produced object as a monograph, addressing overlapping and intersecting issues, we can trigger a curiosity and encourage new readers for this publication—first and foremost today's Black women photographers. This chapter is an attempt to shed some light on the publication, seeing it as a unique capsule in the visual and textual history of Black feminism. Working around what comes to light and what remains in the shadows, Fred Moten wrote, "The mark of invisibility is a visible, racial mark; invisibility has visibility at its heart. To be invisible is to be seen, instantly and fascinatingly recognized as the unrecognizable, as the abject, as the absence of individual self-consciousness, as a transparent vessel of meanings wholly independent of any influence of the vessel itself."[127]

Notes

1. I would like to thank Molly Shinhat, Anita McKenzie, Mumtaz Karimjee, Amina Patel, Joy Gregory, Sharron Wallace, and Ingrid Pollard for their contributions to this piece.

2. The reproduction of its cover is probably the only reference one can find when undertaking research to find out more about *Polareyes*' publication context. It is mentioned in *Shades of Black*'s chronology of key 1980s events (2005). It is also mentioned as part of another chronology in *Ten.8*'s 1992 issue entitled *Critical Decade*, edited by Stuart Hall and David A. Bailey. Its presence in both chronologies might indicate a critical role, or at least some sort of importance, but to my knowledge no substantial writing exists about this singular, avant-garde publication.

3. "Editorial," *Polareyes* 1 (1987): 3.

4. Sean O'Hagan, "Britain's Photographic Revolution," *Guardian* (30 October 2011).

5. Abigail Solomon-Godeau, *Photography after Photography: Gender, Genre, History* (Durham, NC: Duke University Press, 2017), 1.

6. Anthias Floya, Harriet Cain, and Nira Yuval-Davis, *Racialized Boundaries: Race, Nation, Gender, Colour and Class and the Anti-racist Struggle* (London: Routledge, 1992); Fiona Williams, *Social Policy: A Critical Introduction: Issues of Race, Gender and Class* (Cambridge: Polity, 1989).

7. Graham Stewart, *Bang! A History of Britain in the 1980s* (London: Atlantic Books, 2013), xi.

8. Andy McSmith, *No Such Thing as Society: A History of Britain in the 1980s* (London: Constable, 2010); Alwyn Turner, *Rejoice, Rejoice! Britain in the 1980s* (London: Aurum, 2010).

9. Jenny Bourne, "'May We Bring Harmony'? Thatcher's Legacy on 'Race,'" *Race & Class* 55.1 (2013): 87–91.

10. For more information see Sunil Gupta, "The Foundation of Autograph ABP: Diary Notes," *Autograph Newsletter* 34 (October 2007): 1.

11. Maxine Walker reported: "Black women knew they could do things for themselves but aligning with white women (whom I felt we could potentially share a great deal with) was counter productive if first they had not dealt with their racism," in Maxine Walker, "We Do Not Wish to Do It Quietly," *Ten.8* 27 (1987): 43. Coincidently, the conference "Women & Photography" was held in Syracuse, New York, in the same year, where leading photography historians Abigail Salomon-Godeau and Deborah Willis spoke.

12. "Faced with the construction of a women's liberation movement that overlooked racism, many black women have rejected (white) feminism and turned to black community struggles," in Julia Sudbury, "(Re)constructing Multiracial Blackness: Women's Activism, Difference and Collective Identity in Britain," *Ethnic and Racial Studies* 24.1 (2001): 32. See also Natalie Thomlinson, *Race, Ethnicity and the Women's Movement in England, 1968–1993* (Basingstoke, Hampshire: Palgrave Macmillan, 2016).

13. Jenny Bourne, "When Black was a Political Colour: A Guide to the Literature," *Race & Class* 58.1 (July–September 2016): 122–130.

14. Rob Waters, *Thinking Black: Britain, 1964–1985* (Oakland, CA: University of California Press, 2019); Kennetta Hammond Perry, "Black Britain and the Politics of Race in the 20th Century" *History Compass* 12.8 (2014): 651–663.

15. Maxine Walker, Molly Shinhat, Mumtaz Karimjee, Jenny McKenzie, Amina Patel, Samena Rana, Similola Coker, Brenda Agard, and Leslie Mitchell, "Editorial," *Polareyes* 1 (1987): 3.

16. Rina Arya, "Rethinking Black Art as a Category of Experience," *Visual Culture in Britain* 18.2 (2017): 163–175.

17. See Jade Bentil, "'We were fire-fighting against Thatcher and the system she was putting forward': The Black Women's Movement and the Boundaries of Nationhood in Thatcher's Britain," in this volume.

18. Matthew Worley, "Punk, Politics and British (Fan)zines, 1976–84: 'While the world was dying, did you wonder why?,'" *History Workshop Journal* 79.1 (Spring 2015): 76–106; Teal Triggs, "Alphabet Soup: Reading British Fanzines," *Visible Language* 29.1 (1995): 72.

19. Nadia Nelson, the designer also worked for *The Voice* at the time.

20. Marsha Rowe, *Spare Rib Reader* (Harmondsworth, Middlesex, England: Penguin Books, 1982); Melanie Waters, "'Yours in Struggle': Bad Feelings and Revolutionary Politics in Spare Rib," *Women* 27.4 (2016): 446–465.

21. Marsha Rowe and Rosie Boycott, "Editorial," *Spare Rib* 1 (July 1972): 3.

22. To learn more about *Spare Rib*, see Charlotte Lydia Riley's chapter in this volume.

23. Chila Kumari Burman, "There Have Always Been Great Blackwomen Artists (1986)," in *Why Are We 'Artists'? 100 World Art Manifestos*, ed. Jessica Lack (UK: Penguin Books, 2017).

24. Lubaina Himid, "Mapping: A Decade of Black Women Artists 1980–1990," in *Passion: Discourses on Blackwomen's Creativity*, ed. Maud Sulter (Hebden Bridge, UK: Urban Fox Press, 1990), 63–72.

25. "Editorial," *Polareyes* 1 (1987): 3.

26. "Editorial," *Polareyes* 1 (1987): 3.

27. Daniel C. Blight, *The Image of Whiteness: Contemporary Photography and Racialization* (London: SPBH Editions, 2019).

28. They were probably thinking of *Spare Rib*'s "Black Women's Issue" published in October 1983 or the *Feminist Review*'s black women's special issue in 1984, "Many Voices, One Chant."

29. Isaac Julien and Kobena Mercer, "De Margin and De Centre," *Screen* 29.4 (Autumn 1988): 2–11.

30. "Editorial," *Polareyes* 1 (1987): 3.

31. The Greater London Council (1965–1986) had a policy of funding black, women's, and gay and lesbian organizations and worked on a diversity of equal opportunities policies. The development of Black women's organizations and campaigns is discussed by Jade Bentil in her chapter in this volume.

32. The "anti-racism" attempts of the Greater London Council included the creation in 1982 of an Ethnic Minorities Committee that declared London as an "anti-racism zone" and declared 1984 "the anti-racism year." See Richard Hylton, *The Nature of the Beast—Cultural Diversity and the Visual Arts Sector: A Study of Policies, Initiatives and Attitudes 1976–2006* (Bath: ICIA, 2007).

33. "Editorial," *Polareyes* 1 (1987): 3.

34. Maxine Walker, "We Do Not Wish to Do It Quietly," *Ten.8* 27 (1987): 42–45.

35. Marina Prentoulis, "The Construction of the Black British Community in *The Voice* and the *New Nation*," *Journalism* 13.6 (2012): 731–749.

36. Michael Ann Mullen, "The Cockpit Gallery," *Ten.8* 26 (1987): 54–56.

37. Jenny McKenzie, "Review," *Polareyes* 1 (1987): 13.

38. A year earlier, Deborah Willis-Thomas published *Black Photographers, 1840–1940: An Illustrated Bio-bibliography* (New York: Garland, 1985), but the book is either not mentioned or unknown to the editors.

39. The existence in the United States of the publication *Black Photographers Annual* (1973–1980) should also be noted.

40. One of Mumtaz Karimjee's poems serves as the epigraph for this chapter.

41. Some of them had already decided to write about their practice and continued after the end of the journal. For example, photographer Mumtaz Karimjee also published, in the journal *Mukti* in 1987, an article entitled "Black and Asian: Definitions and Redefinitions," deploying her field of expression from poetry to critical essay to photography. Laura Forster, "'Our Culture in a Racist Society': Mukti," in *Magazine Movements Women's Culture, Feminisms and Media Form* (London: Bloomsbury, 2015), 111–146.

42. See also David A. Bailey, Ian Baucom, and Sonia Boyce, eds., *Shades of Black Assembling Black Arts in 1980s Britain* (Durham, NC & London: Duke University Press, 2005); Nick Aikens and Elizabeth Robles, eds., *The Place is Here: The Work of Black Artists in 1980s Britain* (Berlin: Sternberg Press, 2019).

43. Naseem Khan, *The Arts Britain Ignores: The Arts of Ethnic Minorities in Britain* (Arts Council of Great Britain, Fundação Calouste Gulbenkian, Great Britain, Community Relations Commission, London: The Commission, 1976); Naseem Khan, "Choices for Black Arts in Britain over 30 years," in *Shades of Black—Assembling Black Arts in 1980s Britain*, eds. David A. Bailey, Ian Baucom, and Sonia Boyce (Durham, NC & London: Duke University Press, 2005).

44. Stuart Hall, "Assembling the 1980s: The Deluge—and After," in *Shades of Black Assembling Black Arts in 1980s Britain*, eds. David A. Bailey, Ian Baucom, and Sonia Boyce (Durham, NC & London: Duke University Press, 2005), 19.

45. Stuart Hall, "The Scarman Report," *Critical Social Policy* 2.2 (Fall 1982): 66.

46. Stuart Hall, "Black Diaspora Artists in Britain: Three Moments in Post-war History," *History Workshop Journal* 61.1 (2006): 1–24.

47. Keith Piper, "Wait, Did I Miss Something? Some Personal Musings on the 1980s and Beyond," in *Shades of Black Assembling Black Arts in 1980s Britain*, eds. David A. Bailey, Ian Baucom, and Sonia Boyce (Durham, NC & London: Duke University Press, 2005), 35–40.

48. Juliette Jarette, "Creative Space? The Experience of Black Women in British Art Schools in Reconstructing Womanhood," in *Reconstructing Feminism: Writings of Black Women* (London & New York: Routledge, 1996), 126.

49. Beverly Bryan, Stella Dadzie, and Suzanne Scafe, "Chain Reactions: Black Women Organising," *Race & Class* 27.1 (1985).

50. As early as its fourth issue *Camerawork* addressed issues such as "Black stereotyping," and the subject of its eighth issue was the "Battle of Lewisham"; as for *Ten.8*, since its first issue in February 1979 the representation of race was discussed, and then throughout the 1980s this discussion largely occupied the pages of the magazines; the editorial board's diversity was also addressed.

51. Walker, "We Do Not Wish," 42–45.

52. It is worth mentioning that in 1987 the art magazine *ArtRage* published a portfolio entitled "Measuring Britain—Women photographers": *ArtRage* 18 (Autumn 1987).

53. Susan Kismaric, *British Photography from the Thatcher Years* (New York: Museum of Modern Art, 1991).

54. For example, a year after the publication of the journal, key figures of the movement published, in *Third Text*, an article now considered seminal, entitled "Black Art: A Discussion," which consisted of a conversation between Karachi born, London-based conceptual artist Rasheed Araeen and Wolverhampton-born artist, curator, and art historian Eddie Chambers. Even if a year prior to its publication tens of Black British women photographers had made *Polareyes*, they finished their twenty-six-page article with a banner disclaimer stating, "We are acutely aware of the gap in the discussion here, as well as in the journal as a whole, about the issues concerning black women artists. We hope, nevertheless, that this initiative will stimulate further debates; and we will welcome unsolicited material in particular about the contributions of black women artists." See Eddie Chambers and Rasheed Araeen, "Black Art: A Discussion," *Third Text* 5 (Winter 1988–1989): 77.

55. Eddie Chambers and Rasheed Araeen, "Black Art: A Discussion," *Third Text* 5 (Winter 1988–1989): 77; Aubrey Williams, "Seeking a Black Aesthetic," in *Creation for Liberation* (1987), n.p.; Rasheed Araeen, "Preliminary Notes for a Black Manifesto," in *Making Myself Visible* (London: Kala Press, 1984), 7–97.

56. Stuart Hall, "Assembling the 1980s," 11.

57. Born in England of Indian descent, Molly Shinhat graduated from Concordia University (Canada) and in 1987 she worked at the Cultural Studies Department of the Cockpit Art Gallery in London.

58. Molly Shinhat, "I'm the Problem, I'm Not White," *Polareyes* 1 (1987): 32–33.

59. Simon Peplow, *Race and Riots in Thatcher's Britain* (Manchester: Manchester University Press, 2019); Michael Keith, *Race, Riots and Policing: Lore and Disorder in a Multi-Racist Society* (London: UCL Press, 1993); Martin Kettle and Lucy Hodges, *Uprising! The Police, the People and the Riots in Britain's Cities* (London: Pan Books, 1982); Robin D.G. Kelley and Stephen G.N. Tuck, *The Other Special Relationship: Race, Rights, and Riots in Britain and the United States* (Basingstoke, Hampshire: Palgrave Macmillan, 2015); Kennetta Hammond Perry, "Race Riots and the Mystique of British Anti-Racism," in *London Is the Place for Me: Black Britons, Citizenship and the Politics of Race* (Oxford: Oxford University Press, 2016).

60. Rhona Hariette, "Young gifted and black," *Polareyes* 1 (1987): 16–17.

61. Laurel Forster, *Magazine Movements: Women's Culture, Feminisms and Media Form* (New York: Bloomsbury Academic, 2015), 1.

62. Nancy Fraser, "Rethinking the Public Sphere: A Contribution to the Critique of Actually Existing Democracy," *Social Text* 25/26 (1990): 56–80.

63. Adelaide Bannerman, "Introduction. Time Lines," in *Shades of Black Assembling Black Arts in 1980s Britain*, eds. David A. Bailey, Ian Baucom,

and Sonia Boyce (Durham, NC & London: Duke University Press, 2005), 205.

64. Centre for Contemporary Cultural Studies, *The Empire Strikes Back: Race and Racism in Seventies Britain* (London: Hutchinson, 1982), which includes Hazel V. Carby's essay "White Woman Listen! Black Feminism and the Boundaries of Sisterhood."

65. Hazel V. Carby, *Reconstructing Womanhood: The Emergence of the Afro-American Woman Novelist* (New York & Oxford: Oxford University Press, 1987).

66. Elizabeth Edwards and Janice Hart, *Photographs Objects Histories: On the Materiality of Images* (London: Routledge, 2004), 1.

67. Bill Jay established the first gallery dedicated to photography in the UK with the Do Not Bend Gallery in London and he was the first director of photography at the Institute of Contemporary Arts (ICA) in London. Whilst there he founded and directed the first Photo-Study Centre.

68. Mathilde Bertrand, "The Half Moon Photography Workshop and Camerawork: Catalysts in the British Photographic Landscape (1972–1985)," *Photography and Culture* 11.3 (2018): 239–259.

69. But the magazine was reborn from its ashes a few years later, in 1987, with the launch of the journal *Third Text*.

70. In her work Laurel Forster investigates the significance of print cultures to the Women's Liberation Movement and sees these publications as feminist interventions into a male-dominated publishing industry. See Laurel Forster, "Spreading the Word: Feminist Print Cultures and the Women's Liberation Movement," *Women's History Review* 2.5 (2016): 812–831; Laurel Forster, *Magazine Movements: Women's Culture, Feminisms and Media Form* (New York: Bloomsbury Academic, 2015).

71. Maria DiCenzo, Lucy Delap, and Leila Ryan, *Feminist Media History: Suffrage, Periodicals and the Public Sphere* (Basingstoke: Palgrave Macmillan, 2011); Barbara Green, *Feminist Periodicals and Daily Life: Women and Modernity in British Culture* (Switzerland: Palgrave Macmillan, 2017); Simone Murray, *Mixed Media: Feminist Presses and Publishing Politics* (London: Pluto Press, 2004); Catherine Clay, *Time and Tide: The Feminist and Cultural Politics of a Modern Magazine* (Edinburgh: Edinburgh University Press, 2018).

72. Natalie Thomlinson, "'Second-Wave' Black Feminist Periodicals in Britain," *Women: A Cultural Review* 27.4 (2016): 432.

73. Rachel Schreiber, *Modern Print Activism in the United States* (Farnham, Surrey: Ashgate, 2013).

74. Laurence Leamer, *The Paper Revolutionaries: The Rise of the Underground Press* (New York: Simon & Schuster, 1972).

75. Valerie Amos, Gail Lewis, Amina Mama, and Pratibha Parmar, "Editorial," *Feminist Review* 17 (Autumn 1984): 2.

76. Leonidas K. Cheliotis, *Roots, Rites and Sites of Resistance: The Banality*

of Good (Basingstoke & New York: Palgrave Macmillan, 2010).

77. bell hooks, "Marginality as Site of Resistance." In *Out There: Marginalization and Contemporary Cultures* (New York: New Museum of Contemporary Art; Cambridge: London: MIT Press, 1990), 341–343.

78. Akwugo Emejulu and Francesca Sobande, eds., *To Exist Is to Resist: Black Feminism in Europe* (London: Pluto Press, 2019).

79. In the 1980s in England, the critical discourse on photography and the Marxist history of photography was echoed particularly in two publications: *Photography / Politics One* (1979) and *Photography / Politics Two* (1986).

80. Simone Murray, *Mixed Media: Feminist Presses and Publishing Politics* (London: Pluto Press, 2004), 6.

81. Maxine Walker, Molly Shinhat, Mumtaz Karimjee, Jenny McKenzie, Amina Patel, Samena Rana, Similola Coker, Brenda Agard, and Leslie Mitchell, "Editorial," *Polareyes* 1 (1987): 3.

82. Walker, "We Do Not Wish, 45.

83. Sandra Harding, *The Feminist Standpoint Theory Reader: Intellectual and Political Controversies* (New York & London: Routledge, 2004).

84. Later, between 1996 and 2006, McKenzie would go on to create the McKenzie Heritage Picture Library.

85. On this subject see Kate Turner's chapter in this volume, "Thatcherism, the Black Women's Movement, and the Politics of Motherhood in Britain."

86. Jenny McKenzie, "Visual Perceptions of a Two Year Old," *Polareyes* 1 (1987): 5.

87. In 1987, The Black Art Gallery in London presented a group exhibition entitled "Staring . . . Mummy and Daddy: Photographs of Our Parents" with works by *Polareyes* photographers such as Agard, Pollard, Walker, and McKenzie.

88. The idea of the "double burden" is examined by Angela Davis in *Women, Race and Class* (London: The Women's Press, 1982), 231.

89. bell hooks, "Homeplace (a site for resistance)." In *Yearning: Race, Gender, and Cultural Politics* (Boston: South End Press, 1990).

90. Emily Matchar, *Homeward Bound: Why Women are Embracing the New Domesticity* (New York: Simon & Schuster, 2013).

91. Michael McMillan, *The Front Room: Migrant Aesthetics in the Home* (London: Black Dog Publishing Ltd., 2009).

92. Maxine Walker, "Boxed Gems," *Polareyes* 1 (1987): 42.

93. Elizabeth Robles, "Maxine Walker: Imaging the Homeplace," *Oxford Art Journal* 40.1 (2017): 172.

94. Walker, "Boxed Gems," 42.

95. Gilane Tawadros, "Redrawing the Boundaries," *Ten. 8* 2.3 (Spring 1992): 89.

96. Gloria Walsh, "Celebrating the Joys of a Grandmother Disabled or Otherwise," *Polareyes* 1 (1987): 24.

97. Roland Barthes, *Camera Lucida: Reflections on Photography* (London: Vintage Classics, 1993).
98. Similola Coker, "Thoughts on Creating/Recreating Ourselves in Film," *Polareyes* 1 (1987): 32–33.
99. Samena Rana, "Disability and Photography," *Polareyes* 1 (1987): 14–15.
100. Her advocacy led to policy changes at the Institute of Contemporary Art (ICA) and in Camerawork's darkroom in East London.
101. Nasa Begum, "Disabled Women and the Feminist Agenda," *Feminist Review* 40 (1992): 72.
102. Zarina Bhimji, "And then I woke up," *Polareyes* 1 (1987), 8.
103. Kimberlé Crenshaw, "Demarginalizing the Intersection of Race and Sex: A Black Feminist Critique of Antidiscrimination Doctrine, Feminist Theory and Antiracist Politics," *University of Chicago Legal Forum* 1 (1989).
104. Walker, "We Do Not Wish," 43.
105. Intersectional thinking, as it can be understood and translated into the British context, was also widely discussed in the article "Challenging Imperial Feminism" by Amos and Parmar where they frame the necessity of crossing dominations. Valerie Amos and Pratibha Parmar, "Challenging Imperial Feminism," *Feminist Review* (Autumn 1984): 18.
106. Thomlinson, "'Second-Wave,'" 433.
107. Crenshaw, "Demarginalizing."
108. Kimberlé Crenshaw, "Mapping the Margins: Intersectionality, Identity Politics, and Violence against Women of Color," *Stanford Law Review* 43.6 (1991): 1282.
109. Walker, "Boxed Gems," 42.
110. Joy Kahumbu, *Polareyes* 1 (1987): 38–39.
111. Thomlinson, "'Second Wave,'" 432.
112. Patricia Hill Collins, *Black Feminist Thought: Knowledge, Consciousness, and the Politics of Empowerment* (New York & London: Routledge, 2000).
113. For American histories, see the action of the Combahee River Collective, active from 1974 to 1980 in Boston.
114. Hazel V. Carby, "White Woman Listen! Black Feminism and the Boundaries of Sisterhood," *Black British Cultural Studies*, eds. Houston A. Baker Jr., Mathia Diawara, and Ruth H. Lindeborg (Chicago: University of Chicago Press, 1996), 71.
115. Other publications were essential to the creation of a field related to Black, postcolonial, and anti-racist feminism in England. F. Anthias and N. Yuval-Davis, "Contextualising Feminism—Gender, Ethnic and Class Divisions," *Feminist Review* (Winter 1983); Beverly Bryan, Stella Dadzie, and Suzanne Scafe, *The Heart of the Race: Black Women's Lives in Britain* (London: Virago Press, 1985).
116. Thomlinson, "'Second-Wave,'" 432–445.
117. Heidi Safia Mirza, *Black British Feminism—A Reader* (London: Routledge, 1997), 3.

118. Barbara Jones, "Lenthall Road Workshop," *Polareyes* 1 (1987): 22.
119. Walker, "We Do Not Wish," 43.
120. Walker, "We Do Not Wish," 43.
121. Linda Nochlin, "Why Have There Been No Great Women Artists?" In *Women, Art, and Power: And Other Essays*, ed. Linda Nochlin (New York & London: Routledge, 2018), 148.
122. Walker, "We Do Not Wish," 43.
123. Pratibha Parmar, "Hateful Contraries: Media Images of Asian Women," *Ten.8* 16 (1984): 71–78.
124. Walker, "Boxed Gems," 42.
125. Barbara Smith, "A Press of Our Own Kitchen Table: Women of Color Press," *Frontiers: A Journal of Women Studies* 10.3 (1989): 11.
126. Quote from a conversation between McKenzie and the author, 16 March 2021.
127. Fred Moten, *In the Break. The Aesthetics of the Black Radical Tradition* (Minneapolis: University of Minnesota Press, 2003), 68.

Works Cited

Aikens, Nick, and Elizabeth Robles, eds. *The Place Is Here: The Work of Black Artists in 1980s* Britain. Berlin: Sternberg Press, 2019.

Amos, Valerie, and Pratibha Parmar. "Challenging Imperial Feminism." *Feminist Review* 17 (Autumn 1984): 18.

Anthias, Floya, and Nira Yuval-Davis. "Contextualising Feminism—Gender, Ethnic and Class Divisions." *Feminist Review* (Winter 1983).

Anthias, Floya, Harriet Cain, and Nira Yuval-Davis. *Racialized Boundaries: Race, Nation, Gender, Colour and Class and the Anti-racist Struggle*. London: Routledge, 1992.

Araeen, Rasheed. "Preliminary Notes for a Black Manifesto," in *Making Myself Visible*. London: Kala Press, 1984. 7–97.

Arya, Rina. "Rethinking Black Art as a Category of Experience." *Visual Culture in Britain* 18.2 (2017): 163–175.

Bailey, David A., Ian Baucom, and Sonia Boyce, eds. *Shades of Black Assembling Black Arts in 1980s Britain*. Durham, NC & London: Duke University Press, 2005.

Barthes, Roland. *Camera Lucida: Reflections on Photography*. London: Vintage Classics, 1993.

Begum, Nasa. "Disabled Women and the Feminist Agenda." *Feminist Review* 40 (1992): 72.

Bertrand, Mathilde. "The Half Moon Photography Workshop and Camerawork: Catalysts in the British Photographic Landscape (1972–1985)." *Photography and Culture* 11.3 (2018): 239–259.

Blight, Daniel C. *The Image of Whiteness: Contemporary Photography and Racialization*. London: SPBH Editions, 2019.
Bourne, Jenny. "'May We Bring Harmony'? Thatcher's Legacy on 'Race.'" *Race & Class* 55.1 (2013): 87–91.
Bryan, Beverly, Stella Dadzie, and Suzanne Scafe. *The Heart of the Race: Black Women's Lives in Britain*. London: Virago Press, 1985.
Burman, Chila Kumari. "There Have Always Been Great Blackwomen Artists (1986)," in *Why Are We "Artists"? 100 World Art Manifestos*, ed. Jessica Lack. Harmondsworth, Middlesex, England: Penguin Books, 2017.
Carby, Hazel V. *Reconstructing Womanhood: The Emergence of the Afro-American Woman Novelist*. New York & Oxford: Oxford University Press, 1987.
Carby, Hazel V. "White Woman Listen! Black Feminism and The Boundaries of Sisterhood," in *Black British Cultural Studies*, eds. H. Baker, M. Diawara, and R. Lindeborg. Chicago: University of Chicago Press, 1996. 71.
Chambers, Eddie, and Rasheed Araeen. "Black Art: A Discussion." *Third Text* 5 (Winter 1988–1989): 77.
Cheliotis, Leonidas K. *Roots, Rites and Sites of Resistance: The Banality of Good*. Basingstoke & New York: Palgrave Macmillan, 2010.
Clay, Catherine. *Time and Tide: The Feminist and Cultural Politics of a Modern Magazine*. Edinburgh: Edinburgh University Press, 2018.
Centre for Contemporary Cultural Studies. *The Empire Strikes Back: Race and Racism in Seventies Britain*. London: Hutchinson, 1982.
Crenshaw, Kimberlé. "Demarginalizing the Intersection of Race and Sex: A Black Feminist Critique of Antidiscrimination Doctrine, Feminist Theory and Antiracist Politics." *University of Chicago Legal Forum* 1 (1989).
Crenshaw, Kimberlé. "Mapping the Margins: Intersectionality, Identity Politics, and Violence against Women of Color." *Stanford Law Review* 43.6 (1991): 1282.
Davis, Angela. *Women, Race and Class*. London: The Women's Press, 1982.
DiCenzo, Maria, Lucy Delap, and Leila Ryan, *Feminist Media History: Suffrage, Periodicals and the Public Sphere*. Basingstoke: Palgrave Macmillan, 2011.
Edwards, Elizabeth, and Janice Hart. *Photographs Objects Histories: On the Materiality of Images*. London: Routledge, 2004.
Emejulu, Akwugo, and Francesca Sobande, eds. *To Exist Is to Resist: Black Feminism in Europe*. London: Pluto Press, 2019.
Fraser, Nancy. "Rethinking the Public Sphere: A Contribution to the Critique of Actually Existing Democracy." *Social Text* 25/26 (1990): 56–80.
Forster, Laurel. *Magazine Movements: Women's Culture, Feminisms and Media Form*. New York: Bloomsbury Academic, 2015.
Forster, Laurel. "Spreading the Word: Feminist Print Cultures and the Women's Liberation Movement." *Women's History Review* 2.5 (2016): 812–831.

Gramsci, Antonio. *Selections from the Prison Notebooks*. London: Lawrence and Wishart, 1971.
Green, Barbara. *Feminist Periodicals and Daily Life: Women and Modernity in British Culture*. Switzerland: Palgrave Macmillan, 2017.
Hall, Stuart. "The Scarman Report." *Critical Social Policy* 2.2 (Fall 1982): 66.
Hall, Stuart. "Black Diaspora Artists in Britain: Three Moments in Post-war History." *History Workshop Journal* 61.1 (2006): 1–24.
Hall, Stuart, and Martin Jacques. *New Times: The Changing Face of Politics in the 1990s*. Marxism Today. London: Lawrence & Wishart, 1990.
Harding, Sandra. *The Feminist Standpoint Theory Reader: Intellectual and Political Controversies*. New York & London: Routledge, 2004.
Hammond Perry, Kennetta. "'Race Riots' and the Mystique of British Anti-Racism," in *London is the Place for Me: Black Britons, Citizenship and the Politics of Race*. Oxford: Oxford University Press, 2016.
Hammond Perry, Kennetta. "Black Britain and the Politics of Race in the 20th Century." *History Compass* 12.8 (2014): 651–663.
Hill Collins, Patricia. *Black Feminist Thought: Knowledge, Consciousness, and the Politics of Empowerment*. New York & London: Routledge, 2000.
Himid, Lubaina. "Mapping: A Decade of Black Women Artists 1980–1990," in *Passion: Discourses on Blackwomen's Creativity*, ed. Maud Sulter. Hebden Bridge, UK: Urban Fox Press, 1990. 63–72.
hooks, bell. "Homeplace (a Site of Resistance)," in *Yearning: Race, Gender and Cultural Politics*. Boston: South End Press, 1990. 41–49.
hooks, bell. "The Oppositional Gaze: Black Female Spectators," in *Black Looks: Race and Representation*. Boston: South end Press, 1992. 115.
hooks, bell. "Marginality as Site of Resistance" In *Out there: Marginalization and Contemporary Cultures*. New York: New Museum of Contemporary Art; Cambridge: London: MIT Press, 1990. 341–343.
Hylton, Richard. *The Nature of the Beast—Cultural Diversity and the Visual Arts Sector. A Study of Policies, Initiatives and Attitudes 1976–2006*. Bath: ICIA, 2007.
Keith, Michael. *Race, Riots and Policing: Lore and Disorder in a Multi-Racist Society*. London: UCL Press, 1993.
Jarette, Juliette. "Creative Space? The Experience of Black Women in British Art Schools in Reconstructing Womanhood," in *Reconstructing Feminism: Writings of Black Women*. London & New York: Routledge, 1996. 126.
Julien, Isaac, and Kobena Mercer. "De Margin and De Centre." *Screen* 29.4 (Autumn 1988): 2–11.
Kelley, Robin D.G., and Stephen G.N. Tuck, *The Other Special Relationship: Race, Rights, and Riots in Britain and the United States*. Basingstoke, Hampshire: Palgrave Macmillan, 2015.

Khan, Naseem. *The Arts Britain Ignores: The Arts of Ethnic Minorities in Britain*. Arts Council of Great Britain, Fundação Calouste Gulbenkian, Great Britain, Community Relations Commission. London: The Commission, 1976.

Kismaric, Susan. *British Photography from the Thatcher Years*. New York: Museum of Modern Art, 1991.

Kettle, Martin, and Lucy Hodges. *Uprising! The Police, the People and the Riots in Britain's Cities*. London: Pan Books, 1982.

Leamer, Laurence. *The Paper Revolutionaries: The Rise of the Underground Press*. New York: Simon & Schuster, 1972.

Malik, Sarita. *Representing Black Britain: A History of Black and Asian Images on British Television*. London & Thousand Oaks, CA: Sage, 2002.

McSmith, Andy. *No Such Thing as Society: A History of Britain in the 1980s*. London: Constable, 2010.

Mirza, Heidi Safia. *Black British Feminism—A Reader*. London: Routledge, 1997.

Moten, Fred. *In the Break: The Aesthetics of the Black Radical Tradition*. Minneapolis: University of Minnesota Press, 2003.

Murray, Simone. *Mixed Media: Feminist Presses and Publishing Politics*. London: Pluto Press, 2004.

Nochlin, Linda. *Women, Art, and Power: And Other Essays*. New York & London: Routledge, 2018.

O'Hagan, Sean. "Britain's Photographic Revolution." *The Guardian* (30 October 2011).

Peplow, Simon. *Race and Riots in Thatcher's Britain*. Manchester: Manchester University Press, 2019.

Prentoulis, Marina. "The Construction of the Black British Community in *The Voice* and the *New Nation*." *Journalism* 13.6 (2012): 731–749.

Robles, Elizabeth. "Maxine Walker: Imaging the Homeplace." *Oxford Art Journal* 40.1 (2017): 169–183.

Rowe, Marsha. *Spare Rib Reader*. Harmondsworth, Middlesex, England: Penguin Books, 1982.

Rowe, Marsha, and Rosie Boycott. "Editorial." *Spare Rib* 1 (July 1972): 3.

Schreiber, Rachel. *Modern Print Activism in the United States*. Farnham, Surrey: Ashgate, 2013.

Stewart, Graham. *Bang! A History of Britain in the 1980s*. London: Atlantic Books, 2013.

Solomon-Godeau, Abigail. *Photography after Photography*. Durham, NC: Duke University Press, 2017.

Sudbury, Julia. "(Re)constructing Multiracial Blackness: Women's Activism, Difference and Collective Identity in Britain." *Ethnic and Racial Studies* 24:1 (2001): 32.

Tawadros, Gilane. "Redrawing the Boundaries." *Ten. 8* 2.3 (Spring 1992): 89.

Thomlinson, Natalie. *Race, Ethnicity and the Women's Movement in England, 1968–1993*. Basingstoke, Hampshire: Palgrave Macmillan, 2016.
Thomlinson, Natalie. "'Second-Wave' Black Feminist Periodicals in Britain." *Women: A Cultural Review* 27.4 (2016): 432–445.
Triggs, Teal. "Alphabet Soup: Reading British Fanzines." *Visible Language* 29.1 (1995): 72.
Turner, Alwyn. *Rejoice, Rejoice! Britain in the 1980s*. London: Aurum, 2010.
Walker, Maxine. "We Do Not Wish to Do It Quietly." *Ten.8* 27 (1987): 43.
Ward, Jesmyn. *The Fire this Time. A New Generation Speaks about Race*. London: Bloomsbury Circus, 2018.
Waters, Melanie. "'Yours in Struggle': Bad Feelings and Revolutionary Politics in Spare Rib." *Women* 27.4 (2016): 446–465.
Waters, Rob. *Thinking Black: Britain, 1964–1985*. Oakland, CA: University of California Press, 2019.
Willis-Thomas, Deborah. *Black Photographers, 1840–1940: An Illustrated Bio-bibliography*. New York: Garland, 1985.
Williams, Aubrey. "Seeking a Black Aesthetic," in *Creation for Liberation*, 1987.
Williams, Fiona. *Social Policy: A Critical Introduction: Issues of Race, Gender and Class*. Cambridge: Polity, 1989.
Williams, Val. "Post-War Women's Photography and Independent Imagery," in *Through the Looking Glass: Photographic Art in Britain 1945–1989*. London: Barbican Art Gallery, 1989. 111–115.
Wills, Clair. *Lovers and Strangers: An Immigrant History of Post-war Britain*. London: Allen Lane, 2017.
Worley, Matthew. "Punk, Politics and British (Fan)zines, 1976–84: 'While the world was dying, did you wonder why?'" *History Workshop Journal* 79.1 (Spring 2015): 76–106.

The Business of Feminism Endures
Four Decades of Spinsters Ink and Aunt Lute Books Publishing Lesbian-Feminist Books in the United States

JULIE R. ENSZER

Founded in conjunction with the US women-in-print movement of the 1970s, Spinsters Ink and Aunt Lute Books are the only two feminist publishers still publishing independently today.[1] Both gained their footing as publishers during the 1980s, including a handful of years when they merged and published under a single imprint. Together, the story of Spinsters Ink and Aunt Lute demonstrates both the visionary and intersectional components of feminism as well as feminism's practical, economic commitments. For Spinsters Ink and Aunt Lute Books, publishing books is a way to both engage with capitalism as a form of feminist and lesbian empowerment and through that engagement challenge and resist capitalist economic orders.

Publishing for feminists and lesbian-feminists was a vital form of activist engagement during the 1970s and 1980s. Trysh Travis's work on the women-in-print movement explores the broad feminist history in conjunction with work by Simone Murray and Catherine Riley that explores feminist publishing in the United Kingdom. Work by Kate Adams and Stephanie Foote explores engagements by lesbians in book publishing, while work by Jan Whitt explores similar movements in magazine publishing. Kristen Hogan and Lucy Delap's work on bookstores explores the political stakes of bookselling for lesbians and the centrality of anti-racist engagements, picking up important nodes of thought also explored by Katie King, Linda Garber, and Kim Whitehead. In this volume, Taous Dahmani's chapter on *Polareyes* and Flora Dunster's on the *Lesbians Talk Issues* series elaborate further activist print cultures. The stories of Spinsters Ink and Aunt Lute Books echo and extend this work on feminist and lesbian print culture.

Today, Aunt Lute Books, started in Iowa City, Iowa, and headquartered since the early 1980s in the San Francisco Bay area, is an independent, nonprofit, multicultural, feminist publisher. The publisher of Gloria Anzaldúa's *Borderlands/La Frontera: The New Mestiza* and a canon-changing anthology of multicultural US women's writing, Aunt Lute does not demonstrate success through wild profits; rather, it maps the increasing presence of intersectional feminist principles in the (non-profit) third sector. A hybrid enterprise, Aunt Lute amplifies feminist social change through multicultural book publishing and supports and nurtures young women of color as they begin their careers as writers, artists, and activists.

Spinsters Ink survived by being passed among activist publishers and editors who nurtured and sustained it through the past forty years. Spinsters Ink is a story of change and negotiation in a variety of different locations that demonstrates the tenacity and resiliency of lesbian-feminist publishing. Like Aunt Lute, Spinsters Ink demonstrates the importance of adaptability and of feminist principles of sharing and collaboration in lesbian and feminist print culture. The story of Spinsters Ink begins in 1977 in upstate New York, in a small community called Argyle, where two women, Maureen Brady and Judith McDaniel, live in an old farmhouse at the end of a long, dirt road. Brady and McDaniel are lovers, feminists, writers, and risk-taking visionaries. The beginning of Spinsters Ink is their story.

Spinster: A Woman Who Whirls, Twirls, and Turns Everything Upside Down

Throughout 1977 and 1978, Brady circulated her manuscript, *Give Me Your Good Ear*, to agents. She wanted to go the traditional route for publication: find an agent, have the agent sell the manuscript to a New York publishing house, and reap personal and financial rewards from the deal. During the late 1970s, there was an appetite among commercial publishers for feminist novels. Commercial New York publishers picked up Rita Mae Brown's *Rubyfruit Jungle* (Daughters, 1973; Bantam, 1977), the Redstockings' *Feminist Revolution* (Random House, 1978), and Sherry Thomas's *Country Women* (Doubleday, 1976); feminist fiction and feminists books made money for publishers and agents. More important, for feminists and lesbian-feminists, the platform of a commercial publisher expanded the audience for feminist and lesbian-feminist ideas. Brady wanted this larger platform, but ultimately a contract was not forthcoming. Finally, Brady "got sick of sending it around."[2]

Frustrated by the experience with commercial publishing, Brady and McDaniel talked about starting their own publishing company. They were "friends with Joan Larkin, Jan Clausen, and Elly Bulkin," lesbians in Brooklyn who all were involved in compelling publishing projects, including *Conditions* and Out & Out Books.[3] Brady and McDaniel talked with them about publishing and were inspired. Finally, they thought, "Why not take publishing into our own hands?"[4] Why not stop sending around *Give Me Your Good Ear* and publish it ourselves? Spinsters Ink was born.

The name Spinsters Ink came to Brady and McDaniel when they were driving home to Argyle after a visit with McDaniel's family in Atlanta. They had recently heard Mary Daly read from *Gyn/Ecology* (1978) where "she re-defined the word 'spinster' [as] a woman who whirls, who twirls, who turns everything upside-down."[5] They liked the possibilities that suggested, so they took Spinsters as the name of the press, and, knowing that they wanted to incorporate, said Spinsters Ink, laughing, "because of course we were going to spell it I-n-k!"[6] This pun, riffing between the business and legal term and the liquid of pens and printing presses, suggests one way feminists imagined remaking the business world: uniting the material realities of their lives with business concepts.

With a name selected, Brady and McDaniel proceeded to publish their first two books: Brady's *Give Me Your Good Ear* (1979), a perfect-bound novel of 125 pages and priced at $4.50, and McDaniel's *Reconstituting the World: The Poetry and Vision of Adrienne Rich* (1978), a saddle-stitched book sold for $1.50. McDaniel describes the publishing process as "seat of your pants."[7] McDaniel and Brady outsourced the physical production of the books to typesetters and printers but handled the labor of distribution, marketing, and promotion of the books themselves. Since they didn't have much money to capitalize the publishing company, they created a pre-publication order form emblazoned with "We need your orders NOW to help with Printing Costs." They distributed this form among friends and colleagues and also to feminist bookstores. McDaniel recalls, "There was a feminist bookstore list" and they had good networks as a result of the movement and the women-in-print network. On that first promotional flyer, Adrienne Rich testified to the importance of Spinsters Ink noting, "I feel so strongly that we need new presses starting . . . and perhaps by starting with Maureen's novel, Spinsters, Ink can begin to define, in the way that action defines itself, what writers and readers have a right to expect from feminist presses." Rich's words, along with the early promotional strategies of McDaniel and Brady, demonstrate the ways that feminist publishers, readers, and writers understood themselves as collectively reliant upon and responsible to one another. Presses not only published books of interest to feminist readers, they also nurtured the work of feminist writers, building a vibrant intellectual community through the material practice of publishing.

Their farm house provided space to store the large shipment of books from the printer, though McDaniel remembers, "I will never forget the semi-trailer coming down our dirt road in the snow. He said, 'So where's the loading dock?'" McDaniel laughed; there was no loading dock. Together, she and Brady unloaded the books into their home. They unpackaged them from the boxes and then repacked them in individual carriers, mailing them out themselves at the local post office to women's bookstores and mail order customers.

After they published the first two books successfully, Brady and McDaniel let women know through their networks that they were accepting manuscripts to consider for publication. McDaniel remembers reading Lynn Strongin's novel *Bones & Kim*, and liking it, particularly because it included a woman with a disability and politically she and Brady were interested in furthering that theme. *Bones & Kim* was the third book published by Spinsters Ink; *The Cancer Journals* by Audre Lorde was the fourth. McDaniel was friends with Lorde, and Lorde told her that she had a book about cancer. Although represented by Charlotte Sheedy, in 1980, Lorde networked with feminist publishers to find a home for *The Cancer Journals* herself; she made the deal with McDaniel and Brady to publish *The Cancer Journals* without input from Sheedy.[8] *The Cancer Journals* was published in the fall of 1980 with a plain yellow cover and no photograph of Lorde, at her request.[9] McDaniel remembers, "We did a lot of publicity for it; we pushed it at conferences; we let people know it was available."[10] She also remembers that "we gave Audre the cover she wanted. She didn't want her picture, and she loved the color yellow. So we had a plain yellow cover with the title on it. That was exactly what Audre wanted." Unfortunately, that cover didn't make the book easy to recognize in bookstores. McDaniel remembers, "At the women in print conference, a bookstore owner said to us, 'I have customers who are standing next to a stack of *The Cancer Journals* and they ask me where it is!' "[11] The book was a success, however, and for the second printing Lorde agreed to have a photograph on the cover; that photograph of Lorde remains the cover of *The Cancer Journal*, still in print today.

In 1981, Spinsters Ink published a novel by McDaniel, *Elegy from a Hill in Hebron*, and, in 1982, Spinsters published Barbara Sjoholm's novel *Ambitious Women*. Barbara Sjoholm is a pen name for Barbara Wilson, one of the founders of Seal Press, another independent feminist publishing house.[12] While building Spinsters Ink, the home of Brady and McDaniel became "a center for literary activity and lesbian and feminist activity in the entire [upstate New York] region." McDaniel recalls "readings at our old farm house," including readings by Michelle Cliff, Melanie Kaye/Kantrowitz, and Joy Harjo.[13] In addition to networking with authors, McDaniel and Brady networked with editors and publishers of feminist journals and magazines. McDaniel recalls the close relationship they had with Brooklyn-based *Conditions*, the New York–based art journal *Heresies*, and North Carolina–based *Sinister Wisdom*.[14]

These lesbian and feminist networks emerged out of political and intellectual necessity and out of the shared commitments of writers, publishers, and readers. While they ran Spinsters, Brady and McDaniel both worked full-time jobs. Brady worked as a physical therapist and McDaniel was an assistant professor of English at Skidmore College. McDaniel was the chair of the gay caucus of the Modern Language Association (MLA); she recalls audiences with hundreds of people at the MLA panels on feminism. "Sometimes up to 700 people would come and hear [writers] read or give papers." At one panel in San Francisco, McDaniel recalls hearing Susan Griffin and Melanie Kaye/Kantrowitz and a few other women, but "what was really amusing was that they were talking, they were not reading, they were giving papers about lesbian feminist writers, and I think every writer that was being talked about was in the audience. Tillie Olsen was in the audience, Joanna Russ was in the audience . . . we knew one another. We weren't strangers. We just knew one another. We talked on the phone, we wrote letters."[15] This highly networked group shared political, social, and cultural commitments—and lesbian-feminist publishing work reflects the highly networked reality of these women.

While other lesbian-feminist publishers approached publishing as a business, as a means of generating income to support themselves, Brady and McDaniel never approached Spinsters as a for-profit venture; they incorporated Spinsters Ink as a nonprofit organization in 1978. As a nonprofit organization, Spinsters required a board of directors that met at least once a year. Brady and McDaniel both served on the board along with their dear friends Adrienne Rich and Michelle Cliff. Both Brady and McDaniel remembered having board meetings two times a year to talk about the publishing work. For Spinsters, nonprofit status enabled the publisher to apply for and secure grant funding. In 1982, the New York State Council of the Arts (NYSCA) awarded Spinsters a grant to publish two books. Brady and McDaniel selected Kitty Tsui's poetry book, *The Words of a Woman Who Breathes Fire*, and Paula Gunn Allen's novel, *The Woman Who Owned the Shadows*, for publication in 1983 with support from the NYSCA grant. Support from a publicly funded state arts organization, combined with the revenue from individual readers, enabled Spinsters to grow and publish more books.

By mid-1982, however, Brady remembers, Spinsters "just got bigger and bigger" and eventually it needed more time than Brady or McDaniel had.[16] Also, Brady and McDaniel separated as intimate partners. While they remained connected doing the work of the press, they were growing in other directions. Through feminist print networks, Brady and McDaniel knew Sherry Thomas, who was a partner in the Oakland-based feminist bookstore, Old Wives' Tales; they knew she was thinking about starting a publishing company. Brady recalls that she felt that Thomas had "similar literary taste" to her and Judith, so they proposed to Thomas, "Why don't you take over Spinster's Ink?"[17] During the summer of 1982, Brady, McDaniel, and Thomas wrote letters, talked on the telephone, and worked out how to transition Spinsters Ink from a New York–based nonprofit organization to a California-based business run by Thomas.

The three negotiated a legal agreement for Brady and McDaniel to sell Spinsters Ink to Thomas for $2,000 on December 13, 1982; Thomas also paid Brady and McDaniel a small royalty on the stock of books sold over the next few years through a consignment arrangement. Brady recalls, "That was the only money we made from Spinsters Ink! When we were publishing, we didn't make any money."[18] Reflecting the capacious forms of economic engagement that feminists made with feminist mission-driven projects, Thomas organized Spinsters as a for-profit corporation in California. The final transition was complete in January 1983 when Thomas began filling orders for Spinsters Ink in the San Francisco Bay Area. During the transition, Thomas highlighted the need to meet face to face with Brady and McDaniel to have "some long talks about substance . . . what constitutes oppressiveness to women in literature; what is racism, classism, antisemitism in fiction? What have been your visionary commitments to the press, to what you will publish and won't? What will my active commitments be?" Thomas summarized this as "All of what Spinsters is 'really' about, it seems to me."[19] While there were important economic considerations for feminist publishers, the political issues and the belief that publishers provided a vision for feminism were the most important ones for Brady, Thomas, and McDaniel.

Spinning a Successful Business: Alone, Then Together

In 1983, Thomas published the two books that Brady and McDaniel had committed to publish, Kitty Tsui's poetry collection, *The Words of a Woman Who Breathes Fire*, and Paula Gunn Allen's novel, *The Woman Who Owned the Shadows*. Building her own list of books, Thomas also published Jean Swallow's anthology, *Out from Under: Sober Dykes and Our Friends*, and Barbara MacDonald and Cynthia Rich's *Look Me in the Eye: Old Women, Aging, and Ageism*. For Thomas these two books, along with Paula Gunn Allen's novel, embodied her vision for Spinster's Ink: serious feminist fiction that "give voices to stories that would never otherwise be heard" and nonfiction books that addressed important and emergent feminist political issues.[20]

In 1984, Thomas published her most successful and bestselling book: JoAnn Loulan's *Lesbian Sex*. In its first nine months, *Lesbian Sex* sold 15,000 copies.[21] Loulan's book became the economic engine for Spinsters Ink. Thomas eventually published three of Loulan's books, *Lesbian Sex*, *Lesbian Passion*, and *The Erotic Dance*. Thomas worked closely with Loulan to assemble the books from Loulan's workshops in the Bay Area, and eventually around the country. Like the challenges that Persephone Press experienced a few years earlier, Thomas struggled to pay the bills even with the successful Loulan sales.[22] She recalls printing in lots of three and five thousand and needing to go back to press constantly. "I just didn't have the cash to print 10,000 at a time, which would have saved me a lot of money."[23]

In a 1985 profile of Spinsters Ink in *Bookpaper*, Thomas reflected, "When I took over Spinsters less than three years ago, I had $6,000, my life savings out of royalties from *Country Women*, a book I did with Doubleday in the 1970s. And now look," she says pointing to the glossy four-color covers on the new fall titles.[24] In addition to books, Thomas produced a "line of contemporary women's art work on four-color notecards and blank books for journals."[25] While successful, a new chapter of Spinsters began through a merger with another feminist publisher, Aunt Lute.

Dear Auntie:
A Publishing Company in the Middle of the United States

Many different communities—South Asian, Filipinx, Latinx—use the word "aunt" as an honorific to respect older people, even if they are not blood relatives. That fact, however, was not on the minds of Joan Pinkvoss and Barb Weiser in 1982 when they started Aunt Lute Publishing Company, Inc. Joan Pinkvoss is a scrappy feminist. Originally from Cincinnati, Ohio, she moved to Iowa City for the Writer's Workshop at the University of Iowa, where she received her MFA in fiction in 1969. During graduate school, she worked as a computer programmer. In Iowa City, she joined up with the feminists and began working with the Iowa City Women's Press (ICWP) Collective and met Weiser. Working at ICWP Collective, the two learned the book trade by publishing two manuals, *The Greasy Thumb: Automechanics Manual for Women* and *Against the Grain: A Carpentry Manual for Women*. These two books reflect a commitment of feminists during the 1970s to help women enter the trades and learn skills that are economically remunerative.

When Weiser and Pinkvoss were dreaming about their own publishing company, a name for their new business was elusive.[26] Finally, Weiser suggested that they name the company after her Aunt Lute. Pinkvoss remembers Weiser saying, "She was so amazing and independent, she was a single woman; when her best friend moved to California to teach, she got a job there and got a house right next door to her."[27] Weiser's Aunt Lute was a school teacher and an independent woman. Pinkvoss and Weiser settled on the name, and today Aunt Lute Books emblazons each book spine Pinkvoss publishes.

In 1982, when Pinkvoss and Weiser founded Aunt Lute, the two had a long history as feminist activists in the print movement. Pinkvoss, in addition to being a printer and having publishing aspirations, was also a master electrician. In 1978 or 1979, she came out to California and apprenticed with the Wonder Woman Electricity Company, started by Suzanne DeVincenzo. Returning to Iowa City, she worked toward her master electrician license and started her own electrical company in Iowa City.[28] Pinkvoss's work as a master electrician and the two titles by ICWP Collective highlight an important strand of feminist thinking in the 1970s and early 1980s: the trades could provide important economic opportunities for women. Uniting feminist theory with the lived reality of work and the need for material economic support weaves throughout the publishing work of the women-in-print movement. While working as an electrician paid the bills, Pinkvoss wanted to publish feminist books. So did Weiser. Aunt Lute was born.

Aunt Lute published five books during its first four years. In 1983, Aunt Lute published Dodici Azpadu's novel, *Saturday Night in the Prime of Life*, and the first anthology of women's writing on fat oppression, *Shadow on a Tightrope*, edited by Lisa Schoenfielder and Weiser. Aunt Lute published small print-runs of these books, about two thousand copies of each title.[29] In 1984, Aunt Lute published a second novel by Azpadu, *Goat Song*. In 1985, Aunt Lute published two more books, an anthology of lesbian plays edited by Kate McDermott, *Places, Please!*, which contained seven lesbian plays by playwrights including Terry Baum, Sarah Dreher, Julia Willis, Mariah Burton Nelson, and Ellen Gruber Garvey, and Michal Brody's book about *Lavender Women*, a Chicago lesbian newspaper that published from 1971 until 1976, titled *Are We There Yet? A Continuing History of Lavender Women*.

While Iowa City had been Pinkvoss's home for over a decade, she felt there was no traction for the small press in Iowa City, so she began exploring a move to San Francisco. While contemplating her move, Pinkvoss was talking with her publishing colleague, Sherry Thomas, the editor and publisher of Spinsters Ink. The two decided to join forces, combining Spinsters Ink and Aunt Lute into one publishing company, Spinsters/Aunt Lute. Part of the announcement of the merger of Spinsters Ink with Aunt Lute read, "In three years, with support from several other women, Sherry built a list of five books into seventeen titles, and added a new sideline of women's art notecards and blank books. The new publications greatly expanded the diversity of the images and voices represented."

A Feminist Union Marked with a Slash

Aunt Lute and Spinsters completed their merger in June 1986; books between June of 1986 and June of 1991 bear the joint name, Spinsters/Aunt Lute. These five years were productive and successful ones for Spinsters/Aunt Lute. In 1987, Spinsters/Aunt Lute published one of the most iconic books of the feminist movement: Gloria Anzaldúa's *Borderlands/La Frontera*. Pinkvoss met Anzaldúa in Iowa City when she came to speak at a conference organized by an anti-racism committee at the university. After Anzaldúa read, Pinkvoss remembers asking her if she had any plans to publish; Anzaldúa said no. Pinkvoss remembers, "I never liked to be pushy, so I said, Well you know if you ever want some help with that I'm joining Aunt Lute up with Spinsters in the Bay Area and I know that's where you live and I'd be happy to talk to you."[30] When she got out to the Bay Area, Pinkvoss was more direct, and the two agreed to work together on a book.

Originally *Borderlands* was going to include only Anzaldúa's poetry, but Pinkvoss realized that the market for poetry was small and that the corpus of poems that Anzaldúa had was small as well. Pinkvoss asked Anzaldúa if she had any prose, and she said, "Well I have these few essays that I've been working on." Today, of course, the essays are what people know of *Borderlands*. Pinkvoss recalls, "We had the essays, which are poetical, and the poetry which is narrative, and this wonderful mix of form that Gloria did." In *Borderlands*, Anzaldúa wanted to "go someplace beyond *This Bridge Called My Back*" and use "her own life as a metaphor" to explore how women needed to "build a new culture."[31]

Although Anzaldúa's *Borderlands* is now hailed as a germinal text in feminist theory and Chicana thought, when the book published in 1987, it received a tepid response. In fact, another book published by Spinsters/Aunt Lute in 1987 received much more attention. *Tight Spaces* is a collection of writing by three African American women Pinkvoss had met in Iowa City. *Tight Spaces* won the 1988 American Book Award from the Before Columbus Foundation.

While *Tight Spaces* was a prize-winning book, Anzaldúa's *Borderlands* gained increasing readership and celebration over time. Pinkvoss feels that Anzaldúa's travel and lecturing taught people how to read *Borderlands*. Shortly after the book was published, Anzaldúa received an opportunity to teach at University of California-Santa Cruz. This teaching experience was generative for the book *Making Face, Making*

Soul/Haciendo Caras, and helped Anzaldúa to leverage her profile and do more speaking engagements. As she spoke around the country, she taught people how to read and appreciate *Borderlands*.

Shay Brawn, now the managing editor at Aunt Lute, describes *Borderlands* as "a touchstone for us because it's . . . a classic reminder of what our core values are, what our mission is."[32] In the first year, 3,575 copies were sold from a print run of 5,000. By August 31, 1989, 6,462 copies were sold and a total of 8,090 were in print. The book was selling an average of three thousand copies per year. By the end of March of 1990, 7,044 copies were sold and 10,524 were in print. Anzaldúa had earned $4,461.09 in royalties. By 1994, in the NEA grant, Aunt Lute wrote, "These books [by minority women writers] often take several years to find their audiences and to reach readers previously unfamiliar with our press or readers disaffected in general. A good example is our title *Borderlands/La Frontera* by Gloria Anzaldúa, published in 1987. This title, which examines thoroughly the complexity, history and experience of living as a Chicana in the U.S. sells more per month than it did per year its first three years." During the first decade of *Borderlands*, 55,000 copies were sold. From 1998 to January 2012, over 100,000 copies of the book were sold.

In the late 1980s, Pinkvoss realized she wanted to work with writers whose voices were not regularly published, particularly women of color. This decision was grounded in the activism and political commitments of Pinkvoss. Thomas's literary tastes were more focused in the lesbian community; she enjoyed the extraordinary success of Loulan's sex manuals as well as lesbian fiction. Pinkvoss wanted to publish more feminist work that addressed racism and structural inequalities. She wanted to "publish the voices of women who wanted to speak to our communities or speak across to other communities," and often these women "were not accomplished writers" and thus needed a "very intense editorial process."[33] It took a long time to create these books and then to help them find a readership. Pinkvoss wanted to focus "not only on artistic merit but on the ability of the manuscript to educate the public about women and people of color."[34] It was work that Pinkvoss felt was best suited for support from grants. This realization about the process of how she wanted to work and what kind of work she wanted to do corresponded with a change in NEA policy whereby the NEA would no longer use fiscal sponsors; organizations had to have their own 501c3 registration to be eligible for a NEA grant. Pinkvoss decided to incorporate Aunt

Lute as a nonprofit organization. They received nonprofit status on September 12, 1990.

Simultaneously, Pinkvoss and Thomas realized that the benefits of their partnership had reached its end. The two decided to separate Aunt Lute and Spinsters Ink, making them independent entities once again. The malleability of both the partnership and the different forms of structural and economic engagements demonstrate the ways both publishers were first and foremost committed to political visions for their work over the structures of capitalism and entrepreneurial nonprofits. Pinkvoss's goals for Aunt Lute Books as a nonprofit organization were "to create a diverse board, a diverse staff, and an internship program that would speak to that diversity." Aunt Lute and Spinsters Ink officially separated in June 1990.

Aunt Lute: A Life of Her Own

In 1991, Aunt Lute and Spinsters Ink had successfully split as enterprises. Aunt Lute operated as a nonprofit publisher with a focus on multicultural multiethnic books by women—and continues to operate that way today. Aunt Lute described itself as "multiracial, multi-ethnic women's press that has been committed to publishing high-quality, diverse literature for ten years. Our purpose is to bring the richness of culturally diverse women's voices and experiences into print. Further, we support an extensive and culturally sensitive editorial process of bringing those voices to creative fruition, to guarantee that there will be a larger and larger body of quality writing by women authors of all cultures."[35] In 1990, the NEA awarded a two-year $17,000 grant to Aunt Lute. In the early 1990s, the California Arts Council and the San Francisco Foundation also supported Aunt Lute. Throughout the next two decades, public support was crucial to Aunt Lute. Aunt Lute grew in the early 1990s. Cherry Muhanji's novel, Her, was honored with a Ferro-Grumley award for excellence at the 1991 Lambda Literary Awards. In 1992, Aunt Lute had gross sales of $222,276; in 1993, gross sales fell slightly to $200,543, but the organization secured over $70,000 in other sources of income, including government grants, foundation grants, and individual donors. In 1996 and 1997, Aunt Lute had their largest budgets: $300,000 in 1996, and nearly $350,000 in 1997, with about $200,000 in book sales and $150,000 in grant and other private support. The years 1998 and

1999 were difficult for the press; some governmental funders took a brief hiatus from funding the organization, and the effects of the dwindling women's bookstores and the changing book market took their toll.

During the 2000s, however, Aunt Lute returned to its earlier strength, with $239,507 in books sales for 2000, $253,542 in 2001, and $245,564 in 2002. In the first decade of the 2000s, Aunt Lute produced a two-volume set titled *The Aunt Lute Anthology of U.S. Women Writers*. This collection was produced by an editorial collective. The first volume includes women's writing from the seventeenth through the nineteenth centuries; the second volume is twentieth-century women's writing. Focusing on publishing feminist fiction and more recently memoir is a part of the organization's vision for change. Pinkvoss notes, "I have a deep, deep belief that fiction is the way to true understanding. . . . [Fiction] combines the emotional understanding with the lived experience in a way that the reader, if it's done well enough, . . . walks away having learned not just about something but has felt something . . . The only way that we are going to make big dents in women coming together and pushing forward was a pure emotional understand." Another social change strategy was the organization's internship program, which provides opportunities for young women to learn publishing. Every work day at 1 p.m., all of the Aunt Lute folks gather around the lunch table and eat lunch together for an hour. This simple act may be the core of what makes the Aunt Lute internship program successful. Pinkvoss describes the program as "helping young women get the confidence to go forward in their lives."

A variety of market conditions challenge Aunt Lute today. First, the used book market, highly networked and searchable online, cuts into the sales of books, particularly those adopted for courses, such as *Borderlands*. Aunt Lute continues to celebrate the legacy of Gloria Anzaldúa and publishes *El Mundo Zurdo* every eighteen months with papers from the Society for the Study of Gloria Anzaldúa, but no other book published by Aunt Lute generates the same revenue as *Borderlands*. Second, Pinkvoss is aging and looking for a way to potentially exit from Aunt Lute, but she holds most of the debt of the organization. Pinkvoss has worked as a crucial part of the feminist print movement since its earliest days. For over forty years she has been involved in publishing some of the most important feminist and lesbian-feminist books, though with minimal recognition. Gina Gemello, a staff member at Aunt Lute Books for nine years, says of Pinkvoss, "She's just brilliant . . . Joan has managed to keep that place alive in crisis after crisis after crisis. Keep it a great place to work, publishing awesome books . . . She's made a ton of sacrifices. Personally and professionally. . . . She's built something that will sustain behind her." Gemello noted, "Joan would say it was a team, I would say it was a team, but I would say that Joan at the helm of it is why Aunt Lute has survived."[36] Generational transition to a new leader will be a delicate process for Aunt Lute. It has survived by being nimble, able to contract when necessary and expand when market conditions make that possible.

Prize-Winning Books Readers Gobble Up

After Spinsters Ink and Aunt Lute separated, Thomas began to do independent work for the San Francisco Public Library for the gay and lesbian center they were planning. This position "grew into a huge job," so Thomas decided she wanted to get out of publishing.[37] She set out to find a buyer for Spinsters Ink. One of the buyers she had in mind was Joan Drury, an attorney she had met when Drury was living in the Bay area. In 1991, when Thomas called Drury about buying Spinsters, Drury was involved in a number of other projects, including her first novel and a feminist writers fund that Drury founded at Astraea, the national lesbian action fund. Drury was born and raised in Minnesota, where her parents owned and operated a business. The beginning of Drury's life was conventional: she married and had three children. Like her parents, Drury and her husband were entrepreneurial, owning and operating a business together, but during the late 1970s, Drury left her husband and came out as a lesbian. Taken with feminism, Drury went back to school and in 1986 earned a bachelor's degree in women's literature from the University of Minnesota.[38] In 1987 and 1988, Drury lived with her lover in the San Francisco Bay area while her lover went to law school. In 1991, Drury was back at home in Minnesota, working on a number of feminist projects.

Although she originally told Thomas no, she couldn't take over Spinsters, she was intrigued by the possibilities of running a feminist press; she called her daughter, Kelly Kager, who was in Thailand traveling. Ultimately, Drury purchased Spinsters Ink in 1992 from Thomas for $50,000, and Kelly curtailed her travels and came home to Minnesota to run Spinsters Ink. This sale of Spinsters to Drury reflects a high-water mark in feminist publishing: a successful transition of a successful press and economic support for Thomas after nearly a decade of work. Thomas remarked in 2013, "To think that I could sell a lesbian press for $50,000 in those days was pretty remarkable." While the amount is impressive, as happens with most publishers, there was a substantial debt to pay, and most of the money went to cover outstanding account payable, but the sale of Spinsters Ink to Drury did leave Thomas with a little money. Thomas said, it was "actually an enormous gift and I thank Joan Drury from the bottom of my soul." Although the sale demonstrates the economic power of feminist presses, it also demonstrates the importance of accumulated wealth in publishing. According to a Colorado Women's News profile of Drury, "She has taken the $10 million inheritance from her self-made entrepreneurial parents and parlayed it into social activism."[39] Drury's wealth provided a transition for Thomas from her life as a publisher and supported Spinsters Ink over the next ten years, offering an important subsidy to the feminist press. Books published by Spinsters Ink under Drury, as under previous publishers, nurtured both lesbian and feminist writers as well as readers, providing concrete manifestations of activist women's visions for a more egalitarian, less oppressive future.

Drury hired more staff for Spinsters. In addition to employing her daughter Kager as the managing director, Spinsters hired Mev Miller as a sales and marketing manager and employed a production manager. Drury remembers, "Part of what I really wanted to do and how I see as business and feminism and how the two territories work well together is that people, women, lean how to do things they haven't, didn't know necessarily before."[40] In addition to the powerful work that books did on behalf of feminism, feminist publishers also provided employment and training for women.

Spinsters thrived for eight years in Minnesota, publishing forty-two books between 1992 and 2001. During Drury's stewardship of the publishing house, Spinsters Ink won numerous awards for its books. In addition, they sold foreign rights aggressively in Germany and England.[41] Drury was deeply involved in lesbian-feminist publishing and literary work. In addition to Spinsters and the Lesbian Writer's Fund at Astraea, Drury founded and sponsored Norcroft, A Writing Retreat for Women, from 1995 through 2005. In addition, Drury wrote her own novels, completing four of them during the 1990s, all of which were published by Spinsters Ink: *The Other Side of Silence* (1993), *Silent Words* (1996), *Closed in Silence* (199), and *Those Jordan Girls* (2000). Joan Drury is a feminist entrepreneur and one of the examples of what women can do with money to benefit other women when given the opportunity.

In spite of the successes of Spinsters Ink, the 1990s challenged feminist publishers. Writing for Lambda Book Report in 2000, Drury observed, "Several years ago, when lesbian became 'chic,' the mainstream New York houses jumped on the bandwagon and started publishing lesbian works. This hit the smaller presses pretty hard, because we couldn't compete with the large advances and the publicity budgets they had to offer. Over the last few years, the number of lesbian/feminist bookstores declined from 66 to 28. Whether that was a direct result of the mainstreaming of lesbian letters, I couldn't say. But now that the trendiness of lesbian writing has kind of wound down, the smaller presses are going to come back even stronger."[42] Drury recognized that "the new generation will be able to take lesbian publishing into a whole new world with all the major technological breakthroughs: ebooks, Internet publishing, and so on."[43] Drury sold the press to the next generation during this important transitional moment.

A Difficult New Millenium Though Still Fires Burn

In January 2000, two women from Colorado, Katherine Hovis and Sharon Silvas, bought Spinsters Ink from Joan Drury. Together, Hovis and Silvas had been publishing the *Colorado Woman News* since 1988 and two other resources, the *Women's Yellow Page Directory* and *Community Resource Guide for the Rocky Mountain Area*, since 1994. Hovis and Silvas were both business partners and life partners.[44]

Surprising Hovis and Silvas in the sale was the amount of backlist books they purchased from Drury: 80,000 books, which amounted to "two semis full of books!"[45] Storing these books and managing backlist sales is a crucial function of publishers. Hovis and Silvas purchased Spinsters with sixty-two titles on the backlist to manage in inventory and to sell to support the publication of new books. The cash flow challenges of book publishing were difficult for Hovis and Silvas to navigate. Three years after taking over Spinsters Ink, Silvas reflected, "Even though we were familiar with magazine and directory publishing, book publishing was new. The learning curve for the first six months was straight up! It was a whole new ballgame; new lingo, and a new process." Most difficult for Hovis and Silvas was the cashflow. They quickly learned, "with books, there's an eighteen-month turnaround [from publication date] before you ever see the cash back." This contrasted with a three- to six-month turn around for magazine and director publishing.[46]

Hovis and Silvas published important new titles, including work by Val McDermid, Elana Dykewomon, Katherine V. Forrest, Anita Mason, and Darlene O'Dell. They also reprinted a book by Sally Miller Gearhart. Ultimately, however, it was neither the economic challenges of publishing nor changes in the field of feminist publishing that stalled Spinsters Ink under Hovis and Silvas—it was cancer. Publishing slowed as the women grappled with cancer, and, in 2005, Linda Hill of Bella Books acquired the vital back list from Spinsters and nurtured the publishing operation back to life. Today, Katherine Forrest acquires and edits books for Spinsters Ink as a part of Bella Books.

For almost forty years, Spinsters Ink has been publishing lesbian books. The list of books published by Spinsters is widely variable. In the earliest years, the editors of Spinsters focused on literary quality. During the 1980s, the imprint was synonymous with lesbian-made erotica; in the 1990s, genre fiction dominated the list, with mysteries and romances winning a number of awards. More recently, editor Katherine V. Forrest has published a handful of significant books under the Spinsters Ink imprint at Bella Books that suggest the continuing need for and importance of lesbian-feminist books. Reflecting on Spinsters Ink thirty-five years later, Maureen Brady says, "I think of it as having survived. That is the best legacy we could give it: to live."

Feminist Publishing Embraces and Resists Capitalism

Survival in terms of Aunt Lute and Spinsters is not about the success of wild profits, and it is not about a publisher having revenue to pay for a lavish second home, two measures that capitalism traditionally uses to evaluate success. For Aunt Lute and Spinsters, survival is about continued presence in the world, the ongoing production of books, building a life that supports change through book publishing, and sustaining a company that supports and nurtures young women—and in the case of Aunt Lute, young women of color, as they begin their careers.

Both Aunt Lute and Spinsters are critically engaged in marketplace capitalism as book publishers. They create books within the capitalist milieu of book publishing that demands market standards for the book object (eye-catching covers, carefully designed and edited interiors, adherence to quality standards of paper and binding, among other benchmarks) and then sell them using distribution systems such as book distributors and independent and chain bookstores, including online megasellers, to feminists in the world, the envisioned end-use consumers. Each publisher must earn enough revenue every year across their books to pay for printing and binding of books, royalties to authors, operational expenses, and salaries, however modest, for the staff. Whether incorporated as a for-profit enterprise or nonprofit organization, these publishers undoubtably are rooted in consumer-based market capitalism. Yet, as these histories of the publishers demonstrate, each publisher both embraces and resists the capitalist system in which they operate. While both Aunt Lute and Spinsters began as projects of passion and expressions of feminism without regard to the economics of publishing, as they grew, both also pursued, if not profit, economic viability to continue the work. Through the stories of each publisher, the women running Aunt Lute and Spinsters map different forms of economic engagements at different times, experimenting with capricious forms of capitalism as the environment makes such trials possible. While I resist viewing people or publishers as economic failures because either the press closed or did not provide enough economic support to its principles, another undeniable measure of success within capitalism is survival. Both Aunt Lute and Spinsters continue to survive, and at different points thrive, within capitalism, even as they publish books and authors that challenge capitalist orders. This paradox of both embracing capitalism, producing objects of value within the system, and resisting capitalism as a structure that dictates far too much in human lives is one of the profound achievements of both Spinsters and Aunt Lute.

Notes

1. I extend my heartfelt thanks to Joan Pinkvoss of Aunt Lute for her generosity and openness during the research process and for the decades of work she has devoted to sustaining the dreams of feminist publishing, and further gratitude to the staff of Aunt Lute and Spinsters Ink, now and in the past, for their work and dedication.

2. Judith McDaniel, telephone interview by Julie R. Enszer, August 14, 2013.

3. McDaniel, interview.
4. McDaniel, interview.
5. McDaniel, interview.
6. McDaniel, interview.
7. McDaniel, interview.
8. Alexis DeVeaux, *Warrior Poet: A Biography of Audre Lorde* (New York: W. W. Norton & Company, 2004), 264.
9. DeVeaux, *Warrior Poet*, 264.
10. McDaniel, interview.
11. McDaniel, interview.
12. Seal Press is now an imprint of Hachette Book Group.
13. McDaniel, interview.
14. McDaniel, interview.
15. McDaniel, interview.
16. Maureen Brady, telephone interview by Julie R. Enszer, May 30, 2013.
17. Brady, interview.
18. Brady, interview.
19. Letter from Sherry Thomas to Maureen Brady and Judith McDaniel, July 17 [1982], personal collection of author.
20. Thomas letter.
21. Publisher Profile: Spinsters Ink." *Bookpaper* (December 1985): 32.
22. Julie R. Enszer, *The Whole Naked Truth of Our Lives*. PhD dissertation, University of Maryland, Lanham, Maryland, 2013.
23. Sherry Thomas, interview by Julie R. Enszer, New York City, November 1, 2013.
24. Publisher Profile: Spinsters Ink." *Bookpaper* (December 1985): 32.
25. Publisher Profile: Spinsters Ink." *Bookpaper* (December 1985): 32.
26. Agatha Beins and Julie R. Enszer, "We Couldn't Get Them Printed, So We Learned to Print: Ain't I a Woman? And the Iowa City Women's Press," *Frontiers* 34.2 (Fall 2013).
27. Pinkvoss, Joan. Interview by Julie R. Enszer. San Francisco, June 26 and 27, 2013.
28. Interview with Joan Pinkvoss.
29. From box 401 "Iowa City/Aunt Lute."
30. Pinkvoss, interview.
31. Pinkvoss, interview.
32. Shay Brawn, Skype interview by Julie R. Enszer, July 29, 2013.
33. Pinkvoss, interview.
34. "Ten Women in a Tiny Office." Fundraising piece from Aunt Lute Books. Personal collection of the author.
35. "Ten Women in a Tiny Office."
36. Gina Gemello, Skype interview by Julie R. Enszer, July 25, 2013.

37. Thomas, interview.
38. Suzanne Kelsey, "The End of a Dream," in *Minnesota Women's Press*.
39. Sharon Silvas, "Joan Drury—Prolific Writer, Feminist Activist, Change Agent," *Colorado Woman* (January 31, 2001): 38.
40. Joan Drury, telephone interview by Julie R. Enszer, September 27, 2013.
41. Letter from Joan Drury and Nancy Walker to Maureen Brady, February 3, 1997, personal collection.
42. Joan Drury, "Joan Drury on the State of Lesbian Publishing, *Lambda Book Report* 9.2 (September 2000): 13.
43. Drury, "Joan Drury on the State of Lesbian Publishing, 13.
44. Lisa C. Moore, "A Whole New Ball Game," *Lambda Book Report* 11.6 (January 2003): 31.
45. Moore, "A Whole New Ball Game," 31.
46. Moore, "A Whole New Ball Game," 31.

Works Cited

Adams, Kate. "Built Out of Books—Lesbian Energy and Feminist Ideology in Alternative Publishing." *Journal of Homosexuality* 34.3 (1998): 113–141.

Delap, Lucy. "Feminist Bookshops, Reading Cultures and the Women's Liberation Movement in Great Britain, c. 1974–2000." *History Workshop Journal* 81.1 (Spring 2016): 171–196.

DeVeaux, Alexis. *Warrior Poet: A Biography of Audre Lorde*. New York: W. W. Norton & Company, 2004.

Foote, Stephanie. "Deviant Classics: Pulps and the Making of Lesbian Print Culture." *Signs: Journal of Women in Culture and Society* 31.1 (2005): 169–190.

Garber, Linda. *Identity Poetics: Race, Class, and the Lesbian-Feminist Roots of Queer Theory*. New York: Columbia University Press, 2001.

Hogan, Kristen. *The Feminist Bookstore Movement: Lesbian Antiracism and Feminist Accountability*. Durham, NC: Duke University Press, 2016.

King, Katie. "Audre Lorde's Lacquered Layerings: The Lesbian Bar as a Site of Literary Production." *Cultural Studies* 2 (October 1988): 321–342.

Murray, Heather. "Free for All Lesbians: Lesbian Cultural Production and Consumption in the United States during the 1970s." *Journal of the History of Sexuality* 16.2 (2007): 251–275.

Murray, Simone. *Mixed Media: Feminist Presses and Publishing Politics*. London: Pluto Press, 2004.

Riley, Catherine. *The Virago Story: Assessing the Impact of a Feminist Publishing Phenomenon*. Oxford: Berghahn Books, 2018.

Travis, Trysh. "The Women in Print Movement: History and Implications." *Book History* 11 (2008): 275–300.

Whitehead, Kim. *The Feminist Poetry Movement*. Jackson: University Press of Mississippi, 1996.
Whitt, Jan. "A "Labor from the Heart": Lesbian Magazines from 1947–1994." *Journal of Lesbian Studies* 5.1/2 (2001): 229–251.

Lesbians Talk
British Lesbian Politics and the Sex Wars

Flora Dunster

In a 1984 issue of *Signs: Journal of Women in Culture and Society*, the American philosopher Ann Ferguson reflected on, and stated the terms of, an unfurling debate within feminism. Titling her article "Sex War: The Debate between Radical and Libertarian Feminists," Ferguson wrote of an "increasing polarization" between the two eponymous camps, though quickly noting that radical and libertarian feminisms need not be exclusive positions.[1] Nonetheless, Ferguson's phrasing would be adopted on both sides of the Atlantic, and "the sex wars" understood as a division between two ideologically opposed feminist kinds. Radical feminists espoused that "women's heterosexual sexual activity, whether imagized in pornography or actually practiced, becomes a tool of sexual violence against women."[2] Conversely, sex radicals (as I will refer to them) argued against what they saw as radical feminism's moralistic and anti-sex stance, advocating for the free pursuit of sexual experimentation.

Both as they occurred and in successive analysis, the sex wars have been narrated as a protracted breaking point over the course of the 1980s. Sarah Green's late-1980s ethnography of London's Lesbian Archive identifies feelings within the space that the strife generated by sex wars debate would prompt the end of organized feminism, a "falling apart at the seams" aggravated by political difference.[3] Political scientist Lorna N. Bracewell summarizes that a "widely accepted view" of the sex wars defines them as a period of "sororicidal conflicts."[4] This repeated characterization of conflict and collapse has contributed to the ensuing erasure of the decade from feminism's generational modeling.

Rather than positing the sex wars as an end, this chapter argues that looking to their rhetorical complexity underscores feminism's mutability, and the incapacity of its temporal framing as generations or waves to account for the capricious nature of ideology and identification. As such, my contribution to this volume intervenes in the historicization of the feminist 1980s by situating the book series *Lesbians Talk Issues* as a continuation of their mood. Though published from 1992 to 1996 by London's Scarlet Press, the series is linked in content and concerns to the decade just passed. I demonstrate that the books are testimony to the complex lived experiences of lesbians considering the relationship between their sexuality and subjects such as Blackness, socialism, gender transition, AIDS activism, and domestic violence. They extend the space for conversation opened by the sex wars, hosting a dialogue wherein the overlaps and inconsistencies between participant accounts allow for "lesbian" to skirt around the rigid meanings established by radical/sex radical debate.

My analysis intersects with an ongoing conversation around the renegotiation of feminism's temporality, and I am indebted to the work of Catherine Grant, Clare Hemmings, and Sam McBean, among other academics and activists.[5] Exploring the divide marked by Ferguson and its subsequent mythologization, I seek to trouble beliefs that classify lesbian and feminist politics in the 1980s as static or regressive, linked to the description of "sororicidal conflicts" engendered by interfeminist disputes.[6] I propose that this can be achieved by re-animating the sex wars, and expanding their historicization beyond the radical/sex radical split. *Lesbians Talk Issues* provides an archive from which to begin this work, evidencing the centrality of topics otherwise outside the parameters of what might be expected as the central concerns of a lesbian politics, refuting contemporary and generationally bound stereotypes. These include the assumed irreconcilability between lesbian and queer, and lesbian and trans. Two volumes from the series, *Lesbians Talk Queer Notions* and *Lesbians Talk Transgender*, go to the roots of these tensions and counter them through the interweaving of diverse and nuanced perspectives. Returning to *Lesbians Talk Issues* amidst increasingly violent interfeminist and transphobic strife is therefore also a reminder of lesbian solidarities past, which might be drawn on in the present to complicate and strengthen the way politicized identities are inhabited.

To begin, I establish the 1980s as a decade of upheaval, and situate the sex wars within a wider turn toward social and political conservatism. My focus is on the less frequently discussed British context, and this chapter seeks to map it as distinct from—albeit informed by—events taking place in America. To this end, I foreground the writing of Susan Ardill and Sue O'Sullivan, who tracked and explained events in London as they happened.[7] While in tracing the edges of this history for the sake of succinct narration I risk describing the sex wars through the same split I am seeking to trouble, I maintain that an insistence on its precision obfuscates the diverse political and ideological positions at play. This is made clear by *Lesbians Talk Issues*, to which the second half the chapter turns. A rethinking of the feminist 1980s is overdue, and the wide ideological range and loose temporal scope of *Lesbians Talk Issues* offer a generous starting point.

Feminism at War

The 1980s saw rapid change on both sides of the Atlantic, structured by the 1979 election of Conservative Party leader Margaret Thatcher as prime minister of the United Kingdom, and the 1980 election of Republican Ronald Reagan as president of the United States. Swinging the political pendulum to the right, both countries entered the 1980s with the promise of a return to the conservative principles thought lost during the heady post-war years, with a focus on fiscal responsibility, economic growth, and family values. Accounts of the 1980s have foregrounded this shift and its consequences, in the United Kingdom emphasizing the nationalist rhetoric of the Falkland war, the repercussions of the 1984–1985 miner's strike, and the 1988 passing of Section 28 that made illegal the "promotion" of homosexuality by local councils. In the United States, emphasis falls to the War on Drugs, the Cold War, and imperialist incursions in Central America. Both countries have been scrutinized for their deadly response to HIV/AIDS, and transition to a neoliberal model of governance. Feminism rarely emerges as a point of focus, despite being (as Ferguson identified) also at war.

Though looking to the sex wars shifts the feminist 1980s back into view, they have been sidelined by broad narrations of the period and by the standard distillation of white, Western feminism, which focuses on the suffragettes ("first wave") and the rise of women's liberation in the late 1960s and 1970s ("second wave"). The 1990s follow as the moment feminism was compelled to diversify, with the mainstreaming of queer and, following pressure by Black feminists, the intersectional thinking that marks the "third wave" we have been understood as occupying since.[8] If the 1980s are mentioned, it is typically in relation to the framing of a "post-feminist" era during which some level of equality (professional, sexual) is posited as having been achieved, prompting—as American journalist Susan Faludi put it—a backlash, and resulting in what historian Elizabeth Wilson described in 1991 as feminism's "trough of despond."[9]

This mapping (though deliberately reductive) demonstrates how the 1980s have been excluded from the wave model that is used to organize and contain feminist time, and that has persisted despite its pitfalls, including an incapacity to account for politics and events that surpass blocky periodization.[10] This is also a problem of lesbian history's absorption into feminism's, and feminist history's maintenance as a specialist interest. That the sex wars unevenly effected and were fought by lesbians, "a sexual revolution under feminism's own roof," has curtailed their circulation beyond interfeminist and lesbian circles.[11]

Over the course of the 1980s, the sex wars were fought around women's sexual practices, with the two groups identified by Ferguson—radical feminist and sex radical—understood as opposing sides. Radical feminists aligned themselves against pornography, sadomasochism (S/M), sex work, penetration, and butch/femme, all labeled as "male identified." Sex radicals argued for freedom of choice, suggesting that the emphasis on sexual *danger* from within feminism had negated the possibility of sexual *pleasure*. They contended that this had simultaneously worked to desexualize the lesbian, located as the idealized subject of a radical feminist politics.

The sex wars are often recognized as formally beginning with the 1981 publication of a special "Sex Issue" of American magazine *Heresies: A Feminist Publication on Art and Politics*, and the 1982 conference "The Feminist and the Scholar IX: Towards a Politics of Sexuality" at New York City's Barnard College. Both foregrounded difficult conversations regarding the sexual preferences claimed and desired by feminists of different stripes. Meant to initiate and foster debate, *Heresies* and the Barnard conference instead opened onto conflict. Women opposed to taboo sexual proclivities (particularly pornography and S/M) protested the conference and the magazine, which at Barnard resulted in pickets, the confiscation of a conference workbook accused of pro-S/M bias, and an audit by the university. Gayle Rubin, a presenter at Barnard, has reflected on "the horror of having been there . . . a particularly repellent episode in what was unfortunately a repetitive pattern of conduct."[12]

But the opposition to sex radical politics can be better described as having *coalesced* around *Heresies* and Barnard rather than having emerged from them; as B. Ruby Rich details, in 1978 San Francisco hosted a conference on "Women Against Violence in Pornography," and the lesbian BDSM group Samois marched in the city's Gay Freedom Day Parade.[13] Both anti-pornography *and* pro-sex politics were already gaining ground, via consciousness-raising groups, journals and newspapers, and at demonstrations. In the United Kingdom, the sex wars consolidated around different pressure points like the failure to quickly apprehend Peter Sutcliffe, "the Yorkshire Ripper," who murdered thirteen women between 1975 and 1980. A transatlantic dialogue opened between these "sides," who shared resources and outrage.

As the 1980s wound on, so too did the imperative to grapple with gender and sexuality. And though the sex wars implicated a range of topics and sexual practices, S/M and pornography emerged as the issues to play for, tied to the question of what can be defined as feminist and/or lesbian, and to calls for censorship that followed. In 1986, editors and activists Susan Ardill and Sue O'Sullivan, who met working at feminist magazine *Spare Rib*, began writing about the sex wars as they occurred in London. Their article "Upsetting an Applecart: Difference, Desire, and Lesbian Sadomasochism" analyses a series of arguments in 1985 over whether S/M groups should be permitted to meet at the since-closed London Lesbian and Gay Centre (LLGC) in Farringdon.[14] Ardill and O'Sullivan's mapping unpacks key nodes of sex wars debate in a British context, setting up the important and sometimes uneasy conversations carried through in *Lesbians Talk Issues*.

Ardill and O'Sullivan propose that the atmosphere that roused the LLGC dispute evolved from the merging of lesbian separatism with revolutionary feminism (what Lynne Segal has termed a "magnification" of radical feminism), beginning in the late 1970s.[15] This merging formalized calls for political lesbianism, a tactic associated with American theorist and poet Adrienne Rich's 1980 tract "Compulsory Heterosexuality and Lesbian Existence," though the Leeds Revolutionary Feminist Group had published their own statement a year prior, "Political Lesbianism: The Case Against Heterosexuality," which centered on the claim that "sex is the problem; avoiding heterosexual contact is the solution."[16]

Heterosexual contact extended beyond the romantic or sexual and into everyday interactions, while lesbianism was extended beyond the desire of women for women, indicating a choice to extract oneself from relationships with men. This alienated many from women's liberation, which had been understood as espousing sisterhood in a broader sense inclusive of heterosexual feminists, while also alienating lesbians who saw their desires as overshadowed by political correctness. "Suddenly," Ardill and O'Sullivan write, "everyone was grappling with compulsory heterosexuality and political lesbianism, separatism, non-monogamy, lesbian lifestyle, lesbianism as the practice of feminism."[17]

As in the United States, divergent perspectives on sex and sexuality were developing. *Heresies* made its way to the United Kingdom, helping trigger a move to re-eroticize sex.[18] Ardill and O'Sullivan write that "whereas the British revolutionary feminists appeared to see sex as a pleasant possibility between women who had withdrawn from men, *Sex Heresies* underlined the deep and confusing currents of desire between women."[19] The stakes of these "confusing currents" are laid bare in a 1981 essay for the London-based *Revolutionary and Radical Feminist Newsletter*, wherein commentator Jayne Egerton declares that the "Sex Issue" "gives room to the kind of pleasure-seeking politics which justifies pedophilia, pornography," and "the institution of heterosexuality."[20] Feminists on both sides of the Atlantic countered that the impulse to stifle pornography, erotica, and transgressive sexual practices could establish an "unholy alliance" with the censorious political right.[21]

The year 1983 saw radical and revolutionary feminists in London advertise for a "Lesbian Sex and Sexual Practice Conference," picking up the threads left dangling at Barnard, and soliciting speakers with the exclusionary closing sentence, "no transsexuals, the conference is for lesbians only."[22] Around 1985, a "Lesbians Against Sado Masochism" flyer began to circulate. The increased visibility of S/M lesbians propelled debates forward, resulting in the 1985 confrontations as to whether S/M practitioners should be allowed to meet at the LLGC and other shared community spaces. Ardill and O'Sullivan distil this friction, and the resultant climate between radicals, sex radicals, and those who fell elsewhere:

> Because of the negative connotations of sadism and masochism (linked to actual torture, cruelty and emotional suffering), and the hegemony of political lesbianism, they [S/M lesbians] have been come down on—hard—by large sections of

lesbian feminists. Other lesbians, including many socialist lesbians like ourselves, have acted in defence of S/M dykes around issues of censorship and exclusion. This defence has necessarily broadened into an intense struggle over definitions of feminism and lesbianism, the rights and wrongs of lesbian sexual practice, desires and fantasies in general.[23]

Defense-in-solidarity was also staked from a trans perspective. During a 1992 conference at the Institute for Contemporary Arts (ICA) in London, science fiction writer and poet Roz Kaveney proposed that S/M stemmed from a utopian idealism, which was important to cultivate given the climate of conservatism previously outlined. Identifying as a "transsexual lesbian S/M switch," Kaveney noted that attacks on trans women and those on S/M dykes tabled from a feminist position were being made by the same people.[24] By self-identifying as a trans lesbian in support of the S/M community, Kaveney challenges what "feminist" and "lesbian" can signify and thus perform, undermining the ideological base from which some feminisms have tried to define their limits.[25] These expressions of alliance and affinity modulate the radical/sex radical divide, and establish precedent for the synchrony of trans and lesbian.

In a follow-up to their 1986 essay, Ardill and O'Sullivan propose that tensions in London peaked in 1988. Against the backdrop of the recently passed Section 28, the summer of 1988 saw a string of controversial events. Sheila McLaughlin's film *She Must Be Seeing Things* (1987) was screened at the Lesbian Archive's Lesbian Summer School, where the projection was blocked by anti-pornography activists who felt its depiction of heterosexual fantasies, jealousy, and obsession indicated abusive power dynamics; American author, archivist, and activist Joan Nestle (a proponent of butch/femme relationships) gave a reading; and the panel discussion "Putting the Sex Back into Sexual Politics" underscored that disputes over how to conceptualize a feminist approach to sex and sexuality were ongoing. Ardill and O'Sullivan explain that "the summer of '88 signaled a groundswell of openness, an urge to have difficult, knotty discussions . . . the rarified purists were experiencing a backlash. To us it seemed as if they were stuck somewhere back in the 1970s, oblivious to new realities."[26] In 1989, Feminists Against Censorship (FAC) was founded in London as a response to the Primarolo Bill's proposal to sequester all pornography to specially licensed shops, carrying these conversations into the 1990s.[27]

Lorna N. Bracewell has begun complicating how the sex wars are framed in an American context, positing their history as a clash between anti-pornography feminism and liberalism, augmenting the available vocabulary and complicating their standardized portrayal.[28] I follow Bracewell by insisting that to distil the sex wars' history into radical and sex radical camps ignores socialist feminism, cultural feminism, Black feminism, anti-war feminism, trans feminism, and (in the UK) revolutionary feminism, to name a few, and in addition to their shifting relationships with each other *and* with the sign "lesbian." These positions are not discrete, but permissive in their sharing of ideas and ideals—a point made by Kaveney's expression of solidarity, and O'Sullivan's later reflection that she and Ardill "could not neatly find ourselves on one side or another."[29] Identifying with an ideology rarely reduces a subject to a coherent set of beliefs, and what is meant by a signifier or name is unavoidably subjective. What bears consideration is therefore not the terms in play but the lives lived through them: a personal that is political, mutable, and inconsistent. Lee Damsky affirms that "in retrospect, the sex wars can be seen as a struggle over what the relationship between the personal and political should be."[30]

One need not look far to argue for the complexity of this period, with the residue of knotty conversations and multi-hyphenate identifications hindering a simplified narrative. Many of the women associated with London's sex radical scene participated in (and came out at) the Greenham Common Women's Peace Camp, a long-term occupation of an RAF base in Berkshire established in 1981 to protest its housing of American nuclear weapons. Greenham was a largely separatist space that instrumentalized an association between women and nonviolence in objecting to a masculine culture of war, a tendency that lives alongside the radical queer politics some of its attendees would develop.[31] A 1978 feature in *Spare Rib* further captures the ambivalence of being against misogynistic male-oriented pornography *and* arguments for censorship. Author Ruth Wallsgrove explains, "I like to be sexually aroused, but I don't like pictures of women handcuffed, submissive and inviting the reader to be brutal with them."[32] Additionally, expansive queer desires were articulated at the sex wars' beginning. This is evidenced by an anonymous contributor's "schedule" of multiple, sexually fluid experiences titled "Typical Week and a Half," which was printed below the editorial letter in the *Heresies* "Sex Issue."[33] These examples sit uneasily within the generational temporalization of feminism, particularly that which spokes off from a streamlined account of the sex wars.

By looking to the 1980s as a maelstrom of inconsistencies, continuities, and leaps of faith, we can begin unworking the containment of feminist time that has obfuscated the era. Ardill and O'Sullivan's essays read as an effort to process and digest ongoing events, and to work through their finer points. Some thirty years on, their writing sheds light on the particularities of the sex wars in a British context, contextualizing the conversations that ensued in *Lesbians Talk Issues* by detailing the energy that permeates these later publications, sometimes stated, others as an unspoken electric charge. In the sex wars' aftermath, the books introduce a sense of their texture and that of the context which informed, contradicted, and specified it. *Lesbians Talk Issues* speaks to the reconfiguration of feminist and lesbian politics during the 1980s and into the 1990s, and reveals the inadequacy of categorizing the period as one of inertia between the second and third waves, or as defined by a clash between two poles—assumptions that have themselves become linked. Rather than offering a complete history of the books' writing and publication, or an in-depth analysis of each volume, in this chapter's second half I pull at the threads connecting *Lesbians Talk Issues* to the debates around sex and sexuality outlined by Ardill and O'Sullivan. This reveals the 1980s' elastic duration and the shifting nature of lesbian and feminist identification within them, opening each position to more flexible readings.

Lesbians, Talking

In January 1992, an appeal was made in *City Limits*, London's alternative weekly listings magazine. In the lesbian and gay section (and below an ad for the British Film Institute's forthcoming Jodie Foster season) is a short paragraph detailing the arrival of Scarlet Press, "a new feminist publisher looking for contributors to a collection they are planning around the theme of lesbianism and popular culture."[34] As the collection would later market itself,

> Lesbian politics in the 1990s is producing a fast-changing agenda of issues and debates, contradictions and differences of opinion. The **Lesbians Talk Issues** series is designed to

provide a forum in which topics of current interest within the international lesbian community can be dissected and discussed with immediacy and flexibility.[35]

Approximately six months later, a slim paperback titled *Lesbians Talk Queer Notions* hit bookstore shelves.

Seven books were released in all: *Queer Notions* (1992), *Safer Sex* (1992), *Making Black Waves* (1993), *Left Politics* (1994), *Violent Relationships* (1995), *Transgender* (1996), and *Detonating the Nuclear Family* (1996).[36] While each has an author (sometimes two) who penned an introduction and cohered the volume with comments and analysis, they unfold as their titles suggest: lesbians, primarily in the United Kingdom, offer thoughts on the topic at hand, often leaking into others which might not immediately seem related. They include quotes from books, newspapers, and films, and testimony given to the author(s) in charge of collecting these diverse, and often divergent, exchanges.

In an interview following the publication of *Queer Notions*, author Cherry Smyth describes a desire for dialogue as the upshot to the push for censorship at the forefront of anti-S/M and pornography organizing. She explains that "the debate gave women the opportunity to develop a means of talking explicitly and publicly about sexual practice. It created a demand for explicit information on and cultural representation of lesbian sexual practices, by and for lesbians."[37] *Queer Notions* establishes precedent for the six volumes that follow. Through a cut-and-paste, multivocal conversation Smyth probes the complicated relationship of lesbianism to the recuperation of queer as a politicized identity in the early 1990s. As the speakers attest, this was met with both enthusiasm and suspicion, the latter often due to a feeling that queer would become synonymous with cis gay men, or that it accounted for a white experience.

But while "queer" centers the book, it assembles a range of opinions out of which frictions and harmonies emerge. Smyth's tone is both "exploratory" and ambivalent, asking questions that might not yet have answers.[38] Her interlocutors cross generations; for instance, in a quote from *A Restricted Country*, Joan Nestle reestablishes queer within a pre-women's liberation history of lesbian experience, when lesbians were "queer" to the women they would later become allied with, and butch/femme more ubiquitous (albeit classed). Such interjections unmoor queer from its later reclamation and connect it to an expanded narrative of feminist and lesbian feeling—identifications that the book's contributors also take to task. Dispensing with the idea that radical and sex radical feminisms are magnetized by generational difference, ideological characterizations of the second and third waves are confused, opening queer, lesbian, and feminist to broader interpretation.

Though not every volume is directly linked to the sex wars (e.g., *Detonating the Nuclear Family*), the desire for dialogue described by Smyth weaves through each, converging with what Ardill and O'Sullivan described as the "groundswell of openness" that occurred in the summer of 1988. This speaks to the climate of crisis felt across local contexts, and the need to resituate lesbian identity against it. A review of the developing series in the American publication *The Lesbian Review of Books* asked, "What is going on, and how can lesbians contribute to discovering our way out of this conservative morass? One thing we can do is exchange notes with our sisters from the UK."[39] Author Jennifer Rycenga concludes, "the entire *Lesbians Talk Issues* series is valuable in setting a dialogic tone, because neither lesbians, nor queers, (nor anyone) can afford to separate thought from activity at this time."[40] The books suture these two procedures, presenting informally edited conversations that introduce the aforementioned sense of immediacy and flexibility into the relationship between lesbian identification and its politics.

This is conspicuous in Sue O'Sullivan and Pratibha Parmar's *Safer Sex*, which reads the sex wars alongside the ongoing AIDS crisis. Contributor Beth Zemsky proposes that "lesbian sex, in all its forms and in all its diversity, is almost unspeakable. And without a workable discourse concerning lesbian sex, it is almost impossible to have a reasonable discussion about the risk of lesbian sexual transmission of HIV."[41] Zemsky flags that the discussions identified by Smyth as critical to framing a new lesbian subjectivity were also pressing in their implications for lesbian health. The assumption, Zemsky writes, is that only certain lesbians need practice safer sex, namely, those engaged with "deviant" behaviors like S/M or penetration.[42] As a corrective, *Safer Sex* lists two-and-a-half pages of acts and words, ranging in physical and emotional intensity from looking at a partner to having sex with them, with everything from kissing, stroking, and slapping in-between. O'Sullivan and Parmar explain that their aim is not to impose a standard of political correctness but to provide enough information that readers can "make more than theoretical choices" regarding sexual practice.[43] Like *Queer Notions*, *Safer Sex* unmoors a talking point central to sex wars debate from the purview of a singular politics, asking contributors and readers to consider it in terms of their experiences and desires. This is similarly achieved by Joelle Taylor and Tracey Chandler's *Violent Relationships*, which ventures to make abusive lesbian partnerships a feminist matter, and extends its conversation across race, substance abuse, and class. The political is shown to be personal, rather than vice versa, a substitution that marks variability within even the most resolute ideologies.

Zachary I. Nataf, author of *Transgender*, notes the influence of consciousness-raising. He writes that despite efforts from some feminist camps to deride transgender men and women as self-serving or reactionary in their perceived pursuit of "traditional" gender stereotypes, "applying the lessons learned from early feminism that the personal is political, with "consciousness-raising" around shared experiences and oppression, a process of politicization began in some of the support networks and in the alternative therapeutic/social groups during the 1980s."[44] The book privileges reflections from trans, intersex, and nonbinary perspectives, with contributors including Del LaGrace Volcano, Kate Bornstein, Pat Califia, and Jack Halberstam. As with *Queer Notions*, in *Transgender* the designation "lesbian" is claimed and dispensed with in equal measure. Both installments see lesbians talk under and against the sign on topics that challenge and open it, while retaining it as an organizing principle. Positioning "lesbian" alongside both queer *and* transgender needles at their respective frictions, creating the sense that incompatibilities are at least partly a consequence of inherited misunderstandings and consequent prejudices. Nataf writes that this was a deliberate approach, which sought to forge alliances between groups marginalized on the basis of sexual preference and gender identity, the same solidarity described by Kaveney (another contributor to Nataf's volume).[45] The strategies of "early feminism" are decoupled from a specific agenda, bearing on lesbian, queer, and transgender in turn and together.

But rather than establishing new party lines, *Lesbians Talk Issues* exposes inconsistencies in opinion and experience. This could raise the charge that individualism (identity politics) in the 1980s and '90s superseded the collectivity that provided the so-termed second wave its strength: that difference divides. *Left Politics* takes this view, framing the 1980s as the genesis of "sisterhood's" collapse, and mapping the infighting that led to what author Kristina Studzinski describes as a mood of irreconcilable difference. While this description of organized feminism's downfall has been repeated, leading to Bracewell's characterization of "sororicidal conflicts," taken together *Lesbians Talk Issues* makes apparent that feminisms continued developing, and that the variability within them did not necessarily produce structural fracturing. Speaking to the flourishing of Black feminism, editor and publisher Araba Mercer conversely remembered that "there seemed to be so much more going on in the 1980s, everything was new, things were possible,"[46] while Labour MP Diane Abbott has reflected that "in the 1980s there was a belief in sisterhood, and we saw real change."[47]

The capacity of the individual books to balance internal differences is critical to their mapping of this affective landscape. In conjunction with their consideration of topics made peripheral by the maintenance of a radical/sex radical binary, they expand the period beyond that split. As the 1980s unfolded, white feminism's entrenchment in gender and sexuality underscored preexisting conversations among Black and/or working-class feminists that questioned the urgency of the sex wars' main talking points, pushing for an intersectional dialogue that prioritized other facets of identification. Reappearing as a commentator in *Left Politics*, Smyth proposes that "feminism was a rallying call for many of us until we realised as white women that it had failed to address the needs of black women."[48] At the same time, and contradicting Studzinski, Abbott explains that this ongoing interrogation returned feminism to the left politics out of which, in Britain, it had developed, citing the 1984–1985 miner's strike as a key organizing moment for working-class women and their allies.

Making Black Waves clarifies the differing concerns of Black feminism—defined broadly and politically—but also its internal divergences. Authors Valerie Mason-John and Ann Khambatta describe how some Black lesbians supported London's lesbian S/M communities in alignment with sex radical arguments for freedom of choice, while others protested against their racism, adapting a form of radical feminism to support this analysis. Regardless, Mason-John and Khambatta determine that the tenor of the sex wars obscured a need for conversation about sexuality in relation to race, writing that "black lesbians need to create a space where we can discuss these issues openly and generously . . . Our sexuality and sexual practice should not be concerned with scoring points for being radical or right-on, but with understanding the complexity of our whole experiences."[49] The need to talk openly is reiterated by a questionnaire the authors circulated in anticipation of the book. These documents identify a consistent dearth of Black lesbian groups and events, and that respondents subsequently experienced a mix of excitement and nervousness attending both local gatherings and larger ones like the Zami conferences in 1985 and 1990.[50]

Beyond S/M and pornography, Mason-John and Khambatta center the relationship of Black lesbianism to a differently prioritized compendium of feminist issues. These include Black lesbian separatism, argued for by Aqeela Alam on the lines that "your chances of being able to become a whole person are more if you're not relating to White people at close quarters,"[51] while Mercer conversely attests that "I don't subscribe to Black lesbian separatism because I would like to have a much wider view of the world."[52] Such positions are held in tandem, an editorial decision that resists generalization. Separatism, often associated with "bad" radical feminism, instead opens onto survival for some Black lesbian feminists.

In *Transgender*, Nataf approaches the same topic from a different angle, writing that

> at a time in our culture when gender is a burning issue, separatism seems an obsolete tool for making sense of the world. All difference, not just men, maleness and patriarchy, has become a target of suppression. Inevitably the unique and complex experiences of and the differences between lesbians can not be subsumed within the boundaries of the "pure lesbian."[53]

Tying the book back to the sociopolitical landscape described by Rycenga, Nataf draws attention to the strand that coheres *Lesbians Talk Issues*: each uses the experience of lesbian and feminist subjectivity to question the limits imposed on them by political imperatives calcified over time through fidelity, stereotyping, and historicization. Neither lesbian nor feminist—queer, Black, transgender or otherwise—is reducible. Preferences like separatism become supplemental, rather than intrinsic, to the meaning of the signs "lesbian" and "feminist," which are shown to be malleable, contestable, and capable of cutting across time.

The format and content of *Lesbians Talk* complicate presumptions regarding feminism and lesbianism in the 1980s, which I understand as a long decade, the events and effects of which hold (and are held by) these books. The 1980s should not be classified as the static between feminism's second and third waves, nor should they be situated as a moment of collapse. Though it has been proposed that the '80s ushered in a post-feminist decade of power suits and lipstick lesbians, the pressures of the sex wars make clear that feminism was operational throughout, even—and especially—as its meaning was contested. Rosa Ainley observes in her 1995 collection of edited interviews *What is She Like? Lesbian Identities from the 1950s to the 1990s* that "the backlash against feminism has been at least as strong from within as from outside feminist circles. Given this, I was surprised that almost all the interviewees talked about feminism. If the mainstream backlash against feminism is positive evidence of its importance and effectiveness, perhaps there is a parallel strand amongst lesbians."[54] This is an uneven, but telling, equivalence. Where feminism's contestation of deeply engrained misogyny spurred external backlash from right-wing politicians, press, and punters, backlash from *within* was directed at feminism's inability to account for internal differences when figuring itself as a fixed ideological position. *Lesbians Talk Issues* grapples with these disparities while talking around the sign itself, parallel and contemporaneous with a desire to recognize the importance of feminism *and* interrogate its remit.

Contesting the meaning of "lesbian" and "feminist" was central to sex wars debate, a practice that *Lesbians Talk Issues* makes evident. The authors of *Violent Relationships* contextualize the volume by explaining that "this book is set against renewed attacks upon feminism."[55] They affirm Ainley's proposition that though feminism was in a moment of definitional flux, conversation and the processing of personal and group politics continued through and beyond the sex wars' apex, an undertaking indebted to strategies like consciousness-raising that were borne of the women's liberation movements in which many had come of age. This processing is legible across the books, which, though published in the early 1990s, present opinions forged in the crucible of the decade prior.

Conclusion

Emphasizing the relationship between *Lesbians Talk Issues* and the sex wars reestablishes the 1980s as a critical period of conversation around what it means to be a feminist and/or a lesbian, and one that extends beyond the decade's conventional end. The series makes apparent that these signs are not easily defined or homogenized, whether vis-à-vis sexual practice or political affiliation. The sex wars constellated around questions regarding sexuality and gender, a focus that has facilitated their characterization as a battle between radical and sex radical feminisms. Foregrounding the mercurial nature of identification pushes against the sex wars' mapping as a split, which has contributed to obscuring the 1980s from recent feminist focus. Astrid Henry suggests that women who came of age between the late 1970s and mid-1980s—those speaking in *Lesbians Talk Issues*—have been "subsumed under the category 'second wave' . . . As they can be understood as neither 'mothers' nor 'daughters' within feminism's imagined family structure, such feminists are frequently absent from recent discourse on feminism's (seemingly two) generations."[56] But Rosalyn Deutsche reminds us that "generations are not internally homogenous."[57] Thinking the sex wars as an opening rather than a split, their voices, and this period, are brought back into focus, effecting what Deutsche has termed an effort to "move away from casual linearity toward multidirectional models of history."[58] Instead of correlating politicized identifications with the period in which they are lived, Deutsche articulates a more generous way of thinking identity and ideology. Without disavowing their material realities, narrating the sex wars as a disorderly unfolding of feelings and arguments loops the 1980s into the decades that preceded and followed, complicating the presumed specificity of each, and demanding new narratives be written.

Notes

I would like to thank Catherine Grant, Laura Guy, and Amy Tobin for productive conversations that occurred as this chapter was prepared, and Sue O'Sullivan for the insights that pushed it to completion. Additional thanks to Sarah Crook and Charlie Jeffries for their generous editing.

1. Ann Ferguson, "Sex War: The Debate between Radical and Libertarian Feminists," *Signs: Journal of Women in Culture and Society* 10.1 (1984): 106.

2. Ann Ferguson, "The Sex Debate in the Women's Movement: A Socialist-Feminist View," *Against the Current* 2.3 (Fall 1983): 11.

3. Sarah F. Green, *Urban Amazons: Lesbian Feminism and Beyond in the Gender, Sexuality and Identity Battles of London* (London: Palgrave Macmillan, 1992), 2.

4. Lorna N. Bracewell, "Beyond Barnard: Liberalism, Antipornography Feminism, and the Sex Wars," *Signs* 42.1 (2016): 25.

5. See Catherine Grant, "A Time of One's Own," *Oxford Art Journal* 39.3 (2016); Clare Hemmings, *Why Stories Matter: The Political Grammar of Feminist Theory* (Durham, NC & London: Duke University Press, 2011); Sam McBean, *Feminism's Queer Temporalities* (London & New York: Routledge, 2016).

6. Throughout, I refer to lesbian *and* feminist rather than lesbian feminist. The latter has sometimes been seen as synonymous with radical feminism, whereas this chapter attempts to decouple the two signs from that expectation and trace the ways in which they were opened to new interpretation over the course of the 1980s.

7. Interestingly, Ardill and O'Sullivan wrote about British feminism as transplants to the country: Ardill moved to London from Australia, and O'Sullivan from the United States. While this ties the British context back to the international nature of feminist conversation, both women were embedded in London by the time of the sex wars, and recognized it as home. See Sue O'Sullivan, *I Used to Be Nice: Sexual Affairs* (London: Cassell, 1996).

8. The term "intersectionality" was coined by American academic Kimberlé Crenshaw in 1989 in her paper "Demarginalizing the Intersection of Race and Sex: A Black Feminist Critique of Antidiscrimination Doctrine, Feminist Theory and Antiracist Politics," *The University of Chicago Legal Forum* 1 (1989).

9. Elizabeth Wilson, "Feminism without Illusions?," *New Left Review* 190 (November/December 1991): 119. See Susan Faludi, *Backlash: The Undeclared War Against Women* (New York: Crown Publishing Group, 1991).

10. For further analysis of feminism's wave model, see Astrid Henry, *Not My Mother's Sister: Generational Conflict and Third-Wave Feminism* (Bloomington & Indianapolis: Indiana University Press, 2004); Rosalyn Deutsche, Aruna D'Souza, Miwon Kwon, Ulrike Müller, Mignon Nixon, and Senam Okudzeto, "Feminist Time: A Conversation," *Grey Room* 31 (Spring 2008).

11. Flora Dunster, "Sexual Revolution," in *The Art of Feminism*, eds. Luci Gosling, Helena Reckitt, Hilary Robinson, and Amy Tobin (London: Tate Publishing, 2019), 174.

12. Gayle Rubin, "Blood Under the Bridge: Reflections on 'Thinking Sex,'" *GLQ* 17.1 (2011): 16. The conference proceedings are collected in Carol Vance, ed., *Pleasure and Danger: Exploring Female Sexuality* (Boston & New York: Routledge & Kegan Paul, 1984).

13. B. Ruby Rich, "Review: Feminism and Sexuality in the 1980s," *Feminist Studies* 12.3 (Autumn 1986): 526.

14. Susan Ardill and Sue O'Sullivan, "Upsetting an Applecart: Difference, Desire and Lesbian Sadomasochism," *Feminist Review* 23.1 (1986).

15. Lynne Segal, *Is the Future Female? Troubled Thoughts on Contemporary Feminism* (Virago: London, 1987), 96. Revolutionary feminism—a position primarily articulated in the UK—understood its struggle as against men, focusing on the sexual practices and ideals that subordinate women. It perceived a transhistorical male sexuality as the core of women's oppression, interpreting pornography as a cause of male violence, therefore itself a form of violence against women, and justifiably censorable. Sarah Green recounts being "jokingly"

told that "radical feminists believe men are the enemy and hope that one day they'll change; revolutionary feminists believe that men are the enemy and home that one day they'll all *die*" (*Urban Amazons* 18, emphasis in original.) In the US, radical feminists—whose position emphasized abolishing gendered differences—were understood as the vanguard in the fight against S/M and pornography; in the UK, both self-identified revolutionary *and* radical feminists rallied against sexualized representations, though the former became synonymous with a more stringently anti-sex—and anti-men—position.

16. Segal, *Is the Future Female?*, 96.
17. Ardill and O'Sullivan, "Upsetting an Applecart," 39.
18. For further discussion of lesbian erotica's transatlantic circulation, see Laura Guy, "Wanting Pictures after Feminism: Re-reading *On Our Backs*," *Women: A Cultural Review* 30.3 (2019).
19. Ardill and O'Sullivan, "Upsetting an Applecart," 40.
20. Jayne Egerton, "The Goal of a Feminist Politics . . . The Destruction of Male Supremacy or the Pursuit of Pleasure?," in *Sweeping Statements: Writings from the Women's Liberation Movement 1981–83*, eds. Hannah Kanter, Sarah Lefanu, Shaila Shah, and Carole Spedding (London: The Women's Press, 1984), 198.
21. Tessa Boffin, "The Blind Leading the Blind: Socialist-Feminism and Representation," *Feminist Review* 29 (1988): 160.
22. "Let's Talk about It!" *Gay News*, February 3–16 (1983), p. 9.
23. Ardill and O'Sullivan, "Upsetting an Applecart," 40–41.
24. Roz Kaveney, "Sado-Masochism as Art and Practice," panel discussion, "Preaching to the Perverted," Institute of Contemporary Arts, London, July 11, 1992.
25. "Switch" indicates someone comfortable assuming the role of top or bottom, or dominant or submissive, who switches between the two at will.
26. Susan Ardill and Sue O'Sullivan, "Sex in the Summer of '88," *Feminist Review* 31.1 (1989): 129.
27. Sue O'Sullivan and Roz Kaveney were members of FAC, as were others cited in this chapter, including Lynne Segal and Elizabeth Wilson. FAC's minutes, held in the Hall-Carpenter Archives at the London School of Economics, name a slew of sex radical artists, activists, and academics, and evidence the social network that coalesced around these conversations.
28. See Bracewell, "Beyond Barnard."
29. Sue O'Sullivan, introductory talk at "Feminism and Censorship," Feminist Duration Reading Group, February 11, 2021.
30. Lee Damsky, introduction to *Sex and Single Girls: Straight and Queer Women on Sexuality*, ed. Lee Damsky (Seattle: Seal Press, 2000), xvi.
31. "Meet the lesbian punks who've been written out of London's history," *Time Out London*, 25 April 2017. www.timeout.com/london/blog/meet-the-lesbian-punks-whove-been-written-out-of-londons-history-042517

32. Ruth Wallsgrove, "Pornography: Between the Devil and the True Blue Whitehouse" *Spare Rib* 65 (1978): 44.

33. "Typical Week and a Half," *Heresies* 12 (1981): 1.

34. "Scarlet Press," *City Limits*, January 9–16 1992, 51.

35. Sue O'Sullivan and Pratibha Parmar, *Lesbians Talk Safer Sex* (London: Scarlet Press, 1992), 64. Bold font in original.

36. An eighth book, *Lesbians Talk about Gay Men*, was listed by Scarlet Press, though I suspect as a hypothetical future release. I have found no material evidence that this installment was published.

37. Amy Hamilton and Cherry Smyth, "Interview: Queer Notions" *off our backs* 22.9 (October 1992): 13.

38. Cherry Smyth, *Lesbians Talk Queer Notions* (London: Scarlet Press, 1992), 12.

39. Jennifer Rycenga, "Lesbian Talk," *The Lesbian Review of Books* 2.2 (Winter 1995–96): 6.

40. Rycenga, *Lesbian Talk*, 6.

41. O'Sullivan and Parmar, *Lesbians Talk Safer Sex*, 28.

42. O'Sullivan and Parmar, *Lesbians Talk Safer Sex*, 31.

43. O'Sullivan and Parmar, *Lesbians Talk Safer Sex*, 41.

44. Zachary I. Nataf, *Lesbians Talk Transgender* (London: Scarlet Press, 1996), 26.

45. A feeling of solidarity is also articulated by cisgender contributors, including the London-based filmmaker Annette Kennerley, who went on to make *Boys in the Backyard* (1997) and *Matt* (1998). Kennerley's documentaries picture the subjects and politics of San Francisco's communities of trans men during the 1990s, and serve as further testimony to the sometimes productive, sometimes arduous conversations that took place in the sex wars' wake.

46. Ann Khambatta and Valerie Mason-John, *Lesbians Talk Making Black Waves* (London: Scarlet Press, 1993), 53.

47. Diane Abbott, "Diane Abbott on Feminism in the 1980s: 'It was so exciting being in a hall full of black women,'" *The Guardian*, 1 February 2018. www.theguardian.com/lifeandstyle/2018/feb/01/women-1980s-diane-abbott-black-women-radical-feminism

48. Kristina Studzinski, *Lesbians Talk Left Politics* (London: Scarlet Press, 1994), 17.

49. Khambatta and Mason-John, *Lesbians Talk Making Black Waves*, 51.

50. These questionnaires are held in Valerie Mason-John's papers as part of the ruckus! Black, Lesbian, Gay, Bisexual and Trans (BLGBT) cultural archive, at the London Metropolitan Archives.

51. Khambatta and Mason-John, *Lesbians Talk Making Black Waves*, 28.

52. Khambatta and Mason-John, *Lesbians Talk Making Black Waves*, 28.

53. Nataf, *Lesbians Talk Transgender*, 40.

54. Rosa Ainley, *What is She Like? Lesbian Identities from the 1950s to the 1990s* (London & New York: Cassell, 1995), 46–47.

55. Joelle Taylor and Tracey Chandler, *Lesbians Talk Violent Relationships* (London: Scarlet Press, 1995), 8.

56. Henry, *Not My Mother's Sister*, 4.

57. Deutsche et al., "Feminist Time," 55.

58. Deutsche et al., "Feminist Time," 56.

Works Cited

Abbott, Diane. "Diane Abbott on feminism in the 1980s: 'It was so exciting being in a hall full of black women.'" *The Guardian*, 1 February 2018. www.theguardian.com/lifeandstyle/2018/feb/01/women-1980s-diane-abbott-black-women-radical-feminism

Ainley, Rosa. *What Is She Like? Lesbian Identities from the 1950s to the 1990s.* London & New York: Cassell, 1995.

Ardill, Susan and Sue O'Sullivan. "Upsetting an Applecart: Difference, Desire and Lesbian Sadomasochism." *Feminist Review* 23.1 (1986): 31–57.

Ardill, Susan and Sue O'Sullivan. "Sex in the Summer of '88." *Feminist Review* 31.1 (1989): 126–134.

Bracewell, Lorna N. "Beyond Barnard: Liberalism, Antipornography Feminism, and the Sex Wars." *Signs* 42.1 (2016): 23–48.

Brosnan, Julia. *Lesbians Talk Detonating the Nuclear Family.* London: Scarlet Press, 1996.

Boffin, Tessa. "The Blind Leading the Blind: Socialist-Feminism and Representation" *Feminist Review* 29 (1988): 158–161.

Crenshaw, Kimberlé. "Demarginalizing the Intersection of Race and Sex: A Black Feminist Critique of Antidiscrimination Doctrine, Feminist Theory and Antiracist Politics." *The University of Chicago Legal Forum* 1 (1989): 139–167.

Damsky, Lee. Introduction to *Sex and Single Girls: Straight and Queer Women on Sexuality*, ed. Lee Damsky. Seattle: Seal Press, 2000. xi–xx.

Deutsche, Rosalyn, Aruna D'Souza, Miwon Kwon, Ulrike Müller, Mignon Nixon, and Senam Okudzeto. "Feminist Time: A Conversation." *Grey Room* 31 (Spring 2008): 32–67.

Dunster, Flora. "Sexual Revolution," in *The Art of Feminism*, eds. Luci Gosling, Helena Reckitt, Hilary Robinson, and Amy Tobin. London: Tate Publishing, 2019. 174–175.

Egerton, Jayne. "The Goal of a Feminist Politics . . . the Destruction of Male Supremacy or the Pursuit of Pleasure?," in *Sweeping Statements: Writings from the Women's Liberation Movement 1981–83*, eds. Hannah Kanter,

Sarah Lefanu, Shaila Shah, and Carole Spedding. London: The Women's Press, 1984: 198–202.
Faludi, Susan. *Backlash: The Undeclared War Against Women*. New York: Crown Publishing Group, 1991.
Ferguson, Ann. "The Sex Debate in the Women's Movement: A Socialist-Feminist View." *Against the Current* 2.3 (Fall 1983): 10–16.
Ferguson, Ann. "Sex War: The Debate between Radical and Libertarian Feminists." *Signs: Journal of Women in Culture and Society* 10.1 (1984): 106–112.
Grant, Catherine. "A Time of One's Own." *Oxford Art Journal* 39.3 (2016): 357–376.
Green, Sarah F. *Urban Amazons: Lesbian Feminism and Beyond in the Gender, Sexuality and Identity Battles of London*. London: Palgrave Macmillan, 1992.
Guy, Laura. "Wanting Pictures after Feminism: Re-reading *On Our Backs*." *Women: A Cultural Review* 30.3 (2019): 319–341.
Hamilton, Amy, and Cherry Smyth. "Interview: Queer Notions." *off our backs* 22.9 (October 1992): 12–15.
Hemmings, Clare. *Why Stories Matter: The Political Grammar of Feminist Theory*. Durham, NC & London: Duke University Press, 2011.
Henry, Astrid. *Not My Mother's Sister: Generational Conflict and Third-Wave Feminism*. Bloomington & Indianapolis: Indiana University Press, 2004.
Kaveney, Roz. "Sado-Masochism as Art and Practice." Panel discussion at "Preaching to the Perverted," Institute of Contemporary Arts, London, July 11, 1992.
Khambatta, Ann, and Valerie Mason-John. *Lesbians Talk Making Black Waves*. London: Scarlet Press, 1993.
McBean, Sam. *Feminism's Queer Temporalities*. London & New York: Routledge, 2016.
"Meet the lesbian punks who've been written out of London's history." *Time Out London*, 25 April 2017. www.timeout.com/london/blog/meet-the-lesbian-punks-whove-been-written-out-of-londons-history-042517
Nataf, Zachary I. *Lesbians Talk Transgender*. London: Scarlet Press, 1996.
O'Sullivan, Sue. Introductory talk at "Feminism and Censorship." Feminist Duration Reading Group, February 11, 2021.
O'Sullivan, Sue. *I Used to Be Nice: Sexual Affairs*. London: Cassell, 1996.
O'Sullivan, Sue, and Pratibha Parmar. *Lesbians Talk Safer Sex*. London: Scarlet Press, 1992.
Rich, B. Ruby. "Review: Feminism and Sexuality in the 1980s." *Feminist Studies* 12.3 (Autumn 1986): 525–561.
Rubin, Gayle. "Blood Under the Bridge: Reflections on 'Thinking Sex.'" *GLQ* 17.1 (2011): 15–48.
Rycenga, Jennifer. "Lesbian Talk." *The Lesbian Review of Books* 2.2 (Winter 1995–96): 6.

"Scarlet Press." *City Limits*, 9–16 January 1992.
Segal, Lynne. *Is the Future Female? Troubled Thoughts on Contemporary Feminism.* Virago: London, 1987.
Smyth, Cherry. *Lesbians Talk Queer Notions.* London: Scarlet Press, 1992.
Studzinski, Kristina. *Lesbians Talk Left Politics.* London: Scarlet Press, 1994.
Taylor, Joelle, and Tracey Chandler. *Lesbians Talk Violent Relationships.* London: Scarlet Press, 1995.
"Typical Week and a Half." *Heresies* 12 (1981): 1.
Vance, Carol, ed. *Pleasure and Danger: Exploring Female Sexuality.* Boston & New York: Routledge & Kegan Paul, 1984.
Wallsgrove, Ruth. "Pornography: Between the Devil and the True Blue Whitehouse." *Spare Rib* 65 (1978): 44–46.
Wilson, Elizabeth. "Feminism without Illusions?" *New Left Review* 190 (November/December 1991): 119–126.

Epilogues

Looking Back, Thinking Forward

Grassroots Activism and Modern Histories

Sarah Crook

This volume was first conceived in early 2018, at the middle point of Donald Trump's presidency and two years after the fractious Brexit vote. In both Britain (with the exceptions of Scotland and Northern Ireland, neither of which voted for Brexit) and in the United States, it appeared that nationalism, conservatism, and machismo were on the rise. It was not a time that augured well for progressive or marginalized communities. There were exceptions, of course, and glimmers of light, shone by those willing to protest political and social injustices. The city in which this volume originated, Oxford, was witnessing an important conversation about the importance of decolonizing its university's structures, instigated by the Rhodes Must Fall movement—which itself was born at the University of Cape Town, again demonstrating the ways that activism and protest reverberate across and between nations; in America the Black Lives Matter movement continued to provoke urgent reflection about the violence imposed on people of color through structural racism. Both the Rhodes Must Fall and the Black Lives Matter movements arose from injustices. Both, too, were pioneered and led by Black activists. Both—at the time of writing this epilogue—have posed critical challenges to systems of racial injustice and have provoked vitally necessary cultural introspection. Their impact on social movements in the years since should act as a reminder that now, as then, activism is enduring, effective, and necessary.

Resist, Organize, Build entered its final stages amid the Covid-19 pandemic that convulsed the world across 2020 and 2021. That it reached publication is a testament to the hard work of a myriad of people, not least our contributors and our editor at SUNY. It is worth highlighting here the vital labor of those who enabled the volume to be finished but who will not find their names in the table of contents: for me, this was Tracey Knuszka and her team at the Swansea University Student Union Day Nursery (thank you, childcare workers).

This edited collection emerged from both a scholarly need—the volume has provided new ways of understanding our work, something that Charlie discusses in more detail in her editor's note—and a teaching need. The students we have both worked with across a range of Higher Education institutions have been at the forefront of pushing for institutional change. They have turned to the past to explain some of the fissures of the present: we hope this volume, then, will find its way into their hands, and will provide some of the explanations they demand. Nonetheless, *Resist, Organize, Build* has not sought to provide an all-encompassing account of activism in the 1980s. Indeed, broad swathes of vitally important activism are not discussed in detail. Instead, the collection seeks to give a snapshot of some of the scholarship ongoing in this area, and to gesture to parts of the legacy of the activism of this era. The volume has shown that, by putting examples of activism in Britain and the United States alongside one another, we can build a more textured picture of the 1980s as a time of resistance, creativity, and community building. It has sought to look beyond well-known sources, organizations, and geographies of protest to highlight local, grassroots contributions: book series, magazines, and publishers that provided a platform for activist voices; campus activisms, legal cases, and radio, to name just a sample. The authors in this collection have shown that, in feminist and queer resistance to the right in both contexts, their urgent, immediate struggle would also in many cases be foundational to future activisms.

Today the need to fight for women's rights and for queer people's safety remains urgent in both the United States and the United Kingdom. Progress has been made, but both societies remain deeply unequal. In the United States and the United Kingdom today, activists—described by the chapters in this book in their 1980s iterations—seek to secure safer, more expansive futures. Student activists campaign for inclusive campuses. Women defend and demand access to their reproductive rights, and to affordable, flexible, accessible childcare. The arts, including underground and online publishing, and those enabled by new technologies, have remained an essential site for community. These struggles, alongside and overlapping with other contemporary social movements, are fighting against the historic injustices that continue to plague both nations. The fight goes on.

The scholarship that tracks this organizing goes on too. *Resist, Organize, Build* has consciously given a platform to early career scholars alongside historians who occupy more secure academic positions. These emerging scholars will be a part of the movement to establish new intellectual arcs: raising new lines of enquiry and establishing new understandings of the past.

Critically Reflecting (on) the 1980s

CHARLIE JEFFRIES

Our volume emerged out of a period of increased scholarly and societal interest in the history of late twentieth-century social movements. It was compiled in a time of emergency, one that has allowed for easy comparisons with the 1980s, particularly on the resurgence of the right and activist resistance in the United States and the United Kingdom in both periods. The impulse to draw through-lines between the culture wars of the 1980s with those of the early twenty-first century became more intense still after the emergence of the Covid-19 pandemic in early 2020. The government mishandling and activist response to this pandemic, as well as the memories of grief and resistance that it brought up, resonated with those in queer communities who had lived through the AIDS pandemic when it emerged in the 1980s.[1] These resonances—and the important differences between the two ongoing pandemics—have been explored in the US context by Che Gossett and Eva Hayward and in the UK context by Matt Cook.[2] Significantly, the mutual aid groups and mass social movements that were recharged over the course of 2020 and 2021 were able to mobilize as they did in part because of the roots of anti-racist, feminist, and queer organizing established in the late twentieth century.

Drawing these links, however, can of course lead to potential problems and oversights. Does focusing on the 1980s and their reverberations in the 2010s and 2020s suggest that the crises of both periods could be cleared up with a new government or a new decade? Does it imply that their symptoms—nationalism, health crises, anti-Blackness, homophobia, transphobia, violence against women, constant attacks on reproductive justice,³ to name only a few—existed only in these periods in which the right was dominant in the halls of power? In the US context, we know that the New Right was gestating for decades in the run up to Reagan's election, that social conservatism was rampant in the Democratic Clinton presidency—amongst the population as a whole, Republicans in Congress, and Clinton himself—and that none of the social crises that were exacerbated by Trump's toxic presidency will easily subside with Biden and Harris in the White House. The ideologies espoused by the right in the 1980s and in the recent past have been percolating since the beginning of the nation's history, and will be fought against for a long time yet.

It is sometimes the role of historians and other kinds of researchers to hone in as the authors of this collection have here—to focus on specific periods and reach a deeper understanding of their significance. However, as their writing also shows, it is important to see the struggles outlined here as long struggles that neither began with the organizations in these pages nor ended with them. Lisa Levenstein's book on feminisms of the 1990s, *They Didn't See Us Coming*, is a further example of inspiration for future research in this field, in the way that it seeks to better understand a specific underexplored angle of a relatively short period of time, without ever losing sight of the larger picture.

The chapters in this volume have, in this way, made me reflect in new ways on my own research. The four parts of *Resist, Organize, Build* spoke to four crucial sites of the activism of the era: the college campus, the family, the arts, and the nation's borders. These chapters have pushed me to think about and characterize the era in new ways in my own work. For example, Katherine Rye Jewell's and Michael S. Hevel and Charles J. Thompson's chapters on LGBTQ+ campus activism have encouraged me to think about the way we have not collectively understood the 1980s as one of urgent campus activisms, in the way that we do epochs like the 1960s.⁴ The contributions on the use of radio programming (Jewell) and grassroots publishing (Dunster, Enszer, and Dahmani) to advance feminist, queer, and anti-racist politics in this era have also inspired me to trace the longer histories of the grassroots, artistic scenes that I study in my own research: namely, that of zines and feminist and queer music-based social movements.

The chapters mentioned above are just a few examples of how this volume's authors have provided new lenses on my work and have developed my understanding of how this era fits into the longer—and ongoing—stories of overlapping state, societal, and interpersonal violence in both contexts, and the stories of resistance from activists. The writing in these pages suggests that while we might, as researchers, need to hone in on one era, we should recognize the right as consistently antagonizing, often showing up where it isn't expected, and the grassroots struggles outlined in this book as never "between waves."[5] The legacy of the activism in this book's chapters shows not only the resistance of queer and feminist organizers to their immediate conditions, but the longevity of their contributions, and therefore the relevance and importance of the feminist and queer activism of the 1980s to the world we live in, no matter when it is you are picking up this book.

Notes

1. See Matt Cook, "It's a Sin: Revisiting AIDS in the Era of Covid," in "Histories of the Present," *History Workshop*, 6 February 2021. www.history-workshop.org.uk/its-a-sin-revisiting-aids-in-the-era-of-covid

2. See Cook, "It's a Sin," and Che Gossett and Eva Hayward, "Trans in a Time of HIV/AIDS," *Transgender Studies Quarterly* 7.14 (November 2020).

3. The term "reproductive justice" was created and put forward by the group Women of African Descent for Reproductive Justice in June 1994. See "Reproductive Justice," SisterSong: Women of Color Reproductive Justice Collective. www.sistersong.net/reproductive-justice

4. See Katherine Rye Jewell's chapter "'Specialty' Listening: Creating Space for Queer Programming on American College Radio in the Long 1980s" and Michael S. Hevel and Charles J. Thompson, "'Aggies are Not Queers': A History of *Gay Student Services v. Texas A&M University*, 1975–1985," both in this volume.

5. For more on the problems of understanding feminisms in waves, see Kimberly Springer, "Third Wave Black Feminism?" *Signs* 27 (Summer 2002); the contributions to *No Permanent Waves: Recasting Histories of U.S. Feminism*, ed. Nancy Hewitt (New Brunswick, NJ: Rutgers University Press, 2010); and Jade Bentil, "'We were fire-fighting against Thatcher and the system she was putting forward': The Black Women's Movement and the Boundaries of Nationhood in Thatcher's Britain," in this volume.

Works Cited

Bentil, Jade. "'We were fire-fighting against Thatcher and the system she was putting forward': The Black Women's Movement and the Boundaries of

Nationhood in Thatcher's Britain," in *Resist, Organize, Build*, eds. Sarah Crook and Charlie Jeffries. Albany, NY: SUNY Press, 2022.

Cook, Matt. "It's a Sin: Revisiting AIDS in the Era of Covid," in "Histories of the Present," *History Workshop*, 6 February 6 2021. www.historyworkshop.org.uk/its-a-sin-revisiting-aids-in-the-era-of-covid

Gossett, Che, and Eva Hayward. "Trans in a Time of HIV/AIDS." *Transgender Studies Quarterly* 7.14 (November 2020): 527–553.

Hevel, Michael S., and Charles J. Thompson. "'Aggies are Not Queers': A History of *Gay Student Services v. Texas A&M University*, 1975–1985," in *Resist, Organize, Build*, eds. Sarah Crook and Charlie Jeffries. Albany, NY: SUNY Press, 2022.

Hewitt, Nancy, ed. *No Permanent Waves: Recasting Histories of U.S. Feminism*. New Brunswick, NJ: Rutgers University Press, 2010.

Jewell, Katherine Rye, "'Specialty' Listening: Creating Space for Queer Programming on American College Radio in the Long 1980s," in *Resist, Organize, Build*, eds. Sarah Crook and Charlie Jeffries. Albany, NY: SUNY Press, 2022.

Levenstein, Lisa. *They Didn't See Us Coming: The Hidden History of Feminism in the Nineties*. New York: Basic Books, 2020.

Springer, Kimberly. "Third Wave Black Feminism?" *Signs* 27 (Summer 2002): 1059–1082.

"Reproductive Justice," SisterSong: Women of Color Reproductive Justice Collective. www.sistersong.net/reproductive-justice

Contributors

Charlie Jeffries is a British Academy Postdoctoral Research Fellow at Birkbeck, University of London. Her research focuses on the history of sexuality and the history of social movements in the late twentieth century and early twenty-first century United States. She has work published in the *Journal of American Studies*, and she is the author of *Teenage Dreams: Girlhood Sexualities in the U.S. Culture Wars* (Rutgers University Press, 2022). Correspondence to: Dr Charlie Jeffries, Department of History, Classics and Archaeology, Birkbeck, University of London, 26 Russell Square, London, WC1B 5DQ. email: c.jeffries@bbk.ac.uk

Sarah Crook is senior lecturer in post-1800 European social and cultural history at Swansea University. She has research interests in the modern history of psychiatry and the history of modern activisms. Her work has been published in *Medical Humanities*, *Contemporary British History*, and *Women's History Review*, among other places. Correspondence to: Dr Sarah Crook, Department of History, Swansea University, Singleton Campus, Swansea, SA2 8PP. email: s.r.e.crook@swansea.ac.uk

Katie Batza is an associate professor in the Women, Gender, and Sexuality Studies Department at the University of Kansas. Her research explores the intersection of sexuality, health, and politics in the late twentieth-century United States. She is currently engaged with several research projects: a book project that explores the experiences of the early AIDS crisis in the Heartland, a walking tour and podcast project on reproductive justice in Boston, and a cross-disciplinary analysis of access to health care for gender nonconforming and disabled individuals. Her first book, *Before AIDS*, was published by the University of Pennsylvania Press in February 2018 and explores gay health activism in the period before AIDS. She also has published on the history of lesbians and the fertility industry, mapping queer health history and neoliberalism, and partnered in the National Park Service's LGBTQ initiative that aids in identifying, preserving, and interpreting historic sites of particular meaning to the LGBTQ communities. Her work has been funded by Point Foundation, the National Endowment for the Humanities, the American Council of Learned Societies, the American Philosophical Society, a Mellon-Schlesinger fellowship from Harvard University, the Whiting Foundation, and numerous internal grants.

Jade Bentil is a Black feminist historian and DPhil candidate at the University of Oxford. Her scholarship uses oral history methodologies to center the experiences of women of African and African Caribbean descent in Britain and their long history of rebellion, resistance, and refusal. Jade's debut book, *Rebel Citizen*, uses oral history interviews to explore the lived experiences of Black women who migrated to Britain following the Second World War and is forthcoming from Allen Lane.

Taous Dahmani is a PhD fellow in the Department of Art History (specializing in photography) at the Panthéon Sorbonne University (Paris 1). She is interested in visual and migration studies. Her research focuses on Black British Art and Black feminism. Her PhD considers the relationship between photography and postcolonial migration in England from the 1950s to the 1980s. More specifically, her work examines the power of photography to construct or disrupt dominant narratives on the subject. Since the beginning of her PhD she has given several papers in England and France, and had several articles published. From September 2018, she was a scholar at the Maison Française d'Oxford (England).

Flora Dunster is an art and social historian. Her PhD thesis, titled "Hurled Toward the Future: The Queer Subjunctive in British Lesbian Photography, 1987–1996," was completed in 2019 at the University of Sussex and funded by CHASE/AHRC. In 2020, she was a Paul Mellon Postdoctoral Fellow. She lectures on art, photography, and critical theory at Central Saint Martins, amongst other institutions across the United Kingdom. Recent publications include the essay "Do You Have Place? A Conversation with Sunil Gupta" in *Third Text* (2021). She is currently preparing a book on the intertwining of queer politics and lesbian photography in London during the 1980s and 1990s.

Julie R. Enszer is a scholar and a poet. Her book manuscript, *A Fine Bind*, is a history of lesbian-feminist presses from 1969 until 2009. Her scholarly work has appeared or is forthcoming in *Southern Cultures*, *Journal of Lesbian Studies*, *American Periodicals*, *WSQ*, and *Frontiers*. She is the co-editor of *OutWrite: The Speeches that Shaped LGBTQ Literary Culture* (Rutgers University Press, 2022). She is the author of four poetry collections, most recently *Avowed* (Sibling Rivalry Press, 2016), and the editor of *Fire-Rimmed Eden: Selected Poems of Lynn Lonidier* (Nightboat Books, 2022), *The Complete Works of Pat Parker* (Sinister Wisdom/A Midsummer Night's Press, 2016), which won the 2017 Lambda Literary Award for Lesbian Poetry, *Sister Love: The Letters of Audre Lorde and Pat Parker 1974–1989* (Sinister Wisdom/A Midsummer Night's Press, 2018), and *Milk & Honey: A Celebration of Jewish Lesbian Poetry* (A Midsummer Night's Press, 2011), which was a finalist for the 2012 Lambda Literary Award in Lesbian Poetry. She has her MFA and PhD from the University of Maryland. Enszer edits and publishes *Sinister Wisdom*, a multicultural lesbian literary and art journal. Read more of her work at www.JulieREnszer.com.

Michael S. Hevel is an associate professor of higher education at the University of Arkansas. His research focuses on the history of college students in the United States, especially how their identities shaped their experiences in higher education. His research has been published in the *History of Education Quarterly*, *Journal of Higher Education*, and the *Journal of College Student Development*.

Tamar Holoshitz holds a JD from Yale Law School, an MSt in Women's Studies from Oxford University, and an AB in linguistics from Harvard College. Her research interests include feminist legal theory, constitutional law, reproductive rights, statutory interpretation, and family law, as well as the interplay of language and gender. Tamar has worked as a lawyer, served as a gender-based violence prevention advocate, and currently lives in New Haven, Connecticut.

Katherine Rye Jewell is a historian and author of *Dollars for Dixie: Business and the Transformation of Conservatism in the Twentieth Century*, published by Cambridge University Press (New York) in 2017. She received her PhD from Boston University and she is currently associate professor of history at Fitchburg State University. She received the Fitchburg State

University Faculty Research Award in 2018. Her research focuses on the intersection of culture and politics in the United States. Her current research project examines regulation, student and university politics, the music industry, and college radio. Tentatively titled *Live from the Underground: College Radio and the Culture Wars*, this book will explore through archival research how college radio participated in and shaped evolutions in modern musical culture, the culture wars, and the business of music in the post-1970s era.

Nora Kassner (she/they) is a doctoral candidate in history of public policy at the University of California, Santa Barbara. Her dissertation, titled "Hard to Place: Queer Foster Families and the Remaking of U.S. Family Policy, 1975–1996," explores the transformation of US family policy in the late twentieth century through the experiences of queer foster parents and their foster children. Nora combines oral histories with archival research to capture the impacts of public policy on daily life in the United States. Prior to coming to graduate school, Nora worked as a community organizer, and a commitment to publicly engaged scholarship remains central to their work.

Charlotte Lydia Riley is lecturer in twentieth-century British history at the University of Southampton. She is the editor of *Free Speech Wars: How Did We Get Here and Why Does It Matter?* (Manchester University Press, 2021) and is currently writing *Imperial Island*, an exploration of how the empire shaped British society, politics, and culture, to be published by Bodley Head/Belknap.

Charles J. Thompson is a doctoral candidate in higher education at the University of Arkansas. His research is centered on minoritized college students' experiences at U.S. institutions of higher education, with a particular focus on college students with minoritized sexual and gender identities.

Kate Turner is a historian of gender, race and capitalism in modern Britain. She holds a master's in women's studies from the University of Oxford and is a PhD candidate in history at the University of Wisconsin-Madison. Today she lives on Haudenosaunee and Mahican land, in an area otherwise known as Albany, New York.

Index

Note: **Bold** type indicates contributors to this volume.
Page numbers followed by "n" indicate numbered endnotes.

Abbott, Diane, 319
abortion. *See* reproductive rights
ACT-UP, 8, 232, 242
Adair, Carolyn, 35, 36
Adams, Kate, 285
Agard, Brenda, 259, 260, 262
AIDS activist movement (US), 8–9, 11–12, 232, 242. *See also* DOORWAYS project (St. Louis); HIV/AIDS pandemic
Ainley, Rosa, *What Is She Like?*, 321
Alam, Ageela, 320
Alexander, Claire, 183
Allen, Michael, 234
Allen, Paula Gunn, *The Woman Who Owned the Shadows*, 290, 291
American Civil Liberties Union (ACLU): Reproductive Freedom Project (RFP), 203–209; Women's Law Project of Pennsylvania and, 209, 210
American Psychological Association, 39–40
Americans United for Life, 209, 214
Amosu, Akwe, 132
Angelides, Steven, 13
anti-militarism/peace activism, 10

Anzaldúa, Gloria, 9; *Borderlands / La Frontera*, 4, 15, 286, 294, 295, 297; *Making Face, Making Soul / Haciendo Caras*, 294–295
Araeen, Rasheed, 261, 263, 275n54
Ardill, Susan, 309, 311–322
Astraea (US), 298, 299
Aunt Lute Books (US), 4, 5, 292–298; engagement in marketplace capitalism, 296–298, 301–302; merger with Spinsters Ink books, 285, 293–296; as nonprofit corporation, 295–296; origins, 286, 292–293; publications, 293–295, 296–298; separation from Spinsters Ink books, 296
Azpadu, Dodici: *Goat Song*, 293; *Saturday Night in the Prime of Life*, 293

Bannerman, Adelaide, 262
Barrett, Amy Coney, 213
Barthes, Roland, 266
Batza, Katie, 8, 15, 151, **229–251**
BBWG. *See* Brixton Black Women's Group (BBWG)
Bean, Gerlin, 183, 185–186

344 | Index

Bell, Jonathan, *Beyond the Politics of the Closet*, 11
Bella Books (US), 301
Bellos, Linda, 95–97
Benshoof, Janet, 203–205, 209–210
Bentil, Jade, 4–5, 6, 10, 14, **75–116,** 183, 257
Berhane-Selassie, Tsehai, 117–118, 128–130, 132, 133–134
Bhimji, Zarina, 267
Black Cultural Archives (BCA, UK), 78–79
Black Liberation Front, 10
Black Nationalist Movement (UK), 91–93
Black Power Movement (US), 6, 11, 79, 91–93, 180
Black Women's Movement (BWM, UK), 4–6, 10, 14, 75–105, 171–187; "Black" as term, 78; Black lesbian feminists in, 94–98, 194–195n75; Black Power Movement (US) and, 79, 91–93, 180; Black single mothers and, 176–178; Black Women's Centre, 98–100, 103; British Women's Liberation movement (WLM) vs., 77, 80, 87–90, 95–98, 178–179; Brixton Black Women's Group (*see* Brixton Black Women's Group); Census boycott in London (1980), 180–181; East London Black Women's Organisation (ELBWO), 78, 82, 93–94, 101, 103; end of, 103–104, 184; Greater London Council (GLC) and, 100–102, 103, 259, 273nn31–32; *The Heart of the Race* (Bryan et al.), 179–184, 191n46, 193–194n68, 193n62, 194nn73–74; international dimensions of, 85–86; intersectionality and, 78, 86–89, 104; legacy of, 104–105; National Black Women's Conferences, 1, 75–76, 80, 82, 90, 95–96, 171; oral history methodology, 77–79; origins of Black feminist organizing, 79–80; OWAAD (*see* Organisation of Women of Asian and African Descent); "personal as political," 87–90, 91–96; Thatcherism and Black socialist feminist resistance to, 75–76, 77, 81, 83–94, 97–105, 171; uprisings of 1981, 85–86, 92. *See also* lesbian-feminist print culture
Bogle, Marlene T., 99
Bost, Darius, 238
Boyd, Roisin, 133
Boyle, Ed, 154
Bracewell, Lorna N., 307–308, 314
Brady, Maureen, 286–292, 301; *Give Me Your Good Ear*, 286–287; work as physical therapist, 289. *See also* Spinsters Ink books (US)
Brawn, Shay, 295
Breyer, Stephen, 213
Brian, Riley, 46
Bridgeland, Kathleen, 160
Briggs, Laura, *How All Politics Became Reproductive Politics*, 11
British Nationality Act (1981), 83–84, 190n29
British Women's Liberation Movement (WLM), 14; Black socialist feminist responses to, 77, 80, 87–90, 95–98, 178–179; defined, 122; nature of, 77, 89, 178; print cultures in (*see* lesbian-feminist print culture); Thatcher and, 175. *See also* UN Decade for Women
Brixton Black Women's Group (BBWG), 5, 78, 80–82, 88–93, 94; Black socialist feminism as

term and, 81; *On Black Women Organising* (1983 editorial), 92, 93, 96, 97–98; community-based initiatives, 81; formation (1973), 80, 180; links to other Black women's groups in Britain, 81–82; Sisters in Study, 97; *Speak Out* (newsletter), 80, 84–86, 89, 97, 103, 263, 268; state funding issues, 98–101
Brody, Michal, *Lavender Women*, 293
Brooke, Stephen, 10–11, 172
Brown, Glynn, 42
Brown, Jerry, 149–150
Brown, Rita Mae, 287
Bruce, Margaret K., 120
Bruley, Sue, 122
Bryan, Beverley, 80, 84, 85, 88, 91, 101, 102
Bulkin, Elly, 287
Bunch, Charlotte, 124, 125

Cameron, Paul, 39–40
Campaign for Nuclear Disarmament (UK), 1–2
Carby, Hazel V., 80, 265
Carter, Jimmy, 2
Castle, Barbara, 124
Centers for Disease Control (CDC, US), 8
Centre for Contemporary Cultural Studies (UK), 262–263
Chambers, Eddie, 261, 275n54
Chandler, Tracey, 318
City of Akron v. Akron Center for Reproductive Health (1983, US), 199–200, 203, 204–208, 211
civil rights movement, 2, 6
Clausen, Jan, 287
Cliff, Michelle, 290
Cohen, Cathy, 238
Coker, Similola, 259, 260, 262, 266

Cold War politics, 124, 131, 309
Combahee River Collective (Boston), 86
conservatism: HIV/AIDS pandemic and, 240–243; New Right rise in UK and US, 1–2, 8, 10–11, 14; under Reagan (*see* Reagan, Ronald); under Thatcher (*see* Thatcher, Margaret)
Convention on the Elimination of Discrimination Against Women (CEDAW, UK), 127, 136–137n15
Coombs, Kay, 126–127
Cooper, Lynn, 237
Crenshaw, Kimberlé, 5, 86, 267–268. *See also* intersectionality
Crook, Sarah, 1–27, 331–333
"culture wars": HIV/AIDS and (*see* HIV/AIDS pandemic); homophobia in (*see* homophobia / lesbophobia; queer foster parenting); in radio programming (*see* student radio programming [US]); in reproductive rights (*see* reproductive rights); sex wars (*see* lesbian-feminist print culture; sex wars)

Dadzie, Stella, 78–79, 82, 84, 90, 95, 100, 101–102, 105, 179–180, 182–183, 186, 187
Dahmani, Taous R., 5, 6, 15, 255–283, 286
Dallas Buyers Club (2013 film), 7
Daly, Mary, *GynEcology*, 287
Damsky, Lee, 314
Davis, Angela, 130, 265
DeCrescenzo, Terry, 151–156, 158, 160–161
Delap, Lucy, 285–286
Depo-Provera, 10, 86–87, 132
Deutsche, Rosalyn, 322

"developing world" / "development," as terms, 122–124, 130–133, 135–136n7
DeVincenzo, Suzanne, 293
DOORWAYS project (St. Louis), 229–243; "closet" and, 240–241; conservatism and, 240–243; Effort for AIDS (EFA, St. Louis) and, 234–236, 241, 242; fundraising, 230–231, 233–237, 239–240; Heartland as geographical region, 229–232, 243–244n2; nature and role of, 230–236; religious institution support for, 230–242; women and children in, 231, 238–239, 243
Doughty, Frances, 124, 125
Drury, Joan: at Astraea (US), 298, 299; buys Spinsters Ink books, 298–300; and Norcroft, A Writing Retreat for Women (1995–2005), 299; sells Spinsters Ink books to Colorado publishers, 300–301
Dunster, Flora, 13–14, 15, 286, **307–328**

East London Black Women's Organization (ELBWO), 78, 82, 93–94, 101, 103
Edelman, Ed, 152, 153, 155–156
Edland, Michael, 230–231
Effort for AIDS (EFA, St. Louis), 234–236, 241, 242
Egerton, Jayne, 312
Enszer, Julie R., 4, 5, 15, **285–305**
Evans, Tanya, 175–176

Faderman, Lilian, 13
Falklands War (1982), 177, 256, 309
Faludi, Susan, 310
Family Policy Group (FPG, UK), 174–177, 186–187

FCC v. Pacifica (1978, US), 65
female genital mutilation (FGM), 128, 130
feminist movement, 2, 18n24; backlash, 53, 310, 313, 321; consciousness-raising in, 6, 61–62, 88, 92, 264, 268; "first wave," 309–310; "second wave" (1960s and 1970s), 7–8, 77, 309–310, 318, 320, 322 (see also *Spare Rib* (magazine, [UK]); sex wars and, 307–308, 309–315; "third wave" (early 1990s), 8, 9, 310, 320. See also lesbian-feminist print culture; UN Decade for Women
Feminists Against Censorship (FAC, London), 313
Ferguson, Ann, 307–310
Fisher, Tracy, 77, 90, 96, 100, 104
Flier, Daniel, 235
Foote, Stephanie, 285
Ford, Gerald, 37–38
Foreign Commonwealth Office (FCO, UK), 124–125
Forrest, Katherine V., 301
Forster, Laurel, 122, 262, 263, 274n41, 276n70
foster care: nature of US, 148; queer foster parenting in Los Angeles (*see* queer foster parenting [US]); shortage of homes for, 149–155
FOWAAD! (OWAAD journal, UK), 84, 184–185, 263, 268
Francis, Amelia, 10
Fraser, Nancy, 262

Gallimore, Olive, 91–92
Garber, Linda, 286
Garnham, Nicholas, 54
"gay," as term, 13
Gay Alliance of Students v. Matthews (1976, US), 44

gay liberation movement, 2, 7; Gay Liberation Front (1970–1973, UK), 7, 151; *Gay Student Services v. Texas A&M University*, 5, 31–32, 35–46. See also queer foster parenting
Gay Lib v. University of Missouri (1977, US), 44
Gay Men's Health Crisis, 8
Gay Student Services (GSS, Texas A&M University), 5, 35–46; early trials and appeals, 37–43; Gay Line, 33, 34, 36, 39, 45; and *Gay Student Services v. Texas A&M University* (1975–1985), 5, 31–32, 35–46; legacy of, 45–46; legal costs, 41; recognition as student organization (1985), 45; renamed Gay, Lesbian, Bisexual, and Transgender Aggies (1997), 45–46; Supreme Court decision, 43–45, 46
Gemello, Gina, 297–298
Gilroy, Paul, 177–178, 186
Ginsburg, Ruth Bader, 213
GLASS (Gay and Lesbian Adolescent Social Services, US), 154, 160
Global North / Global South, 10, 118, 122–123, 125–126, 128, 130–133, 135–136n7
Gossett, Che, 11–12, 14, 335
Graham, Shirley, 181
Grant, Catherine, 308
Gray, Aleema, 10
Gray, Madi, 132
Greater London Authority (GLA), 259
Greater London Council (GLC), 100–102, 103, 259, 260, 273nn31–32
Green, Sarah, 307
Greenham Common Women's Peace Camp (UK), 314, 332

Gregory, Joy, 256, 260
Groce, Cherry, 102
Gueye, Ama, 76, 82, 88, 90, 91, 93, 96, 101, 104, 105

Hajovsky, Ted, 44
Hall, Stuart, 83, 260, 261
Hanisch, Carol, on "personal is political," 6
Harding, Sandra, 265
Hart, Judith, 124
Healy v. James (1972, US), 42
Heart of the Race, The (Bryan et al.), 179–184, 191n46, 193–194n68, 193n62, 194nn73–74
Hemmings, Clare, 308
Henry, Astrid, 322
Heresies: A Feminist Publication on Art and Politics (US), 310–312, 314–315
Hevel, Michael S., 5, 13, 14, **31–52**
Hill, Linda, 301
HIV/AIDS pandemic, 2, 15; AIDS activist movement, 8–9, 11–12, 232, 242; conservatism and, 240–243, 309; and Dallas Doctors Against AIDS (US), 40–41; films concerning, 7; history in the US Heartland, 229–232 (*see also* DOORWAYS project [St. Louis]); medical treatments, 8, 235–236; *Safer Sex* (*Lesbians Talk Issues* series), 316, 317–318; student radio programming and, 64–65; women and children and, 231, 238–239, 243
Hobbs, Lola J., 158, 159
Hogan, Kristen, 285–286
Holoshitz, Tamar, 5–6, 15, **199–227**
homophobia / lesbophobia: Black lesbian feminists and the Black Women's Movement, 94–98,

348 | Index

homophobia / lesbophobia *(continued)* 194–195n75; Gay Liberation Front (UK) and, 7, 151; *Gay Student Services v. Texas A&M University,* 5, 31–32, 35–46; HIV/AIDS pandemic and, 232–234, 237–238; queer foster parenting and, 151–161; Section 28 (UK) and legislative homophobia, 7, 189n7, 309, 313, 332
hooks, bell, 9, 264, 265
Houlbrook, Matt, 12
housing: DOORWAYS project (St. Louis), 229–243; group homes for homeless youth in Los Angeles, California, 13–14, 153–155; queer foster parenting in Los Angeles, California, 147–162
Hovis, Katherine, 300–301
How to Survive a Plague (2012 film), 7

immigration: race and national identity under Thatcherism, 176–178; Vagrancy Act (1824, UK) as cover for harassment of Black people, 181
Institute for Contemporary Arts (ICA, London), 313
International Monetary Fund (IMF), gender issues and, 131
International Women's Year (IWY, 1975), 119–126
intersectionality (Crenshaw), 5, 86, 267–268; Black Women's Movement (BWM, UK) and, 78, 86–89, 104; intersectional approach to long 1980s, 172; racist and sexist repression, 86–87, 88; representational intersectionality, 267–268

Iowa City Women's Press (ICWP) Collective, 292, 293
It's a Sin (2021 BBC series), 7

Jarette, Juliette, 261
Jay, Bill, 263
Jeffries, Charlie, 1–27
Jennings, Rebecca, 12
Jewell, Katherine Rye, 14, 32, 53–72
Jones, Barbara, 269
Julien, Isaac, *Screen–Polareyes* (with Mercer), 258–259
June Medical Services L.L.C. v. Russo (2020, US), 211, 213–214

Kager, Kelly, 298–299
Kahumbu, Joy, 268
Karimjee, Mumtaz, 255, 256, 259, 260, 262, 274n41
Kassner, Nora, 13, 14, 147–169
Kavanaugh, Brett, 213
Kaveny, Roz, 313, 314, 318
Khambatta, Ann, 319–320
Khan, Naseem, *The Arts Britain Ignores,* 260–261
King, Katie, 286
Kishwar, Madhu, 127
Kitchen Table Press (US), 270
Koestenbaum, Wayne, 12
Kolbert, Kathryn, 209
Koldus, John, 34–38, 41–42, 44–45

Landsman, Stephen, 205
Larkin, Joan, 287
Leeds Revolutionary Feminist Group (UK), 311
Lemos, Sue, 10
"lesbian," as term, 13
lesbian-feminist print culture, 285–302; Aunt Lute Books (*see*

Aunt Lute Books [US]); Bella Books (US), 301; *FOWAAD!* (OWAAD journal, UK), 84, 184–185, 263, 268; *Heresies: A Feminist Publication on Art and Politics* (US), 310–312, 314–315; Iowa City Women's Press (ICWP) Collective (US), 292, 293; Kitchen Table Press (US), 270; *The Lesbian Review of Books* (US), 317; *Lesbians Talk Issues* series (see *Lesbians Talk Issues* [UK]); *Mukti* (journal, UK), 263, 274n41; Old Wives' Tales (US bookstore), 290–292; *Polareyes* (UK), 15, 255–271; *Revolutionary and Radical Feminist Newsletter* (UK), 312; Scarlet Press (UK), 308, 315–316; Seal Press (US), 289; Sheba Feminist Press (UK), 1; *Spare Rib* (see *Spare Rib* (magazine, [UK]); *Speak Out* (BBWG newsletter, UK), 80, 84–86, 89, 97, 103, 263, 268; Spinsters Ink books (see Spinsters Ink books [US]); *Trouble and Strife* (journal, UK), 89. *See also* names of specific authors

Lesbian Review of Books, The (US), 317

Lesbians Talk Issues (UK book series, 1992–1996), 14, 15, 286, 308–309, 311, 315–322; *Detonating the Nuclear Family* (1996), 316, 317; *Left Politics* (1994), 316, 318–319; *Making Black Waves* (1993), 316, 319–320; *Queer Notions* (1992), 308, 316, 318; *Safer Sex* (1992), 316, 317–318; *Transgender* (1996), 308, 316, 318, 320; *Violent Relationships* (1995), 316, 321

Lewis, Brian, *Queer British History*, 12, 13

Lewis, Gail, 80, 83, 86, 89–90, 92, 94, 98, 99, 103, 104, 178–179

LGBTQ youth, 13, 14; constitutional rights, 32; "LGBTQ" acronym and, 46–47n2; literature review, 47–48n3; at Texas A&M University, 31–46. *See also* queer foster parenting (US); student radio programming (US)

Livingstone, Ken, 259

Lockhart, Judith, 185

London Lesbian and Gay Centre (LLGC), 311, 312

"long 1980s," as term, 12–13. *See also* 1980s / long 1980s

Lorde, Audre, *The Cancer Journals*, 288–289

Los Angeles Gay and Lesbian Community Services Center, 150–155, 159–160

Loulan, Joann, sex manuals, 291, 295

MacDonald, Barbara, *Look Me in the Eye* (with Rich), 291

Manchester Black Women's Group (UK), 1

Mason-John, Valerie, 95, 319–320

Mattox, Jim, 43

May, John L., 233–234, 236, 238

McBean, Sam, 308

McCarthy, Helen, 124

McDaniel, Judith, 286–292; *Elegy from a Hill in Hebron*, 289; *Reconstituting the World*, 287; work as English professor, 289. *See also* Spinsters Ink books (US)

McDermott, Kate, *Places*, 293

McGreivy, Susan, 153

McKenzie, Anita, 256, 257–258, 270–271

McKenzie, Jenny, 259, 262, 265

McKeon, Sean, 62
McLaughlin, Sheila, 313
Mercer, Araba, 319, 320; *Lesbians Talk Making Black Waves*, 1
Mercer, Kobena, *Screen–Polareyes* (with Julien), 258–259
Middleton, Mark, 64
Miller, Mev, 299
Miller, Millie, 124, 125
Mindich, Stephen, 63
miner's strike (1984–1985, UK), 7, 10, 256, 309, 319
Minton, Michael, 36–37, 38
Mirza, Heidi Safia, 77, 268–269
Mitchell, Leslie, 259, 262
Moraga, Cherríe, 9
Moten, Fred, 271
motherhood: Black single mothers and, 175–178, 181–182, 231, 238, 243; communalist matriarchy of Black motherhood, 171–172, 178–187; DOORWAYS project (St. Louis) and, 231, 238; HIV/AIDS pandemic and, 231, 238–239, 243; Thatcherite / Victorian politics of, 171–178, 184–187. *See also* parenthood; reproductive rights
Mount, Ferdinand, 174
Moutoussamy-Ashe, Jeanne, 260
Muhanji, Cherry, *Her*, 296
Mukti (journal, UK), 263, 274n41
Murray, Simon, 264
Murray, Simone, 285
Museum of Modern Art (US), *British Photography from the Thatcher Years* (1991), 261

Nadasen, Premilla, *Household Workers Unite*, 11
Nataf, Zachary I., 318, 320
National Association for the Advancement of Colored People (NAACP), 207

National Black Women's Conferences (UK), 1, 75–76, 80, 82, 90, 95–96, 171
National Front (UK), 76, 83, 84
National Network of Abortion Funds (US), 212
National Organization of Women (NOW), 207
neoliberal conservatism, 2, 11
Nestle, Joan, 313; *A Restricted Country*, 316–317
Nestlé baby formula controversy, 132
New Right, rise of, 1–2, 8, 10–11, 14
Nicholls, Jill, 126–128, 132
1980s / long 1980s: counternarrative to, 179; intersectional approach to, 172; "long 1980s," as term, 12–13; as "Me Decade," 171, 186, 187; political agitation, 7–8; rise of New Right in UK and US, 1–4, 8, 10–11, 14
Nochlin, Linda, 269

O'Connor, John, 232–233
O'Connor, Sandra Day, 202, 204–205
Ogle, Albert J., 150–155, 159–161
Olcott, Jocelyn, 120, 121, 125
Old Wives' Tales (US bookstore), 290–292
120 Beats Per Minute (2017 film), 7
Oram, Alison, 12
Organisation of Women of Asian and African Descent (OWAAD, UK), 6, 90–96, 97, 182–183, 268; demise (1983), 77, 96, 100–101; *FOWAAD!* (journal), 84, 184–185, 263, 268; lesbophobia in, 95–98; National Black Women's Conferences, 1, 75–76, 80, 82, 90, 95–96, 171; organization against police violence, 85, 185
O'Rourke, Chris, 12
Osamor, Martha, 181

O'Sullivan, Sue, 309, 311–322
Ouseley, Herman, 99

Pacifica Foundation, 53, 61, 65
parenthood, 147–162, 171–172, 178–187. See also motherhood; reproductive rights
Parmar, Pratibha, 269–270, 317
Patel, Amina, 256, 259, 262
Pennington, Bruce, 59
Pennsylvania Abortion Control Act, 199–200, 203, 208–211
"personal is political" (Hanisch), 6; Black Women's Movement and, 87–90, 91–96; in challenging white bourgeois feminism, 87–90; *Polareyes* (magazine, UK) and, 265–266; reproductive rights and, 88–89
Phelps, Fred, 238
Phoenix, Laeticea, 260
Pinkvoss, Joan, 292–298; merger of Spinsters Ink books with Aunt Lute Books, 293–296; separation of Spinsters Ink books and Aunt Lute Books, 296–298; work as master electrician, 293. See also Aunt Lute Books (US)
Planned Parenthood v. Casey (1992, US), 199–200, 201–203, 213
Polareyes (magazine, UK), 15, 255–271
police aggression: Black Lives Matter movement (US), 331–332; OWAAD (UK) organization against, 85, 185; queer foster parenting and, 156–161; Vagrancy Act (1824, UK) as cover for harassment of Black people, 181
Political Blackness, 183, 188n1, 261–262
political lesbianism, 311–312
Pollard, Ingrid, 256, 260

pornography, 310–311, 312, 316
Potter, Claire Bond, 12
Powell, Enoch, 177
Pride (2014 film), 7
print culture. See lesbian-feminist print culture
publishers / publications. See lesbian-feminist print culture

"queer," as term, 13
queer foster parenting (US), 147–162; group homes vs., 13–14, 153–155; homophobia and, 151–161; legal recognition in Los Angeles, 147–148; Los Angeles Gay and Lesbian Community Services Center activism and, 150–155, 159–160; police encounter and lawsuit, 156–161; social worker activism in, 149, 155–161; youth homelessness and, 148, 149–156, 159–162
queer historical studies, 11–12

"race women" (US), 11
racism, conservatism and, 2
radio programming. See student radio programming (US)
Rana, Samena, 259, 262, 266–267
Rao, Amiya, 124–125
Rathbone, Jenny, 124–125
Rayford, Robert, 229–230
Reagan, Ronald (1981–1989): conservative Reagan Revolution and, 1–4, 8, 9, 11, 14–15, 147–148, 309; election as president (1980), 309; reproductive rights and, 199, 208
religious conservatism, 2; Religious Right in the US, 199, 215n2, 232–233; reproductive rights and, 199, 215n2; support for the DOORWAYS project (St. Louis), 230–242

Reproductive Freedom Project (RFP, US), 203–209
reproductive rights, 5–6, 15, 199–215; *City of Akron v. Akron Center for Reproductive Health* (1983, US), 199–200, 203, 204–208, 211; Depo-Provera, 10, 86–87, 132; factual balancing test, 202, 208–215; female activism in the Global South and, 132; fetal-protective legislation and, 213–215; *June Medical Services L.L.C. v. Russo* (2020, US), 211, 213–214; "personal as political" in, 88–89; *Planned Parenthood v. Casey* (1992, US), 199–200, 201–203, 213; privacy as constitutional right, 200–202; religious right and, 199, 215n2; Reproductive Freedom Project (RFP, US), 203–209; restriction trend in, 211–215; right of consent, 86–87, 205–206, 209–211; *Roe v. Wade* (1973, US), 2, 199–204; *Thornburgh v. American College of Obstetricians and Gynecologists* (1986, US), 199–200, 203, 208–211; trimester framework for abortion, 201–208, 212; undue burden framework, 202–211, 213, 214; *Whole Women's Health vs. Hellerstedt* (2016, US), 211–214
Rich, Adrienne, 287, 288, 290, 311
Rich, B. Ruby, 311
Rich, Cynthia, *Look Me in the Eye* (with MacDonald), 291
Riley, Catherine, 285
Riley, Charlotte Lydia, 10, 14, **117–143**
Roberts, John, 213
Roberts, Marco, 41–45
Robles, Elizabeth, 266

Roe v. Wade (1973, US), 2, 199–204
Rogers, Adrian, 177
Rogers, Barbara, 131–133
Romano, Renee C., 12
Rothschild, Ken, 59
Royles, Daniel, 238
Ruben, Rabbi, 234
Rubin, Gayle, 311
Rycenga, Jennifer, 317, 320

El Saadawi, Nawal, 132
Saltzman, Rob, 152, 155–156
Samantrai, Ranu, 77, 84
Samuel, Raphael, 173
Sasson, Tehila, 132
Scafe, Suzanne, 76, 84, 85, 87, 93, 194n73
Scarlet Press (UK), 308, 315–316. See also *Lesbians Talk Issues*
Schoendfelder, Lisa, *Shadow on a Tightrope* (edited with Weiser), 293
Schofield, Camilla, 177
Schulte, Steve, 151–152
Schwab, Robert, 41
Seal Press (US), 289
Section 28 (1988, UK), 7, 189n7, 309, 313, 332
Segal, Lynne, 311
Sexual Offences Act (1967, UK), 7
sex wars, 307–322; and "The Feminist and the Scholar IX" conference (1982, Barnard College, US), 310–311; and *Heresies: A Feminist Publication on Art and Politics* (US), 310–312, 314–315; pornography and, 310–311, 312, 316; radical feminists vs. sex radicals, 307–315; sadomasochism (S/M) and, 310–313, 316. *See also* lesbian-feminist print culture
Sheba Feminist Press (UK), 1
Sheedy, Charlotte, 288

She Must Be Seeing Things (1987 film), 313
Shinhat, Molly, 256, 259, 260, 261–262, 264
Shope, Gertrude, 132
Silvas, Sharon, 300–301
Sipilä, Helvi, 120
Sjoholm, Barbara (Barbara Wilson), *Ambitious Women*, 289
Skinner, Sheri, 31–36, 39
Sleeman, Kenneth K., 56–59
Slomowicz, Ron (DJ Ron), 64–65
Smith, Barbara, 9, 270
Smyth, Cherry, 316, 317, 319
Snorton, C. Riley, 14
social conservatism, 2
Solomon-Godeau, Abigail, 256
Sorenson, Rosalie, 157–158, 161
Southall Black Sisters (UK), 6, 183
Spare Rib (magazine, UK), 14, 121–135, 258, 311, 314; comparison with *Ms.* magazine (US), 138n31; critiques of "development" and, 130–133, 135–136n7; Global North / Global South and, 10, 118, 122–123, 125–126, 128, 130–133, 135–136n7; origins and description, 117–119, 121–122; relationship between British women's movement and transnational context, 122
Speak Out (BBWG newsletter, UK), 80, 84–86, 89, 97, 103, 263, 268
Spinsters Ink books (US), 4, 5, 286–292, 298–302; backlist acquired by Linda Hill, 301; engagement in marketplace capitalism, 301–302; lesbian and feminist network supporting, 289–292; merger with Aunt Lute Books, 285, 293–296; as nonprofit corporation, 290; origins, 286–287; publications, 287–292, 299; sale to Colorado publishers, 300–301; sale to Joan Drury, 298–300; sale to Sherry Thomas, 290–291; separation from Aunt Lute Books, 296
Standpoint theory, 265
Sterling, Ross, 37–40, 41–42, 44
Stewart, Graham, *Bang! A History of Britain in the 1980s*, 256
Stewart, Keith, 36–37
Stonewall uprising (1969, New York City), 7
Strongin, Lynn, *Bones & Kim*, 288
Stryker, Susan, 14
Stuart, Erin, 128
student activism. *See* LGBTQ youth; student radio programming (US)
student radio programming (US), 14, 53–66; DJs in, 54–58, 60–61, 63–65; emergence of queer media activism, 54, 65–66, 66–67n2; FCC regulation of, 53, 55–59, 65–66, 66n1, 67n3; license-holder control and, 53–54, 55, 57–61, 63; Pacifica Foundation and, 53, 61, 65; public service commitment in, 54–65; WGTB-FM (Georgetown University), 55–61; WRSU (Rutgers University) *Gaybreak* program, 61–63; WRVU (Vanderbilt University) *Out of the Closet* program, 63–65, 66; WXPN (University of Pennsylvania) license revocation, 58–59
Studzinski, Kristina, 318–319
Sudbury, Julia, 77, 79, 91, 102
Sutcliffe, Peter, 311
Sutcliffe-Braithwaite, Florence, 10
Swallow, Jean, *Out from Under*, 291

Taub, Nadine, 204
Tawadros, Gilane, 266

Taylor, Joelle, 318
Texas A&M University, 31–46; Alternative community organization, 32–35, 36, 38, 39; conservatism of, 32–37; Corp of Cadets, 33, 34, 39; described, 32–33; Gay, Lesbian, Bisexual, and Transgender Aggies, 45–46; gay sex as illegal in Texas, 36–37; Gay Student Services (GSS), 35–46; *Gay Student Services v. Texas A&M University* (1975–1985), 5, 31–32, 35–46; GLBT Resource Center, 45–46
Thane, Pate, 175–176
Thatcher, Margaret (1979–1990), 10–11, 14, 15; Conservative government, 1–5, 8, 76, 83–84, 87–88, 95, 97–105, 171–178, 256; *The Downing Street Years*, 175–176; election as Prime Minister (1979), 1, 76, 99, 171, 184–185, 256, 309; Falklands War (1982), 177, 256, 309; Family Policy Group (FPG) and, 174–177, 186–187; miner's strike (1984–1985), 7, 10, 256, 309, 319; second term, 94, 172–178; Section 28 passage (1988), 7, 189n7, 309, 313, 332; third term, 103
Thomas, Sherry: buys Spinsters Ink books (US), 290–291; *Country Women*, 287, 292; merger of Spinsters Ink books with Aunt Lute Books, 293–296; sells Spinsters Ink books to Joan Drury, 298–299
Thomlinson, Natalie, 10, 77, 81, 86, 91, 94, 178, 268
Thompson, Charles J., 5, 13, 14, 31–52
Thompson, Joe, 151–152
Thornburgh, Dick, 210

Thornburgh v. American College of Obstetricians and Gynecologists (1986, US), 199–200, 203, 208–211
Tourmaline, 12
trans histories, 13–14, 45, 64, 318, 320
Travis, Trysh, 285
Trouble and Strife (journal, UK), 89
Trump, Donald, 11, 331, 336
Tsui, Kitty, *The Words of a Woman Who Breathes Fire*, 290, 291
Turner, Kate, 6, 14–15, 171–198

Umoren, Imaobong, *Race Women Internationalists*, 11
UN Decade for Women (1975–1985), 10, 14, 117–135; Commission on the Status of Women, 119–120, 125–126, 136–137n15; Copenhagen conference (1980), 118, 120, 121, 126–128, 129–130; Global North / Global South and, 10, 118, 122–123, 125–126, 128, 130–133; International Women's Year (IWY, 1975) and, 119–126; Mexico City conference (1975), 118, 120, 121, 124–126; Nairobi conference (1985), 117–118, 120, 121, 126, 128–130; NGOs associated with conferences, 118–121, 124–130; *Spare Rib* collective and, 117–119, 121–135
United Kingdom (UK): Conservative government under Thatcher (*see* Thatcher, Margaret); Falklands War (1982), 177, 256, 309; feminist publishers (*see* lesbian-feminist print culture); miner's strike (1984–1985), 7, 10, 256, 309, 319; National Front, 76, 83, 84; Section 28 passage (1988), 7, 189n7, 309, 313, 332; sex wars and, 307–315 (see also *Lesbians Talk Issues*); uprisings

of 1981, 10, 85–86, 92, 100, 260, 262. *See also* Black Women's Movement (BWM, UK)
United Nations. *See* UN Decade for Women
United States (US): conservative movement under Reagan (*see* Reagan, Ronald); *Gay Student Services v. Texas A&M University* (1975–1985), 5, 31–32, 35–46; lesbian-feminist print culture (*see* lesbian-feminist print culture); queer foster parenting in (*see* queer foster parenting [US]); reproductive rights in (*see* reproductive rights); sex wars and, 307–308, 310–311, 314–315; student radio programming in (*see* student radio programming [US])

Walker, Maxine, 257–260, 261, 262, 265–269, 270
Wallace, Sharron, 256
Wallsgrove, Ruth, 314
Walsh, Geraldine, 259, 260
Walsh, Gloria, 266
Walsh, James, 59, 60
Warburton, Anne, 127
We Are Here, 263, 268
Weiser, Barb, 292–298; *Shadow on a Tightrope* (edited with Schoenfelder), 293. *See also* Aunt Lute Books (US)
welfare rights activism, 11
WGTB-FM (Georgetown University), 55–61; closing (1979), 61; Committee to Save Alternative Radio, 59; FCC investigations, 57–59; *Friends* (program for the gay community), 56–58, 59; Jesuit license owner and, 55, 57, 59–61, 63
White, Jessica, 10

Whitehead, Kim, 286
Whitt, Jan, 285
Whole Women's Health vs. Hellerstedt (2016, US), 211–214
Wilson, Elizabeth, 310
Wilson, Melba, 79, 81, 89, 91–92, 96, 99, 103, 104
Women's International Democratic Federation (WIDF), 119
Women's International League for Peace and Freedom (WILPF), 130
Women's Law Project of Pennsylvania, 209, 210
women's liberation movement: in Britain (*see* Black Women's Movement; British Women's Liberation Movement); defined, 122; Mexican Women's Liberation Movement, 125; print cultures in (*see* lesbian-feminist print culture); reproductive rights (*see* reproductive rights). *See also* feminist movement; UN Decade for Women
Wooldridge, Patricia, 36–37
World Bank, gender issues and, 131
WRSU (Rutgers University), 61–63
WRVU (Vanderbilt University), 63–65, 66
WXPN (University of Pennsylvania), 58–59

youth homelessness: decriminalization of runaway teens in California, 149; group housing in California, 13–14, 153–155; rise of queer foster parenting and, 148, 149–162; Triangle Project for queer homeless youth, 159–160

Zemsky, Beth, 317
Zinsser, Judith P., 120
Zweiniger-Bargielowska, Ina, 83–84

www.ingramcontent.com/pod-product-compliance
Lightning Source LLC
Chambersburg PA
CBHW031426230426
43668CB00007B/455